Salience

Salience is both central to human life and relatively underexplored as a philosophical topic. Whether it bothers you that the picture on your wall is wonky, whose advice you take, whether you notice the homeless person at your feet as you squeeze your way down Oxford Street: these are all a function of salience. Salience is clearly of significance for a broad range of philosophical problems but rarely, if ever, has salience itself been the theme. This volume makes it so in an attempt to learn more about the place of salience in philosophy.

All 13 chapters have been specially commissioned for this volume, and are written by an international team of leading philosophers.

Salience: A Philosophical Inquiry is essential reading for students and researchers in philosophy of mind and psychology, epistemology, and ethics. It will also be of interest to those in related subjects such as psychology, politics, and law.

Sophie Archer is Lecturer in Philosophy at Cardiff University, UK. Her primary research interests are in philosophy of mind, philosophy of psychology, and epistemology. She is currently working on a book about belief.

Salience
A Philosophical Inquiry

Edited by Sophie Archer

Routledge
Taylor & Francis Group
LONDON AND NEW YORK

First published 2022
by Routledge
2 Park Square, Milton Park, Abingdon, Oxon OX14 4RN

and by Routledge
605 Third Avenue, New York, NY 10158

Routledge is an imprint of the Taylor & Francis Group, an informa business

© 2022 selection and editorial matter Sophie Archer; individual chapters, the contributors

The right of Sophie Archer to be identified as the author of the editorial material, and of the authors for their individual chapters, has been asserted in accordance with sections 77 and 78 of the Copyright, Designs and Patents Act 1988.

All rights reserved. No part of this book may be reprinted or reproduced or utilised in any form or by any electronic, mechanical, or other means, now known or hereafter invented, including photocopying and recording, or in any information storage or retrieval system, without permission in writing from the publishers.

Trademark notice: Product or corporate names may be trademarks or registered trademarks, and are used only for identification and explanation without intent to infringe.

British Library Cataloguing-in-Publication Data
A catalogue record for this book is available from the British Library

Library of Congress Cataloguing-in-Publication Data
Names: Archer, Sophie, editor.
Title: Salience: A Philosophical Inquiry / edited by Sophie Archer.
Identifiers: LCCN 2021040601 (print) | LCCN 2021040602 (ebook) | ISBN 9780815385196 (hbk) | ISBN 9781032199474 (pbk) | ISBN 9781351202114 (ebk)
Subjects: LCSH: Knowledge, Theory of. | Perception. | Attention.
Classification: LCC BD161.S255 2022 (print) | LCC BD161 (ebook) | DDC 121--dc23
LC record available at https://lccn.loc.gov/2021040601
LC ebook record available at https://lccn.loc.gov/2021040602

ISBN: 978-0-815-38519-6 (hbk)
ISBN: 978-1-032-19947-4 (pbk)
ISBN: 978-1-351-20211-4 (ebk)

DOI: 10.4324/9781351202114

Typeset in Goudy
by MPS Limited, Dehradun

Contents

Contributors   vii

Introduction: Salience and philosophy   1
SOPHIE ARCHER

1 Life through a lens: Aesthetic virtue and salience vs
  Kantian disinterest   10
  DAN CAVEDON-TAYLOR

2 Attention, salience, and the phenomenology of visual
  experience   24
  HEMDAT LERMAN

3 Beyond 'salience' and 'affordance': Understanding
  anomalous experiences of significant possibilities   50
  MATTHEW RATCLIFFE AND MATTHEW R. BROOME

4 On salience-based theories of demonstratives   70
  ELIOT MICHAELSON AND ETHAN NOWAK

5 The ethics of attention: An argument and a framework   89
  SEBASTIAN WATZL

6 Salience and what matters   113
  SOPHIE ARCHER

7 Salience, choice, and vulnerability   130
  SOPHIE GRACE CHAPPELL

8	The moral psychology of salience CHRISTOPHER MOLE	140
9	The unquiet life: Salience and moral responsibility SABINA LOVIBOND	159
10	On salience and sneakiness MARY KATE MCGOWAN	177
11	Harmful salience perspectives ELLA WHITELEY	193
12	Salient alternatives and epistemic injustice in folk epistemology MIKKEL GERKEN	213
13	Salience principles for democracy SUSANNA SIEGEL	235
	Index	267

Contributors

Sophie Archer is Lecturer in Philosophy at Cardiff University. Her primary research interests are in philosophy of mind, philosophy of psychology, and epistemology. She is currently working on a book about belief.

Matthew R. Broome is Professor of Psychiatry and Youth Mental Health, and Director of the Institute for Mental Health at the University of Birmingham and Distinguished Research Fellow, Oxford Uehiro Centre for Practical Ethics, University of Oxford. Matthew's research interests include youth mental health, the prodromal phase of psychosis, delusion formation, mood instability, functional neuroimaging, interdisciplinary methods, and the philosophy of psychiatry.

Dan Cavedon-Taylor is a lecturer in Philosophy at the Open University. His research centrally concerns topics in aesthetics and philosophy of mind, but extends to issues in ethics, social epistemology, and normative topics more generally.

Sophie Grace Chappell is Professor of Philosophy at the Open University. She is the author of a number of books, including *Knowing What To Do* (2014). With the support of a three-year Leverhulme Trust Major Research Fellowship (2017-2020), she has recently completed a new book, provisionally entitled *Epiphanies: an ethics and metaethics of experience*.

Mikkel Gerken is Professor of Philosophy at the University of Southern Denmark. He works on epistemology, philosophy of science, philosophy of mind and cognitive science but he has broad interests that include philosophical methodology and science communication. He is the author of *Epistemic Reasoning and the Mental* (2013) and *On Folk Epistemology* (2017). Currently he is working on a book, *The Significance of Scientific Testimony* (under contract with OUP).

Hemdat Lerman is a teaching fellow and a member of the Warwick Mind and Action Research Centre at the Philosophy Department at the University of Warwick. She is co-editor of *Perception, Causation, and Objectivity* (2011), and the author of papers in the philosophy of perception.

Sabina Lovibond is an Emeritus Fellow of Worcester College, Oxford, where she taught philosophy from 1982 to 2011. She is the author of *Realism and Imagination in Ethics* (1983), *Ethical Formation* (2002), *Iris Murdoch, Gender and Philosophy* (2011), and *Essays on Ethics and Feminism* (2015).

Mary Kate McGowan is the Margaret Clapp '30 Distinguished Alumna Professor of Philosophy at Wellesley College. She works in metaphysics, philosophy of language, feminism, philosophy of law, and their various intersections. She is the author of *Speech and Harm: Controversies Over Free Speech* (2012), co-edited with Ishani Maitra, and *Just Words: On Speech and Hidden Harm* (2019).

Eliot Michaelson is a Senior Lecturer in the Department of Philosophy at King's College London. His work focuses largely on non-ideal approaches to language use, approaches which give up on assumptions like: that the speaker is be understood, that the speaker knows her own mind, or that there is a single best way for a listener to interpret a bit of speech.

Christopher Mole is Professor of Philosophy and Chair of the Programme in Cognitive Systems at the University of British Columbia, Vancouver. He is the author of *Attention is Cognitive Unison* (2011), and *The Unexplained Intellect* (2016), and is co-author, with Daniel Lafleur and Holly Onclin, of *Understanding Mental Disorders* (2019).

Ethan Nowak is Associate Lecturer in the Department of Historical, Philosophical, and Religious Studies at Umeå University. Most of his work has to do with language in one way or another. Some focuses on detailed questions about context-sensitivity in semantics and meta-semantics, while some takes up broader questions about how we use language to construct our identities and shape our communities. His contribution to the present volume was partially supported by the Leverhulme Trust, grant number ECF-2019-608.

Matthew Ratcliffe is Professor of Philosophy at the University of York, UK. Most of his recent work addresses issues in phenomenology, philosophy of mind, and philosophy of psychiatry. He is author of *Rethinking Commonsense Psychology: A Critique of Folk Psychology, Theory of Mind and Simulation* (2007), *Feelings of Being: Phenomenology, Psychiatry and the Sense of Reality* (2008), *Experiences of Depression: A Study in Phenomenology* (2015), and *Real Hallucinations: Psychiatric Illness, Intentionality, and the Interpersonal World* (2017).

Susanna Siegel is author of *The Contents of Visual Experience* (2010) and *The Rationality of Perception* (2017). She is Edgar Pierce Professor of Philosophy at Harvard University.

Sebastian Watzl is associate professor of philosophy at the University of Oslo. He currently heads a Centre for Philosophy and the Sciences. Watzl works in the philosophy of mind and psychology with a focus on attention, the theory of action, and the relationship between normative and descriptive theories of the mind. He is the author of *Structuring Mind* (2017), as well as a range of articles on attention, perception, consciousness, and action. He has recently been awarded an ERC Consolidator Grant for the study of attention norms.

Ella Whiteley is a Fellow in Philosophy at the London School of Economics. Their primary research interests are in ethical and political philosophy, the social dimensions of epistemology and language, and the philosophy of biology. Ella is currently writing on the epistemic and linguistic dimensions of salience. They are also writing on the "invisible labour" performed in universities, and have a forthcoming co-authored paper *Invisible Labour: Time and Hermeneutical Injustice*. This latter research has emerged from their previous research role in 'The Invisible Labour Project' at the University of Cambridge.

Introduction: Salience and philosophy

Sophie Archer

Salience is both central to human life and relatively underexplored as a philosophical topic. Whether it bothers you that the picture on your wall is wonky, whose advice you take, whether you notice the homeless person at your feet as you squeeze your way down Oxford Street: these are all a function of salience. Salience is clearly of significance for a broad range of philosophical problems but rarely, if ever, has salience itself been the theme. This volume makes it so in an attempt to learn more about the place of salience in philosophy.

The chapters that follow often address familiar questions, such as 'What is aesthetic judgement?', 'What is demonstrative reference?', 'What is practical wisdom?', and 'What is epistemic injustice?' but, out of these treatments, a novel set of questions also begins to emerge about salience itself. What exactly is it? Indeed, is there a unified phenomenon here at all? What is the relationship between salience and attention? Are there norms of salience? Are we responsible for what is salient to us? If so, how, and to what extent? Is it something that we stand in an active or passive relationship to? What is it for salience to be pathological? An exciting new topic begins to present itself in this volume, which represents a first attempt at articulating and addressing some of these questions. No doubt more will become clear in time.

In the opening chapter, Dan Cavedon-Taylor discusses what he calls the 'Kantian thesis of aesthetic disinterest'. According to this thesis, aesthetic judgements involve perceptual contemplation for its own sake, necessarily divorced from the individual judger's particular concerns. This view has been challenged in various ways, but Cavedon-Taylor focuses on the charge that it pays insufficient attention to the perspective of the artist. Doesn't the artist make aesthetic judgements concerning their work with a view to modifying it as they are creating it? Cavedon-Taylor argues that the photographer, at least, does make such practically-engaged aesthetic judgements, citing Cartier-Bresson as his central example.

In order to make his case, Cavedon-Taylor draws on a distinction of Susanna Siegel's (2014) between what he calls 'weak' and 'strong' salience. Aesthetic qualities that are weakly salient are attention-grabbing and yet the agent is not moved to action by them whereas those that are strongly salient are attention-grabbing in a

DOI: 10.4324/9781351202114-1

way that "mandates" action (Cavedon-Taylor, 2022, p.14). The cry of their baby will typically be strongly salient to its parent, for example. What Kantian disinterest rules out is any strongly salient aesthetic experience. But Cavedon-Taylor argues that the picture that emerges from the photography and writings of Cartier-Bresson is of aesthetic judgements that cannot be separated from the motivation to photograph. Human life is strongly aesthetically salient for Cartier-Bresson: the aesthetic appreciation of it *is* an experience of a "photo *opportunity*" as Cavedon-Taylor (2022, p.19) puts it.

In Chapter 2, Hemdat Lerman discusses the difficulties in determining whether, and if so how, visual attention to a seen object can contribute to its visual phenomenal salience. She begins by considering the evidence from introspection. She points out that although there does seem to be introspective evidence that visual attention can affect the phenomenology of our visual experience, there is a problem inherent in such introspection. To try to introspect one's experience of an object or property that one is *not* visually attending to, one must attend to it. So, we cannot get clear, via introspection, on what it is like to experience something unattended and therefore how this might differ from the experience of something to which one is attending.

She turns then to empirical work on visual attention. As she points out, there is of course no simple entailment from empirical findings regarding the operation of the visual system to claims about phenomenology. Nonetheless, focusing attention on an object enables further visual processing of information from the object. Lerman suggests then that, at the very least, we can rely on empirical findings as to the results of further processing in order to learn about the ways in which focused visual attention affects phenomenology. Some potential results of further visual processing are greater, "clarity, detail, object-coherence, visual recognition" (Lerman, 2022, p.32). Lerman tentatively advances the hypothesis that at least some of these contribute to making the object visually salient.

Assuming this to be the case, she turns to consider the idea that there is more to the effect of visual attention on its visual phenomenal salience, bringing her to what she calls the 'distinctiveness claim'. This is the claim that, "'focused visual attention has a saliency effect on the phenomenology of visual experience which is distinctive of attention, and thus cannot be fully-captured in terms of changes in appearance (where 'appearance(s)' is understood as referring to ways an experience represents or presents the environment as being)." (Lerman, 2022, p.33). She focuses on Sebastian Watzl's (2017) argument for this claim and finds it wanting.

Next, Matthew Ratcliffe and Matthew R. Broome consider both appeals to 'salience dysregulation' or 'aberrant salience' and 'affordances' in understanding psychiatric illness. They argue that these terms lack the necessary discriminatory power to be anything more than a starting point.

What is 'phenomenologically salient' (what is experienced as salient) can be aberrant in wildly different ways. Ratcliffe and Broome outline a multitude of distinctions between different experiences of aberrant salience, along various different dimensions. Consider the vast difference between something's appearing salient as threatening, versus its appearing salient as fascinating, for example. Or, contrast experiencing something as salient in an aberrant fashion and experiencing its salience *as aberrant*.

Affordances are understood to involve our perceptions of aspects of the environment as salient in ways that are intimately bound-up with our dispositions to act. Ratcliffe and Broome prefer appeals to affordances as opposed to mere salience insofar as they think of the concept of affordances as sensitive to at least some of the distinctions they draw with respect to salience. Nonetheless, they argue that it too is a blunt instrument. As Ratcliffe (2015, p.61, f.n.24) puts it, "Things do not simply 'afford' activities; they appear significant to us in all sorts of different ways." Indeed, what about cases in which something is salient in no longer affording something or not affording what it should, for example? The precise content of an affordance is also difficult to specify along both interpersonal and temporal dimensions, Ratcliffe and Broome argue. Can I experience an object as affording something to you but not me? Or, as affording such-and-such, which will enable so-and-so, that will in turn allow for X?

These, and many more difficulties besides, lead Ratcliffe and Broome to conclude that we need a taxonomy much more nuanced than one containing merely 'salience' and/or 'affordances'. As things currently stand, the extent to which different kinds of aberrant salience are included in, and cut across, our existing diagnostic categories is unclear. And which of the variables Ratcliffe and Broome identify will be the most informative in understanding psychiatric illness is also unclear. But, what is clear, according to Ratcliffe and Broome (2022, p.53), is that at a certain point in our investigation, the concepts of salience and affordances become "swamped" by all the dimensions of variation Ratcliffe and Broome identify and lose their explanatory power.

In Chapter 4, Ethan Nowak and Eliot Michaelson discuss the role of salience in fixing the reference of demonstrative expressions. Roughly speaking, 'salience-based' theories claim that a given demonstrative expression refers to whatever is maximally salient in the context of utterance. So, as Nowak and Michaelson put it, one can imagine as many iterations of these theories as there are answers to the question, 'Salient for whom?'.

The first answer they consider in detail is Allyson Mount's (2008), according to which a demonstrative refers to what is, "mutually recognized as maximally salient" (Nowak and Michaelson, 2022, p.75). They reject Mount's view on the grounds that it renders reference "extraordinarily brittle" (Nowak and Michaelson, 2022, p.80). What is salient to a given individual will often depend on various idiosyncratic facts about them, and if but one person in a group does not find salient what everyone else does, the speaker's reference fails entirely, according to Mount's view. Nowak and Michaelson also encounter problems with both the idea that it is only what is salient to the speaker that counts in fixing demonstrative reference, as well as with the view that it is only what is salient to the listener(s). This leads them to consider whether the appeal to an idealised listener could plausibly be made but problems lurk here too – not least that there often *is* no ideal listener: is it better to find cars salient as opposed to motorbikes, *ceteris paribus*? Finally, a 'random person in the street' will not do either, according to Nowak and Michaelson, as in many cases coordination is achieved thanks to some specialised knowledge that both speaker and listener share.

Nowak and Michaelson conclude that in spite of the initial intuitive appeal of salience-based theories of demonstrative reference, it seems unlikely that one will be ultimately satisfactory. This is not to say, however, that salience won't play an important role in our understanding of the meaning of demonstratives: Nowak and Michaelson anticipate that it will.

In his contribution to the volume, Sebastian Watzl argues that we need an 'ethics of attention'. Since William Clifford published the 'The Ethics of Belief' in 1877, there has been a flourishing field of study dedicated to questions about belief's normativity. Watzl argues that attention is at least as descriptively central to human life as belief and the public also clearly cares about normative guidance concerning attention. So, it too should have its own 'ethics'. One question he thinks would arise in the field is how salience and attention are related and what this tells us about the respective normative pressures on each.

According to Watzl's 'Priority View' of attention, which he develops in his *Structuring Mind* (2017), attention has this descriptive centrality that is plausibly subject to norms insofar as it is a unified phenomenon, consisting in the person's activity of regulating 'priority structures'. These priority structures order the parts of the person's mental life by their relative priority to the person. On this view, the salience of a mental state is a passive phenomenon and consists in the degree to which it commands prioritisation.

Watzl then uses the second part of his chapter to set out a framework for the ethics of attention: for the systematic investigation of the potential norms that, by his lights, would be the norms for the regulation of priority structures. He classifies such norms in accordance with three aspects. First, whether they are norms that pertain to which object is to be attended to or to the manner in which it should be attended to. Second, whether the norms are instrumental or non-instrumental. And, third, whether the source of the norm is moral, prudential, or epistemic.

Our own discussion takes a normative turn at this point. In my contribution to the volume, in Chapter 6, I consider the fact that you can be accountable – be it morally, rationally, or in some other way – for what is and is not salient to you. I try to understand what salience is in the light of this fact.

The sort of responsibility I am interested in is what I call 'direct' or 'intrinsic'. It is *for finding something salient*, or *for failing to do so*. So, it cannot be explained in terms of any indirect voluntary control you might exert over what is salient to you, such as by practising attending in certain ways. Rather, I argue that it is to be explained in terms of your 'evaluative control' over what is salient to you. You evaluate what matters and therein control what is salient to you. According to the 'Naïve Constitutive View' of this evaluative control, in the kinds of cases I am concerned with, the salience of something to you is *constituted* by your occurrent evaluation that it matters in the situation. This captures the direct nature of your responsibility for what is salient to you. However, focusing as it does on a particular occurrent evaluation, it cannot do justice to another important feature of the type of accountability for what is salient to you I am concerned with – that this salience is reflective of your character, more broadly speaking. A mere one-off occurrent evaluation, considered on its own, cannot explain this.

With this in mind, I turn to what I call the 'Separate States View' of your evaluative control. On this view, the salience of something to you is not constituted by an occurrent evaluation. Rather, salience, in itself, is a mere 'standing out' or eliciting of your attention. But such salience is caused and rationalised by your standing evaluations about what matters in general. This account captures the idea that your responsibility is grounded in your character. However, I argue that it cannot properly explain the direct nature of your responsibility for noticing or for failing to notice. As such, I propose what I call the 'Sophisticated Constitutive View' of your evaluative control. I argue that the salience of something to you, in the kinds of cases I am interested in, is constituted by your occurrent evaluation that it matters in the situation and emerges from your standing evaluative worldview about what matters in general.

Next is Sophie-Grace Chappell's succinct chapter on moral philosophy in which she argues that a list of possible actions at a time (an 'option range') is not an objective given. When the trolleyologist, for example, presents us with a dilemma in which we *must* choose between either killing the one or the ten, this is a hopeless fiction. In fact, there are always infinitely many possible actions at a time: "in between any two possible actions there is a third." (Chappell, 2022, p.131) As such, we choose between the possible actions that are salient to us. And, which are salient to us is itself a value-laden matter. Chappell argues that which possible actions are salient to us is in part contingently determined by various psychological and social-historical factors. But it is also, in part, a question of our determining them in accordance with practical wisdom. She asks, "What psychological mechanisms bring it about, in people of good character, that the right options are salient to them – and the right other options silenced? To raise this question is to ask for an account of practical wisdom." (Chappell, 2022, p.138) Chappell herself does not attempt to provide such an account in this volume (though she has said much about it elsewhere [see e.g. 2009, 2014, and forthcoming]. But, in the next chapter, Christopher Mole sets about making a contribution to this task.

Mole begins by drawing on decision theory to argue that an option's being salient does not, in itself, provide us with a *reason* for choosing it. This is not the role of salience in moral decision making. Rather, Mole agrees with Chappell that its role is in framing our options in the first place. We often, Mole thinks, behave badly simply because an important aspect of a situation is not salient to us and we sometimes behave well only because of the lack of salient temptations to do otherwise. To understand the development of practical wisdom then, Mole thinks that we need to answer Iris Murdoch's (1970, p.53) question as to whether there are, "any techniques for the purification and reorientation of an energy which is naturally selfish, in such a way that when moments of choice arrive we shall be sure of acting rightly".

According to Mole, we can begin to understand what such techniques could be by looking to the past few decades of psychological research on attention and its impact on what is salient to us. This research reveals that salience is in part determined by the regularities in the things to which we direct our attention. Salience structures can be laid down fairly easily in this way and, once this has happened, they "display inertia" (Mole, 2022, p.156). However, the research also reveals that we need not be consciously aware of the factors determining such a structure, nor need they feature in our intentions. As Murdoch (1970, p.36) says then, attending "imperceptibly... builds up structures of value around us". But Mole argues that this need not be thought of as cultivated by "an obscure system of energies" (Murdoch, 1970, p.52) – we are beginning to remove the obscurity thanks to psychological research on attention.

In Chapter 9, Sabina Lovibond is also interested in the role of salience in practical wisdom. She reorientates us slightly though by focusing on how we might avoid what she calls "involuntary wrongs" (Lovibond, 2022, p.161). That is, wrongs that we have no voluntary control over – they are not even the foreseeable consequences of our voluntary acts and omissions, for example. In particular, she is interested in Robert Adams' (1985) claim that failing to respond (consciously or unconsciously) to ethical data that are rich enough to enable an appropriate ethical response can constitute an involuntary wrong. To understand Adams' claim, Lovibond (2022, p.172) thinks that we need to know when ethical data counts as "objectively salient" such that they would be subjectively salient to the practically wise person.

She advances the ambitious idea that everything that can be assumed to be available to someone with the normal abilities at a given time and place (adjusted for age, physical or mental abnormality and other considerations of this kind) count as objectively salient ethical data. This idea seems to enable us to capture, "the moral shadow that hangs over ordinary (bourgeois) life even when no one seems to be doing anything amiss", as Lovibond (2022, p.165) beautifully puts it. However, she worries about the charge of over demandingness. Ultimately, she rejects this charge though, on the grounds that our objective should be understood to be progressing in the right direction towards a better perception of saliences, even if we cannot reasonably expect ever to meet the ultimate, ever-retreating standard. We will always be liable to a 'surprise attack of conscience' in this regard, even grounded in remote historical events, for example. She closes though with an example of our responsibility for what is salient offering the possibility for voluntary agency. The example she gives is the topical one of making a political intervention in the form of making others acknowledge as salient sexual harassment that has for too long been objectively salient.

In her chapter, Mary Kate McGowan (2022, p.178) discusses some "sneaky" consequences of altering what is salient. In particular, she is interested in harmful salience-altering speech actions that pertain to group-based injustice.

Her central example involves a white male doctor, Dr Green, who was the chair of the hiring committee that just hired a Black female doctor, Dr Tilson. In the course of a conversation between the two at a reception to welcome Dr Tilson to the medical practice, Dr Green says to Dr Tilson, of hiring her, "[It was a very easy decision] for us too. We wanted to diversify our staff and many of our patients are also Black. They'll relate to you." (McGowan, 2022, p.185) Whatever his intention, Dr Green's speech action makes Dr Tilson's race salient (or more salient) in the social context they are in. However, that doing so has such significant consequences is not salient: it is sneaky (even though the consequences themselves can of course be all too salient for some).

McGowan explores two ways in which Dr Green's salience-altering speech action might harm Dr Tilson: it might *constitute* a harm to her, and it might *cause* her harm. According to McGowan's use of the term, to say that a speech action 'constitutes' harm is to say that the action enacts a norm, which is followed, and harm results from following that norm. In addition to constituting a harm to Dr Tilson in this sense, McGowan argues that Dr Green's remarks might also simply cause her harm. They might do so by triggering stereotype threat, for example, or by activating relevant implicit associations of those around her concerning Black women.

Ella Whiteley is also concerned with harming someone by making certain aspects of them salient. But Whiteley is primarily interested in the idea that we can harm someone *simply* in virtue of making certain aspects of them salient – regardless of what attitudes or actions this might cause in addition. So, unlike McGowan, when Whiteley talks about making something salient as 'constituting' harm, they are not talking about a "norm-driven way of causing", as McGowan puts it. Rather, Whiteley's main claim is that there can be patterns of salience that are harmful in and of themselves, as this is ordinarily understood. Whiteley calls these 'harmful salience perspectives' and says that they involve attention on things that should not be salient, or not enough attention on things that deserve to be made salient.

Whiteley draws upon a powerful example of a harmful salience perspective: when the fact that someone has been raped becomes the most salient about them. Simone Biles, 4 times Olympic gymnastics champion, recently expressed a concern along these lines when she announced that she had been sexually abused by her USA Olympic national team doctor. According to Whiteley, it is a problem for the fact that someone has been raped to be the most salient thing about them when it is in their interests for something else to be instead. It is in Biles' interest, for example, for her athletic prowess to be the most salient thing about her. Whiteley claims that this is because this prowess is a personhood-related trait, whereas having been raped is not. Indeed, they suggest that making someone's "*thing*-like properties" (Whiteley, 2022, p.202) more salient than their personhood-related properties is a form of objectification to be added to Martha Nussbaum's (1995) famous list. They raise but do not attempt to resolve the vexed issue that arises here concerning the relationship between what one *wants* to be salient about oneself and what it is in one's interests to be. Finally, Whiteley concludes with an interesting consequence of their view. Hate speech – in addition to being false and often inciting violence – might be harmful simply insofar as it brings to salience certain traits of an individual (*qua* their group membership).

Mikkel Gerken's chapter considers how salience can be implicated in 'discriminatory epistemic injustice'. This consists in someone's being, "wronged specifically in her capacity as an epistemic subject" (Gerken, 2022, p.222). He opens by arguing that what is known as the 'salient alternatives effect' on knowledge ascriptions can lead to such epistemic injustice. The 'salient alternatives effect' is the name given to the fact that we are less prepared to ascribe knowledge that *p* to someone when a particular possibility (an 'alternative') that is incompatible with *p* is salient. I might be less prepared to ascribe someone knowledge that it is three o'clock when the possibility that their clock has stopped has been suggested and hence made salient, for example. Now, Gerken assumes in his chapter that whether or not someone can properly be said to 'know' something does *not* depend on which alternatives are salient. Rather, the salient alternatives effect is best understood as a cognitive bias. He then puts this idea to work in identifying a "distinctive route to epistemic injustice" (Gerken, 2022, p.213).

He explores two main ways in which social stereotypes, associated with characteristics like race, can result in discriminatory epistemic injustice via the salient alternatives effect on knowledge ascriptions. First, he argues that whether someone is regarded as having ruled out a salient alternative may be affected by these phenomena in a way that leads to discriminatory epistemic injustice. Second, he argues that social stereotypes and in-group/out-group psychology may also influence judgements about knowledge by their effect on the salience of alternatives, leading to discriminatory epistemic injustice.

Susanna Siegel closes the volume by exploring her sense that considering the case of journalism in 'aspirational democracies' might best illuminate norms of salience. She proposes what she calls a 'Salience Principle of Importance', which states that journalists in democracies should make salient information that is important for the public to know about. However, this principle generates what she dubs the 'Problem of Democratic Attention': democracy imposes an attentional demand upon the public that cannot easily be met. The public often faces substantial bars of various kinds to attending to a lot of the important information that should be made salient to them, even when it is. In particular, such information may not be particularly exciting, as is evidenced by the divergence between what is important and what 'trends' on social media, for example.

To address the Problem of Democratic Attention, what we need, Siegel (2022, p.249) claims, is "a way to orient the reader". We need to know which attitudes facilitate democracy and how newspapers can select and present the news in a way that fosters these attitudes. Her 'Public-as-Protagonist Principle' of salience, she claims, can help. It requires journalists to frame and select stories in a way that invites readers to see themselves as potential participants in public life – to make clear their stake in a situation and how they could make a difference with respect to it. This, she suggests, will cultivate attitudes that facilitate democracy as well as making the news more likely to attract attention in the first place.

References

Adams, R. 1985. Involuntary Sins. *Philosophical Review* 94(1): 3–31.
Broome, M. R. and Ratcliffe, M. 2022. Beyond 'Salience' and 'Affordance': Understanding Anomalous Experiences of Significant Possibilities. In S. Archer (Ed.), *Salience: A Philosophical Inquiry* (pp. 50–69). Routledge, Abingdon.
Cavedon-Taylor, D. 2022. Life Through a Lens: Aesthetic Virtue and Salience vs Kantian Disinterest. In S. Archer (Ed.), *Salience: A Philosophical Inquiry* (pp. 10–23). Routledge, Abingdon.
Chappell, T. 2009. *Ethics and Experience*. Acumen, London.
Chappell, S. G. 2014. *Knowing What To Do*. Oxford Univeristy Press, Oxford.
Chappell, S. G. 2022. Salience, Choice, and Vulnerability. In S. Archer (Ed.), *Salience: A Philosophical Inquiry* (pp. 130–139). Routledge, Abingdon.
Chappell, S. G. forthcoming. *Epiphanies*.
Clifford, W. 1999. The Ethics of Belief. In T. Madigan (Ed.), *The Ethics of Belief and Other Essays* (pp. 70–96). Prometheus, Amherst, MA.
Gerken, M. 2022. Salient Alternatives and Epistemic Injustice in Folk Epistemology. In S. Archer (Ed.), *Salience: A Philosophical Inquiry* (pp. 213–234). Routledge, Abingdon.
Lerman, H. 2022. Attention, Salience, and the Phenomenology of Visual Experience. In S. Archer (Ed.), *Salience: A Philosophical Inquiry* (pp. 24–49). Routledge, Abingdon.
Lovibond, S. 2022. The Unquiet Life: Salience and Moral Responsibility. In S. Archer (Ed.), *Salience: A Philosophical Inquiry* (pp. 159–176). Routledge, Abingdon.
McGowan, M. K. 2022. On Salience and Sneakiness. In S. Archer (Ed.), *Salience: A Philosophical Inquiry* (pp. 177–192). Routledge, Abingdon.
Michaelson, E. and Nowak, E. 2022. On Salience-Based Theories of Demonstratives. In S. Archer (Ed.), *Salience: A Philosophical Inquiry* (pp. 70–88). Routledge, Abingdon.
Mole, C. 2022. The Moral Psychology of Salience. In S. Archer (Ed.), *Salience: A Philosophical Inquiry* (pp. 140–158). Routledge, Abingdon.
Mount, A. 2008. Intentions, Gestures, and Salience in Ordinary and Deferred Demonstrative Reference. *Mind and Language* 23(2): 145–164.
Murdoch, I. 1970. *The Sovereignty of Good*. Routledge, London.
Nussbaum, M. 1995. Objectification. *Philosophy and Public Affairs* 24(4): 249–291.
Ratcliffe, M. 2015. *Experiences of Depression: A Study in Phenomenology*. Oxford University Press, Oxford.
Siegel, S. 2014. Affordances and the Contents of Perception. In B. Brogaard (Ed.), *Does Perception Have Content?* (pp. 51–75). Oxford University Press, Oxford.
Siegel, S. 2022. Salience Principles for Democracy. In S. Archer (Ed.), *Salience: A Philosophical Inquiry* (pp. 235–266). Routledge, Abingdon.
Watzl, S. 2017. *Structuring Mind: The Nature of Attention and How It Shapes Consciousness*. Oxford University Press, Oxford.
Whiteley, E. 2022. Harmful Salience Perspectives. In S. Archer (Ed.), *Salience: A Philosophical Inquiry* (pp. 193–212). Routledge, Abingdon.

1 Life through a lens: Aesthetic virtue and salience vs Kantian disinterest[1]

Dan Cavedon-Taylor

1.1 Introduction

Kant's thesis of aesthetic disinterest casts a domineering shadow over contemporary aesthetics. According to Kant, aesthetic judgement entails pleasure in an object's perceptual appearance. This pleasure is said to be 'disinterested' insofar as it is free from practical interests and desires. (Kant's theory is most often discussed as a theory of beauty. I shall be rather liberal in my understanding of the view and take it as a theory of aesthetic judgement more generally.) For Kant, aesthetic judgement is a matter of contemplating perceptual form, with our sensory and cognitive faculties operating in complete absorption, to the exclusion of all else. In not being based upon personal interests or desires, this pleasure is not one of idiosyncratic preference or mere liking, what Kant calls 'the agreeable' (§3). Nor is it pleasure in a thing's objective utility, it's being fit for its function, what Kant calls 'the useful' (§4). Rather, aesthetic judgement entails pleasure in a thing's looking good (or sounding good, etc.) purely for looking at it (or the hearing of it, etc.), entirely, that is, for its own sake. Objects that occasion pleasure in this way are experienced as if made not just for the viewer's perceptual gratification, but for everyone's. Kant writes: 'attached to the judgement of taste, with the consciousness of an abstraction in it from all interest, [is] a claim to validity for everyone' (§6).

Close cousins of Kant's thesis are defended to this day. Edward Bullough (1912), Clive Bell (1914), Jerome Stolnitz (1960), Jerrold Levinson (1992) and Bence Nanay (2016) all defend views that draw inspiration from Kant in affirming that aesthetic judgement is, necessarily, free from personal interest and idiosyncrasies. It is therefore entirely non-practical in character. Aesthetic judgement, for these philosophers, entails experiencing objects and events in a uniquely detached way. Here is Bell, motivating his aesthetic formalism and, 100 years later, Nanay, demarcating aesthetic attention:

> Those who find the chief importance of art or of philosophy in its relation to conduct or its practical utility... will never get from anything the best that it can give. Whatever the world of aesthetic contemplation may be, it is not the world of human business and passion; in it the chatter and tumult

DOI: 10.4324/9781351202114-2

of material existence is unheard, or heard only as the echo of some more ultimate harmony.

(Bell, 1914, p.26)

There is a very clearly defined difference between aesthetic attention and non-aesthetic attention—one of them is distributed across properties but focused on one object, whereas the other one is not… [T]hinking of aesthetic attention as distributed attention does capture the original Kantian importance of disinterest in our aesthetic experiences. Practical interest in an object… could be described as attention focused on a limited number of its features—the ones we are interested in from a practical point of view.

(Nanay, 2016, p.26)

Kant's concept of aesthetic disinterest contains idiosyncrasies of its own. If aiming to be accurate to Kant, then one should be careful to keep his notion of disinterest distinct from the views of others (Zangwill, 1992; Crowther, 2008, pp.70–72). Nonetheless, the above philosophers clearly do follow directly in Kant's footsteps. We can therefore justifiably use the term 'Kantian disinterest' in a stipulative manner to cover all such views, and related ones, that distinguish what goes on in the mind of one who is considering an object or event aesthetically, with one who is considering that object or event in a more practical or engaging way, i.e., via the lens of their personal interests.

Kantian disinterest has recently been challenged from a number of directions. Judgements of sexiness may be thought to be at once aesthetic, yet partially constituted by the judge's practical interests, i.e., sexual desires (Lintott and Irvin, 2016). Moreover, some encounters with beauty are significant not because they cause one to shed one's idiosyncratic interests, values and desires, but because they reveal and transform those interests (Riggle, 2016). Kantian disinterest has also been challenged for its failure to acknowledge conceptual overlaps between the aesthetic, the moral and the social (Carroll, 1996; Berleant, 2010; Saito, 2016).

All of the above challenges focus on the aesthetic judgements of spectators. I will explore a quite different problem for the thesis of Kantian disinterest, one that is fruitfully approached via the notions of perceptual attention and salience: that it pays insufficient attention to the psychology of creators of art, and so can be challenged from the point of view of art-making and not only art-viewing. As a preview: what is salient (broadly: attention-grabbing) in one's perceptual experience on a given occasion is a function of one's interests, values, desires, expectations and beliefs at that time. Crucially, I shall argue that aesthetic qualities may be experienced by artists as salient not merely in the sense of being attention-grabbing, but also as mandating action as part of an artistic response to those qualities. Beauty moves us, not necessarily to tears or rapt contemplation, but to practical action. Beauty may inspire deeds, and it may do so as part and parcel of its appreciation. Or so I shall argue. To help fix ideas,

I focus on the art of photography, though I believe similar claims would hold for other art forms, e.g., poetry/literature, music and painting, though no doubt the details would need handling differently. In addition, I will argue that a virtue-based approach to aesthetics supplies a useful background against which to address these matters insofar as the link between salience and interests is suggestive of a link between salience and character, one that has already been explored fruitfully in the moral domain (Chappell and Yetter-Chappell, 2016).

1.2 Art-making vs disinterest?

Theories of Kantian disinterest are unduly spectator-based in their analysis of aesthetic judgement. That will be the take-home message. By attempting to divorcee aesthetic judgement from practical action, they view such judgement through the lens of passive observation, rather than active creation. Indeed, an underappreciated problem for such theories is that they rule out certain judgements on the part of artists as *bona fide* aesthetic. Berys Gaut (2007, p.31) has drawn attention to this problem. Gaut writes:

> If we insisted that a contemplative (non-practical) attitude is necessary for an attitude's being aesthetic, then any artist at all would count as not taking up an aesthetic attitude to her work while making it. For her attitude towards her work is certainly practical while she makes it: she is concerned to create it and to revise it in various ways so as to improve its quality. The contemplative criterion for the aesthetic attitude here reveals itself as rooted in the audience's perspective on the artwork and neglects the viewpoint of its maker, which has at least as good a claim to be an aesthetic one as does the audience's.

Gaut's idea is that at least two things are true of artists when they create their works: (i) they make aesthetic judgements about those works and (ii) such judgement are made from a practical point of view; they are not made from a passive, disinterested perspective of calm contemplation, but from an interested perspective as to whether certain actions need performing, i.e., on the work currently being created. For instance, producing a still life, a painter may pause to judge the composition not dispassionately, but by way of deciding if further work is necessary and where. Finding the composition only somewhat balanced, they may be further prompted to judge whether the proportions are quite right and whether the colour scheme needs rethinking. The ensuing aesthetic judgements are practical in character, having a conceptual connection to action: the proportions *are* off a tad and require retouching; a darker shade of red *would* better accentuate the contrast between the objects; etc. Thus, artists' aesthetic judgement of their works pose a counterexample to Kantian disinterest.

No doubt artists are interested in modifying their works on the basis of their aesthetic judgements. But whether there is a compelling challenge here to Kantian disinterest is less clear. Defenders of Kantian disinterest can reasonably attempt to separate in these cases the artist's aesthetic judgement from the artist's interests. For in reaching a verdict on whether their work requires modification, the artist may consider the work from the point of view of a dispassionate spectator, thereby flipping between interested and disinterested perspectives and keeping the two separate. The (dis)pleasure taken by the painter in their composition need not be (dis)pleasure that is grounded in their idiosyncratic interests, e.g., to refine the work or make it better fit the vision they initially had in mind. That is, the interest and the (dis)pleasure need not in fact 'mix' (§2) in the way that Kant thought problematic. Only if the (dis)pleasure in the object of creation is partially constituted (or grounded, etc.) in the artist's idiosyncratic interests, while remaining intuitively aesthetic, will Kantian disinterest be challenged. But as the possibility of switching between disinterested/interested perspectives and thereby keeping them distinct shows, this way of understanding the cases Gaut has in mind is not mandatory.

So, if Gaut is right to highlight a clash between art-making and Kantian disinterest, then that clash requires a much fuller defence. This is the aim I set myself in this paper. I shall attempt to elucidate the tension between art-making and Kantian disinterest by considering the art of photography and works by one of its great masters: Henri Cartier-Bresson. But to do so will first require detours via the concepts of both salience and virtue.

1.3 Salience

Philosophical discussions of the concept of 'salience' are few, but where they are found, they typically take their lead from a body of literature in perceptual psychology on the mechanisms of perceptual attention (Wu, 2014; Chappell and Yetter-Chappell, 2016; Watzl, 2017; though see Greco, 2003 and Lackey, 2007 for discussion of 'explanatory salience'). By and large, discussion of what is salient for an agent is bound up, either implicitly or explicitly, with the discussion of how perceptual attention alights on a region, object or feature in a non-involuntary, automatic way (sometimes called 'exogenous' or 'exogenously-driven' attention). This aligns with a very natural reading of the term 'salient' as referring to that which is attention-grabbing. Things that are salient for an agent are things that capture, divert or take command of the agent's attention. Such involuntary shifts of perceptual attention will be my focus and contrast with shifts of spatial-, object- or feature-based attention that occur intentionally (sometimes called 'endogenous' or 'endogenously-driven' attention).

First point: involuntary shifts of attention, while automatic and unwilled, are still causally responsive to idiosyncratic aspects of the agent's psychology (for some exceptions, see Wu, 2014, pp.37–38). A crying voice may automatically draw your auditory attention away from a conversation only because you recognise the voice to be your child's. A water cooler may draw your visual attention only because you are thirsty. Focusing on the conversation, you weren't listening out for your child's voice. Not believing a water cooler to be located in the building, you weren't looking for one. Rather, these things struck you. They were salient for you, exerting an involuntary tug on your attention, but only given your particular background beliefs, desires, interests, etc.

An example from beyond the armchair: in experimental conditions, Yi Jiang and their colleagues (2006) found that erotic pictures either involuntarily capture or repel subjects' spatial attention, dependent on the sex and sexual orientation of the subject participant: the attention of heterosexual males was involuntarily captured by female nudes yet repelled by male nudes, while heterosexual females' and gay males' attention was involuntarily grabbed by male nudes (though not repelled by female nudes in quite the same manner). Similar patterns of attentional repulsion/capture were observed for bi-sexual and gay females.

A second point: to the extent that what an agent finds salient is a product of their particular psychology, salience patterns can imply facts about character. For instance, we may find others morally blameworthy to the extent that certain morally-relevant facts are not salient to them. Failing to have one's attention diverted by the surrounding poverty when visiting an exotic holiday destination seems to imply obliviousness to others' needs. But we also find people morally blameworthy to the extent that certain morally-relevant facts *are* salient to them, exerting a pull on their attention, and yet fail to provide any motivational influence. Having one's attention grabbed by the sound of one's child calling out in pain, but without being moved to check on the child, implies at best pitilessness and at worst malevolence. As Chappell and Yetter-Chappell put it (2016, p.452): 'In cases where the needs of others are especially *salient* to an agent, any altruistic desires in that agent can be expected to function at full efficacy'. Such an expectation is normative in character and not merely causal.

A third point: one way to understand episodes of perceptual salience, as a form of non-voluntary attention-grabbingness, is that they involve an experience of the world as attempting to solicit a response from you. Susanna Siegel (2014, pp.55–56) distinguishes among such soliciting experiences ones in which attention is grabbed by a stimulus and the agent fails to be moved by the solicitation, from cases where the motivation to do what is solicited is present. Siegel calls the latter cases ones of 'experienced mandates'. For hopefully very many parents, hearing their child crying in pain involves an experienced mandate and is not a mere soliciting experience: the child sounds as if it is to-be-checked-on *and* the parent feels compelled to do so. Siegel (Ibid., p52) characterises the phenomenology of experienced mandates as follows: 'From your point of view, the environment pulls actions out of you directly, like a force moving a situation, with your actions in it, from one moment to the next'.

I will mark this distinction of Siegel's by talking of experiences where a stimulus is *weakly salient*, in contrast with experiences in which a stimulus is *strongly salient*. The parent whose attention is grabbed by the sound of their crying child, but is not moved to check on its wellbeing, has a *weakly salient* experience of their crying child. The parent whose attention is grabbed by that sound and, in hearing it, is motivated to check on the child has a *strongly salient* experience of their crying child. The first is a blameworthy agent. The second is intuitively more admirable.

Now, theories of Kantian disinterest claim that aesthetic judgements of, e.g., beauty, elegance, harmony, proportion, unity, etc. are partially constituted by a contemplative experience in which one sheds one's idiosyncratic interests and is perceptually absorbed in an object's appearance for its own sake, absent practical concerns. Insofar as attributions of strongly salient experiences imply both idiosyncratic interests of the agent, combined with motivational elements, Kantian disinterest entails that there can be no strongly salient aesthetic experiences of, e.g., beauty, elegance, harmony, proportion, unity, etc. A *strongly salient aesthetic experience* is had by an agent just in case they experience an object to be, e.g., beautiful, elegant, harmonious, proportioned, unified, etc. in an attention-grabbing way that implicates one or more idiosyncratic psychological features of that agent and where a high degree of motivation to act on that experience is present. Such experiences, of beauty and other aesthetic qualities, are conceptually tied to the agent and their peculiar interests in ways that Kantian disinterest says is incompatible with them being *bona fide* aesthetic in character. Yet strongly salient aesthetic experiences are not only possible, but are plausibly attributed to aesthetically virtuous artists, photographers in particular.

1.4 Virtue aesthetics

In philosophical aesthetics, the locus of aesthetic evaluation has traditionally been taken to be objects. A shift away from this tradition has occurred in the shape of virtue-based approaches to aesthetics. Like virtue-based approaches in ethics and epistemology, these aim to direct evaluative focus onto agents, with emphasis on the skills, emotions, character traits, motives and intentions that manifest in artistic activity, where this includes the appreciation, performance and creation of works of art.

This approach has been developed in a number of ways (see Woodruff, 2001; Goldie, 2007; Lopes, 2008; Kieran, 2010; Ransom, 2019). My focus will be the distinction drawn by Tom Roberts (2018) between faculty and trait aesthetic virtues, principally in relation to artistic creation. This distinction takes inspiration from a familiar one in epistemology at the heart of the dispute between reliabilism and responsibilism. According to reliabilism, intellectual virtue is constituted by mere *faculties* of the agent: a good memory, finely detailed powers of perception, keen powers of inference and reasoning, etc. (Sosa, 2007) According to responsibilism, intellectual virtue is constituted by aspects of an agent's character: *traits* of open-mindedness, adaptability, carefulness, humility, fairness, etc. (Zagzebski, 1996)

Roberts notes that we can, accordingly, consider aesthetic virtues of creation to be constituted by *faculties*, e.g., perfect pitch, a steady hand, a sense of harmony and rhythm, an eye for detail, a vivid imagination, a rich vocabulary etc. or by *traits*, e.g., that reflect a concern for the aesthetic, including the courage to push boundaries, receptivity to and open-mindedness about novel sources of aesthetic value, and a concern for honesty and authenticity in the expressive or representational properties of one's works.

Artworks that are the product of aesthetic faculty virtues instantiate *achievement value*, according to Roberts. For instance, hyperrealistic portraits by Chuck Close are finely executed, requiring a keen eye for detail and refined motor-skills. The song 'Parakeet' by the band Faraquet is complex in terms of its individual riffs and its changes in time signature, requiring a dexterous memory to switch between such changes.

Trait aesthetic virtues, by contrast, are ones that the agent is more fully responsible for and constitute more deeply who the agent is as a person. Chiefly, this is through such virtues revealing core concerns, values and principles to which the agent is evaluatively committed. Attributions of these aesthetic virtues thus imply facts about the agent's motives in ways that attributions of mere faculty virtues do not. Such works have, according to Roberts, *motivational value*. The chief idea is that artworks can be aesthetically evaluated not simply for their intrinsic formal qualities, nor for how they are the product of an agent's remarkable aesthetic faculties or skills, but for being 'shaped and crafted according to what she cares about' (Ibid., p.443). Denis Dutton makes a similar point when discussing the concept of authenticity in art:

> It is more than just formal quality that distinguishes the latest multimillion-dollar Hollywood sex-and-violence blockbuster or manipulative tearjerker from the dark depths of the Beethoven Opus 131 String Quartet or the passionate intensity of The Brothers Karamazov. These latter are meant in a way that many examples of the former cannot possibly be: they embody an element of personal commitment normally missing from much popular entertainment art and virtually all commercial advertising. (2003, p.271)

The concept of aesthetic trait virtues dovetails neatly with the concept of strongly salient aesthetic experiences. Recall: a strongly salient aesthetic experience is had by an agent just in case they experience an object to be, e.g., beautiful, elegant, harmonious, proportioned, unified, etc. in an attention-grabbing way that implicates one or more idiosyncratic psychological features of the agent and where a high degree of motivation to act on that experience is present. What an agent finds strongly salient in this aesthetic sense likewise reflects the agent's concerns, values and interests.

We saw in the discussion of the parent who has a strongly salient experience of their crying child that they are morally admirable, to some extent, for being motivated to check on its wellbeing. The parent who is not so motivated, and who has a weakly salient experience of their crying child, is morally blameworthy. (Caution: do not think that all weakly salient experiences entail a deficit of virtue, nor that all strongly salient experiences entail its possession. Some attributions of strongly salient experiences, where an agent is motivated to act maliciously, entail viciousness and some attributions of weakly salient experiences entail commendable restraint.)

Likewise, I suggest, artists are sometimes *aesthetically* admired for their strongly salient aesthetic experiences; that is, for having their attention grabbed by a stimulus and being motivated to produce works of art as a result. When artists are so admired, they are thereby admired for their *trait* aesthetic virtues, aesthetic virtues that, unlike mere faculty virtues, imply motivational facts: that the artist was moved to produce *that*. To make this idea concrete, I now turn to photography, first discussing its relation to aesthetic faculty virtues before moving on to the manifestation in photography of aesthetic trait virtues.

1.5 The photographer's eye

Consider talk of 'the photographer's eye' or of someone's having 'a photographer's eye'. These are terms that praise an agent for having a relatively unique way of seeing the world, one that is manifest in their photographs. It might be thought that to have a photographer's eye is merely to possess certain aesthetic *faculty* virtues, e.g., to visually discern spatial forms or to imagine how a 3-D scene will appear in the 2-D surface of the resulting photograph, etc. We can also add here the practical skills to knowledgeably control certain variables, like shutter speed, focal length and lighting conditions. Consider as well how an agent with a photographer's eye may perceptually categorise objects in such a way that entails awareness of those objects' typical temporal dynamics, thus enabling such objects to be tracked through the viewfinder (Maynard, 2008, p.203). This latter skill is especially important for capturing the scene in its full dynamics, what Henri Cartier-Bresson famously called 'the decisive moment'.

Cartier-Bresson's writings are a rich source of reflection on the nature of photography. Some of these seem to describe the act of photographing from the perspective of aesthetic faculty virtues. Consider the following:

> Photography is the simultaneous recognition, in a fraction of a second, of the significance of an event as well as of a precise organization of forms which give that event its proper expression. (2004, p.42)

> Sometimes it happens that you stall, delay, wait for something to happen. Sometimes you have the feeling that here are all the makings of a picture—except for just one thing that seems to be missing. But what one thing? Perhaps someone suddenly walks into your range of view. You follow his progress through the viewfinder. You wait and wait, and then finally you press the button. (Ibid., p.33)

> After developing and printing, you must go about separating the pictures which, though they are all right, aren't the strongest. When it's too late, then you know with a terrible clarity exactly where you failed... Was it simply that you did not take into account a certain detail in relation to the whole setup? Or was it (and this is more frequent) that your glance became vague, your eye wandered off (Ibid., pp.25–27)

> Memory is very important, particularly in respect to the recollection of every picture you've taken while you've been galloping at the speed of the scene itself. The photographer must make sure, while he is still in the presence of the unfolding scene, that he hasn't left any gaps, that he has really given expression to the meaning of the scene in its entirety, for afterwards it is too late. He is never able to wind the scene backwards in order to photograph it all over again. (Ibid., p.25)

> [Photography] requires concentration, a discipline of mind, sensitivity and a sense of geometry. (Ibid., p.15)

For Cartier-Bresson, the photographer's eye involves a kind of flexibility of seeing, quick reactions, a keen memory, and, above all, a sense of space and form. Looking at some of Cartier-Bresson's best-known works of winding streets and alleys there can be no doubt that he is, as Gérard Macé, put it, 'a geometrician without a sliderule'. (See Cartier-Bresson's *Aquila degli Abruzzi*; *Sifnos, Greece*; and *Hyères, France*.) Indeed, Cartier-Bresson's photographs merit admiration not just for their striking formal features, but for the achievement involved in skilfully capturing such fleeting geometrical patterns; Cartier-Bresson's photographs are not merely formally interesting, but *well-timed* (Cavedon-Taylor, 2021).

But there is another strand in these writings, and others, of Cartier-Bresson's and that point to the importance he placed on aesthetic trait virtues and the *motivational* value that may be possessed by the resulting photographs. Indeed, talk of 'the photographer's eye' can attribute not only certain remarkable faculties or skills. It can implicate aspects of the photographer's character, their concerns and motivation. Talk of 'the photographer's eye' is thus not always talk about a skill-based type, but something more trope-like: a particular, unrepeatable way of seeing the world. Cartier-Bresson's photographer's eye, for instance, is not that of Nan Goldin's or Ansel Adams's. Some photographs are the product of agents who see the world in playful, absurd or ironic ways. Others are the product of agents who see things more seriously.

The photographic eye of Cartier-Bresson was a humanistic one. The above remarks are made by someone with patience for, and open-mindedness to, the beauty of human life. Crucially, they express Cartier-Bresson's concern to faithfully record the intricacies of human, lived experience, with all of its details, both messy and minute. Cartier-Bresson, in his own words, sought to accept humanity 'in all its reality', reporting that his aim, above all else, was 'to be attentive to life' (2004, p.66). On visiting Moscow, he revealed his particular aesthetic concerns as follows: 'I explained that my main interest was in people and that I would like to see them in streets, in shops, at work, at play, in every visible aspect of daily life'. Cartier-Bresson's photographs of crowds and persons appear evidence of his finding beauty in fleeting moments of ordinary life. (See his *Boy Carrying a Wine Bottle*; *portrait of Alberto Giacometti*; *On the Banks of the Marne*.) As E.H. Gombrich (1978, p.10) writes, Cartier-Bresson's photographs 'will make us look at people and situations anywhere with a heightened sense of sympathy and compassion. He is a true humanist'.

So, Cartier-Bresson possessed a photographer's eye that was not merely geometrically exacting, but also deeply humane. Accordingly, his photographs merit admiration, among other reasons, insofar as they were produced from the aesthetically virtuous motivations of open-mindedness to, and patience with, a certain kind of beauty: that of human life. Again in his own words: 'In photography, the smallest thing can be a great subject. The little, human detail can become a leitmotiv' (2004, p.29).

Here, then, is the key claim: examining Cartier-Bresson's photographs and reading his thoughts on photography, it is natural to think that human life was *strongly* aesthetically salient for him. That is, the aesthetic aspects of everyday life did not take command of his attention, yet leave him unmoved; that would be to attribute to Cartier-Bresson mere *weakly* salient aesthetic experiences of human life. Rather, it is plausible that he found beauty, serenity, and other aesthetic qualities in small details of human life in an attention-grabbing way that entailed a desire to faithfully and sympathetically record such details with his camera. For Cartier-Bresson, the beauty of human life may have been salient in the sense that it simultaneously called out to be photographed and moved him accordingly. The environment may have seemed to pull the act of photographing out of him directly, in the manner described by Siegel. So much the worse for theories of Kantian disinterest, since they analyse aesthetic judgement as necessarily free from personal concerns and practical action.

How far can these remarks be generalised? I suspect that they can be generalised quite widely, among both amateur and professional photographers. It is very natural to think that people are moved to take photographs of people, places and events because they find those people, places and events to be objects of aesthetic interest. A tourist may be concerned to capture the breath-taking beauty of their surroundings and, as a result, have their attention grabbed by the magnificence of particular natural scenes and vistas in such a way that these may, phenomenologically, call out to be photographed, thereby moving the tourist accordingly. A doting grandparent at their grandchild's nativity play may be unable to divert their eyes from their grandchild, due to their love for the child, feeling compelled to snap away on their phone as a result. Both count as instances of strongly salient aesthetic experience. Photography is a case where beauty may at once grab and move. For an aesthetically virtuous photographer, like Cartier-Bresson, the appreciation of beauty is the experience of a photo *opportunity*, making judgements of beauty and motivation to act entwined for them.

Now, these examples, including that of Cartier-Bresson, might be construed in a causal way that does not threaten Kantian disinterest. On the causal picture, the photographer's appreciation and judgement of the objects before them is one thing, their being moved to photograph those objects remains quite another. The disinterested judgement merely causes a motivation to act. Indeed, recall the earlier worry about Gaut's way of motivating a clash between Kantian disinterestedness and art-making by focussing on artists' judgements of their works. The worry was that while the artist may appear to be taking an interested, practical stance when judging their work aesthetically, as Gaut suggests, she may in fact be flipping between interested and disinterested stances, again keeping the two distinct.

So, we have two potential responses on the part of the defender of Kantian disinterest to consider. First, the photographer's appreciation of a scene and their motivation to photograph it may be connected, but only casually. Second, the two may not be connected at all; the photographer may simply switch at will between disinterested and interested attitudes.

The problem with these responses is in how they separate the aesthetic judgement of O from the motivation to photograph O. Take the first response. Since it says the two are connected causally, this would entail that the photographer's aesthetic judgement of O and their motivation to photograph O can be understood in isolation from one another. The second response broadly agrees on this matter. For it denies that there is any connection *per se* between the photographer's aesthetic appraisal of the scene before them and their motivation to photograph that scene; instead, a higher-order state in the photographer is responsible for voluntarily switching between the two.

Are either views plausible? The key worry is that there appears little that can be understood of the motivation to photograph O, if fully characterisable in abstraction from an aesthetic judgement of O's qualities, something that both responses claim is the case. For how are we to understand a subject's being motivated at t1 to photograph O, with the aesthetic judgement of O at t1 potentially absent? Where no aesthetic judgement of O is present, motivation to photograph O can be expected to not be present as well. Construing the connection between the photographer's aesthetic judgement and their motivation to photograph either as a mere causal one, as the first response does, or as not connected at all, as the second does, fails to give a plausible account of the strength of the connection between the two. In the case of aesthetically virtuous photographers, like Cartier-Bresson, motivation to photograph seems closer to a criterion for the attribution of aesthetic judgement, rather than something that is at best connected contingently, i.e., via causation.

1.6 Broader concerns

In claiming that (some of) the experiences of (some) photographers are fully salient aesthetic experiences, there is one respect in which I wish to depart from Siegel. Recall that Siegel calls the more general type of experience here, a felt solicitation from the world with accompanying motivational elements, an experienced mandate. What I wish to dispute is Siegel's claim that the object of such experiences is never represented as 'a source of normative constraint' (2014, p.46). Siegel's idea appears to be that in feeling oneself answerable to the world in these experiences one does not simultaneously experience oneself to be under pressure or requirement to act in a relevant way. Siegel claims that this contrasts with how one may feel oneself, for whatever reason, answerable to another person.

Given the connection between salience and character, I think that this last claim is to be resisted. (Recall that having one's attention grabbed by a stimulus, in either weakly salient or strongly salient experiences, aesthetic or otherwise, implies psychological facts about one's interests and concerns.) The parent whose attention is grabbed by the sound of their crying child and is motivated to check on their wellbeing may well experience a 'normative constraint' on the action of checking: it is experienced as *to be done*, morally. Similarly, given what we know about Cartier-Bresson's character via his photographs and writings, it is plausible that he experienced a normative constraint on the action of photographing human life, that photographing human beauty is *the thing to be done*, from the point of view of the aesthetic. Human beauty may have been experienced as requiring faithful documentation. Thus, an agent in either the ethical or aesthetic cases described, who is motivated to act but, for whatever reason does not, may well experience themselves as having failed to live up to normative demands. Inaction may be experienced as the wrong thing to have done. Regret and self-reproach may ensue.

These two cases are individually sufficient to put pressure on Siegel's claim that strongly salient experiences/experienced mandates never involve experiencing a stimulus as imposing a normative constraint. Clearly, the idea that we are subject to *aesthetic* demands is the more controversial claim. But all that I am claiming is that we sometimes *feel* that such constraints are present, either for ourselves or others. One may feel that, from the point of view of the aesthetic (and not simply as a matter of ethics, prudence or etiquette), Jim should have worn a tie, or that Isabelle ought to have updated the décor in her flat by now, or that a colleague is much too old for that hairstyle (see Archer and Ware, 2018 for more examples). Likewise, an aesthetically virtuous photographer, who acts from care and concern for the aesthetic, may feel that they really ought to photograph an object, whether a scene in nature or tender moment between persons, that it would be an 'aesthetic crime' to leave it unrecorded and so allow the photo opportunity to wither away. Furthermore, such a photographer may feel it normatively required of them not merely to photograph some object, say, a particular person, but that, given the person's nature, aesthetic demands require they be photographed in a *specific* way, e.g., sympathetically, glamorously, grittily, etc.

1.7 Conclusion

This paper has many moving parts. In closing, I'll attempt to take stock.

Theories of Kantian disinterest claim that aesthetic judgement is partially constituted by pleasure in an object's appearance that is free from the influence of one's personal interests, desires or values. Aesthetic judgement, on this view, is said to be a wholly contemplative, or non-practical psychological state.

I have first claimed that this view is incompatible with the existence of strongly salient aesthetic experiences; that is, experiences that form the basis of aesthetic judgement in which an object is found to be, e.g., beautiful, elegant, harmonious, proportioned, unified, etc. in an attention-grabbing way that (i) implicates one or more idiosyncratic psychological features of the agent and (ii) where a high degree of motivation to act on that experience is present.

Second, I have claimed that we have good reason to think that there are, in fact, fully salient aesthetic experiences. A motivating thought here is that beauty sometimes inspires action rather than cool observation. Against the background of a virtue-based account, where the character and motives of artists are aesthetically assessable, my example of where we may find strongly salient aesthetic experiences is among the experiences of photographers. A particular case study is Henri Cartier-Bresson, whose photographs and writings suggest both an aesthetic interest in human life and in being motivated to authentically record its minutiae as part of its appreciation. Human life appears to have been strongly aesthetically salient to him.

Many of these claims, about Cartier-Bresson in particular, remain speculative. But the idea that beauty, human or otherwise, may inspire artists to make art and that, second, artists are persons who have unique ways of seeing the world (i.e., in which certain things are salient to them which are not for others), are both familiar ones, however difficult to articulate or make fully precise. If what I have said here is along the right lines, then, at the very least, much more must be done by the defender of Kantian disinterest to show how the two are compatible with their analysis of the aesthetic judgement.

Note

1 Thanks to Sophie Archer, C. Thi Nguyen and Tom Roberts for comments on previous versions.

References

Archer, A. and Ware, L. 2018. Beyond the Call of Beauty: Everyday Aesthetic Demands Under Patriarchy. *The Monist* 101: 114–127.
Bell, C. 1914. *Art*. G. P. Putnam, New York.
Berleant, A. 2010. *Sensibility and Sense*. Imprint Academic, Upton Pyne, UK.
Bullough, E. 1912. 'Psychical Distance' as a Factor in Art and an Aesthetic Principle. *British Journal of Psychology* 5: 87–118.
Carroll, N. 1996. Moderate Moralism. *British Journal of Aesthetics* 36: 223–238.
Cartier-Bresson, H. 2004. *The Mind's Eye: Writings on Photography and Photographs*. Aperture, New York.
Cavedon-Taylor, D. 2021. Arrangement and Timing: Photography, Causation and Anti-Empiricist Aesthetics. *Ergo*. https://philarchive.org/archive/CAVAAT-2v1
Chappell, R. Y. and Yetter-Chappell, H. 2016. Virtue and Salience. *Australasian Journal of Philosophy* 94: 449–463.
Crowther, P. 2008. *The Kantian Aesthetic*. OUP, Oxford.

Dutton, D. 2003. Authenticity in Art. In J. Levinson (Ed.), *The Oxford Handbook of Aesthetics* (pp. 258–274). OUP, Oxford.
Gaut, B. 2007. *Art, Emotion and Ethics*. OUP, Oxford.
Goldie, P. 2007. Towards a Virtue Theory of Art. *British Journal of Aesthetics* 47: 372–387.
Gombrich, E. 1978. Henri Cartier-Bresson. In *Henri Cartier-Bresson: His Archive of 390 Photographs from the Victoria and Albert Museum*. Victoria and Albert Museum, London.
Greco, J. 2003. Knowledge as Credit for True Belief. In M. DePaul and L. Zagzebski (Eds.), *Intellectual Virtue* (pp. 111–134). OUP, Oxford.
Jiang, Y., et al. 2006. A Gender- and Sexual Orientation-Dependent Spatial Attentional Effect of Invisible Images. *Proceedings of the National Academy of Science of the United States of America* 103: 17048–17052.
Kieran, M. 2010. The Vice of Snobbery: Aesthetic Knowledge, Justification and Virtue in Art Appreciation. *Philosophical Quarterly* 60: 243–263.
Lackey, J. 2007. Why We Don't Deserve Credit for Everything we Know. *Synthese* 158: 345–361.
Levinson, J. 1992. Pleasure and the Value of Works of Art. *British Journal of Aesthetics* 32: 295–306.
Lintott, S. and Irvin, S. 2016. Sex Objects and Sexy Subjects: A Feminist Reclamation of Sexiness. In S. Irvin (Ed.), *Body Aesthetics* (pp. 299–317). OUP, Oxford.
Lopes, D. 2008. Virtues of Art: Good Taste. *Aristotelian Society Supplementary* 82: 197–211.
Mace, G. 1996. The Lightest Baggage. Reprinted in H. Cartier-Bresson, *The Mind's Eye: Writings on Photography and Photographs*. Aperture, New York.
Maynard, P. 2008. Scales of Space and Time in Photography: Perception Points Two Ways. In S. Walden (Ed.), *Photography and Philosophy: Essays on the Pencil of Nature* (pp. 187–209). OUP, Oxford.
Nanay, B. 2016. *Aesthetics as Philosophy of Perception*. OUP, New York.
Ransom, M. 2019. Frauds, Posers and Sheep: A Virtue Theoretic Solution to the Acquaintance Debate. *Philosophy and Phenomenological Research* 98: 417–434.
Riggle, N. 2016. On the Interest in Beauty and Disinterest. *Philosophers' Imprint* 16: 1–14.
Roberts, T. 2018. Aesthetic Virtues: Traits and Faculties. *Philosophical Studies* 175: 427–429.
Saito, Y. 2016. Bodily Aesthetics and the Cultivation of Moral Virtues. In S. Irvin (Ed.), *Body Aesthetics* (pp. 225–242). OUP, Oxford.
Siegel, S. 2014. Affordances and the Contents of Perception. In B. Brogaard (Ed.), *Does Perception Have Content?* (pp. 1–28). OUP, Oxford.
Sosa, E. 2007. *A Virtue Epistemology*. OUP, Oxford.
Stolnitz, J. 1960. *Aesthetics and Philosophy of Art Criticism*. Houghton Mifflin, Boston.
Watzl, S. 2017. *Structuring Mind*. OUP, Oxford.
Woodruff, D. 2001. A Virtue Theory of Aesthetics. *Journal of Aesthetic Education* 35: 23–36.
Wu, W. 2014. *Attention*. Routledge, London.
Zagzebski, L. 1996. *Virtues of Mind*. CUP, Cambridge, UK.
Zangwill, N. 1992. Unkantian Notions of Disinterest. *British Journal of Aesthetics* 32: 149–152.

2 Attention, salience, and the phenomenology of visual experience

Hemdat Lerman

2.1 Introduction

We seem to have strong evidence – both introspective and experimental – that visual attention can affect the phenomenology of our visual experience. (By 'the phenomenology of visual experience' I mean the subjective character of one's visual experience – i.e., how things are, visually, from one's own perspective. Henceforth, unless specified otherwise, 'attention' should be read as 'visual attention', and 'phenomenology' as 'phenomenology of visual experience'). However, the exact character of such effects is far from clear. My aim in this paper is to spell out the main difficulties involved in attempting to achieve a clearer view of these effects, and to make some suggestions as to how we can make progress with this issue while avoiding tempting mistakes. I shall do this by discussing the question of whether there is a sense in which attention to a seen object can be said to contribute to the object's apparent or phenomenal saliency.

Several philosophers have recently suggested that focussing visual attention on a seen object renders it phenomenally salient/prominent/central/highlighted/ at the foreground (where it is suggested that these expressions are meant to capture the same aspect of the phenomenology).[1] According to some of the philosophers in question,[2] this effect on the phenomenology is distinctive of attention, and thus it cannot be fully captured in terms of the ways the experience presents (or represents) the environment as being (e.g., the attended object appearing larger or brighter than its surroundings). I'll argue that there are no good reasons for accepting this view. Instead, I'll suggest a more modest sense in which visual attention may contribute to the apparent/phenomenal salience of seen objects.

In 2.2 I focus on introspection as a source of evidence regarding the effect of attention on the phenomenology (where I use 'introspection' to refer to what we commonsensically regard as our ability to learn about our mental life 'from within'). The reader will be offered the opportunity to try to experience effects of visual attention on the phenomenology of visual experience. I'll then point out the inherent limitation on our ability to learn about the effect of attention on the phenomenology by introspection. In 2.3 I turn to the question of

DOI: 10.4324/9781351202114-3

Attention and visual phenomenology 25

whether and how empirical work on visual attention can contribute to our attempt to find out more about the exact character of the effect on the phenomenology. In 2.4 I consider the claim that focused visual attention has a distinctive saliency effect on the phenomenology of visual experience, an effect that cannot be captured in terms of the ways seen objects are presented in the experience as being. I'll look at potential ways of supporting the claim and argue that they do not provide sufficient support.

Before I start on those tasks let me explain the motivation for the discussion in this paper and highlight the significance, in this context, of the questions I'm asking about visual phenomenal salience. My interest in the effect of visual attention on the phenomenology of visual experience arises from an interest in philosophical accounts of visual experience. Such accounts are constrained by facts regarding the phenomenology of visual experience, and thus to be able to evaluate them one needs to get the details of the phenomenology right. The effect of attention on the phenomenology is particularly interesting since (a) we constantly shift visual attention during our everyday interaction with the environment, (b) the effect isn't transparent to us because of the dependence of introspection on attention discussed in 2.2, and (c) the effect potentially creates difficulties for two currently popular accounts of visual experience (namely, representational/intentional and relational accounts).[3] Now, as mentioned earlier, it is a widely held view that there's a kind of phenomenal salience that results from focusing attention on a seen object.[4] Being interested specifically in the phenomenology of *visual experience*, we want not only to clarify exactly what such phenomenal salience involves, but also to make sure we distinguish the effects of visual attention on *visual* phenomenology from coinciding effects on one's phenomenology in general (e.g., arguably, singling out a seen object in thought, intending to keep track of it, etc., contribute to how things are for one 'from the inside' beyond any contribution this might make to how things are for one visually). Thus, our inquiry into the character of the effect of attention on the phenomenology of visual experience involves asking: In what sense(s), if any, are visually attended objects phenomenally salient? To what extent is their phenomenal salience due to the effects of attention on the phenomenology of *visual experience*? And if there are effects on visual phenomenology that contribute to such salience, what more can we say about the exact character of these effects? (Note that this focus on the saliency effect of attention bears directly on current debates in philosophy of perception. One of the ways of arguing that the effect of attention poses a challenge to representational/intentional and relational accounts of visual experience, point (c), is to claim that attention has a distinctive saliency effect on visual phenomenology, which cannot be captured in terms of ways objects are (re)presented as being.[5])

There is also another, somewhat less direct, way in which the effect of attention on the phenomenology bears on accounts of visual experience. Arguably, a further constraint on such accounts is that they should make intelligible the role that visual experience plays in enabling us to entertain demonstrative thoughts about seen objects and in enabling us to gain knowledge about such objects. Visual attention is, arguably, essential to both, and it is plausible that its effect on the phenomenology is relevant to understanding the role it plays in both. One example, to which the present discussion of a saliency effect is relevant, is John Campbell's suggestion (2002) that a kind of saliency due to attention (which he refers to as 'highlighting') plays a role in our ability to entertain demonstrative thoughts about visually attended objects.[6] An immediate question for such a view concerns exactly what the relevant saliency contributes to the explanation of our ability to entertain demonstrative thoughts. And to answer this question we need to have a clearer view about what such saliency involves. Furthermore, it seems that to have such an explanatory role the relevant kind of salience shouldn't depend on 'cognitive attention', in particular on the subject's singling out the object in thought. Thus, for a proposal like Campbell's to be viable, it must be possible to trace the causes of this form of salience to the operation of a form of attention that is distinctively visual, rather than cognitive.

To emphasize, I am not going to defend any particular claim concerning philosophical accounts of visual experience (or demonstrative thought). Similarly, I am not going to defend any specific positive view about the exact character of the effect of attention on the phenomenology and the sense in which this effect may contribute to the visual phenomenal salience of attended objects. My aim is merely to spell out the main difficulties involved in attempting to achieve a clearer view of the effect of attention on the phenomenology (with emphasis on phenomenal saliency), and to distinguish steps that may help us to achieve some further clarity from unhelpful ones.

2.2 Introspection

I said at the start that there seems to be introspective evidence that visual attention can affect the phenomenology of our visual experience. To experience one such effect, try to keep your eyes more or less fixed on the central area of Figure 2.1 and shift your attention to the lighter shape and then to the darker one.

When you shift attention from one shape to another, do you experience a change in the phenomenology (that is, in how things are visually for you)? If so, can you specify exactly what the character of this change is? I asked several people about their experience in this and similar tasks. Many reported that the

Figure 2.1 Overlapping figures (adapted from Rock, 1995, p.144. In the original figure the darker shape is red and the lighter one green).

change in the focus of attention seemed to them to be accompanied by a change in phenomenology (some with more confidence, others with less). However, they are generally unsure about the exact character of this change. Some are happy to accept a description of the change as involving the attended shape 'coming forward' or becoming more salient or prominent, while the unattended one recedes to the background or becomes less salient or prominent; though what exactly is meant by any of these terms is left open.[7] Some say that the attended shape is in some sense seen more clearly, perhaps in more detail (this is especially notable when one is instructed to attend to, say, the lighter shape prior to seeing Figure 2.1, and is then shown the figure for a limited amount of time).

If you experience a change in the phenomenology when shifting attention between the two shapes, you too are likely to be unsure about the exact character of the change. For there is an inherent problem with the attempt to introspect the character of the experience of an object or property when visual attention is focused on a different object or property. We cannot direct introspective attention to an aspect of our visual experience (e.g., the way the lighter shape appears to us) without also directing (visual) attention towards the object or feature this aspect is an experience of (e.g., the lighter shape).[8] Thus, for example, when one's visual attention is focused on the darker shape in Figure 2.1, one's introspective attention isn't simultaneously directed at one's experience of the lighter shape. To introspectively attend to that experience, one will need to increase the amount of visual attention allocated to the lighter shape; but this may, potentially, affect the phenomenal character of the experience. It seems unquestionable that to learn about the exact character of the experience of an object one needs to direct introspective attention toward this experience; and so the dependence of introspective attention to visual experience on visual attention (to aspects of the environment) means that introspection alone can't provide us with a clear view of the exact character of the experience of the unattended object, and thus also of the exact ways in which it differs (if any) from the experience of the object when attention is focused on it.

We may still look for ways in which we can use introspection to gain *some* further information about the way attention affects the phenomenology. For example, it seems that we (or rather some of us) can, sometimes, notice particular effects like increase in apparent size, contrast, or color saturation of an attended object relative to an unattended one, if we shift our attention between two identical stimuli. For example, try, while fixing your gaze on the black square in the middle of Figure 2.2, first to equally attend to both patches, and then to shift your attention to the right-hand patch. (The reason you are asked to shift attention while keeping your gaze fixed on a fixation point mid-way between the two patches is that the direction of one's gaze has a notable effect on the phenomenology. The center of the human retina, called the fovea, is significantly more sensitive to light than its surroundings, and the sensitivity decreases with distance from the fovea. That means that what we direct our gaze towards can be seen more sharply and clearly than other things in our visual

Figure 2.2 A pair of qualitatively identical Gabor patches flanking a fixation point.

field. And the sharpness and clarity decrease the farther the seen thing is from the direction of gaze. When the direction of attention corresponds to the direction of one's gaze we call it 'overt' and when its direction differs we call it 'covert', and the same holds for shifts of attention.) When both patches are attended to equally, you are likely to experience the contrast between the dark and light stripes of the patches to be the same. Then, when you shift attention to the right-hand patch, you might experience the contrast between the stripes of the right-hand patch as higher than that of the stripes of the left-hand patch (note that not everyone has this experience).[9]

However, the identification of specific types of changes in the phenomenology in this and similar cases makes only a limited contribution to our understanding of how attention affects the phenomenology. First, in those cases in which we (or rather some of us) identify a particular type of change, we may lack a clear sense of whether this is the only change in the phenomenology and what other changes occur. Second, it isn't clear whether, and if so how, we can generalize to other cases from the special cases in which the display is designed to bring out the particular type of change – e.g., does it generalize to the shift of attention between the shapes in Figure 2.1? What kind of character will the experience in this case have to have for it to count as manifesting the same effect on contrast? Moreover, as we'll see in 2.3, there is evidence that the effect doesn't even generalize to all the cases in which it is clear what would count as a similar effect on contrast.

There are also reasons to worry about the reliability of introspection on one's experience when shifting attention between objects in displays such as Figures 2.1 and 2.2. The dependence of introspective attention on visual attention raises questions about what we are doing when we try, for example, to keep our attention focused on the darker shape (or the right-hand patch) and at the same time also introspect the character of the experience of the lighter shape (left-hand patch). Perhaps we are increasing the amount of (visual) attention we allocate to the lighter shape. If so, we would like to know to what extent this affects the experience of the lighter shape, and to what extent it involves withdrawing attention from the darker shape.[10] To start addressing these worries we should attempt to introspect our experiences in relevant controlled conditions that require quite a bit of work to set up.[11] For present purposes, though, we can conclude that introspection on cases like the ones discussed above do at least suggest that attention can have an effect on the phenomenology of our visual experience, and that *as a matter of principle* introspection cannot, by itself, reveal to us the exact character of the affect(s). In the next section, I consider how empirical work on visual attention may help us to learn more about the character of the relevant effects.

2.3 Empirical work

Experimental research on visual attention aims to uncover and understand the mechanisms responsible for visual attentional phenomena. Central to such phenomena is the selection of some information (from the available visual information) for further processing or for the control of specific actions.[12] Such selection is what takes place in the visual system in the kind of demonstration we considered in the previous section – that is, very roughly, when we manage to direct attention to the lighter shape rather than the darker one, an underlying mechanism modifies visual processing in such a way that information from the lighter shape (rather than information from other aspects of the scene) is selected for further processing.

Now, if experimental research can provide us with details about what such modifications involve, it seems reasonable to expect that it can help us to form a clearer view about the effect of visual attention on the phenomenology. For example, if we learn that only very general visual information regarding unattended objects is processed (thus, more specific information doesn't get processed) while both general and more specific information regarding the attended object is processed, then we will have further support to our sense that the experience of the attended object was more detailed than it was prior to our shift of attention towards it and that it was more detailed than that of the object which was unattended at the time.

Significant progress has been made in research on visual attention, and the combination of behavioral and neurobiological findings has provided quite detailed information about the mechanisms underlying visual attentional phenomena. We may, therefore, hope that this will allow us to form a quite detailed account of the effect of attention on the phenomenology. I do think that the experimental work can help us to clarify the character of the effect of attention on the phenomenology, but it should be clear that there is no simple entailment from relevant empirical findings to claims about the phenomenology.

The main obstacle is the fact that not every effect at the level of information-processing shows up in the subject's (conscious) experience.[13] This is particularly clear for effects that take place at early stages of visual processing – where the processing of information from a relatively narrow location during a relatively brief period of time is relatively unaffected by information from other locations and other times – because its contribution to the subject's experience may vary according to its relationship with information from other parts of the visual field and with information gathered at subsequent times. It is interesting here to consider, as an example, an effect of attention on early visual processing which, *in certain circumstances*, can show up in the subject's visual experience.

Experimental findings suggest that when attention is directed covertly to a certain location there is an increase in relevant neural responses to stimuli at that location. Thus when one fixes one's gaze on the black square in Figure 2.2 and attends to one of the patches, say the right one, there's an increase in the activity of neurons that respond to the right patch. Marissa Carrasco has suggested that due to this increase in activity the neural response resembles the response to a patch which is of higher contrast when attention is distributed more or less equally over the display, and that the increased activity is interpreted in the visual system as a signal of a patch of higher contrast.[14] Furthermore, in carefully controlled experiments, Carrasco finds that subjects' experiences of the relative contrasts of patches (in displays structurally similar to Figure 2.2, where the patches may differ from each other in contrast) are affected by attention. Attention to a patch increases its contrast relative to the other unattended one – e.g., when the patches are equal in contrast the attended one is experienced as higher in contrast, and when the attended patch is lower in contrast from the unattended one (for a certain amount of difference) they are experienced as similar in contrast.[15] The suggestion then, is that this is due to the effect on the signal at the early stage. Arguably this effect on the signal also explains the effect you may experience when attending covertly to one of the patches in Figure 2.2.

It is tempting to think that since the same increase in neural activity occurs whenever attention is covertly directed towards an object, there should also be a corresponding effect on experienced contrast. However, there is empirical evidence that when subjects view, instead of two still patches, moving stripes (within the bounds of the patches' locations – as if one is viewing the movement through a window) and covertly attend to one of the locations, there is no increase in the apparent contrasts of the stripes, but rather a slight decrease (see Turatto et al., 2007, p.172). Turatto et al. speculated that the reduction in contrast may be the result of blurriness due to the movement.[16] What matters for our purposes, though, is not the exact explanation, but rather the demonstration of how a (presumed) effect on information-processing at an early stage can be canceled out by other factors.[17]

It is worth mentioning that the effects of spatial and especially temporal context on the fate of more local information processed in the visual system aren't confined only to information about simple features like contrast (which are supposed to be processed at an early stage). The phenomena of visual masking and priming enable researchers to identify cases in which relatively complex visual information is processed but doesn't show up in experience. Masking occurs when a stimulus which would have been experienced had it been presented on its own, isn't experienced when it is embedded within a certain context (the mask). E.g., when a gray circle is displayed on a white screen for 40ms and the screen remains empty during the following second, subjects experience a brief appearance of a gray circle on an otherwise white screen. However, if the 40 ms display of the circle is followed by a 20 ms of white screen and then a 40 ms display of a gray ring that encircles the location at which the circle occurred, subjects experience only a brief appearance of the ring on an otherwise white screen.[18] Priming is an effect of a visual encounter with a stimulus on further performance (e.g., the speed of recognition of a similar stimulus when it is encountered again, or an effect on subjects' choice when they are shown the first few letters of a word and asked to complete it with the first word they can think of), where the subject isn't conscious of the existence of the effect. By testing the priming effects of masked stimuli, researchers attempt to find out what information from the masked stimuli (which aren't experienced consciously) has been processed. The research so far suggests, for example, that shape and category information from masked stimuli can be processed.[19] Highlighting the effect that temporal context can have on whether or not visual information shows up in experience is particularly important in this context since many of the empirical findings regarding visual attention concern modulations of visual information-processing at very fine timescales.

The focus, in experimental work, on fine timescale phenomena gives rise to a further complication. It isn't always obvious how such phenomena relate to what we ordinarily think about as phenomena of visual attention – our visually focusing on an object, say, in an attempt to recognize what kind of thing it is, our looking around the room in order to try to find the keys, or what we do when we attempt to shift attention covertly between the two shapes/patches in Figures 2.1 and 2.2. The former type of shifts of attention often occur 3 times per second, and we are, typically, unaware of their occurrence (at least the occurrence of each shift individually). Moreover, what we may view as focusing visual attention on an object may involve several shifts to surrounding objects, and between different aspects of the object.

Given the potential gaps between attentional modulation of information-processing and our conscious visual experience as well as the gap between fine timescale phenomena that the experimental research focuses on and what we ordinarily think of as phenomena of visual attention, it may seem that there is no point appealing to empirical work in order to learn more about the character of the effect of attention on the phenomenology. But this is an overreaction. First, the fact that the relationship between the empirical findings and the phenomenology is rather complex doesn't mean that we can't gain a better understanding of this relationship than we now have.[20] And the same holds for the relationship between the fine timescale phenomena and what we ordinarily regard as visual attentional phenomena. What it means is that we (philosophers) need to be very careful and patient when we attempt to evaluate what we can learn from given empirical findings about the phenomenology. It seems, in particular, that it would be useful to pay more attention to empirical work concerning the integration of information over time and concerning higher-level visual information-processing, as well as empirical studies of (both covert and overt) attention in the natural environment. Second, it seems that, even without addressing all the issues mentioned above, empirical data can reveal constraints on what could be true about the character of the effect of attention. Thus, for example, learning how reduced attention affects information-processing (not only locally at the early stages of visual-processing but more generally) provides constraints on what could be presented in our experience of unattended or less attended objects (at the beginning of the section I mentioned such a suggestion with regard to the processing of details). Furthermore, with sufficient care we can identify selective attentional modulations which are plausibly part of what takes place when we intentionally shift attention in our test cases (e.g., cases in which we shift attention covertly and attempt to introspect the experience as we did in 2.2); thus such constraints could be used to support hypotheses that fit a shaky observation we make on the basis of introspection.

To summarize, I suggest that empirical findings about attentional modulation of visual information-processing can potentially help us to learn more about the effect of attention on visual phenomenology, but that drawing conclusions regarding the effect on the phenomenology from relevant empirical data is a rather complicated matter. For this reason, I do not offer here any specific positive claim about effects on the phenomenology that are supported by empirical findings. Still, I think the programmatic suggestion about how empirical work can provide constraints on the character of the effect of attention enables us to formulate an initial hypothesis about the sense in which the effect of attention may be described in terms of salience.

Consider the selective attentional modulation of information-processing which, plausibly, occurs when we focus attention (overtly or covertly) on one object and so (to some degree) withdrawing attention from others. Such modulations result in the selection of information from the attended object rather than other information for further processing, and thus we can expect that whatever it is that further processing yields – clarity, detail, object-coherence, visual recognition – would be higher for the attended object relative to its unattended (less attended) surroundings. We can then ask whether any of these differences between the experiences of attended and unattended objects (or combinations of the differences) give us a sense in which the attended object is made salient to the subject. An initial hypothesis that doesn't seem implausible is that the experience of an object being visually more clear, coherent, and detailed than its surrounding does make the object stand out visually for the subject.[21] Furthermore, it doesn't seem unreasonable to suggest that this sense of salience of an attended object is relevant to explaining the role that visual attention to objects plays in enabling us to think about them demonstratively, to gain visual information about them and to intentionally direct visually guided actions towards them.[22]

These very general suggestions are meant to be mere hypotheses that may turn out to be wrong on more careful consideration. But let's assume for the sake of the argument that something along these lines is correct. It is still an open question whether this gives us the whole story about the kind of salience people report finding when they introspect the effect of attention in test cases. In the next section, I consider an attempt to argue that it doesn't give the whole story.

2.4 The distinctiveness claim

A number of philosophers have recently suggested that focused visual attention has a saliency effect on the phenomenology of visual experience which is distinctive of attention, and thus cannot be fully-captured in terms of changes in appearance (where 'appearance(s)' is understood as referring to ways an experience represents or presents the environment as being).[23] I'll refer to this suggestion as 'the distinctiveness claim' (to simplify matters I'll understand the claim that the effect is distinctive of attention as equivalent to the claim that the effect cannot be captured in terms of appearance[24]).[25] If there is such a distinctive (saliency) effect, then, arguably, it cannot be due merely to attentional modulations of visual information-processing. For presumably, attentional modulation of information-processing can only result in an effect on the appearance, since ultimately visual information-processing is understood functionally, and its function (in addition to providing information for action) is to account for the appearances. Thus, such modulations may affect whether or not aspects of the visual scene are seen; which ones are experienced as coherent objects; how detailed the presentation of each aspect is; the specificity of the properties and relations that are presented; etc.; and in addition, they may skew appearances (as when two patches of equal contrast are experienced as being different in contrast).[26,27]

What support is there for the distinctiveness claim? Proponents of the view often appeal to introspection of one's experience while one covertly shifts attention between qualitatively identical aspects of a display (e.g., the two patches in Figure 2.2), suggesting that such introspection reveals a phenomenological change that isn't due to any change in the apparent features.[28] Some philosophers (e.g., Speaks, 2010) do so by providing a test case regarding which they argue that no change in appearance is experienced at all, others admit that some changes in appearance occur but that these changes do not exhaust the effect on the phenomenology. However, our discussion in 2.2 and 2.3 suggests that introspection on the relevant experiences simply cannot suffice for supporting such claims. First, due to the dependence of introspection on attention, we do not have a clear enough sense of what the effect of attention on the phenomenology involves. Second, the empirical data do not provide us with a straightforward way of determining the effects of attention on appearance, so we cannot hope somehow to try to subtract what we know about the effect on appearance from what we introspect. Third, since there are, at least in principle, ways in which the effect on appearance can contribute to making an attended object salient, one cannot simply assume or argue a priori that effects on appearance cannot account for the saliency effect one seems to identify introspectively (especially given the lack of clarity about the exact character of effects we notice introspectively).[29]

In his 2017 Watzl attempts to provide an argument for the distinctiveness claim. I will consider this argument in detail both because it is the only detailed attempt I know of to provide such an argument,[30] and because some of the faults of the argument seem to be common faults in philosophers' reasoning about the phenomenology of experience in general and the effect of attention on it in particular.

Before presenting the argument, there is a need for one further clarification. The distinctiveness claim was described above as saying that focused visual attention has a distinctive saliency effect – i.e., an effect that cannot be fully-captured in terms of changes in appearance – on the phenomenology of the subject's experience. Watzl, and some of the other philosophers who discuss the claim, emphasize that they are concerned with focused *subject-level* (or personal-level) visual attention. So from here on I'll understand the distinctiveness claim in this way. This, of course, raises the question of what is meant by *subject-level* visual attention. We can start by pointing out that the activity of attending counts as subject-level when it is an activity of the subject – something the subject is doing. (Note that this doesn't exclude from counting as subject-level cases in which one attends, against one's own will, to a distractive stimulus – e.g., the moving images on a monitor in the background. Attending to a destructive stimulus can be something the subject does just like biting one's nails against one's own will is.[31]) Clearly, this rules out mere attentional modulations of visual information-processing from being considered as subject-level; but things become complicated when we ask whether we can assume that each (fine timescale) attentional modulation is at least a part of the activity that underlies subject-level attentional activity. For lack of space, I will ignore these complications and the potential problems they pose for Watzl.

Let's turn then to Watzl's argument for the distinctiveness claim. In order to show that focused (subject-level) visual attention has an effect on the phenomenology that goes beyond any effect it might have on the appearance, he argues as follows.[32]

Take any set of effects of attention on the appearance which may occur when a subject is experiencing a certain scene s in conditions c, while allocating attention in a certain way a. (Of specific interest to us is the case in which the subject focuses attention on only one out of a number of objects in s). The appearance – that is, the way things in the scene are presented to the subject in that experience as being – is a function of s, c, and a. Call this way w. Whatever the effects on the appearance are (that is, whatever the details of w are), there are always a scene s*, conditions c*, and a distribution of attention a* (a≠a*) which

1   replicates w – i.e, w is the way things in s* are presented to the subject in her experience when she experiences s* in c* while allocating attention in way a*.

For example suppose that a subject is viewing Figure 2.2 (this would be the scene s), in certain conditions (c) which include fixing their gaze on the black square, while covertly shifting attention towards the right-hand patch (this would be way a). And suppose, for the sake of the argument, that as a result of the attention shift the right-hand patch appears slightly higher in

contrast than the left-hand one. The claim is that the appearance w which is due to s, c, and a can be replicated by viewing a modification of Figure 2.2 in which the contrast (between the stripes) of the right-hand patch is higher than that of the left-hand one where the difference in contrast between them is the same as the degree of the apparent difference in contrast in w (this would be s^*), the conditions are the same (i.e., $c^*=c$), and the subject attends equally to both patches (a^*).
2   the phenomenology of the experience of s in c given a, differs from the phenomenology of the experience of s^* in c^* given a^*.

If this is true (or rather, if it is true for all cases in which a is a case of a subject's focusing visual attention on a certain aspect of the scene), then visual attention has a distinctive effect on the phenomenology of the experience (though, as the argument is presented, it is a further question whether the additional effect involves making the attended aspect, in some sense, salient). However, both (1) and (2) are problematic.

To see that (1) is problematic, consider the possibility that the effect of focussing attention on one of the objects in a given scene on the appearance involves an effect on the specificity of the experience – both with regard to how determinate or determinable apparent properties of the attended and unattended properties are (e.g., whether the object is experienced as having a very specific rectangular shape, as merely rectangular, as rectangularish, and so on), and with regard to the amount of details one experiences.[33] (As mentioned in 2.3 such effects are likely results of attentional modulations of information-processing). It is, however, doubtful that such effects can be replicated as required by (1). That is, it is doubtful that there is a way of adjusting the scene and conditions so that a subject who distributes their attention over the adjusted scene in the adjusted condition will have an experience with exactly the same appearance as they have while focusing attention in the original case. Watzl suggests that changes in how determinate/determinable apparent properties are can be replicated with the help of glasses that blur/focus parts of the scene. In addition one might think that lack of details can be easily replicated by erasing details from the scene (e.g., erasing pockets, buttons and creases from a shirt, or the complex texture from a piece of wood). But both suggestions seem mistaken. Consider our experience of objects in the distance. The experience is less specific than the experience of the same object from closer to. But the phenomenology, when the object is seen at the distance is nothing like simply seeing the same thing only somewhat blurred (and with missing details).[34]

It seems, then, that (1) is incorrect.[35] However, let's assume for the sake of the argument that it is correct, and consider (2).

What is the basis for (2)? Watzl starts his discussion of it by claiming that it is 'intuitively obvious' (2017, p.177), and continues:

> There is an obvious phenomenal difference between focusing your visual attention on some small detail, and diffusing attention over the scene as a

> whole. This difference remains even if we suppose that the world appears the same in both scenarios. The relevant phenomenal difference simply doesn't seem to amount to a difference in the apparent world a subject encounters in her phenomenal experience. (2017, p.177)

Note, first, that Watzl isn't asking us to compare two actual experiences – the one we have when we focus attention on 'some small detail' (of a given scene in given conditions) and our experience in the relevant replica situation in which we diffuse attention over the scene. We are merely asked to *suppose* that in a replica situation the appearance (what we called w) is the same as the appearance in the focused attention situation. Furthermore, neither Watzl nor anyone else can attempt to evaluate (2) by comparing actual experiences of the relevant types (at least not given our present knowledge about the effect of attention on the appearance). For we don't know what w in the focused attention situation is, and don't know what a perfect replication should be. Take the simplified example described above (with relation to Figure 2.2). For the purpose of the example I assumed that the only effect on appearance due to attention was an increase in the relative apparent contrast between the patches. However, we have no good reason to assume that this is the only effect on appearance (any aspect of the patch – size, shape of the stripes, character of the blurry bit enveloping the patch, etc. – and the gray background may change in the specificity of its appearance, and there may also be further effects on apparent relative distance, etc.). Furthermore, in my description of the simplified example I only talked about what the relative contrast between the patches should be, but an actual replication requires us to determine the specific degrees of contrast of each patch in the display. This requires that we know the extent to which the appearance of each patch is affected. In addition, it is possible that an accurate replication requires that we take into account small changes in the amount of attention allocated to different aspects of the display over time – changes that occur even when we are attempting to fix attention on one patch only[36] – as these may result in (slight) changes in appearances over time.[37]

Note that one cannot simply attempt to argue that it is unlikely that any of the differences I've just mentioned would explain the effect of attention on the phenomenology, and therefore that a simplified, inaccurate replication can suffice for our purposes. The problem isn't merely that the argument promises to show that no set of changes in appearance can capture the whole effect that attention has on the phenomenology, and thus proponents of the argument can't simply presuppose that some effects on the appearance are irrelevant to capturing the full saliency effect. The further problem is that (i) introspection doesn't give us a clear sense of the character of the change in phenomenology of the test case, and (ii) at least some of the likely potential effects of attention on appearance (including some of the ones missing in the simplified example) may contribute to some sense of saliency of the object on which we focus attention. Consequently, we can't rule out that even fine differences concerning these effects on the appearance can make a difference to whether or not the phenomenology seems to us to involve the relevant sense of saliency of the relevant object.

It is clear, then, that Watzl isn't offering an actual way of introspectively noticing, by comparing relevant actual experiences, that attention has an effect that goes beyond its effect on appearance. Returning then to the above quote, the question is: what basis is there for Watzl's claim that '[the phenomenal difference between the focused and distributed attention episodes] remains even if we suppose that the world appears the same in both scenarios.'? Since it is a claim about the phenomenology, he must rely on introspection in some actual cases. And since ordinarily we direct attention overtly – that is, together with corresponding eye movements – the relevant actual cases have to be ones in which one can be sure that attention is directed covertly, which limits the range of relevant cases to the kind of test cases we mentioned in 2.2.[38] It seems, then, that Watzl, like other proponents of the distinctiveness claim, is simply relying on introspection in the test cases.[39] Consequently, the discussion in 2.2 and 2.3 casts doubts on his basis for (2).

Although Watzl's argument for the distinctiveness claim doesn't advance us beyond reliance on introspection in the test cases, further examination of Watzl's discussion may help us in a different way. Since Watzl allows for the possibility that the effect of attention in the test cases is partly an effect on appearance, perhaps his discussion could point us towards aspects of the experiences in the test cases which might explain how introspection on such cases leads Watzl and others to believe that the effect on the phenomenology in those cases goes beyond the effect on the appearance.[40] There seem to be two such aspects, and in the rest of this section I will consider briefly whether any of them provide immediate support for the distinctiveness claim.

The first aspect is suggested by the last sentence in the above quote – 'The relevant phenomenal difference [between the focused and distributed attention episodes] *simply doesn't seem to amount to a difference in the apparent world* a subject encounters in her phenomenal experience' (my italics). Though this isn't what Watzl is explicitly discussing there, the sentence reminds us that the effect of attention on the phenomenology in the test cases isn't experienced as a change in the world – we aren't even slightly inclined to judge that the shapes and patches in Figures 2.1 and 2.2 have changed (as we might have been if the effect yielded an illusory experience). Thus, for example, if you experience the attended patch as becoming higher in contrast when you shift attention to it, it is most likely that you do not experience the change as a change in the contrast of any of the patches. Perhaps, then, this fact plays some role in explaining how the test cases might seem to involve a distinctive effect of attention.

It should be clear, though, that the fact that the effect of attention on the phenomenology isn't experienced as a change in the world, by itself, doesn't immediately entail that the effect on the (visual) phenomenology goes beyond the effect on appearance. First, some changes in appearance which shifts in attention can potentially cause – e.g., mere changes in specificity – do not correspond to change in the world. Thus the fact that the change in appearance doesn't appear as a change in the world doesn't mean that the effect of attention on the phenomenology goes beyond the effect on appearances.[41]

Second, in the test cases the change in appearance that is due to the shift in attention occurs during our ongoing experience, and thus our experience includes an experience of a certain change. Now, when this is the case, the specific way in which the appearance changes – for example, whether the experience is as of an object in front of one gradually changing shape in a rather natural way, whether the experience is as of an object becoming partly occluded by another object, and so on – can make a difference to whether or not the change appears (visually) as a change in the properties of a certain object. Moreover, a change may appear as one that doesn't involve changes in the object, even when the appearance of the object after (or before) the change is, by itself, potentially misleading (with regard to the object's features).[42] For example, watching a pound coin, which is initially facing you, slowly turning 45°, so that at the end its side is facing you, doesn't appear as a change in the coin's shape, though the appearance from the side could have misled you regarding the shape of the object you see. So again, the mere fact that the change doesn't appear as a change in the world doesn't mean that the effect of attention on the phenomenology goes beyond an effect on appearance.

The point is that there can be different types of changes in appearance which might all be described as a change from appearance A (e.g., an object being round) to appearance B (e.g., the object being an elongated rectangle), but when the change itself is experienced it (visually) appears differently – in some cases as a change in an object's qualities, in others as a change in some environmental conditions, in the subject's condition, or perhaps merely as a change that isn't experienced as a change in the object's qualities (while not experienced as being due to any other factor[43]). Cases of the latter two types may be generally described as cases of visual constancy (at least in a loose sense). And it doesn't seem implausible that such constancy is present in cases of covert shift of attention. Consider again the experience of covertly shifting attention to the right-hand patch in Figure 2.2. It seems that a subject who experiences a change in contrast in this situation doesn't experience it as a change in the actual contrast of the patches. In this particular example, it seems reasonable to suggest that we have a case of the third type: it isn't part of the way the change is visually experienced that it is due to a shift in attention, the experienced change simply isn't experienced as a change in the patch. (This is, at least, how the experience strikes me.[44]) If this description of the appearance in the case in question is correct, then we have a change from the appearance of two patches of equal contrast to an appearance of the right-hand one appearing higher in contrast, while the appearance of the change isn't an appearance of a change in the actual contrast of any of the patches.[45]

When reflecting on how a certain change in appearance is (visually) experienced by us, it can be very difficult to separate the effects of what we believe and know about the situation from what is genuinely an aspect of the experience. This is especially true in what I described above as the third type of case –

where the apparent change isn't experienced as being of a certain kind of change. Thus I am not ruling out the possibility that in the patches' case the appearance of the change isn't sufficient for explaining why it seems to us immediately obvious that the change isn't a change in the patches. And that the explanation requires appeal to a belief that the patches aren't changing, or to one's knowledge that one is shifting attention in the relevant manner. Note, though, that since our aim now is to identify an aspect of *the experience* in the test cases that could account for the impression that the effect of attention goes beyond its effect on appearance, this alternative construal is of interest to us only to the extent that the relevant belief/knowledge is somehow an aspect of or based on a relevant aspect of the phenomenology of the experience which isn't obviously a matter of appearance. One candidate, which seems more promising than alternatives, is one's immediate awareness of how one is attending, which is the second (potential) aspect of the experience we'll consider.

Watzl mentions in his discussion of (2) that the phenomenological difference (between an experience in a focused attention episode and an experience in a replica episode with diffused attention) is due to the fact that in each case the subject is doing something different and the fact that she is aware of what she is doing (from the inside).[46] Now, there is no doubt that in the test cases we are very much aware of how we are directing our attention, since these are cases in which we deliberately (and with some effort) shift attention covertly to a particular object, and attempt to maintain it while we attempt to introspect the phenomenology. It also seems unquestionable that this has an effect on the overall phenomenology of our state at the time (i.e., not merely visual). But it is not at all clear that it affects *visual* phenomenology. In addition, this suggestion raises questions as to whether the effect is genuinely an effect of subject-level focused visual attention, or whether it is merely due to the awareness of how one attends. One way of pressing the latter worry is to ask whether the effect generalizes to all cases of subject-level focused visual attention. There are clear cases in which we aren't aware of shifts of our visual attention. For example, there are several situations in which we shift attention overtly about 3 times per second without being aware of doing so. So to argue that the effect generalizes, one would need to defend a view according to which focused subject-level attention is limited to cases in which we are aware of how our visual attention is directed. In addition, the relevant view would need to regard such awareness as a genuine integral part of one's visually attending, otherwise the effect of the awareness of one's focusing attention would seem similar in type to effects that the awareness of other visual exploratory activities could have on the phenomenology.

A proper discussion of these worries would require consideration of several complex issues that are beyond the scope of this paper. However, I take it that it is far from obvious whether and how the worries could be dealt with. And this is all I want to show at this point. I will, though, make a few brief comments which will highlight some of the difficulties involved in trying to address these worries.

The first worry – whether one's awareness of how one is attending affects the phenomenology of visual experience, rather than merely the overall phenomenology – raises complex issues as to whether there is a useful distinction to be drawn between the phenomenology of visual experience and other aspects of the overall phenomenology, and if so, how to draw it. But for present purposes, we can just focus on two options that seem favorable to the proponents of the distinctiveness claim. First, they could assume (like most philosophers of perception nowadays[47]) that there is a useful distinction to be drawn between the relevant aspect of the phenomenology, and that one's awareness of what one is doing forms part of what we can consider to be non-perceptual phenomenology; and argue that there are cases in which one's awareness of what one is doing can affect visual phenomenology, where awareness of how one is visually attending is such a case. Second, they could argue, specifically, that the phenomenology of our visual experience is a phenomenology of our active visual engagement with the environment, where this cannot be construed as a simple conjunction of a more basic visual phenomenology and awareness of relevant activities.[48]

The second suggestion seems to be in tension with attempting to argue for an effect that is distinctive of visual attention, where visual attention is treated as separable from eye movement and other bodily movement that are normally part of one's active visual engagement with the environment (e.g., moving towards an object to see it more clearly, changing the angle from which an object is viewed in order to gain more information about its shape, and so on). For the suggestion is concerned with subjects' active visual engagement with the environment as it is viewed by the subject. And it doesn't seem that, generally, subjects' awareness of this engagement can be broken down into fine components one of which is the direction of visual attention (independently of eye movement and further bodily movements). That is, the test cases are special in that they involve one's specifically aiming to shift attention covertly, but there is no corresponding element that is a separable component of every ordinary way in which we focus attention on objects during our everyday interaction with the environment.[49]

Let's turn then to the first suggestion – that one's awareness of how one is attending isn't itself an aspect of visual phenomenology but that it has an effect on it. There are two questions we should ask here. Is it reasonable to suggest that such awareness can have an effect on visual phenomenology? And if so, does the relevant effect concern the saliency of attended objects? A potential consideration that might support a positive answer to the first question is this. Awareness of conditions that affect the experience (e.g., the lighting conditions, the subject's location relative to the object) seem to be relevant to determining the character of visual phenomenology. For example, it is clear that information about one's position relative to an object is significant to how one experiences the object. It is also clear that part of the way such information affects one's visual experience is a matter of the visual-system using such information in processing information about shape, size, and so on; a use that is independent of what one is aware of. But there is room for arguing that one's awareness of one's (potentially changing) location relative to objects is integral to how the object is experienced as being. That, for example, the way an object's shape and color are experienced from a long distance is inseparable from its being *experienced* as far away. The thought then, is that the same could be true of the effect of attention – i.e., that in addition to attention's affecting the experience by modulating information-processing, one's awareness of how one is attending can (in some cases) make it the case that the effect (or aspects of it) is experienced as an effect that is due to the way in which one is directing attention. This suggestion doesn't seem completely implausible (especially if it isn't meant to be general), but it is also not obvious that it is correct, and it is not obvious how to decide whether it is. Furthermore, it doesn't seem that this suggestion can help to support the claim that attention has a distinctive *saliency* effect on the phenomenology. For the suggestion merely says that an object one is focusing attention on may be experienced as being attended, and that changes in the way it appears may be experienced as due to changes in the focus of one's attention. This, by itself, doesn't seem to give us a sense in which an object is (visually) experienced as salient.[50] It is, of course, true that the object is singled out by the subject as the object of their attention, and it may be argued that this involves a sense in which the object is salient to the subject. But here a suggestion such as Wu's (2011, 2014) – that this sense of saliency is an aspect of non-visual phenomenology – seems more plausible (unless we return to the second suggestion which seems to be in tension with the project of identifying an effect that is distinctive of visual attention, construed as independent of eye movements, etc.).[51]

As mentioned above, these sketchy comments about the prospects of appealing to the awareness of how one is attending in order to support the distinctiveness claim are only meant to point toward some of the complications one may face when attempting to address the two worries – whether such awareness affects visual phenomenology and whether it is genuinely an effect of (subject-level) visual attention. I do not take them to be sufficient for showing that the worries can't be addressed, but hopefully they help to clarify that addressing them isn't a trivial matter.

2.5 Conclusion

My aim in this paper was to spell out the main difficulties involved in attempting to achieve a clearer view of the effects that visual attention has on the phenomenology of visual experience, and to make some suggestions as to how we can make progress with this issue. Given the prevalence of the view that in the case of focused visual attention such an effect involves, in some sense, an increase in the saliency of the attended object, I approached this task by asking whether there is a sense in which focusing visual attention on a seen object can have a saliency effect on visual phenomenology.

We saw that introspection, by itself, cannot provide more that a very general characterization of such effects, often with limited confidence on the side of the subject. I suggested that empirical work on visual attention can provide some further clarity about the effects of attention on the phenomenology, even though the relationship between the empirical work and facts about the phenomenology is rather complicated. I also suggested that given general considerations regarding the way in which empirical work can put constraints on what could be true about the phenomenology, and regarding the role attention plays in modulating visual processing, the relevant modulation can, potentially, account for a sense in which an object on which attention is focused is made salient relative to its surroundings.

I then turned to consider whether we can find support for the claim that attention has a (further) distinctive saliency effect on the phenomenology – one that goes beyond an effect on appearance, and thus one that isn't merely due to attentional modulation of visual information-processing. The limitations of introspection and of what our current empirical knowledge tells us about the effect on the phenomenology, together with the fact that attentional modulation of visual information-processing might give rise to some sort of saliency effect, make appeal to introspection in the test cases seem hopeless. I therefore considered the argument by which Watzl attempts to support the distinctiveness claim, and argued that it doesn't add any support beyond the support provided by introspection on the test cases. Finally, I considered two potential aspects of the experience in the test cases which might explain why someone who is aware of potential ways in which attention can affect appearances in the test cases might still hold that it has a further distinctive effect. I suggested that neither aspect immediately supports the distinctiveness claim.[52]

Notes

1 For simplicity's sake, I'll just use 'salience' to describe this effect. The claim that attention has a saliency effect isn't new, and recent philosophers who discuss it – e.g., Stazicker (2011), Watzl (2017), Wu (2011, 2014) – usually take the effect to be one that William James emphasized in *The Principles of Psychology* in 1890, and which has been widely acknowledged by both philosophers and psychologists. Part of the reason for my focus on the views of certain recent philosophers is that, in their discussions, they wish to distinguish clearly between, on the one hand, effects of *visual* attention on the phenomenology *of visual experience*, and on the other hand, effects of attention in general (including cognitive attention) or effects on non-visual phenomenology. It's worth emphasizing that the use of 'salience' here is distinct from its use to refer to an aspect of objects in virtue of which they attract one's visual attention (the latter is the way salience is ordinarily used in empirical work on visual attention). The use of 'salience' here differs also from Watzl's (2017 and this volume). Watzl uses 'salience' to refer to an aspect of mental states that (by definition) attracts attention to them; where 'phenomenal salience' is the 'felt' attracting aspect. (In Watzl's words 'Phenomenal salience is a felt command to attend to something...' 2017, p.213)
2 E.g., Speaks (2010), Watzl (2011, 2017), Beck and Schneider (2017).
3 Potential challenges, to these two views, posed by effects of attention are discussed, for example, by Chalmers (2010), Beck and Schneider (2017), Block (2010, 2015), Brewer (2013), Ganson and Bronner (2013), Speaks (2010), Stazicker (2011), Watzl (2011, 2017, 2019), Wu (2011, 2014). Note that in this paper I focus on the way attention affects the experience of *seen* objects. A different (though related) type of challenge to

all accounts of visual experience concerns the effect of attention on the experience of the whole scene, where the focus is on empirical data that suggest that some amount of attention to an aspect of the environment is necessary for it to be seen, and the challenge is to reconcile this with the fact that introspection suggests that we have a fully detailed experience of the whole scene.
4 See fn.1.
5 This challenge is discussed by Chalmers (2010), Speaks (2010), Watzl (2011, 2017), and Wu (2011, 2014).
6 Note that the claim that the saliency in question plays a role in an account of demonstrative thoughts is consistent with Nowak and Michaelson's (this volume) claim that what they call 'salience-based theories of reference' are untenable. The former is a claim about demonstrative *thought*, and it is specifically limited to the role of *visual* attention in enabling *simple vision-based* demonstrative thoughts. In contrast, the latter claim concerns the determination of the reference of demonstrative-involving *linguistic utterances*, and Nowak and Michaelson's considerations in support of it are specific to the use of language in communication. Furthermore, the latter claim isn't limited to cases in which the salience involved in determining reference is due to visual attention, it is meant to apply, equally, to cases in which salience is due to cognitive attention.
7 'Unattended' should be read here as 'not in the focus of the subject's attention (when the subject's attention is focused on some object)'. For even when we focus attention on one object we may still allocate some attention to other seen objects. (In fact, the discussion below suggests that it's likely that in the kind of case we are considering we do allocate attention to the 'unattended' object). In addition, I'd like to stay neutral on Mack and Rock's (1989) claim that some amount of attention to an object is required for having an experience of it.
8 The formulation in the text is meant to capture a phenomenon we all encounter when we attempt to introspect our visual experiences (see Martin, 1998). I'm simplifying here by focusing on the ordinary case, when we aren't hallucinating. What matters for our purposes is that from the subject's perspective, directing their introspective attention towards a certain aspect of their visual experience can't be separated from doing what one does when one shifts visual attention towards the object or property this is an experience of (for a subject who believes they are hallucinating, introspecting an aspect of their experience would involve attempting to shift attention as they would do if they believed the experience wasn't hallucinatory. See Martin, 1998, p.17, Soteriou, 2013, Ch.8). Those who hold that – in contrast to our commonsense view – in the ordinary case our visual experience and visual attention aren't directed towards mind-independent objects/properties would replace the formulation in the text with one that fits their theory, but should still accept the description of how things are from the subject's perspective.
9 The example is based on experiments, conducted by Marisa Carrasco and her collaborators, which are meant to show specific effects of attention on the phenomenology (for an overview see Carrasco, 2009).
10 A further worry concerns the fact that we are using simple, unchanging displays which are visible to us before we start our introspective exercise. As a result, our experience of the unattended object and our introspective judgment about it could both be affected by prior experience we had while we attended to the object. Things are complicated by the fact that often this is also the case in our everyday interaction with the environment. However, it is still the case that ordinarily the scenes we view are dynamic and much more complex. Some further worries will be mentioned in 2.4.
11 Psychologists have been conducting several experiments in relevant controlled conditions in order to determine what information is available to subjects from unattended objects. However, since the psychologists in question aren't interested in

the fine details of the phenomenology, they only aim to determine whether a subject can report (directly or indirectly) the presence of an unattended object and its (coarse-grained) color, shape, etc. (Carrasco's work is an exception to this, I'll return to her findings in the next section). Even if we agreed that the relevant ability to report is a good indication of whether the subject experienced the object and its properties, it doesn't tell us anything about the differences, if any, between the experience, with and without attention, of the objects and properties that the subject can report when not attending to the object.

12 I'm using here 'selection' of information as a general term for processes that yield such selection, while staying neutral on the exact way in which this result is achieved.
13 I understand 'experience' as conscious.
14 For objections to this suggestion see Beck and Schneider, 2017, p.480.
15 See, for example, Carrasco et al., 2004, Cutrone et al., 2014. In the experiments, in order to ensure that the effect is indeed due to attention (e.g., ruling out an effect of eye movement) the patches are viewed for a very short time (e.g., 40 ms – i.e., milliseconds – in the 2004 study). One might raise doubts as to whether this is sufficient time for subjects to actually experience the relative contrast (see Wu, 2014). I leave aside these and other types of doubts that had been raised regarding Carrasco's findings.
16 Turatto et al., 2007, p.176. To be accurate, the study in question showed an effect of attention on the experienced speed, and the speculation was that the increased speed of the attended movement resulted in increased blurriness which, in turn, explains the *decrease* in contrast (rather than merely the fact that no increase in contrast occurred).
17 I also mentioned in 2.2 the difficulty regarding the generalization from an effect experienced when a specially designed display is viewed (e.g., increase in contrast between striped patches) to other types of displays. In this context it is interesting to consider whether the contrast between elements of the scene is always experienced as contrast. (Compare parallax motion, where relative movement is experienced as difference in distance). It's also interesting to note that it seems that the effect might not generalize to cases of overt attention. Try to shift your attention *overtly* between the patches in Figure 2.2 – i.e., shift both attention and your gaze toward one patch, then the other, and so on. My (and others') experience is that the effect disappears.
18 For a rough demonstration see https://warwick.ac.uk/fac/soc/philosophy/people/lerman/backward_masking_demo.ppsx
19 For references see Breitmeyer, 2014, Ch.5.
20 To clarify, the suggestion is that careful experimental research and theorizing can help to clarify the general relationship between visual information-processing and conscious visual experience, and that this can be done without worrying about the character of the experience of unattended objects. Thus such general knowledge can then help us move from findings about attentional modulation of visual information-processing to hypotheses about the character of the experience of unattended or less attended objects. There are, of course, well-known limitations to our ability to draw conclusive conclusions about the general relationship between information-processing and phenomenology, but this is not to say that we can't have better and worse support for particular hypotheses.
21 What about effects of the kind Carrasco has identified: attention (in some circumstances) causing an increase in experienced contrast, size, speed, etc.? Perhaps in some cases they can contribute to making the attended object stand out visually relative to its surroundings (e.g., when the relevant features of the unattended surroundings are similar to that of the attended object, as was the case in Figure 2.2), or perhaps the intensification just after shifting attention may have such effect. But while maintaining attention to an object whose, say, contrast is sufficiently less

intense than that of its surroundings, it seems that the intensification of its contrast won't suffice for making it stand out visually.
22 See Campbell (2002) for the claim that visual attention and the resulting saliency play these roles.
23 It is more common to formulate the claim by using 'representational content' instead of 'appearance'. I adopt Watzl's use of 'appearance' as a way of staying neutral on whether experience has representational content or whether the way aspects of the environment are presented as being is (partly) constituted by their mind-independent qualities. However, my characterization of 'appearance' is slightly different from Watzl's (who explains his use of 'appearance' as referring to 'the way things look to the subject when she has that experience' (2017, p.160)). Neither characterization makes it clear why we can't simply say that 'being salient/prominent/central/highlighted' is itself part of the appearance. Perhaps what proponents of the view have in mind could be captured by saying that the relevant ways of experiential presenting/representing are the aspects of the experience which provide (mis)information about how things are with the relevant aspects of the environment.
24 The effect being distinctive of attention entails that it cannot be captured in terms of appearances, but not vice versa. We can't rule out a priori the possibility that there are other aspects of visual phenomenology that can't be captured in terms of appearance – e.g., blurry vision – and which may play a role in accounting for the effect of attention. For present purposes, we can ignore this complication.
25 Proponents of the claim include Speaks (2010), Watzl (2011, 2017), Beck and Schneider (2017). Chalmers (2010) suggests that it is potentially true, but doesn't commit to it. Note that the view I'm targeting here differs from Block's (2010), as far as I understand it. It is true that Block argues that attention has an effect on the phenomenology that cannot be explained in terms of appearance (in the sense in which the term is used here). However, it doesn't seem that the effect Block has in mind has to do with a kind of saliency that is distinctive of visual attention. In any case, even if I'm wrong about this, his view should be treated separately since his considerations are rather different in kind than those of Chalmers, Speaks and Watzl. I discuss his view elsewhere (work in progress).
26 Beck and Schneider (2017) argue that visual attention to an object makes the object phenomenally salient, and that the salience in question cannot be explained in terms of change in appearances (furthermore, they associate the relevant sense of saliency with what Watzl considered to be the phenomenology that is distinctive of visual attention). However, some of the things they say suggest that they think that the phenomenal saliency in question is explainable in terms of attentional modulations at the level of information-processing (specifically, the fact that they talk about the neural correlate of salience, p.480, and assert that salience is a property of the visual system, p.489). There is no space here to explain why I find their suggestion problematic. What matters for present purposes, though, is that the following discussion bears on their view since it questions the basis for their claim that attention is correlated with *phenomenal* salience rather than some unconscious aspect that realizes what they call 'functional salience'.
27 Note that for the above claim to be entirely accurate (in the light of the point made in fn. 24), we should either consider aspects of the phenomenology such as blurry vision as part of the appearances, or add that attentional modulation of visual information-processing may also result in visual side-effects of the processing (which aren't specific to attention).
28 For example Chalmers (2010), Speaks (2010), Watzl (2011). Wu (2011, 2014) also suggests that such demonstrations seem to reveal an effect on the phenomenology which isn't due to changes in appearance, though he concludes that the effect isn't perceptual. It is worth noting that the example discussed by Nickel (2007), which is

often treated as another example of the same effect, is different in nature since it involves an effect on the phenomenology that is mediated by a change in grouping. Such an effect isn't meant to generalize to all other cases of focused attention.

29 A further problem with reliance on introspection in the relevant test cases is the fact that they have features that are unique to them (e.g., the fact that they involve intentional covert direction of attention, and the fact that we attempt to introspect the experience), where these aspects could mistakenly give the impression of a distinctive effect of attention on the phenomenology. I consider this problem below.

30 The consideration used by Wu (2011) and Watzl (2011) to show that the effect of attention cannot be captured in terms of appearances *presupposes* that attention has a distinctive effect on the phenomenology.

31 Roessler (2011, p.278, in particular fn.6) makes this point.

32 What follows is my way of spelling out Watzl's replicability argument (Watzl, 2017, pp.173–174). Note that the argument is presented as an argument for the existence of some distinctive effect (not specifically a saliency effect). However, Watzl seems to assume that a saliency effect is the only candidate for being the distinctive effect of attention.

33 In some but not all cases these two ways of difference in specificity overlap. Henceforth, when I talk about 'specificity' I mean to refer to both.

34 These points have been made by Stazicker (2011, pp.64–65, 113–114) and Wu (in unpublished drafts). Watzl attempts to provide a general argument for the claim that a replica must always be possible (2017, pp.174–178). However, one of the problems with the argument is that Watzl simply ignores the fact that differences in the specificity of apparent properties are consistent with the different appearances all being veridical.

35 To be accurate, it is incorrect given the very plausible assumption that attention can affect specificity. It may seem that (ignoring the problems with (2)) Watzl could at least use a weakened version of (1) – limited to cases in which there are no such effects – in order to show that there are cases in which attention has a distinctive effect. (Thanks to Sophie Archer for pointing out this option.) However, apart from the worry about the generality of the effect, it also seems rather unlikely (given the considerations discussed in 2.3) that there are cases in which focused attention doesn't have some effect on specificity (at the very least in the sense of information regarding detail).

36 See, for example, Fiebelkorn and Kastner, 2019.

37 A further difficulty concerns the nature of what we do when we are meant to distribute attention equally over the scene or over a number of stimuli. Wu (2019, p.949–950) makes a related complaint about the nature of such distribution of attention.

38 Note that this restriction also means that one can't rely on what we might commonsensically think of as the phenomenology associated with visual attention. For it seems that this is inseparable from the effect of eye movement.

39 In principle there is a further option here – that we can gain insight about the effect of attention on the phenomenology from certain exercises of the imagination. But this doesn't seem an appealing option. First, it seems implausible to suggest that such imagination can provide such insight, as it was not based on relevant experiences in actual situations. Second, we have no basis for trusting such imaginations if we don't rely to some extent on the similarity between actual past experienced and imagined experiences.

40 Watzl (2017, pp.177–180) offers a series of arguments in support of (2). I have various reservations about each of them (some are related to the points made so far about the quote from p.177, others to further assumptions and moves Watzl makes). What I'm doing in the text is extracting from these arguments two aspects of the test cases

which seem to me most likely to give rise to the sense that the effect on the phenomenology goes beyond an effect on the appearances. What I'm interested in, though, isn't whether this *explains* why people are inclined to accept the distinctiveness claim, but rather whether this aspect can justify accepting the claim.

41 This problem is the problem that mars Watzl's attempt to argue that a replica must always be possible (mentioned in fn.32).

42 I'm ignoring here a whole range of subtle differences between different kinds of cases. For present purposes, a very rough indication of a group of phenomena is sufficient.

43 Think about a type of change that can be experienced when watching a magic trick which (visually) appears to involve an unexplained change in an object in clear view (or a similar effect on video).

44 But see the next paragraph for a qualification. Note that I'm not ruling out the possibility that, at least sometimes, other changes in appearance that are due to attention – especially changes in specificity – may, in some sense, be experienced as due to change in the direction of one's attention (in a similar manner to the way we experience difference in clarity that are due to direction of gaze).

45 It is, of course, possible that the appearance of the patches' contrast after the change isn't, by itself, potentially misleading, and thus that even if I'm right about the change's appearance, there's a further aspect of the appearance that can explain why the apparent relative contrast (while attending) does not seem to be their real relative contrast. However, at the moment I'm focusing on the experience of the change (which is present in all the test cases) since it seems to me to play some role in accounting for the fact that we don't take the change in the test cases to be a change in the object. If there is a further aspect which isn't merely a matter of appearance and which makes it the case that even without experiencing the change the apparent relative contrast of the patches wouldn't seem to us to be their actual relative contrast, then this would be what we are looking for. But introspection doesn't offer clear candidates. (It is interesting to note that the results in Carrasco's experiments suggest – though do not conclusively show – that without an experience of the change, the effect of attention on the appearance of the patches is misleading. In the experiments subjects' attention is shifted towards the location of one of the patches just before they are made visible. At least in some of the experiments subjects were required to make an (implicit) judgment as to which of the two patches is higher in contrast, and the results show that the effect of attention yields a systematic mistake: the contrast of attended patches are judged higher than it actually is relative to the unattended patch. (See for example Ling and Carrasco, 2007, p.1051 where they say 'we... asked observers to report the orientation of the stimulus that was higher in contrast'.)

46 Watzl, 2017, p.179.

47 And as I've been doing so far in this paper. For such an assumption is integral to the way in which I formulated the question pursued in the paper.

48 I take this to be Crowther's view in his 2010.

49 To emphasize, the problem arises for this suggestion since the suggestion is that the awareness of one's active engagement with the environment is immediately considered to be part of visual phenomenology.

50 Would it support the claim that visual attention has *some* distinctive effect on visual phenomenology? Not immediately. The claim in the text is that the awareness of how one is attending has such an effect. There is still a further question whether one can argue somehow that such awareness is a constitutive aspect of subject-level focused visual attention.

51 In addition to arguing that the effect of the subject's singling out the object is an effect on non-visual phenomenology, Wu also argues that it doesn't generalize to all cases of subject-level focused visual attention.

52 I am very grateful to Sophie Archer, Thomas Crowther, Richard Dietz, Naomi Eilan, Guy Longworth, Daniel Quesada and Matthew Soteriou for very helpful discussions and comments. Some of the material was presented to the LOGOS group (Barcelona). I am very grateful to the audience for their very helpful comments and questions.

References

Beck, J. and Schneider, K. A. 2017. Attention and Mental Primer. *Mind and Language* 32(4): 463–494.
Block, N. 2010. Attention and Mental Paint. *Philosophical Issues* 20(1): 23–63.
Block, N. 2015. The Puzzle of Perceptual Precision. In J. Windt and T. Metzinger (Eds.), *Open MIND: 5(T)*. Frankfurt am Main: MIND Group. doi: 10.15502/9783958570726.
Breitmeyer, B. G. 2014. *The Visual (Un)Conscious and Its (Dis)Contents: A Microtemporal Approach*. Oxford University Press, Oxford.
Brewer, B. 2013. Attention and Direct Realism. *Analytic Philosophy* 54(4): 421–435.
Campbell, J. 2002. *Reference and Consciousness*. Oxford University Press, Oxford.
Carrasco, M., Ling, S. and Read, S. 2004. Attention Alters Appearance. *Nature Neuroscience* 7: 308–313.
Carrasco, M. 2009. Attention: Psychophysical Approaches. In T. Bayne, A. Cleeremans and P. Wilken (Eds.), *The Oxford Companion to Consciousness* (pp. 1–10). Oxford University Press, Oxford.
Chalmers, D. 2010. The Representational Character of Experience. In D. Chalmers (Ed.), *The Character of Consciousness* (pp. 339–379). Oxford University Press, Oxford.
Crowther, T. 2010. The Agential Profile of Perceptual Experience. *Proceedings of the Aristotelian Society* 110(2): 219–242.
Cutrone, E. K., Heeger, D. J. and Carrasco, M. 2014. Attention Enhances Contrast Appearance via Increased Input Baseline of Neural Responses. *Journal of Vision* 14(14): 1–14.
Fiebelkorn, I. C. and Kastner, S. 2019. A Rhythmic Theory of Attention. *Trends in Cognitive Sciences* 23(2): 87–101.
Ganson, T. and Bronner, B. 2013. Visual Prominence and Representationalism. *Philosophical Studies* 164: 405–418.
Ling, S. and Carrasco, M. 2007. Transient Covert Attention Does Alter Appearance: A Reply to Schneider (2006). *Perception & Psychophysics* 69: 1051–1058.
Mack, A. and Rock, I. 1998. *Inattentional Blindness*. MIT Press, Cambridge, MA.
Martin, M. G. F. 1998. Setting Things Before the Mind. In A. O'Hear (Ed.), *Contemporary Issues in the Philosophy of Mind* (pp. 157–179). Cambridge University Press, Cambridge.
Nickel, B. 2007. Against Intentionalism. *Philosophical Studies* 136: 279–304.
Nowak, E. and Michaelson, E. 2022. On Salience-Based Theories of Demonstratives. In S. Archer (Ed.), *Salience: A Philosophical Inquiry* (pp. 78–93). Routledge, Abingdon.
Rock, I. 1995. *Perception [Rev. ed.]*. Scientific American Library, New York.
Roessler, J. 2011. Perceptual Attention and the Space of Reasons. In C. Mole, D. Smithies and W. Wu (Eds.), *Attention: Philosophical and Psychological Essays* (pp. 274–291). Oxford University Press, Oxford.
Soteriou, M. 2013. *The Mind's Construction: The Ontology of Mind and Mental Action*. Oxford University Press, Oxford.
Speaks, J. 2010. Attention and Intentionalism. *Philosophical Quarterly* 60(239): 325–342.

Stazicker, J. 2011. *Attention & The Indeterminacy of Visual Experience*. PhD thesis, University of California, Berkeley.

Turatto, M., Vescovi, M. and Valsecchi, M. 2007. Attention Makes Moving Objects Be Perceived to Move Faster. *Vision Research* 47(2): 166–178.

Watzl, S. 2011. Attention as Structuring of the Stream of Consciousness. In C. Mole, D. Smithies and W. Wu (Eds.), *Attention: Philosophical and Psychological Essays* (pp. 145–173). Oxford University Press, Oxford.

Watzl, S. 2017. *Structuring Mind: The Nature of Attention and How It Shapes Consciousness*. Oxford University Press, Oxford.

Watzl, S. 2019. Can Representationism Explain How Attention Affects Appearances? In A. Pautz and D. Stoljar (Eds.), *Blockheads! Essays on Ned Block's Philosophy of Mind and Consciousness* (pp. 581–608). The MIT Press, Boston.

Watzl, S. 2022. The Ethics of Attention: An Argument and a Framework. In S. Archer (Ed.), *Salience: A Philosophical Inquiry* (pp. 89–112). Routledge, Abingdon.

Wu, W. 2011. What Is Conscious Attention? *Philosophy and Phenomenological Research* 82(1): 93–120.

Wu, W. 2014. *Attention*. Routledge, London.

Wu, W. 2019. Structuring Mind: The Nature of Attention and How It Shapes Consciousness, by Sebastian Watzl. *Mind* 128(511): 945–953.

3 Beyond 'salience' and 'affordance': Understanding anomalous experiences of significant possibilities

Matthew Ratcliffe and Matthew R. Broome

3.1 Experiencing aberrant salience

This chapter discusses whether and to what extent the concepts of 'salience' and 'affordance' can assist us in understanding anomalous experience in psychiatric illness. First of all, we ask whether types of experience associated with schizophrenia (and potentially other diagnoses as well) are adequately accommodated by appeals to 'salience dysregulation' or 'aberrant salience'. We argue that the concept of 'salience' is insufficiently discriminating and therefore fails to do the required work. We go on to ask whether these and other wide-ranging phenomenological disturbances might be better conceptualized in terms of altered 'affordance'. We show that the same problem arises here.

In addressing the nature of salience dysregulation, we focus on the influential and ambitious account developed by Shitij Kapur and colleagues, which seeks to integrate phenomenology, neurobiology, and pharmacology (Kapur, 2003; Kapur, Mizrahi, and Li, 2005). However, most of our points apply to discussions of salience dysregulation more generally. Kapur's account is concerned with aberrant salience in the early stages of schizophrenia and how it relates to the subsequent formation of hallucinations and delusions. However, it is debatable whether the relevant phenomenology is specific to schizophrenia, with potential implications for the continuing employment of 'schizophrenia' as a diagnostic category. For instance, van Os (2009) proposes 'salience-dysregulation syndrome' as a more encompassing alternative, one that is consistent with the diagnostic non-specificity of certain delusions and hallucinations and also with evidence pointing to the non-specificity of neurobiological changes in psychosis (e.g., Jauhar et al., 2017).[1] The legitimacy of diagnostic categories is not our concern here; we are interested in what experiences of 'salience dysregulation' consist of, regardless of where they might arise. Nevertheless, the answer might well turn out to have implications for psychiatric classification, research, and treatment. Suppose, as we will suggest in what follows, that 'salience dysregulation' accommodates a diverse range of predicaments. Greater sensitivity to these differences could feed into the task of refining or revising diagnostic categories. It may also turn out that different experiences are generated in different ways and amenable to different treatments. Hence the task of phenomenological

DOI: 10.4324/9781351202114-4

clarification is an important one and, in this chapter, we draw a number of distinctions that can feed into it.

We should begin by distinguishing between phenomenological and non-phenomenological conceptions of salience. In the former case, things are experienced as salient, whereas, in the latter, one might instead talk of detection, responsiveness, neural activation, solicitation of behavior, and so forth. We are concerned exclusively with the phenomenology, with *experiences of salience*.[2] We further restrict our discussion to *passive salience*, where things appear conspicuous in one or another way without the prior involvement of active attention or explicit thought. That said, we acknowledge that the distinction between active and passive salience will not be clear-cut and that the two most likely interact in any number of ways.

One might think of an experience of salience in very broad terms, as something or other appearing conspicuous. However, for Kapur, salience involves something more specific than an amorphous 'pop-up' effect. Drawing on work by Berridge and Robinson (1998) and Berridge (2007), he emphasizes 'incentive' or 'motivational' salience. This consists in a basic form of 'wanting', which is both perceptual and motivational in character: 'it transforms the brain's neural representations of conditioned stimuli, converting an event or stimulus from a neutral "cold" representation (mere information) into an attractive and "wanted" incentive that can "grab attention"' (Berridge and Robinson, 1998, p.313). Incentive salience can persist regardless of whether or not one experiences 'reward' or anticipates doing so.[3] Hence it is distinct from both reward-perception and reward-learning. Berridge and Robinson (1998, p.348) extend their account so as to accommodate aversive stimuli as well. Here, they suggest, a positive valence attaches to a perceived alternative. For example, being frightened of something may involve feeling positively drawn to a place of safety. The phenomenology of salience is thus a matter of practically engaged anticipation, something that is either integral to perceptual experience or at least intimately associated with it. In perceiving a current state of affairs as salient in a positive or negative way, we are drawn to act so as to realize or avoid a possibility that it points to, a possibility that *matters to us*.

It is this conception of salience that Kapur (2003) applies to the phenomenology, neurobiology, and pharmacology of schizophrenia. Salience is construed as a kind of motivational pull that attaches to objects of experience, encompassing both attraction and aversion. At the neurobiological level, it is regulated by mesolimbic dopamine, which modulates attraction and aversion. Consistent with this, pharmacological intervention for schizophrenia and psychosis targets the dopamine system. Kapur suggests that psychosis originates in experiences of non-localized, aberrant salience. Things in general may appear more salient than usual. Furthermore, they appear salient in unusual and unstructured ways. These do not map onto the actual physical properties of perceived entities or reflect one's various projects and concerns, but they persist nonetheless. Delusions are an outcome of attempts to make sense of the experience, to impose an interpretation that accommodates the strange and disordered manner in which things appear:

> ....endogenous psychosis evolves slowly (not overnight). For many patients it evolves through a series of stages: a stage of heightened awareness and emotionality combined with a sense of anxiety and impasse, a drive to 'make sense' of the situation, and then usually relief and a 'new awareness' as the delusion crystallizes and hallucinations emerge. [....] It is postulated that before experiencing psychosis, patients develop an exaggerated release of dopamine, independent of and out of synchrony with the context. This leads to the assignment of inappropriate salience and motivational significance to external and internal stimuli. At its earliest stage this induces a somewhat novel and perplexing state marked by exaggerated importance of certain percepts and ideas.
>
> (Kapur, 2003, p.15)[4]

It is not entirely clear from this whether or not an experience of aberrant salience should be regarded as *perceptual* in nature. The answer hinges on whether a liberal or more conservative conception of perceptual content is adopted. We are inclined towards the former. However, even if one resists the designation 'perceptual', our various points can be made just as well with reference to how one's current surroundings are *experienced*, in contrast to what might be inferred from that experience. Nevertheless, it should be added that aberrant salience is not *exclusively* perceptual in nature. According to Kapur's model, dopamine dysregulation underlies the aberrant salience of both external events and one's own mental states. There is, he says, 'aberrant assignment of salience to the elements of one's experience, at a "mind" level'. Hallucinations arise when one's own 'internal representations' are experienced as salient in anomalous ways (Kapur, 2003, p.13).

This approach has been criticized in a number of ways. At the very least, it needs to be supplemented. Even if salience dysregulation is the proximal cause of psychosis and dopamine is a key element of the 'final common pathway' (Howes and Kapur, 2009), a more complicated story needs to be told about a range of distal causes, including – potentially – genetic vulnerabilities, developmental trajectories, traumatic events, social isolation, migration, and substance abuse. Neuroscience can only take us so far and, to accommodate all of these factors, an interdisciplinary approach is needed (Broome et al., 2005). In addition, it remains unclear how, exactly, salience-dysregulation leads to psychosis, in the context of schizophrenia and more widely. It is arguable that additional factors, such as interpretive biases, are also required (Howes and Nour, 2016). However, criticisms generally concern the hypothesized causes and effects of salience dysregulation, rather than the nature of the experience. Even critics of Kapur tend to assume much the same conception of salience. For example, Howes and Nour (2016, p.3), while acknowledging that salience is more 'multifaceted' than sometimes supposed, describe the relevant experience as 'the world seeming pregnant with significance, generating feelings of apprehension and a sense that the world has changed in some as yet uncertain way'. One might think that descriptions like this make it clear enough what an experience of aberrant salience consists of. So we can leave the phenomenology behind at this point and get on with investigating how salience dysregulation is caused, how it contributes to psychosis, and what the implications of this are for classification and treatment. However, that would be premature. 'Incentive salience', as conceived of by Berridge, is equally applicable to the lives of humans and rats (his experimental subjects being the latter).[5] As we will show, it fails to accommodate more subtle phenomenological distinctions that apply in the human case. Likewise, the notion of 'aberrant salience' encompasses considerable diversity, pointing to the likelihood that different kinds of disturbances predominate in different people at different times.

In Section 2, we will suggest that, once one starts distinguishing the various dimensions and types of salience, 'aberrant salience' is revealed as something in need of more detailed and discerning analyses. Then in Section 3, we will turn to recent formulations of J. J. Gibson's 'affordance' concept, which, it has been suggested, have the discriminatory power needed to capture different kinds of phenomenological disturbance. However, we will show that they suffer from similar shortcomings. While both 'salience' and 'affordance' might facilitate initial steps towards an appreciation of the relevant phenomenology, they are blunt tools that only get us so far. At a certain stage in our inquiries, they are swamped by the many important dimensions of variation and lose their explanatory power.

3.2 The subtleties of salience

We can at least assume a distinction between localized and widespread salience dysregulation. While the former involves experiencing something specific as unusually salient or things looking strange in the context of a particular, transient situation, the latter is unbounded and may even involve everything appearing somehow odd, with some things appearing odder than others. Schizophrenia is taken to involve the latter. The claim is that dopamine dysregulation leads to indiscriminate assignments of significance or importance to stimuli. Is this sufficient to identify a singular type of phenomenological disturbance? We suggest not. Consider the following definition of salience dysregulation: 'aberrant assignment of novelty and salience to objects and associations' (Kapur, Mizrahi, and Li, 2005, p.59).[6] Reference to novelty *and* salience suggests that the two are not simply to be identified, and that seems right. Although salience is often associated with novelty, something can be salient without at the same time appearing novel. When watching a film, someone being eaten by a shark that is somehow flying in a tornado might be most salient at a given moment. However, it is neither novel nor surprising when the film is *Sharknado*. A further distinction needs to be drawn between something being novel and its being unexpected, given that a significant change need not come as a surprise. These points apply equally to a range of other situations. For instance, a person you have been waiting for will be experienced as salient when she arrives, even though her arrival at that place and time was anticipated.

Of course, one could respond that the shark is expected to bite and the person to arrive, but not at that *exact* moment. This points to the need for a more refined account of what it is for something to be novel or surprising, as there are many different ways in which something might deviate from the mundane or fail to accord with one's expectations. However, it seems clear that at least some experiences *do* involve salience without surprise. Something can look incongruous and consequently conspicuous even if one knows it is there and has seen it many times. And some things remain salient despite being neither novel nor incongruous, as when the pile of papers sitting on one's desk is experienced as *urgent*. Indeed, what appears salient in a given situation and context of activity is often just what we are most concerned about, where our concerns reflect a range of different commitments, values, habits, and projects. Thus, aberrant salience could involve something appearing novel or surprising in one or another way when it is not, something appearing somehow incongruous in one or another way when it is not, and/or something appearing important in a way that does not reflect its relationship to a wider context of activities and concerns.

There are many other variables at work in our experiences of salience, any of which could feed into the task of distinguishing and categorizing forms of salience, aberrant or otherwise. For instance, it might seem obvious that salience comes in degrees, but it is just as important to appreciate that there are qualitatively different *kinds*. We do not merely experience things as more or less conspicuous in relation to a wider context; they also *matter* to us in different ways. Hence, *salience*, in the relevant sense, is equally a matter of *significance* (Broome et al., 2005, p.26). Something might appear threatening, fascinating, of immediate relevance to current activities, and so forth. Categorization of stimuli as attractive or aversive will not suffice to capture the diversity (an observation that also illustrates the limitations of research on incentive salience in non-human animals, the conclusions of which do not apply in a straightforward way to the complexities of human experience).

One might object that salience and significance/mattering are distinct aspects of experience, that things can appear significant *or* salient *or* both. However, a distinction between salience and significance is most likely an artifact of the language used to describe experiences and should not be taken to indicate that the relevant experiences actually incorporate two dissociable components. If we seek to capture the relevant phenomenology, it is more accurate to say that something appears salient *as* threatening, *as* enticing, *as* useful. That it is experienced as mattering in one of these ways implies that it is also salient – phenomenologically conspicuous. There is no need to postulate an additional property of salience. Pure salience is an abstraction from the experience, not a part of it. That things do, on other occasions, appear salient in some way without at the same time appearing significant does not imply that experiences of significance should be construed additively, in terms of salience plus something else.

Such considerations might well prove important when it comes to the further analysis and categorization of salience dysregulation. Some variants may involve disruption of only certain *types* of significant possibility or at least the predominance of a certain type of disruption. In other instances, those possibilities may be largely or wholly unaffected, with the disturbance focused elsewhere. The alternative would be to insist that dysregulation is completely unstructured in every case, that any kind of significant possibility attaches to anything whatsoever. But salience dysregulation is not simply a matter of anarchic salience (where forms of salience attach to things at random) and/or globally heightened salience. For instance, there is a difference between a world where everything looks somehow menacing and unpredictable, where a strange and pervasive feeling of foreboding predominates, and a world where everything looks somehow unexpected, perceptually fascinating, and oddly cut off from any relationship with practical activities. The former is primarily a matter of anticipation while the latter is more a matter of experienced conflict between what is present and what was previously anticipated. Along with this, ways of mattering differ – one case involves dread and the other fascination. Both forms of experience are compatible with a schizophrenia diagnosis.

There is also considerably more to be said about how salient entities and events can conflict with anticipation. The extent to which and manner in which something is anticipated cannot be extricated from the kind of significance attached to it. For instance, a threat may appear inevitable or merely possible, immediate or far away. Reflecting these differences, things threaten us in different ways – to be terrified in the face of something is different from dreading its arrival. Anticipation also has varying degrees of determinacy. A threat might be specific and concrete or far less determinate (as in a general air of foreboding). When an event is – in some way – unanticipated, there remain several ways in which it might appear *novel*. In one scenario, it negates what was anticipated – one reaches out to pick up a cup of coffee, only to find out that it is filled with water. It should be added that negation comes in different forms: 'it is not what I took it to be'; 'it is not there at all'; 'it does not possess the properties that I took it to possess'. Alternatively, something might conflict with one's expectations and thus appear surprising but without negating them. In such a case, it may or may not appear incongruous. For example, an unanticipated encounter with a friend need not involve any sense of negated expectation, although it can sometimes involve incongruity: 'what on earth are *you* doing *here*?'

As all of this illustrates, salience is not just a matter of experiencing what is *actually present*. Things appear salient in the light of (a) what was anticipated prior to their arrival and/or (b) what is now anticipated from them. Experience is thus permeated with the anticipation, fulfillment, and negation of significant, variably determinate possibilities.[7] Consequently, things appear salient in a range of different ways. In cases of *aberrant* salience, there is an additional distinction to be drawn between experiencing something as salient in a way that *is* aberrant and experiencing it *as* aberrant. For example, there is a difference between experiencing the sofa in one's lounge as menacing and experiencing it as strangely menacing (given a mismatch between that entity's physical properties and the kinds of significant possibilities associated with it). This points to a further question concerning the source and type of normativity at stake when we refer to salience as 'aberrant'. Is it a biological, epistemic, and/or phenomenological 'ought'? One might answer 'all three', but they do not always go together. For instance, a non-localized experience of everything being somehow not right might well be biologically 'normal' or even 'functional' under certain conditions, such as illness or threat perhaps. And whether or not such an experience enhances or interferes with epistemic abilities will depend on the situation, which may or may not be unusual in relevant respects. Conversely, an experience could be somehow biologically 'wrong' or epistemically misleading without itself incorporating any sense of wrongness Regardless of the source of normativity, there are further distinctions to be drawn between different kinds of deviations from a norm. Something's appearing salient *when it should not do so* differs from its appearing salient *when it should, but not in the way that it does* and from its *not appearing salient when it ought to* (according to one or another criterion). In the latter case, the absence of salience can itself be salient.

Another important variable to consider is whether an experience is modality-specific and which modality or modalities it involves. As noted earlier, we might think of salience as principally perceptual in nature – it is a matter of how our surroundings appear to us and how various things relate to our concerns and potential activities. But it is arguably much broader than this. The weak point in an argument might equally be described as 'salient', as might some feature of an imagined situation or remembered event. Furthermore, it is not simply the case that we experience something as 'perceived', 'imagined', 'thought', or 'remembered' and, in conjunction with this, experience it as salient in one or another way. The kinds of salience attached to an experience also contribute to our sense of its being one and not another *type of experience* – an experience of perceiving, anticipating, remembering, imagining, or thinking. To explain further, it seems reasonable to maintain that the hallmark of perceptual experience is a sense of 'presence' (e.g., Noë, 2004). Thus, when we have a perceptual experience of a tree, that experience is not exhausted by its sensory-perceptual content. We also experience the tree as *here, now*. It is this 'here, now' that constitutes our sense of the experience as unambiguously perceptual in nature. However, objects of perception sometimes look strangely unfamiliar, not quite there, somehow unreal, to the point where it no longer feels like an unambiguously perceptual experience. Erosion of the sense that one is having a perceptual experience is attributable – at least in part – to aberrant salience. A perceived entity that does not offer the usual types of salient possibilities associated with specifically *perceptual* experiences may also appear salient in lacking those possibilities. It stands out, in appearing somehow akin to an imagined or remembered entity – not fully there. Alternatively, a type of salient possibility that is more usually specific to perceptual experiences might attach to the contents of memory or imagination. With this, the sense that one is imagining or remembering, rather than perceiving, is eroded (Ratcliffe, 2017). For instance, suppose that you cannot help imagining having done p and feel intense guilt every time you do imagine having done p. The kind of significance attaching to p is likely to diminish, to some degree, your sense of merely imagining rather than remembering p. Salience plays a dual role here: an experience can be anomalous and thus salient, given that it incorporates uncharacteristic forms of salience.

Salience is thus integral to the phenomenological constitution of intentionality, to our grasp of the distinctions between what is currently the case, what was the case, what is not and never was the case, and what might be the case. For that reason, it is not sufficient to refer to 'aberrant salience' within one or another modality. Associated disturbances of intentionality should also be acknowledged. Kapur (2003) takes delusions to be beliefs that are 'highly improbable'. However, wide-ranging salience disruption can erode one's grasp of the distinction between what is and what is not the case and – with this– the *manner* in which one believes. For instance, the relevant phenomenology might straddle the boundaries between experiences of believing and imagining (Ratcliffe, 2017). Such 'beliefs' are not merely anomalous insofar as they have highly implausible contents and are maintained despite evidence to the contrary. They also involve a form of intentional experience that is different in kind from that associated with more typical forms of believing.[8]

A consideration of the modal structure of intentionality also complicates the issue of what it is for something to appear salient in the guise of incongruity. One might think that this involves having a perceptual experience of something that fails to cohere with a wider perceptual experience of one's surroundings. However, something could appear incongruous due to its offering salient possibilities of a kind that are more usually associated with another modality of intentionality, or its pointing to a blend of salient possibilities that more usually belong to distinct modalities. Aberrant salience could thus involve inter-modal tensions and conflicts rather than just intra-modal anomalies. Another potential scenario involves tension between the salient possibilities attached to perceptual experience (which may all remain specific to perception) and the kinds of salient possibilities that concurrently arise in other modalities, such as memory and imagination. For example, suppose that you meet Person A and have a flood of memories involving Person B, while anticipating interactions with Person C. Here, there would be a pervasive sense of incongruity, in terms of which more localized ways in which Person A and her activities appear 'salient' should be understood.

Another important point to keep in mind begins with the uncontroversial observation that salience is often relational in structure: entity x appears salient in relation to potential scenario y, which is itself salient in the context of value z, and so forth. Salience should not be conceived of in an overly atomistic way; it would be more accurate to say that human experience incorporates a variably integrated web of salient possibilities. Kapur (2003, p.15) states that dopamine release is ordinarily 'stimulus-linked' and that schizophrenia involves 'stimulus-independent release of dopamine', where salience is created rather than detected. However, he also acknowledges that 'detection' takes place relative to a backdrop of concerns and activities, which determine whether and how something is salient: 'Under normal circumstances, it is the context-driven activity of the dopamine system that mediates the experience of novelty and the acquisition of appropriate motivational salience' (Kapur, Mizrahi, and Li, 2005, p.61). Hence salience is partly a matter of whether or not something coheres with a wider, structured context. In virtue of what, though, does that larger context hang together?

For a typical adult human being, the kinds of salience that things have are generally symptomatic of variably idiosyncratic sets of cares, commitments, concerns, relationships, projects, norms, habits, and so forth. Something appears salient to me in light of my current activities and requirements, relative to a larger project that is itself intelligible in relation to my cares, commitments, goals, and plans. The fact that our experiences of salience, in all their diversity, are structured and largely consistent is a reflection of the extent to which a human life is structured and consistent. That structure does not just depend on matters internal to the individual; her situation and relations with others are equally relevant. Circumstances such as illness, loss of long-term employment, and bereavement can disrupt entire systems of projects, cares, and concerns, through which things appear significant in consistent and patterned ways. With this, there is a widespread, dynamic, and long-term disruption of salience, which varies in degree and takes different forms. An experience such as that of profound grief can involve disturbances of salience that appear very similar to those (sometimes) implicated in the early stages of schizophrenia. For example, Helen Macdonald describes a kind of 'madness' that she underwent following the death of her father:

> It was a madness designed to keep me sane. My mind struggled to build across the gap, make a new and inhabitable world. The problem was that it had nothing to work with. There was no partner, no children, no home. No nine-to-five job either. So it grabbed anything it could. It was desperate, and it read off the world wrong. I began to notice curious connections between things. Things of no import burst into extraordinary significance. (2014, p.16)

In this case, what might be labeled 'aberrant salience' arises due to losing a life-structure relative to which things formerly appeared salient in temporally consistent, integrated ways. This is quite different, both phenomenologically and causally, from a scenario where a life has structure and, despite this, things start to appear oddly salient. Thus, whether and how a person might be said to experience 'aberrant salience' cannot be extricated from the manner in which she is immersed in the social world. All of those projects, pastimes, commitments, and relationships that are a prerequisite for maintaining a fairly stable, integrated system of significant possibilities depend to some degree on our relations with specific individuals, other people in general, and the social world as a whole. If you lose your marriage, your job, or both, a whole system of significant possibilities is disrupted. And, if you find other people in general untrustworthy, or even threatening, it becomes difficult to embed yourself in a shared world in a way that allows stable patterns of significant possibilities to emerge.[9]

Kapur (2003, p.15) regards the social as a kind of add-on to the more basic phenomenon of salience dysregulation. When delusions eventually occur, he says, 'they are imbued with the psychodynamic themes relevant to the individual and are embedded in the cultural context of the individual'. However, salience is imbued with the social from the outset, reflecting possibilities that depend in multifarious ways on relations with others and on shared projects and commitments that stretch many years into the past and the future. This further complicates the nature of 'aberrance'. Whether salience is aberrant and whether it is experienced as aberrant can both be symptomatic of (a) something failing to cohere with a wider context that is temporal, interpersonal, and social in structure or (b) the erosion of a context that ordinarily structures and stabilizes experiences of salience. Given that new patterns of salience need to be forged when past projects and relations have collapsed, it is not clear what qualifies as aberrant during a period of upheaval and what qualifies as a normal or even unavoidable aspect of adjustment. Such distinctions are surely crucial when it comes to investigating the phenomenology of psychiatric illness, as well as its causes and potential treatment.[10]

The two alternatives we have sketched are not mutually exclusive. Any number of factors could disrupt salience-structuring contexts or interfere with their initial formation. For instance, it could be that certain patterns of social development culminate in relatively unstructured ways of inhabiting the world, which are not framed by cohesive projects and stable commitments. Resultant instability might then render one vulnerable to further salience dysregulation. In short, if something is already precariously balanced, it is easier to destabilize (Ratcliffe and Bortolan, 2020). A range of potential scenarios should therefore be considered, which involve importantly different relationships between context-destabilization and salience dysregulation. This is consistent with various strands of evidence indicating that developmental disruption, social isolation, and anxiety can all contribute to vulnerability to psychosis (e.g., Broome et al., 2005).

To summarize, we started off with 'aberrant salience', but have ended up with a host of interconnected variables, compatible with a wide range of subtly different predicaments. These variables include degree and kind of incongruity; determinacy of anticipation; the kind of significance or mattering involved; whether or not something is experienced *as* anomalous; whether and how an experience relates to disruption of life-structure; and whether and how incongruity involves the modal structure of intentionality. Further dimensions of variation include whether and how the salience of things relates to one's potential actions, the actions of others, or impersonal happenings; whether anticipated happenings appear preventable or inevitable; and whether, how, and to what extent one's experience incorporates motivational force. (We will say more about these in Section 3, in turning to 'affordances'.)

Until the full range of potential experiences are distinguished and it is made clear what, exactly, is at play in a given case, it will remain unclear whether and to what extent (a) current diagnostic categories encompass different kinds of salience dysregulation, and (b) forms of salience dysregulation cut across diagnostic categories. Along with this, it will remain unclear which of these variables are most informative when it comes to classification, research, and treatment. We therefore suggest that the beguilingly simple label 'aberrant salience' should give way to a more nuanced, discerning taxonomy, one that makes use of the various distinctions drawn here, and perhaps others as well.

3.3 Beyond affordance

We have argued that the term 'salience' lacks the discriminatory power required for psychiatric classification, research, and treatment. However, one might respond that there is another term available, one that is currently employed in more discerning ways and capable of accommodating the various different phenomena we have described. We are thinking of the term 'affordance', originally coined by J. J. Gibson (1979). Like 'incentive salience', this term relates to how we perceive aspects of the environment as salient and significant, in ways that are inextricable from our actions and dispositions to act. In a number of recent discussions, Gibson's original use of the term has undergone considerable refinement and revision. Here, we are not concerned with whether one or another formulation applies more widely. What we want to do is focus specifically on the extent to which phenomenological changes in psychiatric illness can be captured in terms of a sophisticated conception of 'affordance'.

Now, it could be maintained that the affordance-concept is of little or no use in this context, given that affordances are non-phenomenological in nature. On one account, they are environmental properties, which the organism's perceptual apparatus is tasked with detecting. More plausibly, though, they are relational in nature. For instance, Chemero (2003, p.189) takes them to be 'relations between the abilities of organisms and features of the environment', rather than environmental properties. In order to accommodate aberrant salience, the concept must also relate to human *experience* and to the possibilities offered by a distinctively *social* world. An approach developed by Rietveld and Kiverstein (2014) seeks to do just that. They maintain that the notion of organismic 'ability' should be broadened to include skills. In the human case, these skills further depend on socio-cultural practices. Borrowing from Wittgenstein, Rietveld and Kiverstein suggest that affordances are relative to 'forms of life'; they are possibilities for action that are offered by the environment, but only given a contingent set of 'sociocultural practices' and associated skills. This account dispenses with some of our concerns about 'salience', by acknowledging the inextricability of opportunities for action from contingent patterns of social relations that are susceptible to disruption. Nevertheless, what Rietveld and Kiverstein call the 'landscape' of affordances remains non-phenomenological in character.[11] If we take an individual with a specific set of skills, confronted with a specific situation, relative to a particular form of life, there is a fact of the matter concerning what that situation does and does not afford. This applies regardless of whether or not the relevant affordances are detected or, more specifically, experienced by that individual.

However, Rietveld and Kiverstein also appeal to a more specific 'field' of affordances, consisting of those affordances that an individual is currently responsive to. This can be construed phenomenologically.[12] De Haan et al. (2013) propose analyzing anomalous experiences of significant possibility in terms of affordance-fields, by introducing three variables. First of all, there is the width of the field – how much appears salient (something that relates closely to a capacity for choice). Second, there is the depth of the field – whether currently experienced affordances are structured by longer-term concerns. Third, there is the height of the field – the degree to which things appear salient.

In addressing the applicability of 'affordance' to forms of anomalous experience (and to human experience more generally), we are not concerned with whether the view is true or false. Rather, what is at stake here is the *utility* of the affordance concept - whether, when, and how it serves to illuminate something that would be murkier without it. There is a pragmatic choice to be made: what is its discriminatory power; how versatile is it; how useful is it in this particular context of inquiry? Our answer is that many of the concerns we have raised about salience also apply here. A refined conception of affordance is an improvement on mere salience, as it is sensitive to at least some of the distinctions we have drawn. Even so, it remains too blunt a tool and only gets us to the beginning of a phenomenological inquiry into how possibilities are experienced. In the book *Experiences of Depression*, Ratcliffe briefly raises the following worry:

> Things do not simply 'afford' activities; they appear significant to us in all sorts of different ways. It is not helpful to say that a bull affords running away from, while a cream cake affords eating. What is needed for current purposes are distinctions between the many ways in which things appear significant to us and, in some cases, solicit activity. Furthermore, the significance something has for us is not just a matter of how we might act. Some significant possibilities present themselves as certain, and thus as impervious to our influence.
>
> (Ratcliffe, 2015, p.61, note 24)

This was picked up on by Roy Dings (2018), who offers a detailed response on behalf of affordances. He allows that such concerns have some basis, but maintains that the affordance concept can be further refined so as to incorporate the required distinctions.[13] Like De Haan et al, Dings distinguishes between affordances and experiences of solicitation involving them, noting – quite rightly – that experiences of affordance are much less stable than the affordances themselves. He further acknowledges that whether or not an affordance solicits action is symptomatic of concerns and needs. These, he says, are inseparable from a kind of bodily responsiveness through which we experience our surroundings as inviting or demanding certain activities. Things are thus experienced as significant in different ways, in light of different concerns.[14] Dings appreciates that Gibson was concerned with more stable ways in which the environment might be said to offer things to an organism. Even so, he maintains that the concept of affordance can be further applied to the associated phenomenology in an informative way. Dings notes that experiences of solicitation are 'rich and nuanced'. He suggests that this diversity can be accommodated by distinguishing between the 'valence' of an experienced affordance (to be identified with the kind of significant possibility it involves), the 'force' of solicitation, and what he calls 'mineness'. This latter term is introduced to capture the extent to which an affordance is experienced as being close to 'who I am' or, more precisely, 'who I take myself to be' – how that affordance relates to one's 'psychobiography'.

This is certainly more discriminating than mere 'incentive salience'. Combining the various points, it can be said that (a) affordances are embedded in forms of life, reflecting not only abilities but also skills and associated norms; (b) experiences of affordance are more fragile and depend on idiosyncratic, contingent, changeable cares and concerns; (c) affordances reflect, to varying degrees, the structure of a life; and (d) the field of affordances can be further analyzed in terms of width, depth, height, and affective coloration. Is that sufficient? In the remainder of this chapter, we will suggest not.

One problem is that experienced affordances are consistently construed in terms of something *soliciting* or *calling for* one or another form of activity. This eclipses the many different ways in which perceptual experiences relate to potential activities. Something might be salient in no longer affording something; it might be experienced as not affording what it should do; it might afford the loss of other affordances; and so on. And what should we say about something that affords the impossibility of acting upon it? It could be re-described as affording the possibility of acting upon something else, but this would be to misconstrue the relevant experience, which is principally one of *not being able to do p*, rather than of *being able to do q*. The fact that *p* does not offer something is *there*, part of the experience. Indeed, the world as a whole can appear in the guise of not offering what it should, what it once did – it is not simply that one's surroundings lack experienced affordances; the lack itself is there.

Questions also arise concerning whether and to what extent we experience affordances as *for other people* but not for ourselves, as when you can see that B has not spotted an opportunity and are desperate for her to realize and act accordingly. Is the experience of affordance any less direct here and, if not, how does this relate to the suggestion that experienced affordances reflect one's 'psychobiography'? Furthermore, just how complicated is the interpersonal structure of affordances – do we experience something as 'affording p for them but not for me', as 'affording p for me, q for her, and r for them', as 'affording p for them and also p for us but only if they don't get there first'?

We could go on, piling on distinction after distinction, so that any appeal to 'affordance' has to be repeatedly qualified in order to pin down the relevant experience and distinguish it from others. However, it is when we further emphasize the temporally elongated structure of human concerns that the concept really starts to give way. For one thing, it is not at all clear where the experience of affordance stops and a longer-term sense of possibility begins: is an experience of affordance restricted to possibilities that can be actualized within the next few seconds or might an affordance concern possible scenarios located in the distant future? In conjunction with this, it is unclear how the content of an affordance is to be specified. And, when our subject matter is *experienced* affordances, the question of content cannot be avoided. We are obliged to provide at least some indication of *what* is experienced when one experiences affordance A or affordance B. Otherwise, we will be unable to distinguish affordance-experiences from one another.

Consider technological affordances. Should it be said that, given a form of life, a set of skills and concerns, an airport, and a plane ticket, we can experience a plane as affording 'getting from London to New York'? If so, does it further afford 'getting to New York in time for a meeting with B' or 'getting to New York in time for a meeting with B, which is important in the context of project X, insofar as it offers the possibility of involving Person C in that project', and so forth? How much of this is built into the experience of possibility? Do we allow that experienced affordances sometimes include a variably determinate sense of longer-term possibilities?

De Haan et al. (2013, p.7) seem to acknowledge that the experience of possibility goes beyond that of affordance: 'one not only perceives the affordances that are immediately present here and now, but one is also pre-reflectively aware of future plans and possibilities for action: the affordances on the horizon that one is responsive to, so to speak'. However, this raises problems for any attempt to capture our experiences of significant possibility in terms of affordance. The intelligibility of affordances that are immediately present depends on other affordances that lurk in the background. A situation offers something now, given that its actualization offers something else, which offers something else, all in the context of a dynamic, structured life. It is unclear where the affordance stops and a more diffuse, temporally elongated sense of possibility begins. Indeed, we see no principled way to settle on a level of description that specifies the content of an 'affordance' but does not go beyond it. To insist on a maximum temporal distance between an experienced affordance and the time of its anticipated actualization would seem rather arbitrary.

The distinction between actual and anticipated affordance-experiences therefore hinges on how much content is imported into the experience of solicitation. We could say that a departure gate affords the possibility of walking through, boarding a plane, boarding a plane to the United States, or getting to one's meeting with B. All of these things could be integral to a current experience of the possible in some way and to some extent. Even if a fully determinate propositional thought about meeting B is not occurring right now, a less determinate sense of that possibility may continue to shape how one's surroundings are currently experienced. In identifying a specific affordance, there is thus a risk of imposing something with an artificially circumscribed content upon experiences that incorporate a whole range of variably determinate possibilities, stretching from the immediate moment into the distant future, experiences that vary along numerous dimensions. If one attempts to avoid this by instead employing a sparse conception of affordance, involving the immediate solicitation of specific activities, one ends up disregarding forms of life, skills, and idiosyncratic life structures, rendering the concept largely irrelevant to human experiences of significant possibility and their aberrations.

As with salience, it can be added that affordance-experiences are not exclusively perceptual. If the concept is applied to human experience, it also seems plausible that memories, imaginings, and paths of thought incorporate affordances. Furthermore, different kinds and patterns of affordances – what is solicited and how it is solicited – are characteristic of different modalities. For instance, something remembered might afford doing something now: 'Oh no – I forgot to collect the children from school; I have to go!' We could also conceive of a pattern of thought as a form of activity afforded by a situation, as when a philosopher stumbles upon a piece of writing or listens to a talk and has the experience of its pointing to certain significant possibilities for thought, certain paths to be followed. More generally, experienced possibilities do not just involve potential happenings that can be actualized by our bodily activities; they point to possibilities for other modalities of intentionality as well. Consider major life events, such as leaving a job that one has done for thirty years, moving to a new country, or ending a relationship. In such cases, something affords the possibility of reconfiguring one's whole landscape – and thus field – of affordances. What is offered is the possibility of something transforming one's possibilities, in a way that is not limited to the perceptual modality. Even in more mundane cases, the content of an affordance might be said to include its implications for other affordances in the same and/or other modalities. This is consistent with the postulation of 'affective affordances', aspects of the social and material environment that offer the prospect of altering one's emotional state in one or another way (Krueger and Colombetti, 2019). Given that other affordances are also, presumably, imbued with affect (insofar as they involve experiencing significant possibilities that relate both to one's concerns and to felt dispositions to act), opportunities to regulate one's emotions can be thought of in terms of affording changes to actual or experienced affordances.[15] Again, it is unclear how to specify the content of these affordances.

In considering the relationship between affordances and modalities of intentionality, it is also evident that the affordance-concept lacks the phenomenological depth required to analyze all-enveloping experiential changes of the kinds associated with severe psychiatric illness. Discussions of affordance-experience take it as given that one's surroundings are experienced as 'here, now' and restrict themselves to the manner in which certain ingredients of the here and now solicit activities. However, as pointed out with regard to 'salience', characteristic patterns of solicitation are integral to the sense that one is perceiving at all, that things are 'here, now'. Insofar as talk of affordances takes an experience of presence for granted, it overlooks a more profound phenomenological achievement, one that is often disturbed in psychiatric illness.

Once all of the phenomenological distinctions required to specify what an affordance-experience consists of have been added on, the term 'affordance' starts to look rather hollow in the middle of it all. Gallagher (2018, p.720) summarizes Gibson's central insight as follows: 'The claim is that perception is intrinsically action-oriented in the sense that we perceive things in terms of our pragmatic possibilities for acting on or with them'. We agree that this is an important insight to feed into work on the phenomenology of possibility. However, all it comes down to in the end is that perceptual experience, in all or almost all cases, relates in one or another way to the potential for action. And the relationship is hugely variable, ranging from an immediate solicitation to act in a more or less specific way to a sense of something as curiously removed from any potential or actual inclination to act. When it comes to describing what, exactly, various experiences of possibility consist of, the word 'affordance' becomes a placeholder, a blank to be filled in. Although it is easy enough to carry on talking in terms of affordances, once a certain point is reached, the term ceases to do any explanatory work. The exercise of defending its applicability to the phenomenology of psychiatric illness becomes analogous to that of building a house around a brick in order to demonstrate that a brick can function as a viable home. To pinpoint what an experience of X affording Y – anomalous or otherwise – actually consists of, at least the following need to be specified:

- The kind of significant possibility involved
- The experienced likelihood of Y's occurrence
- The temporal distance between X and Y
- The degree of determinacy with which Y is anticipated
- Whether X is experienced as offering possibility Y for me, for you, for us, or for them
- Whether, to what extent, and in what ways Y relates to one's longer-term projects and commitments
- The modality or modalities of intentionality relative to which X is experienced as affording Y
- How Y relates to and perhaps integrates a range of other experienced affordances
- Whether X also affords the alteration of other affordances
- Whether certain significant possibilities are experienced as absent
- Whether the possibility of Y is specific to X or more pervasive
- The specificity of any activities solicited by X

- Whether activities are presented as possible, impossible, easy, difficult, efficacious or inefficacious
- Whether one is drawn towards or away from X, in one or another manner

These distinctions are applicable to localized affordances and to all-enveloping shifts in the 'field' of affordances, both of which can come in many different guises. What we have is a pre-reflective, dynamic experience of interconnected possibilities that differ from one another in various respects. Adding that these possibilities consist of experienced 'affordances' and forcing a diverse range of ways in which experienced possibilities relate to potential activities into the formula 'X affords Y' does not tell us anything more. What does the explanatory work is not 'affordance' *per se* but the myriad qualifications that follow it. One could just as well say simply that 'things affect us' or 'we are affected by our surroundings'. Being 'affected' might sound rather too passive. However, by the same token, 'affordance' is too active, at least when we are faced with describing experiences that include the likes of all-enveloping helplessness, perceptual fascination devoid of practical possibility, or a world that no longer elicits activities and appears lacking in a non-localized way.

Granted, the term 'affordance' might prove helpful in instilling a preliminary acknowledgment of the manner in which perception is practically engaged. But, like 'salience', it is at best an initial step in an inquiry concerning experiences of significant possibility, analogous to the first stage of a rocket that is jettisoned at a certain point. Where detailed phenomenological study is concerned, what is required is a more discerning account of how human experience incorporates a complicated, multi-faceted, dynamic, and cohesive anticipation-fulfillment structure, involving various different kinds of significant possibilities. There is ample evidence that it does, but few attempts to go beyond the basics.[16] This might seem unwieldy, but there is no substitute if our goal is an understanding of human experience that is adequate for research and clinical practice in psychiatry.

Acknowledgments

Thanks to Sophie Archer for helpful comments on an earlier version of this chapter.

Notes

1 When the relevant phenomenology is examined, it becomes apparent that the category 'schizophrenia' accommodates a range of different phenomenological predicaments, some of which are difficult to distinguish from forms of experience associated with other psychiatric diagnoses (Ratcliffe, 2017, Chapter 6).
2 A comparable distinction is also made in recent work on 'predictive coding'. For instance, Andy Clark (2016) distinguishes conscious 'surprise' from non-conscious 'surprisal', where what minimizes surprisal can be very surprising.

3 However, Berridge and Robinson (1998, p.341) do acknowledge that the line between incentive salience and hedonic pleasure is sometimes unclear, given that experiences of incentive salience can themselves be pleasurable: 'a person who took a drug that made the world seem a more attractive and rewarding place, by selectively enhancing incentive salience, might find it difficult to describe those effects without invoking hedonic concepts'.
4 The account is thus reminiscent of Jaspers (1963), who maintains that delusions arise when one seeks to escape the uncomfortable tension and indeterminacy of 'delusional atmosphere' (a pervasive and enduring experience of one's surroundings as significant in unfamiliar and incongruous ways) by imposing a more determinate interpretation upon the experience.
5 Howes and Nour (2016) also note the methodological difficulties involved in extrapolating from animal studies.
6 Similar definitions are adopted by others. See, for example, an influential discussion by Fletcher and Frith (2009).
7 It is arguable that a phenomenological account of the manner in which experience incorporates anticipation is complemented in various ways by recent work on predictive coding and predictive processing, work that has also been related to the topic of aberrant salience and dopamine dysregulation in psychosis. See Ratcliffe (2017, Chapter 6) for a discussion.
8 An appreciation of how salience dysregulation can impact on the phenomenology of belief may also help to clarify the relationship between aberrant salience and delusion – how exactly the former disposes one towards the latter.
9 See Ratcliffe (2017, Chapters 5 and 6) for a discussion of how widespread loss of trust in other people implies loss of phenomenological structure and, with this, a widespread change in the experience of significant possibilities.
10 To indulge in a bit of speculation, it could even be that, in some instances, altered dopamine signaling and resultant 'salience dysregulation' operate as a sort of 'system reboot'. Old patterns of significance are no longer viable, given a widespread loss or failure of projects, and so new patterns need to be formed. This is achieved via the loosening of established patterns and the presentation of a plethora of novel possibilities, some of which later coalesce into coherent wholes that reflect new cares, concerns, and projects. Psychosis may arise when this goes awry, for instance, when the person is socially isolated and / or socially anxious in such a way or to such an extent that new patterns form in partial isolation from practical engagement with a consensus world.
11 See also Gallagher (2018) and Krueger and Colombetti (2019) for slightly different but complementary conceptions of an 'affordance space'. For Gallagher, an affordance space includes 'the full range of possible affordance fields relative to an individual, including the current affordance field plus any possible changes in that field due to changes in physical or cognitive skills or environment' (p.722).
12 De Haan et al. (2013, p.7) distinguish landscape from field in the following way: 'The *landscape* of affordances refers to all the possibilities for action that are open to a specific *form of life* and depend on the abilities available to this form of life. The *field* of affordances refers to the relevant possibilities for action that a particular *individual* is responsive to in a concrete situation, depending on the individual's abilities and concerns'.
13 De Haan et al. (2013, p.7. fn.8) also acknowledge that the concept requires further refinement. Hence the disagreement between us concerns prognosis as much as current utility.
14 Similarly, De Haan et al. (2015) add 'affective allure' to 'width', 'depth', and 'height', in order to accommodate the qualitatively different kinds of felt significance that a field of affordances might include.

15 As noted by Broome and Carel (2009), opportunities for the affective manipulation of other affordances, which may be recognized by oneself and / or others, are employed in the context of psychotherapy. However, it can be added that interpersonal regulatory processes of this nature are just as easily described and investigated without reference to 'affordances' (Ratcliffe, 2018).
16 In earlier work, one of us, Ratcliffe, employs the concept of 'existential feeling' to capture a variable sense of the kinds of possibilities that the world incorporates (Ratcliffe, 2008, 2015). He still endorses the concept. However, in this chapter, we adopt a broader perspective upon the experience of possibility, something that cannot be captured in its entirety by appealing to existential feeling.

References

Berridge, K. C. 2007. The Debate over Dopamine's Role in Reward: the Case for Incentive Salience. *Psychopharmacology* 191: 391–431.

Berridge, K. C. and Robinson, T. E. 1998. What Is the Role of Dopamine in Reward: Hedonic Impact, Reward Learning, or Incentive Salience? *Brain Research Reviews* 28: 309–369.

Broome, M. R. and Carel, H. 2009. The Ubiquity of Moods. *Philosophy, Psychiatry and Psychology* 16: 267–271.

Broome, M. R., et al. 2005. What Causes the Onset of Psychosis? *Schizophrenia Research* 79: 23–34.

Chemero, A. 2003. An Outline of a Theory of Affordances. *Ecological Psychology* 15: 181–195.

Clark, A. 2016. *Surfing Uncertainty; Prediction, Action, and the Embodied Mind*. Oxford University Press, New York.

De Haan, S., Rietveld, E., Stokhof, M. and Denys, D. 2013. The Phenomenology of Deep Brain Stimulation-induced Changes in OCD: an Enactive Affordance-based Model. *Frontiers in Human Neuroscience* 7, Article 653.

De Haan, S., Rietveld, E., Stokhof, M. and Denys, D. 2015. Effects of Deep Brain Stimulation on the Lived Experience of Obsessive-Compulsive Disorder Patients: In-depth Interviews with 18 Patients. *PLoS One* 10(8): e0135524. 10.1371/journal.pone.0135524.

Dings, R. 2018. Understanding Phenomenological Differences in How Affordances Solicit Action. An Exploration. *Phenomenology and the Cognitive Sciences* 17: 681–699.

Fletcher, P. C. and Frith, C. D. 2009. Perceiving is Believing: a Bayesian Approach to Explaining the Positive Symptoms of Schizophrenia. *Nature Reviews Neuroscience*, 10: 48–58.

Gallagher, S. 2018. The Therapeutic Reconstruction of Affordances. *Res Philosophica* 95: 719–736.

Gibson, J. J. 1979. *The Ecological Approach to Visual Perception*. Lawrence Erlbaum Associates, Hillsdale, NJ.

Howes, O. D. and Kapur, S. 2009. The Dopamine Hypothesis of Schizophrenia: Version III – the Final Common Pathway. *Schizophrenia Bulletin* 35: 549–562.

Howes, O. D. and Nour, M. N. 2016. Dopamine and the Aberrant Salience Hypothesis of Schizophrenia. *World Psychiatry* 15(1): 3–4.

Jaspers, K. 1963. *General Psychopathology*. Translated from the German Seventh Edition (1959) by J. Hoenig and M. W. Hamilton. Manchester University Press, Manchester.

Jauhar, S., et al. 2017. A Test of the Transdiagnostic Dopamine Hypothesis of Psychosis Using Positron Emission Tomographic Imaging in Bipolar Affective Disorder and Schizophrenia. *JAMA Psychiatry* 74: 1206–1212.

Kapur, S. 2003. Psychosis as a State of Aberrant Salience: a Framework Linking Biology, Phenomenology, and Pharmacology in Schizophrenia. *American Journal of Psychiatry* 160: 13–23.

Kapur, S., Mizrahi, R. and Li, M. 2005. From Dopamine to Salience to Psychosis – Linking Biology, Pharmacology and Phenomenology of Psychosis. *Schizophrenia Research* 79: 59–68.

Krueger, J. and Colombetti, G. 2019. Affective Affordances and Psychopathology. *Discipline Filosofiche* XXVIII: 221–246.

Macdonald, H. 2014. *H Is for Hawk*. Vintage Books, London.

Noë, A. 2004. *Action in Perception*. MIT Press, Cambridge, MA.

Ratcliffe, M. 2008. *Feelings of Being: Phenomenology, Psychiatry and the Sense of Reality*. Oxford University Press, Oxford.

Ratcliffe, M. 2015. *Experiences of Depression: a Study in Phenomenology*. Oxford University Press, Oxford.

Ratcliffe, M. 2017. *Real Hallucinations: Psychiatric Illness, Intentionality, and the Interpersonal World*. MIT Press, Cambridge, MA.

Ratcliffe, M. 2018. The Interpersonal Structure of Depression. *Psychoanalytic Psychotherapy* 32: 122–139.

Ratcliffe, M. and Bortolan, A. 2020. Emotion Regulation in a Disordered World: Understanding Borderline Personality Disorder. In G. Stanghellini and C. Tewes (Eds.), *Time and Body: Phenomenological and Psychopathological Approaches* (pp. 177–205). Cambridge University Press, Cambridge.

Rietveld, E. and Kiverstein, J. 2014. A Rich Landscape of Affordances. *Ecological Psychology* 26: 325–352.

van Os, J. 2009. A Salience Dysregulation Syndrome. *British Journal of Psychiatry* 194: 101–103.

4 On salience-based theories of demonstratives

Eliot Michaelson and Ethan Nowak[*]

4.1 Introduction

Consider the question of what makes it the case that a certain object counts as the referent of a particular utterance of a demonstrative like 'this' or 'that'. One much-discussed possibility is that it is the speaker's intentions which determine this fact, either directly or in conjunction with some further conditions. Another obvious possibility is that it is the fact that some particular object is maximally salient in the context of utterance which makes it the referent. The present essay will be dedicated to working out what this latter suggestion means, why we might prefer it to the former, and why, ultimately, we don't find it tenable.

4.2 Background

To get the salience theory better in view, consider an early exposition by Robert Stalnaker:

> The fact that a speaker is speaking, saying the words he is saying in the way he is saying them, is a fact that is usually accessible to everyone present. Such observed facts can be expected to change the presumed common background knowledge of the speaker and his audience in the same way that any obviously observable change in the physical surroundings of the conversation will change the presumed common knowledge. If a goat walked into the room, it would normally be presupposed, from that point, that there was a goat in the room. And the fact that this was presupposed might be exploited in conversation, as when someone asks *How did that thing get in here?*, assuming that others will know what he is talking about.
>
> (Stalnaker, 1978, p.86, emphasis in original)

Stalnaker's aim in this classic paper was to show how the informational transactions that occur during the course of a conversation might be modeled in broadly set-theoretic terms, not to defend any particular claims about demonstratives or reference. It is nevertheless striking how natural a view about demonstratives is suggested by his example. If we say that the referent of 'that' in a context is whichever object is most salient in the context (or relatedly, that the referent of 'that F' is whichever F is most salient in the context) it seems like we will make the right predictions about this and a host of familiar cases. By walking into the room, the goat makes himself not just salient, but mutually salient—such that we can each rely on the other to recognize that we both take him to be salient. On the model we have just quickly sketched, the referent of 'that thing', as used in the context described, will be the most salient thing, i.e., the goat.

Despite the prima facie appeal of an approach to demonstratives grounded in salience, most of the action in the literature over the last 40 or so years has been focused on the prospects for theories that make a speaker's referential intentions the sole, or at least the primary, determinant of reference. Consider, for instance, the early expression of this sort of 'speaker-intentions' view to be found in David Kaplan's *Afterthoughts*:

> What should we think of as the contextual feature relevant to the evaluation of a demonstrative? In the formal semantics, it may be taken to be the demonstratum. But at the preformal level, I think of it as the *directing intention*. The directing intention is the element that differentiates the 'meaning' of one syntactic occurrence of a demonstrative from another…
> (Kaplan, 1989, pp.587–588)

In other words, in Kaplan's formal model, demonstratives are mapped to whatever counts as 'the demonstratum' in that context. Kaplan's 'demonstratum', however, is just a place-holder. The actual piece of theoretical machinery that is supposed to perform the reference-fixing work is the speaker's 'directing intention', or what Kaplan thinks of as roughly the mental analog of an act of pointing.

A prominent variation on this theme was developed and defended by Kent Bach in a number of contributions in the 1990s. In one typical passage, Bach says that the referent of a demonstrative is fixed by a speaker's referential intention, which he claims:

> …isn't just any intention to refer to something one has in mind but is the intention that one's audience identify, and take themselves to be intended to identify, a certain item as the referent by means of thinking of it in a certain identifiable way.
> (Bach, 1992, p.143)

More recently, the speaker's intentions have been made to play a crucial role in sophisticated metasemantic treatments of demonstratives like the 'coordination account' defended by Jeffrey C. King:

> [T]he coordination account claims that the value of a given use of a demonstrative is that object that meets the following two conditions: 1) the speaker intends it to be the value; and 2) a competent, attentive, reasonable hearer would take it to be the the object that the speaker intends to be the value.
>
> (King, 2014, p.226)

We suspect that part of the reason views built around the idea of salience have not been as common as views that depend on the speaker's referential intentions is that it is easy to acknowledge at least a limited role for salience within the structure of an intention-based theory. Consider Stalnaker's goat again. If someone asks 'How did that thing get in here?' in the context previously described, offering no further indication about which thing she has in mind, reasonable listeners can employ basic Gricean reasoning to determine that she must have intended the goat. If the speaker did not mean to refer to the most salient thing, she would presumably have done something to make that clear. So, the fact that certain objects are mutually known or supposed to be salient in a context can be treated as a clue that indicates something about the speaker's likely referential intentions.[1]

Of course, the fact that salience *could* play a supporting role in a story built on the speaker's referential intentions does not mean that it *should*. Speaker-intention theories face a number of problems that salience-based theories, at least on their face, seem likely to be able to avoid.

Consider, for example, some difficulties raised recently by Christopher Gauker. One of those concerns the nature of the intentions a speaker must have in order for her demonstratives to refer to a particular object. Gauker claims that the ways of characterizing the relevant intentions that are most likely to be empirically successful will be question-begging:

> The content of the pertinent [speaker's] intention is described thus: *to refer to object o in uttering "that"*. *Referring* in this sense is supposed to be an act of the speaker. It is not a semantic relation of reference between an utterance and an object. So it is open to an advocate of the speaker-intention theory to hold that the nature of this act can be explicated without circling back to the semantic relation that is supposed to be explained. But how? It is in answering this question, that the theory is liable, i.e., threatens, to beg the question. That is because a prima facie plausible answer is the following: The speaker intends to use "that" to refer to an object *o* if and only if the speaker intends to use "that" in such a way that his or her *utterance* of "that" does refer to *o*. If we explain the content of the speaker's intention in this way, then we come straight back to the question we were supposed to be answering: What does it mean to say that an utterance of "that" refers to a given object?
>
> (Gauker, 2018, p.116, emphasis in original)

Another worry Gauker raises about the speaker-intention theory is that it is psychologically implausible. When demonstratives can be felicitously used, Gauker claims, interpreters will be able to figure out their referents without having to engage in any reasoning about the speaker's intentions—they will generally be able to track the same objects as the speaker by using heuristics that do not involve reasoning about the speaker's mental states at all (see Gauker, 2018, pp.19–124).

This worry amounts to one particular manifestation of a thought that a number of philosophers have given voice to in different forms. In fact, one of us has previously argued, along lines very similar to Gauker's, that the speaker-intention theory is unnecessarily complicated, since it introduces instructions into the lexicon—i.e., find the object of the speaker's intention—that would not amount to a substantial constraint, given the general framework of the interpretive task.[2] For a long time, philosophers have expressed a related worry about whether children, for example, really engage in the kind of second-order reasoning that the speaker-intention theory would require of them in order to count as users and consumers of demonstratives.[3]

Finally, Gauker gives an argument against the speaker-intention theory of demonstratives that is based on the intuition that we can refer to particular objects in thought without forming an intention to refer to them: If I look at a box of persimmons, some ripe, some not, I can direct my attention to one of them, the one in the lower left-hand corner, and think *That is ripe!* My thought itself contains an occurrence of a demonstrative, which refers to the persimmon in the lower left-hand corner of the box. Or so one might suppose. But if the speaker-intention theory is correct, then that cannot be right. According to that theory, if my thought really contains an occurrence of a demonstrative, then what it refers to can only be what I intend that occurrence to refer to. So the thought *That is ripe!* would have to be accompanied by another thought—an intention—to the effect that the occurrence of a demonstrative in the first thought refers to the persimmon in the lower left-hand corner. But that is absurd. So the speaker-intention theory is mistaken.

Note that one needn't endorse anything so strong as Gauker's claim that we literally think with demonstratives in order to run this sort of argument. If there are merely demonstrative-like elements of thought, regardless of whether they occur in some full language of thought, then the speaker-intention theorist will face this sort of dilemma: either she must endorse the claim that the reference of these demonstrative-like elements of thought is determined by further thoughts, or else she must split her theory of reference for linguistic demonstratives apart from her theory for the demonstrative-like elements of our thought.

While we are skeptical that any of Gauker's objections are likely to convince the committed speaker-intention theorist, we raise them to highlight the potential, and relatively under-appreciated, advantages of the salience-based alternative. In addition to making intuitively correct predictions about the core demonstrative data, a salience-based theory will naturally avoid the kinds of difficulties Gauker raises. If an utterance of a demonstrative in a context picks out the salient object from the context, there is no threat of circular intentions—since there is no intention in the first place that might be circular or not. Similarly, there is no worry about children having insufficiently complex intentions, or about interpreters having to go through epiphenomenal psychological calculations in order to arrive at a referent. Finally, the question of demonstrative reference in thought seems likely to be straightforwardly tractable on a salience-based account—the question of intending that a thought refer to this or that object simply does not arise. Instead, one simply has an element of one's thought that refers, when tokened, to whatever is maximally salient.

Given the intuitive appeal of salience-based treatments of demonstratives, and given the promise they hold out of avoiding some of the serious difficulties that speaker-intention theories face, it is surprising that they have not received more sustained attention in the literature. Here, we hope to remedy that by sketching out a variety of different ways of precisifying the basic idea that salience determines demonstrative reference. Ultimately, we will argue that each of these precisifications faces significant difficulties of its own. But none of this will be obvious until we say much more about what one might mean by 'salience in a context'.

We begin in the next section with a brief review of some recent work on salience-based approaches to demonstratives. Then we will show how a number of alternative views could be derived by modifying the picture that emerges from that work in various ways. Finally, we show how both the basic view we identify and, as far as we can tell, any of its natural derivates are susceptible to a certain class of objections.

4.3 The varieties of salience

Howard Wettstein was the first philosopher we know of to offer a modern-day salience-based approach to demonstratives. The outline of Wettstein's approach is illustrated well by means of a case in which the speaker points at a figure in the distance and says: 'That is a self-destructive man'. The speaker takes the figure to be Jones, but in fact, the person in the distance is Smith. While there are ways for the speaker-intention theorist to handle cases like this one, each involves substantial complications. An approach based on salience, on the other hand, easily makes the natural prediction:

> [R]eference to Smith, the man in the distance, would remain unchanged if the speaker did not point but rather took advantage of the fact that Smith was the only individual in view. The reference would remain unchanged if there were a number of people in view but Smith was somehow prominent, say he was walking towards the speaker and auditor and waving in their direction. There are a host of such contextual features that provide cues to the auditor and, at the same time, enter into the determination of reference.
> (Wettstein, 1984, p.71)

While Wettstein never explicitly uses the term 'salience' here, his remarks clearly allude to something along these lines. According to Wettstein, it is a complex combination of contextual (and also conversational) factors that go into determining the reference of demonstratives in context. Which such factors? Well, apparently those that can serve as cues to the auditor as to which object is the referent. Wettstein never tells us directly exactly which cues these are, but given that he is explicitly arguing against the speaker-intention view, the charitable alternative would seem to be: cues that serve to make a particular object maximally salient.

Still, we might hope for a more detailed explanation of how these cues are supposed to determine a referent. For some clues to how to go about this, we turn now to the most well-developed salience-based treatment of demonstratives of which we are aware, due to Allyson Mount.[4] Here is the core of her position:

> By saying that something is salient, I mean that it is the focus of perceptual or cognitive attention. Salience, on this view, is not some objective feature that can be determined independently of the mental states of conversational participants; it is essentially a mind-dependent matter. An object is *mutually recognized as maximally salient* by conversational participants when all interlocutors have focused their attention on it, and are aware that they have all focused their attention on it. Thus my claim is that a demonstrative refers to the object mutually recognized as maximally salient. When there is no such object, the demonstrative does not refer.
> (Mount, 2008, pp.155–156, emphasis in original)

While this view clearly echoes Stalnaker's suggestion in certain respects, it also offers an important clarification. No longer is 'salience' left unanalyzed. Rather, an object is salient if it is the focus of 'perceptual or cognitive attention'. We take it that Mount has it in mind that, even when one thing is at the focus of one's perceptual attention and another at the focus of one's cognitive attention, there will be some fact of the matter about which of these foci is at the center of one's overall attention. For present purposes, we are happy to set aside cases involving speakers and listeners with divergent and competing foci of their perceptual and cognitive attention.

Now, of course, one could quibble with this way of understanding the nature of salience. For example, one might prefer to say that it is *only* perceptual focus that matters. Or, alternatively, that *only* cognitive focus should count. The latter option strikes us as odd, given that demonstratives are very often used to refer to objects that stand out perceptually in one's proximal environment. The former option, however, does not seem obviously better; after all, it certainly seems possible to use demonstratives to refer to objects that are distant, abstract, or otherwise imperceptible. This would seem to belie a restriction to just perceptual focus.

A second sort of variance in salience-based theories is nicely brought out by considering Mount's particular version of the view alongside Wettstein's. For Wettstein, the condition that an object has to meet in order to count as the referent of a demonstrative in a context is that it be salient to the listener. For Mount, on the other hand, the salience condition is characterized with regard to both the speaker and the hearer. Before we offer specific arguments against positions like Wettstein's and Mount's, it will be worth taking a moment to clarify that still more varieties of the salience view can be derived by varying the nature of the agents with regard to which the salience criterion is implemented. In other words, we can imagine as many versions of the salience view as there are answers to the question: 'Salient for whom?' In addition to views that involve just the actual listener, or the actual speaker and audience, we can imagine views defined solely with regard to the actual speaker, or idealized versions of the speaker, listener, or both of them. We could try putting some hypothetical third party in the context, and ask ourselves how they might react to the demonstrative used. As far as we can tell, all of these variations on the salience view are ultimately susceptible to the same basic problem we will raise for Mount's version of the view, though some certainly fare worse than others.

4.4 Problems for *de facto* mutual salience

Suppose we follow Mount (2008) in saying that the referent of a simple demonstrative in a context is the object that is 'mutually recognized as maximally salient' by all of the participants in a conversation. (For complex demonstratives, we imagine that the corresponding formulation should be that the referent of 'that F' in a context is the F that is mutually recognized as maximally salient in the context.) When applied to cases like that of Stalnaker's goat or Wettstein's distant Smith, this treatment seems like it will make the right predictions. If a goat walks into the room, normal people engaged in conversation will notice, and focus their attention on the goat, at least for a moment. If one of them asks 'How did that thing get in here?', the goat will be mutually recognized to be salient, and thus, on Mount's approach, it will end up being the referent of the demonstrative. If there is only one man in the distance, or if one man is particularly noticeable for whatever reason and someone says 'That is a self-destructive man', that man will be mutually recognized as salient. Thus, he will count as the referent. We see no reason to doubt that this story could be adapted to cover a wide range of other common examples.

At the same time, however, we think covering a wide range of examples is not enough to show that a theory is empirically adequate. The problem is that, at this point, basically every competitor theory can handle most, if not all, of the common examples. To discriminate between those theories, we need to look at cases in which not everything goes right.

The simplest sort of case worth considering is one where the listener simply isn't paying attention. Consider once more a version of Stalnaker's goat case. Only this time, distracted by the commentaries on Kavanaugh's Senate testimony that are blowing up on my Twitter feed, I fail to notice that a goat has entered the room. So transfixed am I that I don't even hear you when you ask me 'How did that thing get in here?' On Mount's theory, this will entail that reference fails and that the speaker's question will end up concerning no particular object at all.[5]

Now, it might be thought that Mount's theory can be qualified in some way so as to require that the listener must be paying attention. (She offers an extended discussion of the criteria by which people who are spatiotemporally near to a demonstrative-tokening might nevertheless fail to count as audience members in the sense relevant for the evaluation of referents on her theory; compare e.g. Mount, 2008, pp.155–156.) We'll return to this suggestion below, but first it is worth demonstrating that there are other sorts of cases that will prove equally problematic for her view.

Consider a case we discuss in Nowak and Michaelson (2021b), which was presented by David Robson, writing for the BBC on September 5, 2014:[6]

> *Superhuman Vision*
> As Concetta Antico took her pupils to the park for an art lesson, she would often question them about the many shades she saw flashing before her eyes. I'd say, 'Look at the light on the water—can you see the pink shimmering across that rock? Can you see the red on the edge of that leaf there?' The students would all nod in agreement. It was only years later that she realised they were just too polite to tell the truth: the colours she saw so vividly were invisible to them.
>
> Today, she knows that this is a symptom of a condition known as 'tetrachromacy'. Thanks to a variation in a gene that influences the development of their retinas, people like Antico can see colours invisible to most of us. Consider a pebble pathway. What appears dull grey to you or me shines like a jeweller's display to Antico. 'The little stones jump out at me with oranges, yellows, greens, blues and pinks,' she says. 'I'm kind of shocked when I realise what other people aren't seeing.'

Imagine that the rock that shimmers pink for Antico is just one among many rocks in a river, the rest of which look uniformly—to both her and her students—the way ordinary rocks do to an ordinary trichromat observer (i.e., an observer with three types of color-sensitive cones instead of four). From Antico's perspective, then, the pink rock stands out clearly. Suppose that she now says:

(1) Everyone sketch a picture of that shimmery pink rock.

If we apply Mount's criterion to this example, we should predict a straightforward failure of reference. Although there is a pink shimmery rock that is salient for Antico, there is no such object (or indeed, any single object at all) that is mutually salient to Antico and her students. So, her demonstrative has no referent.

Our own judgment is that, while we should clearly expect communication to fail in a case like the one just described, it is not so obvious that we should think of Antico's utterance as involving an instance of reference failure. To borrow a locution employed frequently by King (2014), the teacher has 'done what she can' to refer. She is clearly not guilty of the sort of failing a speaker would be guilty of if she uttered a demonstrative with no grounds for thinking that anyone else would have any way of tracking the object she herself was focused on. On the contrary, one of the key features of this real-life case is that Antico's students for decades gave her no reason to doubt that they could see what she saw.

While we would be reluctant to claim that being a responsible demonstrative user is enough to guarantee reference, we think Antico's presumption about her students' visual experience is enough to make a reasonably strong case that her use of the demonstrative 'that' *did* in fact refer to the rock in question.[7] At the very least, we expect that she, after learning the facts of the case, might persist in claiming that she successfully used the demonstrative to refer. Moreover, we cannot imagine a plausible standard by which more could be expected of her; clearly it would be too much to expect her to shuffle a set of color swatches and test her students' spontaneous recall ability before using color terms with them.

We think it is also important to emphasize that Antico's demonstrative *thoughts* presumably refer to the rock in question. So, it seems like we must either allow that the utterances she would take to be vocalizations of those thoughts either fail to correspond to the thoughts in ways that she herself would recognize, or else allow that those utterances involve successful reference. Other things being equal, we prefer the latter option to the former. So long as they are using the language in a broadly competent fashion, we find the idea that a person's utterances amount to an external manifestation of her thoughts to be a broadly attractive one.

If you find that your intuitions with regard to the case presented differ from ours, consider a variation on which the roles are reversed. Instead of Antico's seeing a particular rock that stands out, imagine that all of Antico's trichromat students see a single rock in the riverbed reflecting the last rays of sunlight in a particularly beautiful way. For them, a single rock stands out from among all the rest, bathed in the shimmering pink of the sunset. For Antico, all of the rocks in the river are shimmering pink, equally beautifully, but less uniquely. One of the students says:

(2) Oh wow, everyone look at that amazing pink rock!

We suppose that it will be uncontroversial that all of the students present will track the same rock. Someone might comment on its shape, or position, or apparent weight, and all of the rest will be able to engage in a coordinated exchange. Antico, however, will have no idea which rock is meant, as the rocks all look the same to her. In this case, then, there is no object that counts as mutually maximally salient, so Mount's treatment of demonstratives predicts reference failure. Whatever reference is though, and whatever contextual features determine it (if any do), surely this is a case of it. Of course, Mount's account might be preserved by stipulating that Antico should not count as part of the audience for purposes of determining reference here. That move, however, strikes us as implausibly ad hoc.

Although the example involving tetrachromatic vision is a nice one, both because it involves a real case and because it makes the point so vividly, in general, we think that which objects are salient to the observers in a context will depend a lot on idiosyncratic facts about those observers themselves. Of course, someone who has access to a sensory modality that others do not, or someone whose discriminations in a certain modality are more fine-grained than others will at least sometimes find her attention drawn to different objects in virtue of her experience.

Importantly, however, sensory perception is not the only route by which differing sensitivities to the environment can be revealed. Parallel arguments can be mounted using other mental states that bear on the question of attention. While copyright considerations prevent us from showing it, there is a classic image from Gary Larson's *The Far Side* in which a city is depicted in chaos after an atomic explosion. Flames are everywhere, and the streets are choked with people fleeing on foot and in cars. In one of the cars, a man is driving with his dog in the passenger seat. The dog gazes intently out the window, looking not at the mushroom cloud, or the burning buildings, but at another dog that is visible on a corner. The caption reads "And then Jake saw something that grabbed his attention."

The cartoon is funny because we know that dogs are very interested in other dogs. Indeed, it would not be surprising if some dogs turned out to be more interested in other dogs than in the end of the world. While dogs, as far as we know, should not count as audience members for the purposes of theorizing about demonstratives, substantial variation among humans in terms of their interests is also a widespread phenomenon. Consider the following scenario:

Special Interests
I am a classic car fanatic, whereas you prefer motorcycles. Out for a stroll one day, we come across a 1961 Jaguar E-Type and I am transfixed. I say to you 'Wow, that is so cool!' However, though I've failed to notice it, there is a lovingly-restored 1968 Norton Commando parked right next to the Jaguar. Naturally, you are transfixed by the motorcycle and take that to be mutually salient.

As before, the example will involve a failure of reference according to Mount, whereas we are unconvinced that this is the right result. In fact, this will continue to be the case even if I am leading a tour for a classic car club of which you happen to be a member. You love classic cars, you just happen to love motorcycles even more. Everyone else can take the Jaguar to be mutually salient, but if you happen to fixate on the motorcycle, that's all it will take to undermine reference here. In other words, the mutual salience view makes reference extraordinarily brittle—something we find to be an intolerable conclusion.[8] Particularly with larger audiences, but even with smaller ones, *success* in achieving recognition of mutual salience looks like too strong a requirement on referential success. Uses of demonstratives, it would seem, can succeed in referring even when part—or perhaps even all—of the audience fails to coordinate with the speaker on which object is maximally salient in context.

4.5 *De facto* speaker or hearer salience?

Most of the foregoing problem cases can be avoided by shifting from Mount's criterion of mutual maximal salience to a criterion that only takes one of the conversational roles—that of the speaker—into consideration. So, in the case of the tetra-chromatic teacher who sees an outstanding rock and tries to point it out to her class, if we say that the object that is salient for the speaker is the referent of her demonstratives, we come away with the result that she succeeds in referring. Similarly in the variant of the case where the students are the ones who speak up, seeing a particular reflection of the sunset. Similarly in the case of *Special Interests*. And similarly for the case where the listener is simply failing to pay attention.

What we've now arrived at is actually a much older proposal, due to Bertrand Russell. In his *Human Knowledge* Russell tersely sketches the view as follows:

> 'This' denotes whatever, at the moment the word is used, occupies the centre of attention.
>
> (Russell, 1948, p.107)

In context, it is clear that Russell means by 'the centre of attention' the center of the *speaker's* attention in particular. So what Russell proposes is basically a speaker-oriented version of Mount's view.

But this proposal is untenable for two reasons. First of all, it isn't at all clear how much it in fact differs from the view that it is the speaker's *intentions* that fix reference, rather than her attention. One might, after all, be forgiven for thinking that having an *o*-directed intention is a rather good way to put *o* at the center of one's *attention*. Having noted this, we can now see the second worry: given the similarity of this view to the speaker-intention view, it would seem that the present view will suffer from the same potential drawbacks as an unrestricted version of that latter view. In particular, Russell's view would seem to be subject to a version of the 'Humpty Dumpty Problem': it allows for speakers to use demonstratives to refer to whatever they want, without limit, so long as the referent is something that presently occupies the center of their attention. Part of what originally motivated the salience theory was the thought that this is precisely something that one *cannot* do. Rather, one can only use demonstratives to refer to things that are, in some sense at least, salient. While we've had trouble spelling out that sense, it would seem rather odd for the advocate of the view to abandon this core motivation in order to defend this variant of it—allowing that speakers can succeed in making terms like 'this' refer to things simply by focusing their thought on them while they utter the term.

At least the speaker-oriented version of the view has the potential to deal with our various problem cases, however. The same cannot be said of the listener-oriented version of the view, i.e., a view on which the referent of a demonstrative with regard to a context is whichever object is salient to the listener. That gets the inattention case clearly wrong, as well as making bad predictions about one-on-one versions of *Superhuman Vision* and *Special Interests*. Those examples, after all, are meant precisely to play up the fact that what is salient to a speaker might not be to the listener, and vice-versa. With multi-person audiences, it's not even clear that a listener-oriented view will be well-defined—what should we say if everyone in the audience is such that a different object is salient to them? If we take it that unanimity is required, then reference will again turn out to be extraordinarily fragile. If it is not, then we need some procedure for weighing different responses by different audience members. While there may be room to argue about various proposals, we are inclined to suspect that none of them is likely to result in a successful theory.

4.6 Ideal salience?

The kinds of examples we have used to argue against a Mount-style treatment of demonstratives, on which an object counts as the referent of a demonstrative only if it is in fact mutually known to be salient to the participants in a conversation, all involved a gap between the object at the center of the speaker's attention and the object at the center of her audience's attention. At least in cases where this gap seems not to be the result of speaker negligence, it is hard to defeat the intuition that the speaker's use of 'this' or 'that' succeeds in referring. In the inattention case, we are tempted to think: 'If only the listener had been more attentive, then communication would have succeeded.' In the case of *Superhuman Vision*, we are tempted to think: 'Oh, but if only the students had been the way Antico *took* them—with reason—to be, then communication would have succeeded, in virtue of the fact that their attention would have been focused on the same objects'. And in *Special Interests*, we think: 'Right, but if the speaker's interlocutor had just been a bit more attentive to the speaker's interests rather than her own, then communication would again have succeeded'. In all these cases, then, while actual coordination may be lacking, *potential* coordination on an object as maximally salient seems very much a live possibility.

These intuitions raise an important question: why not, instead of building the salience theory around the actual participants in a conversation, use idealized versions of one or the other of them to fix the facts about reference? If we were to pair the actual speaker with an idealized listener in each of these cases—one with respect to whom we correct for all the deficiencies above—then we would seem to be able to account for all the cases that looked problematic for Mount's theory.

There are a number of things to be said about this proposal. First of all, it's not at all clear that we should want to keep the mutual aspect of it. Consider, for instance, a case along the following lines:

Misguided Hands
I am transfixed by a 1961 Jaguar E-Type in my field of view. However, when I go to point to it and utter 'Wow, that is so cool!' my arm moves off-course and I end up pointing directly at a lovingly-restored Norton Commando some distance away from the Jaguar, and not at all in my field of view—and thus not at all at the center of my attention.[9]

We find it highly unlikely that the speaker's use of 'that' refers to the Jaguar here. Perhaps—as the de facto mutual salience theory would predict—it refers to nothing at all. But another distinct possibility is that it actually succeeds in referring to the Norton Commando. We think this is not at all unlikely, in fact. But if that's right, we would have a much easier time predicting it if we were to abandon the mutual aspect of the salience theory and rely instead just on what a suitably-idealized listener would find maximally salient.

A similar point can be made by means of Kaplan's (1978) classic Carnap-Agnew case. Kaplan asks us to imagine a situation in which the speaker points behind herself to where, previously, her beloved picture of Rudolf Carnap hung. However, unbeknownst to her, that picture has been exchanged for another, this one of Spiro Agnew. Without looking, and having never visually encountered the picture of Agnew, the speaker points behind herself and directly at the picture of Agnew and says:

(3) That is a picture of one of the greatest philosophers of the twentieth century.[10]

Following Kaplan, we take it that the speaker's use of 'that' here refers to the picture which is actually behind her, the picture of Agnew. But there is no way for the speaker's attention to be fixed on that picture *de re*. At best, she might have her attention fixed on *whatever picture happens to be hanging on the wall behind me*. But this seems a rather odd focal point for her attention given the obvious competitor: her beloved picture of Carnap, something with which she is well-acquainted and should easily be able to fixate on *de re*. What's more, the picture could just as easily have been removed and replaced by nothing at all. So, here again, the salience-theorist might do well to jettison the mutual salience requirement and move towards an idealized listener-oriented approach.

Unfortunately, this version of the theory also faces some significant downsides. For one thing, it now looks as though, in order to be good interpreters, listeners need to ask themselves not what's actually salient to them, but rather what a more ideal version of themselves would take to be salient. This, we submit, is to massively ramp up the psychological demands that the theory places on interpreters. Ordinary listeners will typically be able to recognize what's salient to them. Whether they are typically capable of recognizing what would be salient to a more ideal version of themselves is highly questionable. If not, then most listeners will be failing to abide by the norms of interpretation we would expect for them to have to abide by to count as good, attentive listeners. Likewise, we are highly skeptical that small children will be able to engage in this sort of complicated reasoning.

Equally worryingly, it seems to us that no amount of idealization of the listener will be able to handle cases like *Special Interests*. Is it somehow more ideal for the listener to share the speaker's preference for classic cars over classic motorcycles? We fail to see how this constitutes any sort of real possibility. So, if we idealize on the actual listener, we obtain the result that the speaker's use of 'that' refers to the Norton Commando—contrary to her intentions, and contrary to what seems to be the intuitive judgment regarding the case. Likewise, if I am leading a tour for classic car aficionados, one of whom happens to actually be an even bigger classic motorcycle aficionado, then either we'll need to relativize reference to each individual, or we'll need some way of aggregating. Idealization won't solve this problem, since idealization won't coordinate some members' dominant interest in classic cars with others' dominant interest in motorcycles.

Finally, it seems to us unlikely that we should actually prefer this view over a nearby one according to which demonstratives refer to whatever an idealized listener would take them to refer to. While we are inclined to reject this latter view for various reasons, it strikes us as having the advantage of allowing the listener to take account of things like what she takes the speaker to be interested in getting across, or what she takes to be the broader purposes of the conversation, in interpreting the speaker's use of a demonstrative.[11] One might insist that all of this is simply a part of what an idealized listener should take account of in determining what is maximally salient in a context. That, of course, is fine. But then the account has lost another of its purported advantages: now, to be good interpreters, listeners are going to have to try to grasp the speaker's intentions after all—for those are now stipulated to be relevant to the determination of reference.

One might try to avoid these worries yet again by appealing not to an idealized listener, but rather to a 'random person in the street', as it were. But this will yield the wrong result in any number of cases where the speaker and listener manage to coordinate based on some specialized knowledge that both possess. If one paramedic asks another for 'that SAM splint', the first is likely to be handed a particular object. A random person in the street, on the other hand, is likely not to know what a SAM splint is.

Now, one might try iterating the theory yet again by allowing that the random person in the street needs to be a party to the common ground of the conversation. But, again, we can simply revise the case: suppose that the paramedic simply asks a passer-by to hand her that SAM splint, in the hopes that her addressee will be able to identify it—or even, perhaps, in a panic. Now, supposing that the passer-by is also a paramedic, though, in civilian clothes, communication will succeed here—and, we take it, reference as well. But a random person who is party to the common ground of the conversation would not be able to identify the referent here.

Of course, we cannot claim to have cut off every route by which one might try to employ an idealized or everyday listener, in conjunction with a salience-based approach, to generate a theory of demonstrative reference. But we hope to have shown enough to convince the reader that, if such a view can be made to work, it is going to have to be a rather more complicated version of the view than those we began with. The question, at that point, is whether the potential for empirical adequacy is worth the price of this complexity, or whether it can be bought more cheaply elsewhere.

4.7 Conclusion

Salience-based theories of demonstratives have a good deal of intuitive appeal: very often, we use demonstratives to coordinate our thought and talk on objects that are already highly salient in a context. Very often, we do this by relying on our apparent mutual knowledge that these objects are salient to each of us. The problem with this view, we have suggested, is that it can go wrong too easily. All too often, we are going to think that something is mutually salient even when it isn't. Nonetheless, it seems that demonstrative reference can succeed in such cases.

We've investigated a variety of potential responses to this conundrum, mostly focused on refining the notion of salience under consideration—making it idealized in some way, or just the purview of the speaker or listener, individually. We argued on the basis of particular features of each of these ways of going that none of these looked particularly promising. In conclusion, we'd like to step back and offer a broader critique of salience-based approaches of all sorts.

It seems to us that any salience-based approach to demonstratives is based on a fundamental misunderstanding of how we use terms like demonstratives. We do, of course, sometimes use these terms to refer to things that are already salient in a context. But sometimes we also use these terms to *make particular objects salient*. In the SAM splint case we offered above, we don't take it that the SAM splint will have been particularly salient antecedently, unless one has both a great deal of specialized knowledge and a good view of what's wrong with the patient. Asking for the SAM splint serves to make the SAM splint salient—to direct the listener's attention to it, *ceteris paribus*, supposing that she knows what a SAM splint is. That's part of the point of the utterance. Of course, one could further modify the theory so as to try to account for these shifts in salience due to the utterance itself. But then we would need a full theory of how utterances themselves shift what's salient, what is going to tend to draw our attention, in a context. The worry is that to make good on that, the salience theorist might well find herself appealing to things like the speaker's intentions—undermining a good deal of the original motivation for the view.

All that said, while we are pessimistic about the prospects for a salience-based account of demonstrative reference, we are more optimistic that there will be helpful lessons to be drawn from the consideration of such theories. In particular, we find it rather appealing to think that a crucial part of the explanation of why we cannot, in general substitute 'this' for 'that' while preserving (at the very least) felicity, has to do with the ways that we use these particular terms to help structure each other's attention.[12] In our formal linguistic theories, this fact is likely to be reflected in different felicity conditions being attached to each of these terms.[13] But we should ask: what is it that such theories are aiming to represent? On the one hand, we might simply take them to aim at predicting our judgments on felicity and truth. But we take that to be a mistake; plausibly, the reason *why* we make such judgments is because we tacitly understand that we can use 'this' in English to help structure our interlocutors' attention in a certain way, such that more proximal objects are likely to be nudged towards the center of attention. Combined with a gesture and/or a descriptor, in the case of a complex demonstrative, these look like remarkably versatile tools for helping to direct each other's attention in face-to-face contexts. So, even if we reject the thought that demonstratives refer to whatever is maximally salient, worked out in one way or another, there is likely to be an important role for salience to play in our understanding of the meanings of demonstratives.

Indeed, we are inclined to think that the lesson to be learned here extends well beyond the demonstratives. It seems to us that certain other recalcitrant phenomena in the vicinity of linguistic meaning might be amenable to explanations in terms of their tendencies to restructure our attention. So, for instance, it strikes us as plausible that part of what is so contemptible about a variety of slur terms is that they serve to highlight negative ways of interacting with their targets, to invoke a certain perspective that makes actions that would otherwise be ignored as non-options come into focus as options.[14] Likewise, the very *style* of one's speech may serve to highlight a certain class of responses—at least to a particular sort of audience—as anyone who has had to deal with a government bureaucracy in a foreign tongue will be well aware.[15] In both these cases, we suspect that there is much to be gained from thinking about the, often rather subtle, ways that what we say serves to help structure our interlocutors' attention, both intentionally and unintentionally. Again, our claim is not that such structure will provide us with any easy answers to a range of traditional philosophical questions like 'What is meaning?' or 'What determines demonstrative reference in context?' Rather, we hope that thinking in terms of how our speech helps to structure each other's attention will serve to offer us new and richer ways of interpreting extant theories—and perhaps even to direct our attention to some new and as-yet unexplored questions about the interplay between meaning and mind.[16]

Notes

* This work is entirely collaborative and names are listed in alphabetical order.
1. This possibility is mooted in Reimer (1991), who posits that speakers sometimes rely on assumptions about mutual salience to obviate the practical need to point or offer other overt indications regarding their intentions when trying to coordinate with their listener by means of a demonstrative.
2. See Nowak (2021a) section 3.3 for discussion.
3. Note that some people think children can do this, and even do it easily; see Wimmer and Perner (1983), Breheny (2006), Csibra (2010), McEllin et al. (2018), and others for discussion.
4. Una Stojnić, Matthew Stone, and Ernie Lepore have recently defended a sophisticated theory that they call the 'coherence-attention' theory; compare Stojnić et al. (2013, 2017). The notion of 'attention', however, that is at the heart of their theory is a highly technical one that has little to do with psychological salience. As such, we set consideration of their view aside. For a detailed critical discussion, however, compare Nowak and Michaelson (2020).
5. We thank Mount herself for reminding us (p.c.) that there is room for someone to accept reference failure in a case like this, but to downplay the significance of the resulting problem by invoking the distinction between speaker meaning and semantic meaning (see Kripke, 1977 for discussion). So, it might well be that even if the semantic value of the speaker's question is undefined or incomplete, there is a fully-specified question in the vicinity, i.e., the question the speaker *meant* to ask.
6. Available at: http://www.bbc.com/future/story/20140905-the-women-with-super-human-vision.
7. We discuss our reluctance about the 'doing enough' criterion in our Nowak and Michaelson (2021b), and our reluctance to accept the claim that there necessarily be any single criterion of reference in the first place in Nowak (2021a) and Nowak and Michaelson (2021a).
8. Of course, one might disagree with us on this point; perhaps failures of reference really are the norm. Mount (2008, pp.155–156), for instance, seems to embrace this consequence, and Mount (p.c.) has suggested that this can be made more palatable by appealing, once again, to Kripke's distinction between speaker's reference and semantic reference. The idea would be that, even if successful semantic reference involving demonstratives is relatively rare, speaker's reference can be wheeled out to help explain our intuitive judgments on these cases, communicative potential, speaker responsibility, success in coordination, etc. At this point, we find ourselves wondering whether the notion of semantic reference has, at least for demonstratives, become a theoretical third wheel; we would have thought that a notion of demonstrative reference worth having should figure into one or more of these explanatory projects, and we are at a loss for what exactly the salience-theoretic understanding of this notion is actually well-suited to explain. See our Nowak and Michaelson (2021a) for further discussion of the explanatory role—or, on our account, roles—of demonstrative reference and Michaelson (2016, 2021) for a sustained inquiry into a particular explanatory role for meaning and semantic reference to which salience theories look particularly ill-suited.
9. This is basically a variant on the 'keys' case from Reimer (1992, pp.385–386).
10. The original case from Kaplan (1978, p.239) involved his 'dthat' operator. But since that isn't a term of ordinary English, and the semantics of 'dthat' is purely stipulative and thus beyond dispute, we have altered the example slightly.
11. See Nowak and Michaelson (2021b) for our reasons for rejecting the view.
12. See Wolter (2006) for helpful discussion on this point.
13. See, for instance, Elbourne (2008).
14. See Camp (2013) for a view along these lines

15 See Nowak (2022) for an extended discussion of the philosophical import of this sort of phenomenon.
16 For their incisive comments on an earlier draft, many thanks to Sophie Archer and Allyson Mount. For a helpful discussion on these issues, thanks as well to Jonathan Cohen and Sam Cumming.

References

Archer, S. (Ed.). 2022. *Salience: A Philosophical Inquiry*. Routledge, Abingdon.
Bach, K. 1992. Intentions and Demonstrations. *Analysis* 52(3): 140–146.
Breheny, R. 2006. Communication and Folk Psychology. *Mind and Language* 21(1): 74–107.
Camp, E. 2013. Slurring Perspectives. *Analytic Philosophy* 54(3): 330–349.
Csibra, G. 2010. Recognizing Communicative Intentions in Infancy. *Mind and Language* 25(2): 141–168.
Elbourne, P. 2008. Demonstratives as Individual Concepts. *Linguistics and Philosophy* 31(4): 409–466.
Gauker, C. 2018. Against the Speaker-Intention Theory of Demonstratives. *Linguistics and Philosophy* 42: 109–129.
Kaplan, D. 1978. Dthat. In P. French, T. Uehling and H. Wettstein (Eds.), *Contemporary Perspectives in the Philosophy of Language* (pp. 383–400). University of Minnesota Press, Minneapolis.
Kaplan, D. 1989. Afterthoughts. In J. Almog, J. Perry and H. Wettstein (Eds.), *Themes from Kaplan* (pp. 565–614). Oxford University Press, Oxford.
King, J. C. 2014. Speaker Intentions in Context. *Noûs* 48(2): 219–237.
Kripke, S. 1977. Speaker's Reference and Semantic Reference. *Midwest Studies in Philosophy* 2: 255–276.
McEllin, L., Sebanz, N. and Knoblich, G. 2018. Identifying Others' Informative Intentions from Movement Kinematics. *Cognition* 180: 246–258.
Michaelson, E. 2016. The Lying Test. *Mind and Language* 31(4): 470–499.
Michaelson, E. 2021. Speaker's Reference, Semantic Reference, Sneaky Reference. *Mind and Language*. 10.1111/mila.12349.
Mount, A. 2008. Intentions, Gestures, and Salience in Ordinary and Deferred Demonstrative Reference. *Mind and Language* 23(2): 145–164.
Nowak, E. 2021a. No Context, No Content, No Problem. *Mind and Language* 36(2): 189–220.
Nowak, E. 2022. Speech and the Significance of Style. Manuscript.
Nowak, E. and Michaelson, E. 2020. Discourse and Method: Why Appeals to Context Still Won't Go Away. *Linguistics and Philosophy* 43: 119–138.
Nowak, E. and Michaelson, E. 2021a. Meta-metasemantics, or the Quest for the One True Metasemantics. *Philosophical Quarterly*. 10.1093/pq/pqab001.
Nowak, E. and Michaelson, E. 2021b. Who's Your Ideal Listener? *Australasian Journal of Philosophy* 99: 257–270. 10.1080/00048402.2020.1741658.
Reimer, M. 1991. Demonstratives, Demonstrations, and Demonstrata. *Philosophical Studies* 63: 187–202.
Reimer, M. 1992. Three Views of Demonstrative Reference. *Synthese* 93: 373–402.
Russell, B. 1948. *Human Knowledge*. George Allen & Unwin, London.
Stalnaker, R. 1978/1999. Assertion. In R. Stalnaker (Ed.), *Context and Content*. Oxford University Press, Oxford.

Stojnić, U., Stone, M. and Lepore, E. 2013. Deixis (Even Without Pointing). *Philosophical Perspectives* 27: 502–525.

Stojnić, U., Stone, M. and Lepore, E. 2017. Discourse and Logical Form: Pronouns, Attention, and Coherence. *Linguistics and Philosophy* 40: 519–547.

Wettstein, H. K. 1984. How to Bridge the Gap Between Meaning and Reference. *Synthese* 58(1): 63–84.

Wimmer, H. and Perner, J. 1983. Beliefs About Beliefs: Representation and Constraining Function of Wrong Beliefs in Young Children's Understanding of Deception. *Cognition* 13: 103–128.

Wolter, L. K. 2006. *That's That: The Semantics and Pragmatics of Demonstrative Noun Phrases*. PhD thesis, University of California, Santa Cruz.

5 The ethics of attention: An argument and a framework[1]

Sebastian Watzl

5.1 Introduction

Suppose that you had no other information about a person than facts about her attention. The description you have uses only 'attention' and close relatives as a psychological predicate. That is: you have information about what she focuses her attention on; how much attention she pays to certain things; what is salient to her or has a tendency to grab her attention, and what – by contrast – tends to never get her attention. You also know about her capacity to control her attention: how much she has of it and when she exercises it. On the other hand, you are not told what that person believes or desires, what she perceives, what she intends; or what emotions she may have. Only attention; nothing else. I claim that you could still paint an informative picture of her character, her values, and what she cares about; indeed, you could provide decent estimates of many of her other mental states or characteristics. You may infer much about what the person believes or what she sees from what she pays attention to. Information about someone's attention alone, it seems, allows us to give a rich account of the structure of a person's mind, her experiences and what kind of life she likely lives. A psychological theory that uses attention as its only primitive psychological term, in other words, would be comparatively rich in its expressive capacities.

The above exercise illustrates how central attention is in an account of mind and agency: it delineates important contours of a person's life. Several contemporary philosophers (cf. Wu 2011, 2014; Watzl, 2017; Ganeri, 2017; Jennings, 2020) have, relying in part on the large empirical literature on attention in psychology and neuroscience, defended versions of what I will here call the *descriptive centrality of attention*: attention plays an important role in (a) describing an individual's mind and agency, and (b) explaining many central facts about that individual.

This paper argues for a normative implication of the descriptive centrality of attention: given the descriptive centrality of attention, attention should also be *normatively* central. We should develop an ethics of attention that delineates the normative pressures on that central structure of the mind. In this paper, I argue for this claim and sketch a framework for the study of the ethics of attention.

DOI: 10.4324/9781351202114-6

5.2 The argument for the normative significance of attention: From the ethics of belief to the ethics of attention

I use the 'ethics of attention' in this essay in analogy to the 'ethics of belief' that is the title of a seminal paper by William Clifford (1877). Since the resulting debate between Clifford and the psychologist and philosopher William James (1896), 'the ethics of has come to designate an area of philosophy that discusses which normative pressures, if any, govern our practices of forming, maintaining and relinquishing beliefs and how those normative issues relate to the nature of belief (cf. Chignell, 2018). The ethics of belief has evolved to be a rich, multi-faceted and tightly structured field between epistemology, philosophy of mind, action theory, decision theory, and ethics. Some people in this field argue that belief is essentially normative and constitutively governed by – for example – distinctive norms regarding truth (e.g. Shah, 2003); others argue that the nature of belief exactly precludes the existence of belief norms (e.g. Glüer and Wikforss, 2013); and some think that any rational norms of belief flow from general principles of rationality (Rinard, 2017). To speak of the ethics of belief, in my sense, is not to take a specific stance in this debate; it merely indicates a distinctive study of the normative pressures on belief and how they interact with what beliefs are. The ethics of belief is a field that allows a focused discussion of disagreement.

My argument in this paper is that it is at least equally important to have an ethics of attention. Given the descriptive centrality of attention, we need a field of study of which normative pressures, if any, govern our practices of attention: what norms govern what we should attend to; how we should engage our capacity for attention; or when we should begin and when we should stop paying attention to something. Like the ethics of belief, the ethics of attention connects those normative questions to issues regarding the nature of attention, i.e. to what may or may not be subject to such normative pressures. How, for example, are salience and attention related – and what does that tell us about the respective normative pressures on salience and attention? To what degree can we control our attention? How are different forms of attention connected to each other? An ethics of attention will show how those questions impact and are in turn affected by claims about which norms are appropriate for attention. In my sense, the ethics of attention is not only about *moral* pressures on attention. The relative significance of different sources of normative pressures on attention and their interaction, indeed, is one major topic in the ethics of attention (see Section 8 below). The ethics of attention investigates which patterns of attention are rational, epistemically demanded, morally, aesthetically or epistemically blame-, or praiseworthy, ethically right, just or unjust, or prudentially appropriate. Do all such forms of evaluation exist? What is their significance? These are central issues in the ethics of attention. Speaking of the ethics of attention also does not imply that there are *constitutive* norms of attention. This question, again, is one to be debated within the ethics of attention, a field of study that allows a focused discussion of disagreement.

Why believe that there can be and should be an ethics of attention in this sense?

I suggest that we can find an answer by starting with a more general question: which aspects of the mind, generally, can and should be the focus of a sustained normative assessment? Let us look at some examples. We might, for example, think of virtue theorists as developing an ethics of character traits. They tell us what normative pressures there are for maintaining and relinquishing certain character traits and how those normative issues relate to the nature of character traits and the role they play in our individual and collective lives. And we might think of some deontologists as developing an ethics of the maxims that guide our decision-making: they develop a theory of the normative pressures on those maxims and connect this theory with one of the roles such maxims play in action and decision making. In recent years, many further aspects of the mind have become the subject of a field that resembles the ethics of belief – fields that connect the discussion of the nature of those aspects of the mind with discussions of the norms, if any, that may apply to them. We have, for example, discussions of the nature of desire and the question of whether some desires are irrational or immoral, or whether desire can be a source of epistemic insight (e.g. Tenenbaum, 2010). Similar debates have concerned emotion (e.g. De Sousa, 1990, Brady, 2013). In the case of perception, we have seen an intense debate linking questions about the nature of perception and its epistemic role (cf. Lyons, 2017 for a review), and also whether perception itself might be assessible for rationality (e.g. Siegel, 2016). Finally, consider how questions about the nature of concepts have been linked with questions about whether there might be ethical, political, or epistemic pressures to possess or not to possess certain concepts or to change them – a field that often is explicitly described as 'conceptual ethics' (Cappelen et al., 2019).

What, then, is the general principle by which an aspect of the mind becomes a central target of normative analysis? I suggest that the significance of the normative evaluation of an aspect of the mind (or behavior, or social interaction), other things being equal, roughly should be commensurate to its descriptive or explanatory significance. If, for example, one thought that stable, situation-independent, character traits played little role in an account of the mind and in explaining a person's behavior (which is instead largely explained by social structures or situational features), then the evaluation of such character traits should also not be normatively central (cf. Doris, 1998). If, by contrast, character traits, indeed, deeply shaped a person's experience, mind, and action, then it would be appropriate to make them a central object of normative evaluation. Similarly, a focus on the normative role of the emotions is justified to the degree to which the emotions, descriptively, deeply shape a person's life and mind. Finally, the recent focus on conceptual ethics is partly driven by the insight that the concepts we use greatly influences the way we think and feel, how we interact with others, and which lines of inquiry we pursue. Which concepts we use explains many things. Therefore, a normative analysis of concepts is called for. The general principle I suggest is that – other things being equal – normative significance should follow descriptive significance (I will discuss below what the other relevant factors might be).

Note that the idea here is not that (descriptive) psychology determines ethics, or that an *is* in some other way implies an *ought*. Rather, I'm making a normative claim: when we normatively assess a mind, a person, behavior or experience, we should target those aspects of the mind, the person, the behavior or the experience that play important roles in it rather than those that are only of minor explanatory significance.

Now, we are ready to state *the argument for the normative significance of attention*. I will put it as an argument for the conclusion that *if* we should have an ethics of belief, *then* we should also have an ethics of attention. So, here is the argument:

1. Attention and salience are explanatorily central in an account of the mind and in the explanation of experience and behavior to a degree that is, at least, roughly commensurate to the explanatory role of belief. (call this the *descriptive centrality of attention*)
2. If the descriptive centrality of attention holds, then attention and salience should also be normatively central in the following sense: answering normative questions about attention and salience is at least as important as answering normative questions about belief (call this *the descriptive-normative link*)
3. So, Answering normative questions about attention and salience is at least as important as answering normative questions about belief. (this is *the normative centrality of attention*).

Given that many philosophers think that answering normative questions about belief is quite important indeed (as the field of epistemology indicates), it follows from the conclusion of this argument, i.e. the normative centrality of attention, that answering normative questions about attention will be quite important as well. We do, in other words, need an ethics of attention.

In the next sections, I will defend the argument just laid out.

5.3 A further reason for why we need an ethics of attention

Some people might say that, surely, when we, as philosophers, ask about which aspects of the mind or behavior we should make the focus of our normative inquiry, the issue of how much the general public *cares* about getting answers to, or getting guidance regarding normative questions about that aspect of the mind is at least as important as the descriptive centrality of that aspect of the mind. Many people, outside of philosophy, wonder what to believe in an age of fake news; they wonder whether anger is appropriate in a certain situation (cf. Srinivasan, 2018), or what, if anything is wrong with the use of certain concepts (such as racial ones). It is the general public's interest in those questions, one might think, that should drive what philosophers at their normative workbench investigate (just like it's the public's interests that should figure heavily in what kind of machines engineers should develop).

It is not obvious just how heavily the fact that the public is already interested in certain normative questions should figure in which normative questions we as philosophers investigate. Normative innovation might result exactly from realizing the significance of a normative analysis of an aspect of the mind that the general public had tended to overlook. It was, arguably, philosophical insight into the explanatory significance of personal decision-making that first led to philosophical analyses of the normative significance of autonomy and, hence to some of the normative innovations of the enlightenment period.

Yet, a defender of the normative significance of attention can also accept a constraint from public interest in the relevant normative issues. As a matter of fact, the public seems to care a lot more about normative questions regarding attention than normative philosophy does.

In our contemporary context – dominated as it is by mass information and social media—many in the public are faced with pressing challenges about how to organize information, how to individually distinguish what is relevant from what isn't, and how to together agree on what is currently most deserving of collective attention. Accordingly, in the public debate there is no shortage of normative opinions about attention: about what is right, healthy, important, and correct with regard to attention. Social media activity, for example, by many is especially deemed as receiving too much of it. Others argue vigorously that in political debates the particular voices of some persons or groups of persons are getting too much or too little attention. A growing number of self-help and meditation practices, such as mindfulness training, promise help for the proper regulation of attention in an age of distraction (cf. Kabat-Zinn, 2009; Bregman, 2011; Williams and Penman 2011; Newport, 2016). Activists warn of the 'industrialization of [...] attention capture' (Wu, 2017) and some call the liberation of attention the defining moral and political struggle of our 'time' (Williams, 2018). Think also about discussions of spin doctors and troll factories (or certain political actors): they misdirect and distract. Those who criticize either those actors or those who fall for them make claims in the ethics of attention: they argue that it is normatively criticizable to misdirect someone's attention, or that it is wrong to pay too much attention to what is false. Finally, think of the debates about statues, paintings, or history books: the presence of the great men of history in these places gives them a lot of everyone's attention. Our social and physical environments are, literally, engineered and created for certain patterns of attention. Attention in thought, in sympathy, but also in perceptual, in visual or auditory attention: the statues at the central squares are designed to be looked at. Many, in the contemporary public debate, argue that this focus is inappropriate. The painter Titus Kaphar, for example, tries to show with his art that the dreams and hopes of the slave boy, who is depicted in the background of a painting or as leading the horse of a general, they too deserve our attention.[2] Kaphar argues for a claim in the ethics of attention: justice demands changes in our attentional patterns.

The ethics of attention, thus, already is an area of public debate. It is normative philosophy that is lagging behind. While the normative evaluation of our own and other's attention is central to ordinary normative thought and discourse, the majority of contemporary normative philosophy, from moral theory, to epistemology and decision theory, contains no systematic discussion of the ethics of attention.

So, if the public's interest in answers to normative questions about attention and need for guidance in the public debate is indeed an (additional) constraint on whether we, as philosophers, should develop a focused study of the ethics of attention, then we have, indeed, more reason to focus our energies on (developing) such a field of study. Attention is *both* descriptively central and the public cares about normative guidance with regard to it.

5.4 Is attention, in fact, descriptively central?

Let me now look deeper at premise (1) of the argument for the normative significance of attention: the descriptive centrality of attention. Is it really correct that attention is an explanatorily central aspect of the mind and of behavior? If the public's interest in the ethics of attention were driven by a mistaken view of its descriptive significance, then maybe philosophers are right to neglect a normative analysis of attention.

On the face of it, an attack on the descriptive centrality of attention is an uphill battle. In its defense, we can refer to the rich empirical psychology of attention, and to the philosophical accounts mentioned in the introduction. Attention and salience are, arguably, centrally involved in at least the following areas: (a) *Decision making.* A recent review (Orquin and Loose, 2013) emphasizes the 'active role [of attention] in constructing decisions' (p.203), which leads to a host of 'downstream effects' (ibid.). (b) *Intentional agency and agentive control.* Here, Wayne Wu (2011, 2016) has argued for a central role of attention in the explanation of how intentional agency and control over action are possible. (c) *Self-control.* Berkman et al., (2017, p.423) argue that '[a]ttention plays a crucial role in... self-control by gating which options enter the choice set at any one moment and foregrounding their salient attributes' (see also Watzl (forthcoming) where I argue that by appeal to attention, self-control can be fully explained without willpower or a divided mind). (d) *Perception.* Attention is known to affect all aspects of perception, from perceptual precision, response times, to perceptual appearances (see Carrasco, 2011 for a review), and, finally, to whether we perceive certain items at all – as in, for example, Simons and Chabris (1999) famous invisible gorilla experiment. (e). *The Self.* In quite different ways, Dicey-Jennings (2020) and Ganeri (2018) argue that central aspects of the self can be explained by appeal to attention. (f) *Consciousness.* Philosophers have debated which accounts of consciousness are compatible with the effects of attention on consciousness (cf. Block, 2010). And an ongoing debate is about whether attention might be necessary for consciousness (see Watzl (2017) where I argue for a constitutive role of attention with regard to all forms of consciousness). (h) *Memory.* Attention is known to interact with memory in complex ways. What we remember both affects attention, and attention strongly affects what is encoded in memory (e.g. Chun and Turk-Browne (2007) (i) *Introspection.* Several philosophers have argued that introspection either is or is made possible by a special form of attention (e.g. Chalmers, 2003; Goldman, 2006) or relies on attention in a different way (Watzl, 2017) (j) *Emotion.* Philosophers from De Sousa (1990) to Brady (2013) have argued that certain patterns of salience and attention may be 'constitutive of emotional experience' (Brady, 2013, p.181).

To sum up: almost anywhere we look in the mind and in forms of behavior we find plausible arguments to the effect that attention is centrally involved in and complexly interacts with other aspects of the mind. Of course, each particular case to some degree is controversial. But the evidence at least points strongly in the direction of premise (1), i.e. a central role of attention in an account of the mind and of behavior.

Yet, a more subtle attack on the descriptive centrality of attention might be launched. Attention, one might argue, is too variegated to be, itself, descriptively central.

Start by reflecting on the many forms of attention: in one form attention is perceptual: a subject focuses her attention on some perceptually presented items over others. This perceptual attention can be highly focused, or it can be dispersed through a whole scene. But attention also comes in non-perceptual forms: your attention might be occupied by a pain or a feeling; or by a train of thought like planning for your friend's birthday. Finally, your attention might be occupied by an embodied action: consider playing soccer with all your attention, as opposed to kicking some balls while your mind is occupied with the birthday planning. How could there be a normative theory, one might ask, that treats perceptual focus, getting distracted by a feeling of nausea, and the attentive engagement in sports in anything like a unified manner? To make matters worse, some instances of attention are paradigmatic voluntary actions, like when I, just like that, shift my attention, with mental effort from the melody of a guitar solo to the rhythm played by the drums. Some other cases of attention, by contrast, seem passive and involuntary, like when my attention is drawn, against my will, to a beeping phone that disturbs my musical experience. Attention seems to be not one phenomenon at all; but many phenomena.

This commonsense attack on the unity of attention might be supported further by appeal to the science of attention. It has often been treated as a finding of the cognitive science of attention that it 'is not a unitary construct' (Carrasco, 2011, p.1517), best 'considered as a property of multiple, different perceptual and cognitive operations' (Chun et al., 2011, p.76), or 'a label' for several loosely related cognitive processes (Styles, 1997, p.1) (also e.g. Itti et al., 2005, Anderson, 2011, or Hommel et al., 2019). As Jonardon Ganeri (2017, p.25) puts it, one might argue that 'attention ... is not a single psychological kind'.

If attention were indeed disunified in this way, then, it may seem, it cannot be, after all, explanatorily or descriptively central. Consider that if attention were not a single psychological kind, then nothing should be lost by replacing the term or concept 'attention' with terms or concepts referring to the many more specific psychological kinds. But if a term or concept is dispensable in this way, then – one might argue – what it picks out cannot be explanatorily central.

Yet, it does not follow from the fact that there are many forms of attention that those forms have nothing interesting in common. One might, for example, think of them as determinates of a single determinable. Or as multiple realizations of attention. Or, relatedly, one might think of those forms as 'unified by analogy' (cf. McDaniel, 2010): just like a healthy organism, a healthy piece of broccoli, or a healthy circulatory system have something interesting in common, while also – of course – being interestingly different, so different forms of attention might still have the type of unity required for descriptive centrality. Ganeri (2017, p.12), for example, thinks of all of them as 'ongoing [forms of] structuring of experience and action'. Attention, unlike belief or memory, is an ongoing – process like – aspect of mentality, and unlike specific desires or specific perceptual experiences, attention is a structural aspect of mind and action.[3] So, even if attention were not a single psychological kind, several psychological kinds may still share enough similarities so that those kinds form a distinctive aspect of the mind that allows for a targeted normative analysis.

In my view, though, a more direct answer to the disunity worry is available (see also Wu, 2011, 2014, 2016) for a related, though distinct, response). According to the priority structure view I develop in Watzl (2017), all forms of attention consist in the agent's activity of regulating priority structures, which order the parts of the subject's on-going (occurrent) mental life by their relative priority to the subject. This priority structure view unifies the varieties of attention. Perceptual attention consists in prioritizing some parts of a perceptual state over other parts of that state. If the subject's attention is, for example, visually focused on an object, then the state of seeing that object is prioritized. Attention *to* external objects thus gets explained by the relative priority of aspects of the subject's mind. When attention is focused on a feature (like the color of the object or event) then the state of seeing those features is prioritized. The priority structure view allows for degrees of attention as we move up or down the subject's priority ordering. When attention is non-perceptual what is prioritized is a non-perceptual aspect of the subject's ongoing mental life. What is prioritized may be a bodily sensation or feeling, mental images, occurring ideas, and occurrent desires that are constitutive of an embodied action or train of thought. The priority structure view thus unifies all forms of attention by taking as the primary notion that of a mental state's relative priority for the subject. The forms differ only in which aspect of the subject's mind has the highest relative priority.

The priority structure view also unifies passive and active forms of attention, as well as attention and salience. Attention is a mental activity, a personal level on-going process. A person, on this view, is always engaged in that activity. We are constantly regulating our priority structures. Yet, while this is something we are doing, how we are doing what we are doing is subject to both an active and a passive force. The passive force is salience. The salience of a mental state consists in the degree to with that mental state commands prioritization (a type of imperatival content). Salience is a feature of subject-level states, but it is not under the subject's control (just like the content of a perceptual state is subject level but not controlled by the subject). The active force interacts with the passive force and shapes the subject's prioritizing to the degree to which she herself guides her own activity. Such guidance can take all forms that it can also take for bodily action. Attention is subject to deliberation, normative judgment, intention, desire and choice, and fine-grained online control.

The central notion in this framework, to repeat, is the notion of a priority structure, where the parts of the agent's mental life are compared by their relative priority or priority weight. The framework can be expanded in many ways depending on how one thinks of the relevant notion of priority. In my own view, relative priority does not have a reductive definition. We have a grip on the notion through its reflection in conscious experience: here relative priority shapes the field of consciousness into center and periphery. One way to take this is to think of our conscious acquaintance with how peripheral or central a part of our mind is as fixing the reference to an underlying type of relation between those parts of our mind.[4]

A detailed defense of the priority structure view of attention, of course, cannot be provided in this paper (see Watzl (2017) for details). One way to understand the argument of this paper is as conditional on a unified theory of attention, such as the priority structure view. *If* such a view is right, *then* the normative centrality of attention follows. Indeed, I believe that the priority structure view is especially well suited to show how attention is descriptively and explanatorily unified – and, as I will show below, it lends itself well to a structured development of the ethics of attention.

On the other hand, as I suggested above, we might not need a unified view like this in order to defend the descriptive centrality from the threat of disunity (unity by analogy might suffice). In this sense, the argument of this paper is not entirely hostage to objections to a unified theory of attention.

5.5 The wrong kind of object objection

Let me then move to premise (2) of the argument for the normative significance of attention: the descriptive-normative link. I've already mentioned the central motivation behind this premise: an explanatory central aspect of the mind, is – because of that – an important lever in the mind. We want to know how to adjust it properly. If the normative importance of an aspect of the mind would not at least roughly follow its descriptive or explanatory importance, then our normative theories threaten to be parochial: we focus our energies on evaluating an aspect of the mind or of behavior that makes little difference. Suppose you found that an aspect of your mind that is of only little descriptive significance is in normatively bad shape. You would likely respond 'who cares!? It doesn't explain much about me or about what I do'. By contrast, suppose that you became unsure about whether a very significant part of your mind is in normatively good shape: this, clearly would be much more disturbing.

Yet, these general considerations cannot be enough to establish the descriptive-normative link. Many aspects of our physiology, for example, arguably play important explanatory roles regarding our behavior, and, indeed, also with respect to how we feel. But that would not make your physiology an interesting target of normative assessment. If attention is to be an important target of normative analysis, then it must be the kind of thing that permits such an analysis. One might, thus, argue that despite its centrality in the mind attention is not the kind of 'thing' that is amenable to the relevant type of normative assessment. I will call this the wrong kind of object objection. In this section, I will answer two version of this objection.

First, one might argue that while attention is descriptively central, it is *not a phenomenon situated at the right level of description* to allow for normative assessment. Theoretical engagement with attention since the mid Twentieth century has been dominated by a complex, and multi-faceted discussion in cognitive psychology and the neurosciences. This leads naturally to thinking of attention in terms of a set of neuronal or psychological mechanisms. But once we do that, questions about good or bad forms of attention, questions of how attention figures in moral considerations, in the assessment of the character of a person, or its proper role in epistemic inquiry, may appear to be misguided: neuronal or psychological mechanisms may seem not to be the right kind of thing for which such normative questions can be properly posed. Indeed, one might, like Jennifer Hornsby, argue that normative questions about, for example, rationality, responsibility, or moral standing arise only with respect to personal level phenomena (e.g. Hornsby, 2000). Beliefs and transitions between beliefs, according to this view, are assessable for rationality precisely and only because they are personal level. Insofar as other aspects of the mind of a person, like her emotions (De Sousa, 1990) or her perceptual states (Siegel, 2016) also impact the person's normative standing, they, too, must be personal level states or activities.

One could argue against Hornsby that sometimes sub-personal states or activities can also be normatively assessed and impact a person's normative standing.[5] Yet, there is a more direct response: the fact that there exists a rich sub-personal science of attention does not imply that attention is a sub-personal phenomenon. Just consider that much is also known about sub-personal perceptual processes; and yet it is the person who perceives her surroundings (Burge, 2010); the sub-personal processes underpin and enable the subject's perceptual state. Similarly, a person's conscious experience, arguably the paradigm of a personal level phenomenon, is underpinned by sub-personal processes. We should treat attention, like perception and conscious experience, as a personal level phenomenon: attending is something the person does; attentional processes are what underpins the attending. According to the priority structure view, attention, indeed, is a *paradigmatic* personal level psychological phenomenon: priority structures connect all ongoing aspects of the subject's mind and provide them with personal level unity. In addition, attention is constitutively integrated with other personal-level phenomena such as perception, belief, desire, or conscious experience, that form the parts of priority structures. The priority structure framework sketched above thus provides a thoroughly personal level view of attention.

A second version of the wrong kind of object objection might appeal to the claim that at least some forms of attention are not under voluntary control. What is salient to you in a specific situation, and hence what captures your attention, evidently is not something you control. In other cases, a subject may have no awareness of, for example, a subtle shift of attention that occurred to her. Insofar as norms are supposed to provide guidance to the subject, talk of norms for a completely involuntary aspect of the mind, or ones the subject is unaware of may appear to be misguided.

This version of the objection at best targets some types of attention norms. Norms of fittingness for emotions, for example, would apply to the emotions whether or not we control emotions or whether or not we are aware of having those emotions. Similarly, norms of fittingness would apply even to involuntary salience or to shifts of attention we are unaware of. In the literature on the ethics of belief, indeed, some people try to explain our *inability* to control belief by appeal to a constitutive truth norm for belief (Shah, 2003). Even when it comes to *responsibility*, it is highly controversial that we are responsible only for what is under our voluntary control (e.g. Smith, 2005). On the priority structure view, even involuntary forms shifts of attention are always changes to an agent's activity: they are ripples in a sea of agency. This arguably makes attention even more amenable to a normative analysis. Be that as it may, though: how the agential and involuntary aspects of attention interact with the normative assessment of attention is a debate that should, like in the ethics of belief, occur within the ethics of attention. It is not an obstacle to the normative significance of attention.

5.6 Content-based and manner-based attention norms

I hope to have convinced that attention in principle can be assessed normatively. Yet one might still believe that no *systematic* normative investigation can be given. One might argue that we need, at least, a proof of concept, to show that and ethics off attention that resembles the field of the ethics of belief is even possible.

The rest of this paper will – in three sections – respond to this worry, by showing how such a systematic investigation may be provided. I will do so by sketching a framework for such an investigation. We can start with the priority structure view. It gives us a clear target for the normative assessment of attention. Norms of attention are norms for the regulation of priority structures. The proposed framework then classifies potential norms of attention along three dimensions: whether they are manner or object-based, instrumental or non-instrumental, and whether its source is moral, prudential or epistemic. I will use this framework to locate proposals for specific normative pressures on attention in the literature, and in order to situate the normative discussion of attention within the wider field of normative philosophy.

The first dimension, then, is between what I will call *content-based* and *manner-based* attention norms.

We can think of the priority structures I have introduced in two tiers. On tier 1, the elements of the structure are mental states that occupy the subject's attention to various degrees, and the relation between them is their relative priority to the subject (we can allow for ties in relative priority). If I'm paying more attention to the drums than to the instrumental solo, then my hearing the drums has strict priority in my mind compared to hearing the solo. Or if I'm so excited about a possibility that I keep thinking about it and notice little of my surroundings, then my excitement and thoughts about the possibility are prioritized over my experience of the world around me. On tier 2, the elements of the structure, by contrast, are external items and the structure orders them by how much the person attends to them. The ordering in tier 1 determines an ordering in tier 2. Tier 2 characterizes the world as it is according to the attention occupiers. We can think of the structure elements at tier 2 as the intentional objects of the structure elements at tier 1. If there are non-intentional, non-directed aspects of the mind (for example, a feeling of nausea or a headache that occupies your attention), then there is more to tier 1 than can be captured in tier 2. Also, if a part of the world is, as it were, attended 'twice over' like when you both look at rustling leaves and listen to them, then we can capture details in the subject's attention on tier 1 that will be lost if we only consider tier 2.

Note that tier 2 structures in the first place provide an ordering of attended items, but probably do not define an interval scale (we can't define: x receives twice as much attention as y). But, if the structures are 'big enough' we can define rough degrees by the number of actual and potential intermediate elements (cf Watzl, 2017, p.82). Sometimes a normative evaluation may want to say that a person ought to attend much more to one thing rather than another, and not merely pay a little more attention to that thing.

Note also that each priority structure already contains information about what is and what is not included in the subject's current mental life. For the moment neglect the structuring relation, and just think of a tier 1 structure as a set of mental states. We can think of that set as a partitioning of the space of *potential* mental states, into those that the subject actually has and those that she does not have (just like the set of all of a subject's beliefs, i.e. every proposition she believes, partitions the space of possible beliefs into those the subject has and those she doesn't have, i.e. propositions believed and those not believed). Two priority structures can differ simply in that one contains an element that the other does not contain. So, by being given a certain priority structure, we already know what is excluded from it. If you 'overthink' a situation, tier 2 attention norms can express the idea that that thought should not have entered your mind. You should not have attended to that situation at all.

With these two tiers in place, we can now define content-based attention norms as those norms that are exclusively formulated at tier 2. Manner-based attention norms, by contrast, are those that pertain directly to how the person's mind is organized at tier 1.

Content-based norms, then, are what is described when we say that a person should pay more attention to X than to Y, that she should not completely ignore the Fs, that it would be appropriate if people paid more attention to X, or that a virtuous person is one who pays enough attention to certain features of the world.

Content-based norms will ignore in what *way* a person pays attention to something, and instead are concerned with a coarser level of detail: a person should – in some way or other – pay attention to certain features.

As an example where such coarse-graining appears appropriate, consider a hiring process (see Banaji and Greenwald, 2013; see also Siegel, 2016 for discussion). Suppose that person evaluating various résumés harbors an unconscious prejudice against members of a certain group (the out-group). As a result and as a reflection of that prejudice, the evaluator pays little attention to the strong parts of the résumé of outgroup members, while she pays much more attention to weaker parts of their CVs. By contrast, when she considers the résumé of an in-group member, she pays a lot of attention to the strong parts and comparatively little attention to the weak parts. We may want to say that this distribution of attention is normatively criticizable (below I will discuss ways of thinking of the normative source of that critique). Arguably, though, it is normatively irrelevant *how* she re-distributes her attention. She may make sure to perceptually focus her attention equally on all relevant parts of the CVs, she may make sure to give enough thought to all parts after she has looked at them, or she may counteract her bias by directing her attention in her imagination to the qualities that a person with that CV is likely to have.[6]

As a second example, consider gratitude (see Bommarito (2013), and Chappell and Yetter-Chappell (2016)). Someone who possesses the virtue of gratitude (who is a grateful person) must pay a sufficient amount of attention to the value of what others have done for her. Someone who merely knows that others have done something valuable, or is peripherally aware of that value, but pays no attention to that value is not grateful. '[A]ttention is essential to the virtue. We cannot be grateful by simply being aware that someone has helped us', as Bommarito (2013, p.100) puts it. It is thus plausible that good character is characterized by paying enough attention to the value of what others do for us. But arguably it, again, doesn't matter how we pay attention to it: whether we perceptually take it in, when it is happening, by thinking attentively about it, or by often imagining how valuable those deeds were.

Yet, the example of gratitude also illustrates the limits of content-based approaches to attention norms. Suppose that, as Bommarito observes, that a 'teenager under the influence of Nietzsche might attend to the support of his or her parents but take it to be evidence of how disgustingly weak Mom and Dad are'. (ibid.). Such a teenager is attending to the support of his parents, but does not display the virtue of gratitude. So, not all ways of attending to the help of others are a sign of gratitude. There are two ways of taking this observation. On the one hand, we may leave the relevant norm of attention at the content level and provide a fuller characterization of gratitude by supplementing having the right attention structure with, for example, having the right emotions directed at the supporting person. On the other hand, we may take Bommarito's observation as showing that the content-based assessment of attention, in this case, is insufficient. If the subject attends to the value of another's help by prioritizing negative emotions directed at those values, then that distribution of attention makes no contribution to her gratitude. Whether we go one way or the other here plausibly depends on whether we think that a positive contribution of attention can be separated out even if the subject's emotions are misguided: is the person at least partially grateful if she attends to the value of others, even if that attention is accompanied by spite? If yes, then we have a content-based attention norm as a partial component of gratitude. If no, then we are here really dealing with a manner-based attention norm.

Let us then get to manner-based attention norms. Here, as I said, we are concerned not with what the subject pays attention to, but with tier 1 that concerns the organization of the subject's mental life. We thus look in more detail at the *way* a subject pays attention to something.

We have already seen one example of how to distinguish such ways: which mental states are prioritized over others. Suppose, for example, we would like to say, as Iris Murdoch (1970) does, that morality requires that a person should pay attention to the concrete other subjects she is engaged with (a 'just and loving gaze directed on an individual reality', p.33). Staring, perceptually, at others plausibly is not a way of fulfilling that normative requirement: rather what should occupy our attention is reflective thought about others as loci of intrinsic value and worth (though, again, the manner based treatment could be debated: if we can see the intrinsic value and worth, then maybe the prioritization of such seeing *is* a way of encountering the other appropriately; see e.g. Werner (2014) for discussion of whether moral properties are perceptible). As another example, consider the positive evaluation of attentive touch, especially the 'close form of caring touch that forms an essential element of social bonding and human development' (Fulkerson, 2016). There clearly is a good that pertains to the tactile attentive engagement with close others (family, friends, children, and loved ones). Mere inattentive touch does not seem to have the same value; and equally importantly it is attentive *touch* that is valuable, mere attentive thought or seeing does not have the same value (though it may have other values).

Another way of distinguishing ways of attention is by considering *how* a subject's priority structures are regulated. Here we can distinguish, as I mentioned, a passive force on the evolution of those structures in terms of what is salient to the subject and an active force, when a subject guides her attention, for example, with direct and effortful control.

One can argue both that a special value attaches to forms of passively evolving attention structures and to the active control over attention. For the first, consider another example from Bommarito and Chappell and Yetter-Chappell (2016): the role of attention in modesty. Chappell and Yetter-Chappell (2016) argue, correctly I believe, that a modest agent is 'one who is not disposed to find their own positive attributes especially salient' (p.457). She hardly ever finds herself pulled to give attention to those positive attributes. She may have an accurate view of her positive traits but doesn't find them particularly salient. Maybe, indeed, in line with Yetter Chappell and Yetter-Chappell's observations, a modest person actually does spend much of her time attending to her positive attributes: maybe she is paid to look into them and intentionally and effortfully gives them her attention. But such attention requires effort for her. It's painful. For the modest person, attending to her own positive attributes is not automatic (while the immodest person feels the pull to attend to those attributes). Other plausible examples of salience constituted virtues discussed by Chappell and Yetter-Chappell are: being a good friend might be constituted by finding the friend's positive attitudes more salient than her negative attitudes, someone who is able to 'forgive and forget' finds past wrongs not particularly salient (she need not actually have forgotten about them; she is just not drawn to attend to them). These examples illustrate the positive value that may attach to salience, manners of attention that without control evolve in the right direction.

On the opposite side, consider that we may also positively evaluate being in control of our attention. Immanuel Kant (1775-76, p.62) expresses an extreme version of such an evaluation when he says that '[t]he greatest perfection of the powers of the mind is based on our subordinating them to our power of choice ... For this sake, attention ... [is] only the useful for us, if [it is] under the free power of choice, so that involuntary attentiveness ... produce[s] much harm'. While we might not want to follow Kant that attention is 'only useful' if it is 'under the free power of choice', we may still believe that having enough control over our own attention and being able to guide it according to our own values is an important and valuable aspect of self-control and personal integrity.

It is not my goal here to evaluate such proposals, but only to use them as illustrations of norms of attention that pertain to the manner of attention, and not what it is that we attend to.

5.7 Instrumental and non-instrumental attention norms

I now get to a second dimension of the framework: we can distinguish different types of attention norms. We can, on the one hand, evaluate an agent's priority structures and how she regulates them *instrumentally*, i.e. with regard to an end that is achieved through that form of attention, or we can evaluate attention *non-instrumentally*, i.e. evaluate a form of attention on its own without regard to its upshots. A specific form of a non-instrumental attention norm would be constitutive norms of attention. Some people, as I mentioned above, argue that there are constitutive norms of belief or of specific emotions.[7] One important debate in this area then will concern whether there are any non-instrumental or even constitutive attention norms. If so, what are they? If not, why not?

With Immanuel Kant's negative evaluation of 'involuntary attentiveness' we have already seen a clear case of an instrumental attention norm: Kant seems to think that such involuntariness is problematic because it 'produce[s] much harm'. What is normatively problematic thus concerns the consequences of such a manner of attending. For a similarly instrumental, though less one-sided, evaluation of the relative costs and benefits of controlled and uncontrolled forms of attention, consider Chandra Sripada's (2018) discussion of the costs and benefits of mind-wandering (i.e. when our cognitive, non-perceptual attention hops uncontrolled from one thought to the other). Such mind-wandering sometimes may have negative consequences: it prevents you from achieving routine daily goals and may make you feel bad about yourself (Killingsworth and Gilbert, 2010). On the other hand, arguably there are also good consequences: it may distract from boredom, and might lead to escape routines, and lead to insight and deep learning (what Sripada calls the advantages of 'exploration').

Consider also one way of looking at the hiring case I have discussed. One thing that is problematic about the unequal distribution of attention to the good and not so good aspects of the CVs of in-group and out-group members is that as a consequence, a so prejudiced evaluator will tend to not hire the best person for the job. She will miss out on candidates she would have wanted to hire (Banaji and Greenwald, 2013). Her distribution of attention thus is problematic because it is an ill-calibrated instrument for the purpose to which it is put.

Not all instrumental attention norms will have to do with prudence alone: with what best satisfies the desires of the agent. Consider mindfulness meditation. Such meditation is constitutively characterized by certain attention structures: the Oxford English Dictionary, for example, describes meditation generally as ways of 'focus[ing] one's mind for a period of time'[8] in specifically prescribed ways. Mindfulness specifically has been characterized by the idea that the agent intentionally makes higher-order thoughts about her first order experiences a center of her experience (cf. Latham, 2016).

Mindfulness meditation, by its practitioners and advocates, is often described as a good thing. They advocate an ethics of attention. What, though, is supposed to be good about it? It might serve as an epistemic tool, maybe delivering better insight into the true nature of the soul (though see Ratnayake and Merry, 2018 for a critique), and – of course – it is widely promoted as a practical tool, helping to reduce anything from stress, anxiety, to substance abuse and chronic pain, and promoting increased quality of life and increased prosocial attitudes (whether it succeeds in those regards is another matter. See Goyal et al., 2014 for a recent meta-study suggesting skepticism). Many practitioners and many traditions in which mindfulness meditation is important, though, reject the instrumental approach (cf Purser, 2019 for a critique of such uses of mindfulness). They might advocate mindfulness and meditation practices as a good way of life. Mindfulness training ought, they would say, not just help an agent realize goals she antecedently possesses. The instrumental approach, according to this attitude, does not do justice to the transformative effects of mindfulness and meditations practices. They, so the proposal, help the agent to become a better, more virtuous person: they help the agent, for example, to be more compassionate. Through the relevant training at focusing her mind on her own feelings, experiences, and emotions generally, the agent will be in a position to notice anger toward others before it 'takes a hold of her'. It thus helps her realize moral concern and compassion. Such an evaluation of attention would still fall under the instrumental approach: priority structures get evaluated only instrumentally, by how well they serve to realize an independently given good or virtuous trait.

Finally, one might also regard attention as an instrument of inquiry. Suppose that you are trying to find an answer to some question, say how many windows there are on a large skyscraper (cf. Friedman, 2020). If you are trying to find the answer to that question, you must keep your attention focused in the right way. If instead, you started focusing attention, on say, the structure of the pavement, or on the clothes of the people on the sidewalk, your inquiry will likely fail. Attention norms thus might be derived from norms of inquiry, where attention serves as an important zetetic instrument (cf. Friedman, 2020 for a detailed discussion of the shape and importance of norms of inquiry).[9]

Are all norms of attention instrumental norms, i.e. norms that evaluate attention according to its consequences? Arguably this is not so.

An instrumental approach treats the relationship between the attention structures and the relevant good (e.g. compassion) as akin to a means-end relation. But arguably the relationship between the attention structures and certain virtues is closer than that: the virtue is *constituted* in part by certain attention structures. What it is for an agent to have that type of virtue is for her to have certain attention structures – both synchronically as well as diachronically. If an attention structure is constitutive of a virtuous character trait, then it can not only be evaluated instrumentally. It is part of what it is to be an agent with that virtue to have specific attention structures. We have already seen some plausible examples of this type: gratitude and modesty may both be constituted by certain forms of attention (on either tier 1 or tier 2).

Attention thus can be evaluated non-instrumentally if it is a constitutive aspect of a feature or state that can itself be evaluated non-instrumentally. What, aside from virtues like gratitude, may be examples of such features or states? One interesting area of investigation concerns the question of whether some attention structures are constitutive of *epistemically* evaluable states. Among these would be positively evaluated states such as knowledge, justified belief, or understanding, but also negatively evaluated states like prejudice.

For a potential example, consider that (at least) sometimes whether an agent knows something may constitutively depend on whether she has attended in the right way. Consider a doctor aiming to discover whether her patient has cancer. She looks through the patient's files and has only a quick glance at an X-ray (but doesn't pay much attention to it). From the evidence she has considered, it is reasonable to conclude that the patient is healthy. But had she paid more attention to the X-ray, she would have noticed a black spot. While the patient is in fact healthy, let us suppose, had the doctor considered the spot this would have undermined her justification to believe that the patient is healthy. One might argue (see Pollock, 1986; Goldberg, 2017) that the doctor in such as case does not know that the patient is healthy *because she had the wrong tier 2 attention structures*. One might take such cases to show that knowledge of certain facts requires that the agent inquires into the matter properly and responsibly. But in order to inquire into the matter properly and responsibly she must pay attention to the right things (cf. Fairweather and Montemayor, 2017). But now we seem to have a non-instrumentally evaluable attention structure: whether or not the agent cares about knowing anything in this domain, there is a type of epistemic evaluation of the attention structure available.

There is an interesting question of whether some relation less demanding than constitution might also lead to non-instrumentally evaluable attention structures. Return to the hiring example for illustration. One form of evaluation, as we have seen, is instrumental: the evaluator should pay equal attention to the good parts of all CVs because only then will she be able to hire the most qualified person. But arguably there is also another form of evaluation: the prejudiced outlook is irrational (see Siegel, 2016 for further discussion). With no evidence (or indeed against available evidence) the evaluator takes outgroup members to be generally less qualified. Siegel (2016) argues that a tendency to have certain priority structures is itself irrational when it is in a specific sense she defines *based on* having such an irrational outlook: if we would like to say that the irrational outlook is non-instrumentally problematic, then the priority structure that is based on it will itself be non-instrumentally evaluable.

As I mentioned, whether there are any non-instrumental attention norms will be a matter of substantial debate. For now, I hope to have sketched the distinction between instrumental and non-instrumental attention norms enough for such a debate to get started.

5.8 The normative source of attention norms

I now get to a final distinction among different attention norms. This distinction concerns the normative source of the relevant norms.

A first source is prudential considerations. Having certain priority structures, and certain ways of regulating those structures over time can be evaluated according to how good those structures are for the agent who has them. Many instrumental attention norms have such a prudential source. Consider, for example, as we have discussed the costs and benefits of mind-wandering. Mind-wandering may get in the way of an agent's pursuit of long-term goals, and in that sense, it is bad for the agent. But it may also be beneficial if it enables deep learning and serves as a source for welcome distraction.

Prudential considerations generally pertain to the wellbeing of the agent: to what is good for her (see Crisp, 2017). Well-being here may be thought of in terms of desire satisfaction: how well does a priority structure help the agent to satisfy her desires? But well-being can also be thought of in terms of the overall balance of pleasure and pain, or in terms of what is objectively good for the agent (one might, for example, hold that friendship or knowledge and understanding is good for the agent independently of whether it is associated with pleasure or pain or whether the agent has the relevant desires). An interesting question in this area concerns whether some forms of attention may themselves be in this way objectively good for the agent: maybe it is, for example, good for the agent to have enough control over her attention. Or consider when Marcus Aurelius says that 'those who do not observe the movements of their own minds must of necessity be unhappy' (Aurelius, Meditations, 2nd book). Arguably, Aurelius here thinks that reflective attention to one's own mind is objectively good for a person, and not just a means for satisfying her desires or because it will improve the overall balance of pleasure and pain.

A second source of attention norms is moral considerations. We have seen such a source at play when we considered the idea that the attention structures characteristic of meditation and mindfulness may serve as an instrument toward instilling the moral virtue of compassion in an agent. And we have also seen examples of moral virtues, like gratitude or modesty, that may be partially constituted by certain forms of attention. In these cases, the fundamental object of moral evaluation is a certain character trait, and attention gets morally evaluated either instrumentally or because it partly constitutes a morally virtuous character trait.

There is another virtue-theoretically inspired view that does not, though, take this indirect route toward the moral evaluation of attention structures. On this view, the morally virtuous person is constituted by certain attention structures not because those are constitutive of specific character traits. Rather, some patterns of attention and salience just are themselves morally virtuous. Good character requires having the right motivational susceptibilities. We find that aspect of virtue and of morality emphasized in thinkers from Aristotle, Iris Murdoch, John Mcdowell, Lawrence Blum, up to recent work by Seanna Shiffrin.

Which structures then ought the morally virtuous person to have? Arguably, there are several aspects. Arguably, it ought to be salient to her that a situation that has a moral or ethical dimension does have that dimension. For a virtuous person, for example, it will be salient that moral concerns about how we ought to live together are a relevant aspect of her working environment.

Further, the morally virtuous person ought to notice moral wrongs as moral wrongs (they ought to be high enough on her salience ordering). She pays attention to the situation of each individual without needing to consult a moral rule book. Consider a case mentioned by Lawrence Blum (1991). He talks about a situation where two people, John and Joan, are on the subway together. There is another woman who is carrying a heavy shopping bag. John and Joan are both aware of that woman. But the fact that she is uncomfortable is salient to Joan while it isn't particularly salient to John. Blum thinks that the difference between what is salient to John and what is salient to Joan is of moral significance. While Joan's attention is captured by the fact that a morally relevant value is at stake, John is not 'attuned to' that morally significant fact. Blum thinks that the moral difference between John and Joan is not fully captured in how the difference in what is salient is going to make them act. If John is generally like that then this shows a 'defect in his character ... [h]e misses something of the moral reality confronting him'.

Finally, Seanna Shiffrin (2016) argues that there are moral requirements of non-negligence. Those requirements include patterns of attention: 'to be non-negligent is to be both attentive and responsive in thought and agency to how the pursuit of one's (permissible) aims and the state of one's agency affect one's ability to satisfy one's other duties and responsibilities'. On Shiffrin's view, it is an agent's moral responsibility to pay enough attention to the potential side effects of her doing.

A third source of attention norms is epistemic considerations. We have encountered this source when we have considered whether certain priority structures are epistemically evaluable because they are constitutive either of certain forms of irrationality or of positive epistemic states such as knowledge or understanding.

Just like for the case of morality, there is also an interesting question of whether it may be a constitutive feature of an epistemically well-calibrated agent. Maybe, it is part of being epistemically well-constituted that one pays attention to the right things?

Consider the idea that science is not just concerned with knowledge, but with knowledge on matters of interest (Anderson, 1995; Kitcher, 2003). An ideal epistemic agent doesn't just know random facts, but she knows and pays enough attention to *important* facts, facts that objectively merit our attention. This idea is deeply ingrained in how we often think of cultural authority: it purports to identify things that are worth paying attention to – ideas worth considering, books worth reading, creations worth beholding, problems worth solving, histories worth trying to reconstruct – even independent of antecedent social purpose. These things produce pro tanto rational pressure to pay attention to them, regardless of whether or not you have antecedent interest in them, knowledge about them, or desire to pay attention to what someone else says you should pay attention to. The seriousness with which we often debate what exactly belongs in the canon, what it is that 'we all' epistemically speaking ought to pay some attention to here shows that it would be mistaken to simply and quickly attempt to push the relevant epistemic pressures on attention into prudential or moral considerations: it is, at last, a matter of serious debate whether the epistemic value of paying attention to important facts about the world and our place in it can sometimes outweigh moral or prudential considerations regarding what may lead us to improve our lot. Another interesting question here concerns which types of norms are the most fundamental norms. One might, for example, argue that epistemic norms can (or should) be derived from norms of inquiry (Friedman, 2020). Arguably, many attention norms can also be derived from norms of inquiry. If that were so, then epistemic norms and attention norms may be equally non-fundamental.

I will conclude this section, by noting that the three sources of attention norms (prudential, moral, and epistemic sources) need not be exhaustive. They help to structure the debate at the current state of the discussion. Yet if, for example, there were primitive and constitutive attention norms about the conditions under which attention is fitting or apt, then those primitive attention norms would be derivable from any other source. They would instead be constitutive of the nature of attention itself. Whether there are any such constitutive fittingness norms for attention will be one of the central topics a future ethics of attention will need to investigate.[10]

5.9 Conclusion

In this paper, I have argued for the normative significance of attention and attempted to improve our grip on the normative landscape with regard to attention. I have argued that given its descriptive centrality for mind and behavior, attention should be central also in normative philosophy. The public wants answers and guidance with regard to normative questions about attention. Philosophy should develop an ethics of attention that helps to provide guidance and that is commensurate in its richness to the descriptive significance of attention. In the second half of the paper, I have then sketched a framework that may help us to get started at developing the ethics of attention.

Notes

1 This paper has developed out of a presentation initially started with Susanna Siegel. Together we have developed our thinking about attention norms. This material was jointly presented at a workshop on norms of inquiry at NYU. I have also presented it at Umeå University, Stockholm University, and the Rutgers-Columbia Philosophy of Mind Workshop. A presentation resembling more closely the present paper was then presented at a Workshop on Cross-cultural Perspectives on 'Virtues of Attention' at NYU Abu Dabi, at the Colloquium of the Institute of Philosophy in Tübingen, and as a keynote address at a graduate conference on Philosophy of Mind, Language, and Cognition at the University of Western Ontario. The paper received its last changes after a presentation to the Oslo Mind Group. Some material was added from applications for an ERC grant and a grant from the Norwegian Research Council. I would like to thank everyone at those occasions for their feedback, and also everyone who provided feedback on the written material. I would like to single out Susanna Siegel for many inspiring and stimulating discussions and excellent feedback. This result is part of a project that has received funding from the European Research Council (ERC) under the European Union's Horizon 2020 research and innovation programme (Grant agreement no. 101003208).
2 See: https://www.ted.com/talks/titus_kaphar_can_art_amend_history?language=en
3 See Watzl, 2017 for some of the points of this paragraph.
4 The view allows that once reference is fixed the relevant relation may also hold between unconscious mental states.
5 Thanks to Anna Drożdżowicz for helping me to see this clearer.
6 Note that I don't take it as obvious that the critique of the biased assessor of CVs must be situated fully at tier 2. There are probably some ways of attending to the good portions of the ingroup CV that are not an expression of a bias in favor of that group: they might strike a subject as repellent and disgusting and be salient and attract her

attention in that way. A person whose attention is distributed in such a way would arguably *not* be normatively criticizable for paying too much attention to the good portions of those CVs (thanks to Max Kippersund for this point). This example illustrates that there are, in a sense, gradations between tier 1 and tier 2 norms: some norms cover a broad variety of ways of attending, while others cover only a very narrow band.

7 E.g. that a belief is correct only if it is true; cf. Shah, 2003; or that 'anger that p is apt only if p constitutes a genuine moral violation' (Srinivasan, 2018). Thanks to Anders Nes for drawing my attention to those examples.

8 OED.

9 Thanks to Andrew Lee and Jane Friedman for the connection to norms of inquiry.

10 Thanks for comments by Andrew Lee and Anders Nes that helped me in writing this paragraph.

References

Anderson, B. 2011. There Is No Such Thing as Attention. *Frontiers in Psychology* 2(246): 1–8.

Anderson, E. 1995. Knowledge, Human Interests, and Objectivity in Feminist Epistemology. *Philosophical Topics* 23(2): 27–58.

Banaji, M. R. and Greenwald, A. G. 2013. *Blind Spot: Hidden Biases of Good People.* Delacorte Press, New York.

Berkman, E. T., Hutcherson, C. A., Livingston, J. L., Kahn, L. E. and Inzlicht, M. 2017. Self-Control as Value-Based Choice. *Current Directions in Psychological Science* 26: 422–428.

Block, N. 2010. Attention and Mental Paint. *Philosophical Issues* 20(1): 23–63.

Blum, L. 1991. Moral Perception and Particularity. *Ethics* 101(4): 701–725.

Bommarito, N. 2013. Modesty as a Virtue of Attention. *Philosophical Review* 122(1): 93–117.

Brady, M. S. 2013. *Emotional Insight: The Epistemic Role of Emotional Experience.* Oxford University Press, Oxford.

Bregman, P. 2011. *18 Minutes: Find Your Focus, Master Distraction and Get the Right Things Done.* Hachette UK, London.

Burge, T. 2010. *Origins of Objectivity.* Oxford University Press, Oxford.

Cappelen, H., Plunkett, D. and Burgess, A. (Eds.). 2019. *Conceptual Engineering and Conceptual Ethics.* Oxford University Press, Oxford.

Carrasco, M. 2011. Visual Attention: The Past 25 Years. *Vision Research* 51(13): 1484–1525.

Chalmers, D. J. 2003. The Content and Epistemology of Phenomenal Belief. In Q. Smith and A. Jokic (Eds.), *Consciousness: New Philosophical Perspectives* (pp. 220–272). Oxford University Press, Oxford.

Chappell, R. Y. and Yetter-Chappell, H. 2016. Virtue and Salience. *Australasian Journal of Philosophy* 94(3): 449–463.

Chignell, A. 2018. The Ethics of Belief. In Edward N. Zalta (Ed.), *The Stanford Encyclopedia of Philosophy* (Spring 2018 Edition). https://plato.stanford.edu/archives/spr2018/entries/ethics-belief/.

Chun, M. M. and Turk-Browne, N. B. 2007. Interactions Between Attention and Memory. *Current Opinion in Neurobiology* 17(2): 177–184.

Chun, M. M., Golomb, J. D. and Turk-Browne, N. B. 2011. A Taxonomy of External and Internal Attention. *Annual Review of Psychology* 62: 73–101.

Clifford, W. K. 1877 [1999]. The Ethics of Belief. In T. Madigan (Ed.), *The Ethics of Belief and Other Essays* (pp. 70–96). Prometheus, Amherst, MA.

Crisp, R. 2017. Well-Being. In Edward N. Zalta (Ed.), *The Stanford Encyclopedia of Philosophy* (Fall 2017 Edition). <https://plato.stanford.edu/archives/fall2017/entries/well-being/>.

De Sousa, R. 1990. *The Rationality of Emotion*. MIT Press, Cambridge.

Doris, J. M. 1998. Persons, Situations, and Virtue Ethics. *Nous* 32(4): 504–530.

Fairweather, A. and Montemayor, C. 2017. *Knowledge, Dexterity, and Attention: A Theory of Epistemic Agency*. Cambridge University Press, Cambridge.

Friedman, J. 2020. The Epistemic and the Zetetic. *Philosophical Review* 129(4): 501–536.

Fulkerson, M. 2016. Touch. In Edward N. Zalta (Ed.), *The Stanford Encyclopedia of Philosophy* (Spring 2016 Edition). <https://plato.stanford.edu/archives/spr2016/entries/touch/>.

Ganeri, J. 2017. *Attention, Not Self*. Oxford University Press, Oxford.

Glüer, K. and Wikforss, Å. 2013. Against Belief Normativity. In. T. Chan (Ed.), *The Aim of Belief* (pp. 80–99). Oxford University Press, Oxford.

Goldberg, S. C. 2017. Should Have Known. *Synthese* 194(8): 2863–2894.

Goldman, A. I. 2006. *Simulating Minds: The Philosophy, Psychology, and Neuroscience of Mindreading*. Oxford University Press, Oxford.

Goyal, M., et al. 2014. Meditation Programs for Psychological Stress and Well-Being: A Systematic Review and Meta-analysis. *JAMA Internal Medicine* 174(3): 357–368.

Hornsby, J. 2000. Personal and Sub-personal: A Defence of Dennett's Early Distinction. *Philosophical Explorations* 3(1): 6–24.

Hommel, B., Chapman, C. S., Cisek, P., Neyedli, H. F., Song, J. H. and Welsh, T. N. 2019. No One Knows What Attention Is. *Attention, Perception, & Psychophysics* 81(7): 2288–2303.

Itti, L., Rees, G. and Tsotsos, J. K. 2005. *Neurobiology of Attention*. Academic Press, Burlington, MA.

James, W. 1896 [1956]. *The Will to Believe and Other Essays in Popular Philosophy* (pp. 1–31). Dover Publications, New York.

Jennings, C. D. 2020. *The Attending Mind*. Cambridge University Press, Cambridge.

Kabat-Zinn, J. 2009. *Wherever You Go, There You Are: Mindfulness Meditation in Everyday Life*. Hachette Books, London.

Kant, I. 1775–76 [2013]. Anthropology Friedländer (1775–1776). Translated by G. Felicitas Munzel, In: *Lectures on Anthropology* (pp. 37–256). Cambridge University Press, Cambridge.

Killingsworth, M. A. and Gilbert, D. T. 2010. A Wandering Mind Is an Unhappy Mind. *Science* 330(6006): 932–932.

Kitcher, P. 2003. *Science, Truth, and Democracy*. Oxford University Press, Oxford.

Latham, N. 2016. Meditation and Self-control. *Philosophical Studies* 173(7): 1779–1798.

Lyons, J. 2017. Epistemological Problems of Perception. In Edward N. Zalta (Ed.), *The Stanford Encyclopedia of Philosophy* (Spring 2017 Edition). https://plato.stanford.edu/archives/spr2017/entries/perception-episprob/

McDaniel, K. 2010. A Return to the Analogy of Being. *Philosophy and Phenomenological Research* 81(3): 688–717.

Murdoch, I. 1970 [2013]. *The Sovereignty of Good*. Routledge, London.

Newport, C. 2016. *Deep Work: Rules for Focused Success in a Distracted World*. Hachette UK, London.

Orquin, J. L. and Loose, S. M. 2013. Attention and Choice: A Review on Eye Movements in Decision Making. *Acta Psychologica* 144(1): 190–206.

Pollock, J. 1986. *Contemporary Theories of Knowledge*. Rowman and Littlefield, Maryland.

Purser, R. 2019. *McMindfulness: How Mindfulness Became the New Capitalist Spirituality*. Repeater Books, London.

Ratnayake, S. and Merry, D. 2018. Forgetting Ourselves: Epistemic Costs and Ethical Concerns in Mindfulness Exercises. *Journal of Medical Ethics* 44(8): 567–574.

Rinard, S. 2017. No Exception for Belief. *Philosophy and Phenomenological Research* 94(1): 121–143.

Shah, N. 2003. How Truth Governs Belief. *The Philosophical Review* 112(4): 447–482.

Shiffrin, S. 2016. The Moral Neglect of Negligence (April 18, 2016). In David Sobel, P. Vallentyne and S. Wall (Eds.), *Oxford Studies in Political Philosophy*. Oxford University Press, Oxford.

Siegel, S. 2016. *The Rationality of Perception*. Oxford University Press, Oxford.

Simons, D. J. and Chabris, C. F. 1999. Gorillas in Our Midst: Sustained Inattentional Blindness for Dynamic Events. *Perception* 28(9): 1059–1074.

Smith, A. M. 2005. Responsibility for Attitudes: Activity and Passivity in Mental Life. *Ethics* 115(2): 236–271.

Srinivasan, A. 2018. The Aptness of Anger. *Journal of Political Philosophy* 26(2): 123–144.

Sripada, C. 2018. An Exploration/Exploitation Tradeoff Between Mind Wandering and Goal-Directed Thinking. In K. Christoff and K. Fox (Eds.), To appear in *Oxford Handbook on Spontaneous Thought: Mind-Wandering, Creativity, and Dreaming* (pp. 23–34). Oxford University Press, Oxford.

Styles, E. A. 1997. *The Psychology of Attention*. Psychology Press, Oxford.

Tenenbaum, S. (Ed.). 2010. *Desire, Practical Reason, and the Good*. Oxford University Press, New York.

Watzl, S. 2017. *Structuring Mind. The Nature of Attention and How It Shapes Consciousness*. Oxford University Press, Oxford.

Watzl, S. (forthcoming). Self-control Is Not Special. In M. Brent (Ed.), *Mental Action and the Conscious Mind*. Routledge, New York.

Werner, P. 2014. Moral Perception and the Contents of Experience. *Journal of Moral Philosophy* 13(3): 1–24.

Williams, J. 2018. *Stand Out of Our Light: Freedom and Resistance in the Attention Economy*. Cambridge University Press, Cambridge.

Williams, M. and Penman, D. 2011. *Mindfulness: A Practical Guide to Finding Peace in a Frantic World*. Hachette UK, London.

Wu, T. 2017. *The Attention Merchants: The Epic Scramble to Get Inside Our Heads*. Vintage, New York.

Wu, W. 2011. Confronting Many-Many Problems: Attention and Agentive Control. *Noûs* 45(1): 50–76.

Wu, W. 2014. *Attention: New Problems of Philosophy Series*. Routledge, London.

Wu, W. 2016. Experts and Deviants: The Story of Agentive Control. *Philosophy and Phenomenological Research* 93(1): 101–126.

6 Salience and what matters

Sophie Archer

6.1 Introduction

Imagine you are at a political rally, listening to an impassioned speech by a politician whose political outlook you are in general sympathy with. In fact, you are in vehement agreement with their stance on the particular issue at hand. Their central argument in the speech contains a glaring non sequitur but you fail to notice. So concerned are you with the truth, as you see it, of their conclusion that the obviously fallacious nature of their argument does not occur to you. It is not that you notice their logical misstep and dismiss it as insignificant. You do not even notice it at all, despite your attention to the speech. Assuming you are usually pretty competent at reasoning, this failure to notice seems like motivated theoretical irrationality that we would naturally hold you rationally responsible for: "But it's obvious that Y doesn't follow from X! Come on – you can see that!"

Alternatively, imagine you are waiting in a restaurant for a blind date to arrive. They walk in and they are utterly gorgeous. Throughout the date, you continue to be so blindsided by their physical attractiveness that their many and significant character flaws are occluded from your view. They talk about themselves and their accomplishments all the time, never ask you about yourself, and are horrendously rude to the waiter on several occasions. But all you can think about is how good-looking they are. Again, it is not that you do notice their character flaws and do not care. Their physical attractiveness simply dominates the scene, as far as you are concerned. You seem morally criticisable for this: "Don't be so shallow! What about how rude they were to the waiter?"

Finally, imagine you have ambitions to lead a particular project at work. Your boss will decide between you and several other viable candidates for the role. You decide that today is the day you will approach your boss to discuss the matter. You persist, entirely oblivious to their terrible mood. You seem prudentially at fault for this obliviousness: "But didn't it occur to you that they were in a bad mood and it would have been better to wait for a more opportune moment to ask?"

What these examples have in common is that they all involve holding you to account in some way for what you do and do not notice. You are not being held

DOI: 10.4324/9781351202114-7

responsible for what you attend to exactly, but for what is and is not salient to you in the first place. Let us assume that it is legitimate to hold you to account as we do. Rationally, you should have found the non sequitur in the politician's argument salient. Morally, you should *not* have found the person's physical attractiveness so salient that it eclipsed their other important features. Prudentially, you should have found your boss' mood salient if you were to stand a good chance of getting what you wanted.[1] But how are we to understand what it is for something to be salient to you so as to make sense of this responsibility?

I should be clear from the beginning that I intend 'salience' to be understood in what might be called a 'subjective' sense. Sometimes we talk about what is 'salient' in a particular situation, intending this in an objective, or maybe better, intersubjective way. Perhaps the boss' bad mood *was* salient in this sense, even though it was not to you, subjectively speaking.[2] I should also make clear that by 'salience' I do not mean to include some sort of subpersonal sense of the phenomenon. I mean to refer to personal-level salience. And, typically, I have in mind salience that involves full conscious awareness, in either perceptual experience or thought. The question I will be addressing in this essay then is: What is *this kind of salience* if we are to be responsible for it in the sorts of cases I described at the beginning?

As a first stab at defining salience of this kind, one would likely suggest something such as the following: for something to be salient to you is for it to 'stand out' to you, to be 'prominent' or in the 'foreground' of your experience or thought. I will begin, in 6.2 with this idea as developed by Watzl (2017, 2022). Watzl (2022, p.97) describes salience as a "passive force" and, although I will concur that what is salient to you is not subject to your direct voluntary control, I will argue that you must nonetheless be the agent of what is salient to you in some sense, if we are to properly understand your responsibility in the cases with which we began. In 6.3, I will argue that the indirect voluntary control you have over what is salient to you – as when you practise attending to certain phenomena, for example – cannot underpin the kind of direct responsibility you have for something's being salient to you in these cases. In 6.4, I will maintain that the relevant kind of agency is what I will call 'evaluative control'. I will argue that you have evaluative control over what is salient to you insofar as it is intimately connected with your evaluation of what matters. From 6.5, I will turn to the nature of this "intimate connection" and, relatedly, how exactly to understand the relevant evaluation. I will argue for what I will call the 'Sophisticated Constitutive View' of this connection. On this view, something's salience to you in the kinds of cases we are interested in is *constituted* by your occurrent evaluation that it matters in the context of the situation you are in. This enables us to capture your direct responsibility for this salience in itself. The Sophisticated Constitutive View also understands this particular occurrent evaluation as emerging from your standing evaluative worldview about what matters in general. This enables us to explain why it is that we understand your responsibility for what is salient to you in these particular cases in terms of the extent to which it is representative of your broader character.

6.2 The minimal account and direct voluntary control

Let us start with the idea that for something to be salient to you is for it to 'stand out' to you. This could be couched explicitly in terms of attention: something is salient to you insofar as it attracts or 'calls out' for your attention (whether you do in fact attend to it or not). And this happens to a greater or lesser extent, of course: salience is a matter of degree. Watzl (2017) develops precisely this kind of account of salience, in congruence with his 'Priority Structure View' of attention. Roughly speaking, according to Watzl's account of attention, it consists in the regulation of your 'priority structures'. These priority structures order your occurrent mental life in terms of their relative priority to you. According to his 'Imperatival Account' of salience, salient states have, "an imperatival content of roughly the form <put x on top of a priority structure!>" (Watzl, 2017, p.126) What I will call the 'Minimal Account' of salience is something along these lines then: something is salient to you simply insofar as – and to the extent that – it elicits your attention.

Now, according to Watzl (2022, p.97), salience is a "passive force" on your attention:

> Salience is a feature of subject-level states, but it is not under the subject's control (just like the content of a perceptual state is subject level but not controlled by the subject).

It seems clear from what he says elsewhere (e.g., 2017, pp.135–137) that by "passive" and "not under the subject's control", Watzl means simply that what is salient to you is not under your direct voluntary control. This must be right: you cannot simply *decide* that something be salient to you or not as you can decide to raise your arm or not.

Nonetheless, the way in which you are held accountable for what is and is not salient to you in the kinds of cases we started out with would be puzzling, to say the least, if there were no sense in which *you* had 'control' over it at all. If the salience or otherwise of your boss' mood were completely out of your hands, something that just occurred within you – like your heart's beating – how could you be responsible for it in the kind of way you are being held to be in the example? It might be unfortunate, from a prudential standpoint, that their bad mood was not salient to you. But *you* couldn't be held to account over it.[3]

6.3 Indirect voluntary control

Although you cannot simply decide that something be salient to you or not, you *can* decide, even arbitrarily, to focus your attention on a particular aspect of a situation. And doing so may well make it salient to you (and decrease the relative salience of other aspects) with immediate effect. But this is not exercising direct voluntary control over what is salient to you. It is exercising direct voluntary control over what you attend to and therein causing a redistribution in what is salient to you in the situation. It is exercising 'indirect voluntary control' over what is salient to you.

Many of those who discuss the place of salience in moral life think of one's responsibility for it, at least in part, in terms of indirect voluntary control. Typically, this is not with regard to how one directs one's attention at the relevant moment alone, but in terms of the uncountably many decisions over one's lifetime up to that point – some apparently insignificant, others less so – that substantially influence what one finds salient in the moment. Your moral responsibility for what is salient to you is conceived as underpinned by the cultivation of your propensities in this kind of way, particularly in virtue of what you have decided to attend and not to attend to. In the *Sovereignty of Good*, Murdoch (1970, p.37) asks us to:

> ...consider what the work of attention is like, how continuously it goes on... This does not imply that we are not free, certainly not. But it implies that the exercise of our freedom is a small piecemeal business which goes on all the time... Attention is the effort to counteract... states of illusion.

Given that this is so, Murdoch (1970, p.54) wants to know more about the "techniques" we can employ to effectively shape our moral "vision".

When it comes to rational responsibility, Pink (2009, pp.99–100) claims that if someone is to be rationally responsible for failing to notice a non sequitur, for example, this responsibility can *only* be in terms of their indirect voluntary control over this failure:

> What settles whether someone is so responsible? How, for example, to establish that it was through the bad reasoner's own fault that their reasoning was faulty? It is obvious enough how. We would raise questions about their action and omission and about how this might have affected their responsiveness to reason in this case—questions such as the following: what if they had taken greater pains at the time, such as by attending more carefully or taking longer to reflect; or had prepared themselves better beforehand, such as by working harder at practicing this form of reasoning? Did the error arise from their failure to do any of these things?... We are responsible for it only if it arises as our doing.

Now, you *do* have this kind of indirect voluntary control over what is salient to you to some extent.[4] And we do sometimes hold you responsible for its exercise, or lack thereof. "Well, it's no wonder that all you could think to do was punch them. You watch far too many violent films." Here, you are being criticised for your part in shaping yourself into someone for whom punching a person is a maximally salient course of action in such a situation. You are being criticised for voluntarily watching as many violent films as you have and, in so doing, exercising indirect voluntary control over the extent to which a certain, violent, option is salient to you.[5]

Although you might be held responsible in this kind of way in situations such as those I opened with, I think there is another, more direct, way of being held responsible for what is and is not salient to you that these situations illustrate. This involves being criticised *for noticing* or *for failing to notice*, as when you are criticised as rationally at fault for failing to notice the non sequitur. Here, you are being held directly to account for this omission in itself. The expectation you have failed to meet is *that you notice* the non sequitur and appreciate its significance in the context of the politician's speech. For such direct responsibility, indirect voluntary control over what you notice is not to the point.[6] Rather, it seems that noticing itself must be something you can *do*, in a certain sense. Given that you cannot simply decide to notice something, what we need is another form of direct agency over what is salient to you that is not direct voluntary control.

6.4 Evaluative control

Talk of any kind of direct 'control' or 'agency' over what is salient to you might sound inappropriate. But I think that this is only insofar as we understand both in terms of voluntariness. The kind of control I have in mind is emphatically nonvoluntary. It does not involve a decision to do anything. Nonetheless, it is a form of control, which renders that which you control 'yours', in the relevant sense (and hence 'down to you', or your responsibility). It is what I will call 'evaluative control'.[7]

Belief provides us with a good example. Our criticisms of one another's beliefs as 'false', 'off the mark', 'unfounded', 'irrational', 'absurd' etc. are a familiar aspect of everyday life. According to the evaluative control model, these criticisms are to be understood in terms of the control you have over your belief that *p* insofar as it represents your own evaluation concerning *whether p*. You evaluate whether or not *p* is the case, typically in response to your evidence, and therein are in control of what you believe.[8] It is in virtue of this evaluative control that you "make up your mind" when it comes to what to believe, as Moran (2001) famously puts it.

So, on this model, you exercise control over your belief in making an evaluation regarding the truth of the matter. What I would like to suggest here is that, when it comes to what is salient to you in the kinds of cases at the beginning, you exercise control in making an evaluation regarding what *matters* or is of significance in some sense, again typically in response to your reasons that bear on this question. In all of the illustrations I began with, there is an important connection between what is salient to you and what you evaluate as mattering. This mattering could be rational, moral, prudential, or of some other kind. Regardless, the thought is roughly that something's salience to you in such cases aligns with your evaluation that it matters (hence, by implication, its lack of salience to you aligns with the lack of such an evaluation on your part). It is this connection that grounds your direct responsibility for what is and is not salient to you. In being criticised for finding something salient you are being criticised for your evaluation that it matters (at least to the extent that it does, or at the expense of other features of the situation). In being criticised for failing to find something salient you are being criticised for your failure to evaluate it as mattering sufficiently. And, in being expected to adjust accordingly, it is expected that you adjust your evaluation as to what matters. This is something you can *do*, in the relevant sense. The question I will now turn to is how exactly to understand this "important connection" and, relatedly, the precise nature of the evaluation involved.

6.5 The naïve constitutive view

When it comes to belief, it is plausible that your evaluation that *p* is the case simply *is* your belief that *p*. You do not *first* make an evaluation regarding *p*'s truth and then subsequently form the corresponding belief.[9] Your affirmative evaluation as to whether *p constitutes* your belief that *p*. On what I will call the 'Naïve Constitutive View', in the sorts of cases we are interested in, the relationship between your evaluation about what matters and what is salient to you is also a constitutive one. What is salient to you is not merely what commands your attention, as on the Minimal Account we began with. There is more to salience than this. Something's salience to you is constituted by its commanding your attention *in virtue of* your evaluation that it matters (and the degree to which something is evaluated as mattering is constitutive of the degree to which it is salient to you). This evaluation need not be explicit, of course, but it is present, often implicitly, in something's being salient to you in cases like those I opened with.

Unlike belief, which is a standing state, salience is an occurrent phenomenon, in the sense that it occurs in a time-limited manner. So, the evaluation that constitutes the salience, on the Naïve Constitutive View, is also occurrent in this sense. In occurrently finding a certain aspect of your situation most salient, you are occurrently evaluating it as mattering most in that context. You need not be evaluating it as mattering most across all situations or contexts. Your acquaintance, who is currently speaking, might be most salient to you, even whilst your partner sits silently beside you. You also need not be evaluating it as mattering most *sub specie aeternitatis*. You might have a particular penchant for cheese that makes it most salient to you on the menu, without this involving the idea that cheese matters most to one and all.[10]

The Naïve Constitutive View of your evaluative control over what is salient to you (and the degree to which it is) seems to help us make sense of the sort of responsibility for salience we are interested in. When you meet your blind date, for example, your moral responsibility for finding their physical attractiveness so salient that it occludes their other important characteristics makes sense insofar as this salience is constituted by your evaluation that this is what matters in the situation (as opposed to, or more so than, other features of the situation, such as their flawed character). Given that this is a morally objectionable evaluation, you are to be morally criticised *for finding their attractiveness so salient*. And the expectation that you do something directly about what is salient to you in this situation can also be met. You can re-evaluate and *therein* modify the relative salience of your date's physical attractiveness.

When it comes to your responsibility for *failing* to find something salient, such as your rational responsibility for failing to notice the non sequitur in the politician's argument, this can be understood on the Naïve Constitutive View as a failure to evaluate it as mattering in the situation. This, in turn, could of course amount either to your positively having evaluated it as not mattering or, more likely, your failure to make an evaluation. Either way, it seems that the Naïve Constitutive View has an explanation of your direct responsibility here.[11]

However, there is something myopic about trying to understand your responsibility for what is salient to you in a particular situation solely in terms of a snapshot of that situation. As I argued above, when we criticise you for finding your date's physical attractiveness salient above all else, we are criticising you directly for this, in itself, and the indirect voluntary control model cannot capture this. Nonetheless, our criticism can only be properly understood in the context of our understanding of you as a person. This point is revealed, I think, by the fact that it is easy to feel some discomfort about the tone of this blind date example – to hear it as somewhat moralising. Part of the reservation about moral criticism in this case is to do with evolving and ambivalent attitudes to 'purely sexual' encounters between consenting people. But bound up here too is the sense that the description of you in this particular situation is not sufficient to enable us to pass judgement. We want to know whether the salience of your date's physical attractiveness in this situation is reflective of you as a person, or 'out of character'. If it were merely a fleeting episode, unrepresentative of what you evaluate as mattering more broadly speaking, we might not be moved to think particularly poorly of you. On the other hand, insofar as we *are* prepared to offer significant criticism of you for it, we do so, taking it to be representative of some fact about you that is deeper than your having made a one-off, occurrent evaluation in a specific situation. We are not criticising you for having moulded yourself into someone who notices or not, but we *are* criticising you for *being* such a person in this deeper sense. Indeed, relatedly, in holding you to account in the opening cases, we implicitly grant the psychological point that what is salient to you does not spring from nowhere and is representative of your broader character. The problem for the Naïve Constitutive View is that, in focusing solely on particular states of salience themselves (and your occurrent evaluations that it claims constitute these), it omits this richer psychological picture and hence cannot fully and adequately account for your responsibility in these kinds of cases.

6.6 The separate states view

In order to do so, rather than look to your occurrent evaluations, we need to consider what you evaluate as mattering more broadly speaking. This brings me to what I will call the 'Separate States View' of your evaluative control over what is salient to you. On this view, the relationship between your evaluation concerning what matters and what is salient to you is not a constitutive one. Something's salience to you is not constituted by an occurrent evaluation. In itself, salience is simply an eliciting of your attention, as on the Minimal Account we began with. But, in the opening cases, what elicits your attention is caused and rationalised by a separate, more long-standing evaluation of yours as to what matters. 'Rationalised', that is, in the sense that the standing evaluation provides a reason (not necessarily a *good* one) on the basis of which something is salient to you. And it is this causal-rational relationship between your standing evaluation and what is salient to you that explains your responsibility for it.

In an influential article, Smith (2005, p.270) appears to present a version of this view of the nature of your evaluative control over what you "notice and neglect",[12] claiming this to:

> ...indirectly reflect certain judgments or evaluative commitments. There is, if not a conceptual connection, at least a rational connection between these unreflective patterns of awareness and what we care about or regard as important or significant.

The Separate States View seems to allow us to explain why the extent of your responsibility for what is or is not salient to you in a particular situation depends on the extent to which this is representative of your character. Your evaluative control that grounds this responsibility is exercised via your standing evaluations that partially constitute your character, not by mere one-off occurrent evaluations, that may be out of character for you. So, the Separate States View appears to be an improvement on the Naïve Constitutive View in this respect.

The view also seems to offer another advantage over the Naïve Constitutive View: a univocal account of 'salience'. The Naïve Constitutive View claims that in the kinds of cases I opened with, something's salience to you is constituted by your occurrent evaluation that it matters in the situation (and the degree to which something is evaluated as mattering is constitutive of the degree to which it is salient to you). But one might think it implausible that such an understanding of salience can be generalised. What about cases in which what is most salient to you seems to come apart from your evaluation as to what matters most in the situation you are in? To take an example from Watzl (2017, p.135), imagine that:

> A fire alarm captures your attention even if you know that the building is merely testing the system.

You know that the fire alarm does *not* matter to you in the situation – it is only a test. This knowledge does not interfere with its persisting intrusion though. Indeed, it is precisely your knowledge that it does not matter to you now – that you should ignore it – combined with its oppressive presence that makes it so annoying.

The fire alarm case is one in which anyone with a functioning auditory system could find themselves, but other cases that involve irrationality or pathology also suggest themselves. Take someone suffering from Obsessive Compulsive Disorder. An interesting aspect of OCD is that it often includes what psychiatrists call 'good insight'. It seems that someone suffering from OCD might find anything they encounter pertaining to infection, for example, maximally salient. And, strikingly, this is so even though they, in some sense, understand entirely that it does not 'really matter'. It seems it might be maximally salient to them that they have not washed their hands in the last half an hour even though they understand that this does not matter. Indeed, they apparently evaluate it as mattering far less than listening to their child tell them about their day at school, which it seems they evaluate as mattering most at that moment. Nonetheless, they cannot keep their child's stories in view, so distracted are they by their unwashed hands. Somewhat analogously to the fire alarm case above, this kind of insight into their condition can often be part of what makes OCD so frustrating and distressing for someone suffering from the condition.

Both the fire alarm and the OCD with insight cases appear to illustrate the following two possibilities. 1. What is maximally salient to you is not what you evaluate as mattering most in the situation. 2. What you evaluate as mattering most in the situation is not what is maximally salient to you. If it is true that your evaluation and what is salient to you can come apart in both directions like this, then the Naïve Constitutive View cannot provide us with a general account of salience.

The Separate States View, on the other hand, promises to provide an account of salience that is entirely general. According to the Separate States View, what is salient to you *itself* is simply a matter of what 'stands out' to you, or commands your attention, as on the Minimal Account. The fire alarm's salience is its commanding your attention, just as your date's physical attractiveness is its commanding your attention. Neither the salience of the fire alarm, nor of your date's physical attractiveness, is constituted by an occurrent evaluation on your part that it matters in the situation. You are not responsible for the fire alarm's salience to you because you do not have evaluative control over it: *it is not* revelatory of a separate standing evaluation of yours. You *are* morally responsible for the salience of your date's physical attractiveness to you though, insofar as this *is* to be explained by a separate standing evaluation of yours.

In sum, the Separate States View seems to offer two key advantages over the Naïve Constitutive View. First, it appears to enable us to capture the way in which your responsibility for what is salient to you depends on its being representative of your character. Second, in construing salience itself as per the Minimal Account, it promises generality: something's salience to you is simply its eliciting your attention – this is true of both the opening cases and the fire alarm and OCD with insight cases.

However, my concern is that the Separate States View attempts to secure these advantages at the expense of properly doing justice to your direct responsibility for what is or is not salient to you in the kinds of cases I began with. As I argued in 6.3, the indirect voluntary control you exercise over what is salient to you in a given situation cannot explain this. This only allows you to get at what is salient to you via your voluntary actions elsewhere. You voluntarily attend to certain things, for example, and this has a causal influence over what you find salient. But, structurally, at least, it looks as if a similar difficulty arises for the Separate States View. According to the Separate States View, your control over what is salient to you is also exercised via something else – in this case, a separate standing evaluation.

A key difference between your indirect voluntary control over what is salient to you and the kind of evaluative control the Separate States View postulates is that the relationship it alleges between your standing evaluation and what is salient to you is a *rational* one. The indirect voluntary control you exercise over what is salient to you does not involve a rational connection between the voluntary actions you perform in 'training' yourself and what is salient to you. 'Techniques' of the kind Murdoch seeks would seem to involve – at least in abstraction – something like an initial evaluation as to what *should* (she is concerned with the moral sense) be salient to you in a situation of a certain kind and a reliance on the knowledge that humans are such that one can *cause* (without rationalising) the increased salience of something, or some kind of thing, by the practice of repeatedly attending to it, for example. This leaves you in a position of exercising what Hieronymi (2009) calls 'managerial control' over what is salient to you. You *manage* what you find salient in much the same way that you might manipulate a physical object like a book, by picking it up and moving it across the table, relying on the laws of nature to do their bit. *You* are inevitably alienated from that which you control to some extent – there is a merely causal process between you and it. Contrast this with the Separate States View on which what is salient to you does not need to go via such techniques and instead is itself in a direct reasons-relation with your evaluation as to what matters.

Smith illustrates the significance of the rational nature of the relationship between your standing evaluation and what is salient to you with the following example. Imagine you feel nauseous before giving a talk and this nausea is caused by your evaluation of such occasions as, "both important and also fraught with opportunities for failure" (Smith, 2005, pp.257–258). You are not responsible for this nausea in the way you are for what is salient to you, which we are trying to capture. The nausea is merely caused by an evaluation of yours, and not rationalised by it: it is not "(internally) judgement sensitive" (Smith, 2005, p.258). What is salient to you, however, *is*. It is your standing evaluation about the significance of good looks in general that rationalises your date's good looks standing out to you on this particular occasion.

Now, the Separate States View certainly gets you closer (so to speak) to the salience itself than your indirect voluntary control does. Nonetheless, the fact remains that it does not get you all the way in. It does not secure the kind of direct, or *intrinsic*, control over what is salient to you that we are looking for. On the evaluative control model, it is an *evaluation* that something matters that is the seat of your control. If this evaluation is built into the salience itself, you have intrinsic control over that salience. If it is not, you do not. Even if you have a reason to find your date's good looks salient (your own standing evaluation about the importance of looks in general), just as you have reason for that standing evaluation, the difference between the standing evaluation and the salience is that the former *is* itself an evaluation, whilst the latter is not. You can alter your standing evaluation simply in virtue of changing your mind about the significance of physical appearance. However, *ex hypothesi* on the Separate States View, altering the salience of your date's good looks, in this particular situation, is not something you can simply *do* in this way. Rather, it is the rational *upshot* of your changing your standing evaluation. It is an *indication* or *expression* of what you have direct evaluative control over rather than itself an exercise of your evaluative control.

Given that this is so, rather than explaining the criticism we seek to explain of the form, "You should/should not have noticed that *p*!", what the Separate States View gives us is an explanation of a criticism of the form, "You should/ should not evaluate states of affairs like *p* as mattering such that you noticed/did not notice that *p*!". Consider the date example once more. The criticism of you we are trying to understand is not *for being shallow, as evidenced in this case*. Rather, the criticism is of you *for being shallow in this case*.

6.7 The sophisticated constitutive view

So, in order to properly make sense of your responsibility in the sorts of cases I began with, we *do* need to construe something's salience to you as itself constituted by your occurrent evaluation that it matters in the context of the situation. The Naïve Constitutive View has this much right. But, as I have also insisted, this occurrent evaluation will not do justice to the nature of your responsibility if it is a one-off. It needs to be understood as representative of your character, to some extent at least.

The idea that naturally suggests itself at this point is to try to borrow the thought that there is a relationship between your standing evaluations and what is salient to you from the Separate States View. What I will call the 'Sophisticated Constitutive View' does this by understanding the occurrent evaluation that constitutes something's salience to you in a particular situation as emerging from your standing evaluations about what matters in general.

Now, it is clear by everyone's lights that you do not walk around with a fully-articulated, ranked set of standing evaluations about what matters. As Wiggins (1987, p.231) says:

> No theory… can treat the concerns an agent brings to any situation as forming a closed, complete, consistent system. For it is of the essence of these concerns to make competing, inconsistent claims… The weight of the claims represented by these concerns is not necessarily fixed in advance. Nor need the concerns be hierarchically ordered.

Indeed, even if we *were* to conceive of your standing evaluations about what matters on such an implausible model, it is not obvious what explanatory good it would do. It is not as if your ranked set of standing evaluations about what matters would help explain the relative degrees of salience of any corresponding aspects of a given situation. As I touched upon in 6.5, even if we were to imagine a codification on which you evaluate your partner as mattering most, followed by your work etc. it is clear enough that this will not always correspond with the degree of salience each has for you at any given time. Your partner is not *always* the most salient aspect of your experience and/or thought. In fact, precisely in virtue of their 'hinge-like' status in your life, your pressing concerns, such as the work you need to be getting on with that day, will often usurp them in this role, as will someone much less significant to you, generally speaking, who happens to be speaking at that moment.

A far more realistic conception of your standing evaluations about what matters conceives of these as fairly underspecified. What you have is something more like a partially amorphous standing evaluative worldview about what matters (which, of course, is ever-evolving). One could sketch certain aspects of this evaluative worldview more of less accurately, but it is nonetheless far from a fully-articulated ranking of concerns. So, one could say truly of you that you have a standing evaluation that your partner matters, but not what this amounts to exactly. Indeed, with this in mind, it is unclear that the Separate States View can even help itself to the idea that you have a *standing* evaluation that is determinate enough to feature in its account of your responsibility for what is salient to you.

By way of contrast, the Sophisticated Constitutive View allows us to recognise that the content of such standing evaluations can only be fully specified in terms of their application in particular circumstances. On the Sophisticated Constitutive View, it is in relation to a particular situation, with all of its idiosyncrasies, that your evaluative worldview about what matters crystalises into an articulated occurrent evaluation on your part about what matters in that context. Or rather, more accurately, it crystalises into an articulated occurrent evaluative take on the situation as a whole in terms of the degree to which the various aspects of it matter. This constitutes the degree to which you find the different aspects of that situation salient and also helps define your standing evaluations themselves.

Wiggins (1987, p.229) illustrates this relationship between your evaluative worldview about what matters and what is salient to you in a particular situation via appeal to Aristotle's 'Lesbian Rule':

> In fact this is the reason why not everything is determined by law and special and specific decrees are often needed. For when the thing is indefinite, the measure of it must be indefinite too, like the leaden rules used in making the Lesbian moulding. The rule adapts itself to the shape of the stone and is not rigid, and so too a special decree is adapted to the facts.

We might call this account of the relationship between your evaluative worldview about what matters and what is salient to you in a specific situation 'epigenetic', in the sense that what is salient to you in a situation can only be understood in terms of *the meeting of* your previously underdetermined evaluative worldview with the particularities of that specific situation. On the Sophisticated Constitutive View, it is only in context that you get the fully-specified evaluation(s) of the kind you need for evaluative control. And it is such control that enables us to properly explain your responsibility *for noticing* or *for failing to notice*. This responsibility is both specific to the particular act of noticing or failing to notice *and* arises out of (and helps define) your standing evaluative worldview about what matters. So, the sophisticated version of the constitutive view is an improvement upon the naïve insofar as it enables us to capture the idea that the extent of your responsibility for what is salient to you in the kinds of cases we are interested in is determined by the extent to which it is representative of your character. Unlike the naïve version, the Sophisticated Constitutive View is not focused on your occurrent evaluation about what matters in the situation alone, but rather understands this occurrent evaluation as emerging from (and helping define) what you care about, more generally speaking.

6.8 Returning to the problem cases: A univocal account of 'salience'?

If, as I have argued, the Sophisticated Constitutive View provides us with the best understanding of your responsibility for what is or is not salient to you in the kinds of cases I opened with, the question as to what to say about the other sorts of cases involving salience I have mentioned re-emerges. The salience of your date's good looks is constituted by an occurrent evaluation that this matters in the situation. But what about the fire alarm and OCD with insight cases?

Two strategies suggest themselves. First, we could of course simply allow that 'salience' is not univocal. In cases such as those at the beginning, in which you are responsible for what is salient to you, salience is to be understood as per the Sophisticated Constitutive View. In other cases, some of which are irrational or pathological (such as in the OCD with insight example), some of which are what we might call 'biomechanical' (such as in the fire alarm example), what it means for something to be salient to you is to be understood in accordance with the Minimal Account: something is salient to you insofar – and to the extent – that it elicits your attention. Now, these two senses of the word 'salience' would not be unrelated, of course. Both involve something's standing out to you – one in a 'thin' sense, and, the other, in a richer, 'thicker' sense in which this standing out is in virtue of an occurrent evaluation that whatever it is matters in the situation.

Alternatively, we could attempt to preserve the univocality of 'salience' on the Sophisticated Constitutive View, in the face of these problem cases. Indeed, when it comes to the OCD with insight case, the Sophisticated Constitutive View might be thought to help us make sense of the conflict involved in the case along one of the following lines. On the first, the person has insight so occurrently evaluates the fact that they have not washed as not mattering. But, in spite of this evaluation, the fact that they have not washed is also salient to them in the sense that they occurrently evaluate it as mattering. They have conflicting occurrent evaluations: one that it does not matter and one that it does (that is constitutive of its salience to them). On this picture of the case, there is a breakdown in reason-relations between what is salient to the person and their opposing evaluation that this does not matter and they are therein irrational. An alternative picture conceives of the person as failing to maintain a firm grasp on either evaluation. They are prone to evaluate their unwashed hands as mattering (in their being salient), but also to evaluate them as not (in having insight into their condition) and they constantly vacillate between the two, never affirming both at the same time. Their treatment of their reasons on this kind of picture could also leave them open to the charge of irrationality. Finally, one might maintain that the OCD with insight case goes beyond being irrational and is *pathological* precisely insofar as the 'salience' of the unwashed hands is deficient: it is, in fact, a *mere standing out*. This standing out is *not* salience proper (*contra* the Minimal Account) because it is not constituted by their evaluation that it matters and, given that this is the case, the person is not rationally responsible for it. Perhaps our uncertainty as to which option to take here explains our ambivalence over whether, and to what extent, the OCD sufferer is to be held to rational account.

What about the fire alarm case? Here the 'salience' of the fire alarm is not irrational or pathological, it is 'biomechanical'. Any human with a functioning auditory system is such as to have the sound of the alarm continue to dominate their experience in almost any circumstance, whether they like it or not. When it is put this way, it becomes clear, I think, that even on the Minimal Account of salience, this would not be a typical or paradigmatic case of salience. On the Minimal Account, something is salient to you insofar as it attracts or 'calls out' for your attention, *whether you do in fact attend to it or not*. Here we have a case where you have *no option* but to attend to the alarm, in almost all circumstances. It cannot exactly be said to *call out for* or *solicit* your attention, it is not even *commanding* it, it is *enforcing* it. With this in mind, it could be argued that the Sophisticated Constitutive View can comfortably tolerate the idea that this is not a case of salience proper. The fire alarm case involves a *mere standing out* or dominance that is not constituted by your evaluation that it is what matters to you in the situation. The fire alarm is not then, properly speaking, salient to you.[13]

I will not affirm either of these strategies on behalf of the Sophisticated Constitutive View here. We can either restrict its scope to the sorts of cases I have been concerned to explain or not. Either way, what I have argued is that it is the best account of those cases.

6.9 Conclusion

In sum, I set out to understand what it is for something to be salient to you, in light of the fact that you are sometimes responsible for this. The kind of responsibility I have been considering has two interesting features. First, it is 'direct', or 'intrinsic', as I have been putting it: it cannot be understood in terms of any indirect sort of effect you might be able to have on what is or is not salient to you. It is a responsibility *for finding something salient*, or *for failing to do so*. Second, it is grounded in your ongoing character in a certain sense. It is not a responsibility for a one-off noticing or failure to notice, but, rather, is reflective of you as a person.

I have proposed that both features of this responsibility can be understood in terms of what I call the 'Sophisticated Constitutive View'. According to this view, the salience of something to you is *constituted* by an occurrent evaluation on your part that it matters in the situation. Your control over this evaluation *is* your direct, or intrinsic, control over what is salient to you. This occurrent evaluation does not spring from nowhere though. It emerges, by way of interaction with the particular situation you are in, from your more long-standing evaluative worldview about what matters (which only becomes fully specified thanks to these interactions). This explains why we criticise you for what is salient to you to the extent that we consider this to be representative of you and your character more broadly speaking.[14]

Notes

1 The types of responsibility included here are intended as illustrative, not as an exhaustive list.
2 And perhaps one way of expressing our prudential criticism of you is in terms of this mismatch: something was intersubjectively salient and *yet not* subjectively so for you. But it is important to note that a failure to find something subjectively salient that is intersubjectively so will not always be criticisable. Imagine that a certain individual's wealth is the elephant in the room as far as other people are concerned but it is not something that occurs to you: what you notice above all is their warmth. Here you seem morally *praiseworthy* for failing to find subjectively salient what is intersubjectively so. There is much more to be said about the relationship between subjective and objective or intersubjective salience, but I set this aside for the purposes of this essay.
3 Perhaps if you had a particular instantiation of autistic spectrum disorder, for example, it *would* be inappropriate to hold you to account, insofar as it would not have been reasonable to expect that your boss' mood be salient to you. All three cases I offered at the beginning are obviously under-described in all kinds of ways that would affect the appropriateness of holding you to account. I return to this issue later but, for now, I take it that all I need is that there are cases along the lines I outlined at the beginning, the precise details of which could be specified, such that you would be held to account in the sorts of ways I described.
4 See e.g., (Mole 2022, pp.151–157) in this volume on the psychological evidence in support of this kind of indirect voluntary control over what is salient to you. Watzl

(2017, pp.135–137) also discusses the "penetrability" of what is salient to you by various phenomena, some of which are themselves under your direct voluntary control.
5 Obviously, the foreseeability (both for you and in general) of this effect of watching these films is relevant to the extent of your responsibility here too.
6 Indeed, as Smith (2005, pp.267–270) points out, we sometimes hold someone directly responsible in the kind of way I have in mind, *without* also thinking that they are responsible for *coming to be* the person they are in the relevant sense. Imagine someone raised in a deeply racist community (to use one of Smith's example). They might notice something as a result of this upbringing, and be responsible for noticing it, yet not for having contributed to making themselves into one who notices it.
7 I borrow the label from Hieronymi (2009) but she is not the only person to be interested in this form of agency, of course. See, for example, Boyle (2009), Moran (2001), and particularly Smith (2005), when it comes to salience.
8 I say "typically" as I think that there are probably limiting cases of belief on the basis of no evidence. Thanks to Boyle for discussion of this issue.
9 See Boyle (2009) for more discussion.
10 See Smith (2005, p.245).
11 Your responsibility, in this case, will be complicated by the fact that your motivation to fail to find the non sequitur salient is unconscious. This is not, it seems to me, an automatic excuser but the issue does warrant more discussion than I have the space to allow it here.
12 The idiom is Hampshire's (1959, p.91).
13 One might think that you *do* evaluate the fire alarm as mattering, despite your awareness that it is only a test. After all, test or not, you cannot continue with whatever it was you were doing until it is over. (My thanks to both Sabina Lovibond and Joseph Schear for suggesting this idea to me, independently of one another.) The problem with this attempt to resolve the issue though, it seems to me, is that the reason you evaluate the fire alarm as mattering in this way is *because* it is dominating your experience as it is. This, I think, precludes thinking of your evaluation that it matters as constituting its salience.
14 Thanks to an audience at the University of Stirling, to one at UWTSD, and to Sabina Lovibond, and Joseph Schear.

References

Boyle, M. 2009. Active Belief. *Canadian Journal of Philosophy* 39(1): 119–147.
Hampshire, S. 1959. *Thought and Action*. The Viking Press, New York.
Hieronymi, P. 2009. Two Kinds of Agency. In L. O'Brien and M. Soteriou (Eds.), *Mental Actions* (pp. 138–162). Oxford University Press, Oxford.
McDowell, J. 1998. Virtue and Reason. In *Mind, Value, and Reality* (pp. 50–73). Harvard University Press, Cambridge, MA.
Mole, C. 2022. The Moral Psychology of Salience. In S. Archer (Ed.), *Salience: A Philosophical Inquiry* (pp. 140–158). Routledge, Abingdon.
Moran, R. 2001. *Authority and Estrangement: An Essay on Self-Knowledge*. Princeton University Press, Woodstock.
Murdoch, I. 1970. *The Sovereignty of Good*. Routledge, London.
Pink, T. 2009. Reason, Voluntariness, and Moral Responsibility. In L. O'Brien and M. Soteriou (Eds.), *Mental Actions* (pp. 95–120). Oxford University Press, Oxford.

Smith, A. 2005. Responsibility for Attitudes: Activity and Passivity in Mental Life. *Ethics* 115: 236–271.
Watzl, S. 2017. *Structuring Mind: The Nature of Attention and How It Shapes Consciousness*. Oxford University Press, Oxford.
Watzl, S. 2022. The Ethics of Attention: An Argument and a Framework. In S. Archer (Ed.), *Salience: A Philosophical Inquiry* (pp. 89–112). Routledge, Abingdon.
Wiggins, D. 1987. Deliberation and Practical Reason. *Needs, Values, Truth* (pp. 215–237). Blackwell, Oxford.

7 Salience, choice, and vulnerability

Sophie Grace Chappell

7.1 The myth of option ranges

Much contemporary writing in normative ethics, in particular in the consequentialist school and in the ideologically allied fields of economic philosophy and causal decision theory, is dominated by a myth. The myth is this:

> The world just *gives us* option ranges.

More fully:

> In any situation of practical choice, we have a finite, short, and fixed list of available alternatives to choose between. Knowing what the items are on that list, and how many of them there are, is knowing a matter of objective, non-evaluative fact. Actual ethical questions only arise when we consider how to "score" each of the options on the list that "the world gives us", and so, how to choose from that list.
>
> Typical practical deliberation thus becomes a matter of simple disjunctive syllogism: "At t, X must (as a matter of fact) do either A or B or C; but (as a matter of value) not B, and not C; so at t X must do A". And what makes any such disjunctive practical syllogism a sound argument to the conclusion "at t X must do A" is, crucially, the disjunction in its first premiss: the allegedly factual statement of the option range, the listing of the available alternatives.

This myth of option ranges goes back at least to Bentham, Leibniz, Spinoza, and Hobbes, all of whom talk at times in just this sort of way about the choice between alternatives. In contemporary philosophy, the myth is not usually made explicit, but it is implicit in all sorts of places. For instance, it lurks just below the surface in these two familiar recent statements of the consequentialist view—the second of which also, with an all-too-familiar arrogation, implicitly takes "thinking ethically" and "thinking consequentialistically" to be one and the same:

[A] consequentialist theory... tells us that we ought to do whatever has the best consequences... [More formally,] the consequentialist holds that... the proper way for an agent to respond to any values recognised is... in every choice to select the option with prognoses that mean it is the best [i.e., the most probably successful/ highest scoring] gamble with those values. (Pettit, 1991, p.232)

Suppose I then begin to think ethically... I now have to take into account the interests of all those affected by my decision. This requires me to weigh up all those interests and adopt the course of action most likely to maximise the interests[1] of those affected. Thus at least at some level in my moral reasoning I must choose the course of action that has the best consequences, on balance, for all affected. (Singer, 1993, p.13)

Now the myth of option ranges is indeed a myth.[2] Specifically, what is false about it is the contention that any option range, any list of alternative actions available to some agent at some time, could be both objective and finite. If the list of alternative actions *is* objective, then just for that reason it will be infinite. Possibilia are dense; in between any two possible actions, there is a third. In between saluting the flag with *this* amount of respect and *that* amount of respect lies some third possible degree of respect; and different amounts of respect can make "saluting the flag with respect" a name for quite different actions; sarcastically exaggerated respect, for instance, is no respect at all. So in any situation of practical choice whatever, an *objective* list of all the available options would be an infinitely long list. Conversely, if the list of alternative actions is finite, it will not be objective. For any finite list of our options, and in particular, any manageably shortlist of our options, will omit infinitely many alternative possible actions that are nonetheless, given the denseness of possibilia, objectively *there* as possibilities. So its shortness will either be a sign of randomness, or of ideology, or of simple error.

In either case, disjunctive practical syllogisms of the kind described above will be unsound arguments. For all such arguments have to begin from a finitely-long first premiss that says "At t, X must do either A or B or C". And by the argument just given, all premisses of this form are false. There is, then, no way for the world to *give* us option ranges.

7.2 Trolleyology and ticking bombs

One pressure towards the myth of option ranges is generated by a burgeoning philosophical industry in contemporary applied ethics. I refer, of course, to trolleyology, the new(ish)[3] genre of casuistry that invents and explores hypothetical cases involving runaway trams in mines and the like. It is characteristic of trolleyology that the situation is so stipulated that the choosing agent is *not* supposed to have indefinitely many alternatives to choose between, but usually, just two or three alternatives that we are supposed to take as fixed: a lever is in front of her, and it has two and only two settings. (She could of course also refuse to touch the lever at all, thus choosing neither setting. But it is surprising in practice how often even this obvious possibility is treated as an inconvenient wrinkle, finessed away, or just plain ignored.) Maybe this wish to restrict and fix the alternatives is, subliminally, why the scene is so often set in a *mineshaft*. The unspoken assumption is apparently that trolley situations have the "purity" of typical situations in naval warfare, where the combatants' salient alternatives are fewer than they are in land warfare (basically: fight or drown). There's less scope for interfering factors down there in the mine than when one is engaged in other nonetheless-popular trolleyological pastimes, e.g., lethally assaulting fat persons who are so unlucky or so inattentive as to get caught on some railway bridge when a trolleyologist is passing.

But first, it is not actually true, not even in hypothetical trolleyological setups that are expressly designed to make it true, that the deliberator literally has just the option-range that the neo-casuist attempts to stipulate for her. Even at a binary switch-point, and even hypothetically, there are always plenty of other things you might do if you can just think of them. Maybe you can fuse the electrics in the switch-box, causing an explosion that will make all the trolleys in the mine stall on their emergency brakes, right where they are. Maybe you can flip the switches back and forth repeatedly in a way that will be taken as a warning sign by the miners, giving them a chance to place some sort of obstruction on the tracks (possibly one miner is significantly fatter than the others). Maybe you can pray very hard. Maybe you can run out of your signal-box and jump under the runaway tram yourself. Or throw your swivel-chair under it, or a spanner into its gears. Or something else.

Secondly, even if there *was* a finite, small, and fixed option range in any such imaginary scenario, that would only go to show the distance between that imaginary scenario and the real world. A trolleyological case is supposed to give us lessons not just about *other* trolleyological scenarios, but also about "real life". But if trolleyology really is full of cases where there actually are precisely two, or precisely three, alternatives for choice, then trolleyology is so unrealistic that it seems most unlikely to have anything much to teach us about real life at all.

Another way in which the myth of option ranges manifests its power is in discussions of the ticking-bomb scenario.[4] The basic idea is stated by, for example, Anthony Quinton:

> Consider a man caught planting a bomb in a large hospital, which no one but he knows how to defuse and no one dare touch for fear of setting it off. It was this sort of case that I had in mind when I said earlier that I thought torture could be justifiable. (Quinton, 1971, p.757, cited by Allhoff, 2012, p.88)

The point of the example is to direct our minds to one particular possibility, the possibility of torturing the bomber, and to suggest (apparently) that our options are fixed as exactly these two: *torture* and *do nothing*. Yet Quinton's case does not show anything like this; nor does it show anything like what Quinton explicitly says he wants it to show, viz. that "torture could be justifiable". Quinton does nothing at all to show that torturing the bomber will get him to tell us anything useful. Indeed it is hard to make out just what the case *is* that Quinton thinks he is describing, or more exactly underdescribing. (I left nothing out in my quotation; there were no rows of dots in it.) As Quinton puts it, his case simply raises this question: if the bomb is on a timer, and the torture will stop (at least temporarily[5]) when the bomber tells us *something*, then given that the bomber wants the bomb to go off, why would he tell us the truth?

This and other problems are likewise raised by a second ticking-bomb case that is often cited. This one is Michael Levin's:

> Suppose a terrorist has hidden an atomic bomb on Manhattan Island which will detonate at noon… Suppose, further, that he is caught at 10 a.m… but preferring death to failure, won't disclose where the bomb is. What do we do? If we follow due process, wait for his lawyer, arraign him, millions of people will die. If the only way to save those lives is to subject the terrorist to the most excruciating possible pain, what grounds can there be for not doing so? I suggest there are none. (Michael Levin, "The case for torture," *Newsweek*, Feb. 7 1982, p.7, cited in Allhoff; the omissions are Allhoff's not mine)

There is plenty to say about a passage like this, but I will restrict myself to three comments. First, Levin tells us in one sentence that the terrorist prefers "death to failure", and "won't disclose where the bomb is", and in the next asks "What do we do?". Levin himself has just answered his own question. If the terrorist *really* prefers death to failure, and *really* won't disclose where the bomb is, it is not obvious why we should think there is anything much we can do. Not with the terrorist, anyway. Perhaps mobilising mass searches of Manhattan, or mass evacuations, or both, would be a better use of those precious two hours than peeling the terrorist's fingernails off with a pair of pliers.

Secondly, to this mistake, Levin's next sentence ("If we follow due process", etc.) adds a further mistake by insinuating, without actually saying, that the only two alternatives that could possibly occur to us in the scenario he describes are torture and "due process". (The sneer is audible.) Levin thus tacitly claims that opponents of torture can only be saying that, rather than torturing the terrorist, we should go through the standard procedures of law at the standard adagio pace.[6] Once made explicitly, this claim is *obviously* ridiculous.

And thirdly, in his last sentence, Levin helps himself to the conclusion that he has just failed to argue for. *If* the only way to save the millions of lives in question is to subject the terrorist to excruciating pain, then maybe there's a case for doing so; at the very least, if this conditional is true, we need to think about it. But nothing in Levin's own description of Levin's own case gets anywhere near justifying the idea that the antecedent of this conditional is ever true; let alone that it was true in any of the actual cases where he was arguing torture should be used.

For all these reasons—for other reasons too[7]—it is much harder for the ticking-bomb scenario to be realised than philosophers often seem to assume. For sure, we cannot show that a genuine ticking-bomb case is impossible *in principle*. That does not mean that it is mere nit-picking, or what Williams (1981, p.43) calls a "cop-out", to point out how hard it is for such a case to occur. There is a difference in principle between what cases are and what cases are not possible in principle: philosophers can reasonably take cases of the latter sort much less seriously in formulating their general moral views. But there is also a difference in principle between cases that are *easily* possible in principle and cases that are *barely* possible in principle. (Compare the difference, in science, between effects that can happen and characteristically often do, and effects that can happen and characteristically hardly ever do.) Here too philosophers can reasonably take cases of the latter sort much less seriously in formulating their general moral views. An obvious and constantly-recurring type of counter-example to a moral generalisation tends to drive a coach and horses through the plausibility of that generalisation; a rare and recherché type of counter-example need have no such effect. (Sometimes it is *right* to say "It's a universal generalisation, apart from these few cases, but they don't really matter".) If genuine ticking-bomb cases are only barely and not easily possible in principle, they may be no more than rare and recherché counter-examples to the generalisation that torture is wrong. In which case we are entitled not to take them terribly seriously.

7.3 Framing, nudging, and corrupting

Ticking-bomb cases depend on the biasing effect of framing and nudging techniques. Such techniques are, of course, a pervasive feature of the social world. In the real UK, consider the carefully-doctored shortlists of potential archbishops of Canterbury that the Civil Service presents to the Prime Minister. In the fictional UK of *Yes Prime Minister*, consider the two strings of opinion-poll questions that Sir Humphrey Appleby puts to Bernard Woolley:

Sir Humphrey Appleby:	Mr. Woolley, are you worried about the rise in crime among teenagers?
Bernard Woolley:	Yes.
Sir Humphrey Appleby:	Do you think there is lack of discipline and vigorous training in our Comprehensive Schools?
Bernard Woolley:	Yes.
Sir Humphrey Appleby:	Do you think young people welcome some structure and leadership in their lives?
Bernard Woolley:	Yes.
Sir Humphrey Appleby:	Do they respond to a challenge?
Bernard Woolley:	Yes.
Sir Humphrey Appleby:	Might you be in favour of reintroducing National Service?

Bernard Woolley:	Er, I might be.
Sir Humphrey Appleby:	Yes or no?
Bernard Woolley:	Yes.
Sir Humphrey Appleby:	Of course, after all you've said you can't say no to that. On the other hand, the surveys can reach opposite conclusions.[survey two]
Sir Humphrey Appleby:	Mr. Woolley, are you worried about the danger of war?
Bernard Woolley:	Yes.
Sir Humphrey Appleby:	Are you unhappy about the growth of armaments?
Bernard Woolley:	Yes.
Sir Humphrey Appleby:	Do you think there's a danger in giving young people guns and teaching them how to kill?
Bernard Woolley:	Yes.
Sir Humphrey Appleby:	Do you think it's wrong to force people to take arms against their will?
Bernard Woolley:	Yes.
Sir Humphrey Appleby:	Would you oppose the reintroduction of conscription?
Bernard Woolley:	Yes.[does a double-take]
Sir Humphrey Appleby:	There you are, Bernard. The perfectly balanced sample.[8]

As any competent pollster knows, the power to decide, in any deliberative process, what questions are asked—and even more particularly, what questions are *not* asked—is a mighty power. Pretty commonly it is even more important than the power to answer those questions. (Who holds the real power when a witness is cross-examined by a barrister: the witness answering, or the barrister asking? It can be either, depending on particularities; but it is probably oftener the barrister than the witness. "Leading questions" are likelier than "leading answers".) So to buy into the analogous idea that our business in ethics is to decide between a menu of alternatives that the world *just presents* to us is at best a naïve mistake; for consequentialism to buy so frequently and so deeply into this myth evinces at best a remarkable lack of curiosity. At best—and more likely, as appears from the role of the myth in underpinning the standard consequentialist lines about trolleyology and the ticking bomb that I've just been considering, something less benign than mere incuriosity; something worth calling 'ideology'.

The pretence that the world *just gives us* option ranges is a myth, and an ideologically motivated myth. The ideological function of the myth is, quite obviously, to make us take as given what is in fact always contestable, and often highly contentious: the presentation of some particular list of the alternatives facing us as *the one uniquely correct* list of the alternatives facing us. Simply accepting this list plays straight into the hands of whatever power-group is presenting it: often a group that wishes to hypnotise us with some option, in particular, torture or murder for instance, and to make it appear as the option we are *bound* to choose, not just in some extreme and fantastical hypothesis, but in lots of other supposedly similar cases too. Elizabeth Anscombe famously noted the danger of a corrupting spreading-effect when we think about such cases:

> [T]he point of considering hypothetical situations, perhaps very improbable ones, *seems* to be to elicit from yourself or someone else a hypothetical decision to do something of a bad kind. I don't doubt this has the effect of predisposing people—who will never get into the situations for which they have made hypothetical choices—to consent to similar bad actions, or to praise and flatter those who do them, so long as their crowd does so too, when the desperate circumstances imagined don't hold at all. (Anscombe, 1958, p.10)

It is a remarkable fact about our society today that precisely this spreading-effect is quite clearly visible in, in particular, popular attitudes to torture in the US: what works in *Homeland* is assumed to work in the real world too, even though the types of emergency scenarios that routinely happen, or are supposed to happen, in *Homeland* almost never happen in the real world.[9]

7.4 Randomness, vulnerability, and luck

We are faced with—approximately—three alternatives: either the myth that the world just *gives us* option ranges; or we get our option ranges *at random*; or there is some reasonable and rational method for us to arrive at option ranges. Having rejected the first of these three alternatives, we should look harder at the other two.

The first thing to notice about the second alternative, randomness, is that philosophers today are likely to see it as a non-starter, when in fact it may well deserve serious consideration, and to be treated as more than an alternative that is merely there to provoke sceptical relativism. Surely the way we perceive or delimit our option ranges *is* deeply and constitutively shaped by factors that lie deep in our psychological and social history, factors at least some of which may well bear no necessary tracking relationship to the truth. Why should it be thought such a disaster for practical rationality to admit this? Maybe, in fact, some degree of self-knowledge about our own vulnerability to historical contingency is precisely what is needed to overcome our own biases—at least to some degree. But the natural tendency of contemporary ethics is to assume that there are no *degrees* here; that *control is everything*, and also that *control is all or nothing*. Self-conscious, autonomous rational awareness is what we want to be able to ascribe to ourselves, and any limitation at all on that control is—the story goes—as good as a complete annulment of it.

This, ironically, enough, seems to be part of the ideological background that makes the myth of option ranges so attractive to us. The idea is that since the answer to the question of what our options are is *cut and dried*, no space appears, here, in which we might be at the mercy of forces outwith our rational control. And so we remain absolute in our rational autonomy and our deliberative freedom.

My proposal, to the contrary, is that we are indeed at the mercy of history and its determining factors—to some extent. Our rational control and independence are not absolute, though not null either; nor is it fixed—we can and often do become *more* independent of background factors; the free will can be, and perhaps should be, seen as a skill that we can and often do acquire over time. In what we come to see as our option ranges at any given time, we are indeed vulnerable to the contingencies that have shaped us. But the only reasons for thinking this vulnerability a bad thing would have to be either a conviction that, if we are vulnerable to a contingency at all, then we are *completely* vulnerable—which is simply a non sequitur; or a conviction that autonomy and control of our situation are always good, and that it is always bad to be vulnerable to moral luck. This obsession with rational control and independence, and this refusal of vulnerability and contingency, is absolutely characteristic of contemporary moral philosophy. That does not make it any more justified.

7.5 Salience and silence

Alongside the myth that there is no problem or question about how our option ranges are determined for us—the world just gives us them—the second alternative, just reviewed, is that our option ranges arise through randomness, contingency, through factors in one way or another beyond our control. I've just agreed that there is some truth in that. The third alternative is that we ourselves have some broadly rational way of determining our option ranges. And I want to say that there is some truth in this too. What then is this third alternative?

The idea here is just to accept that the way the moral questions are put to us—the way that our option ranges are presented to us—is itself not merely a matter of non-evaluative fact, but inherently morally loaded; but to add that there is some reason to think that we have the ability to pick up the kinds of alternatives for deliberation that it is *morally good* to be able to pick up—and the converse ability to ignore the kinds of alternatives that it is better to ignore. We have to do, in other words, with an account of practical wisdom: contingent, situated, and historically conditioned practical wisdom, but practical wisdom nonetheless. And as just suggested, what practical wisdom will involve will be both a matter of some things' being salient, and also a matter of some other things' being silent.

On deliberative silence, compare Bernard Williams (1985, p.185):

> One does not feel easy with the man who in the course of a discussion of how to deal with political or business rivals says, 'Of course, we could have them killed, but we should lay that aside right from the beginning.' It should never have come into his hands to be laid aside. It is characteristic of morality that it tends to overlook the possibility that some concerns are best embodied... in deliberative silence.

In ordinary English we have the locution *not an option*, meaning that some objectively-available option is not a *serious* option; it is just not something to think about; at the limit, it deserves "deliberative silence". What Williams calls "morality" (or "the morality system") is a family of ways of ethical thinking that seem incapable of deliberative silence in this sense. The morality system says that, if any option is ruled out, it must be ruled out *as the result of* a deliberative calculation, not *in advance of* any deliberative calculation (as Williams thinks should sometimes happen). If it is true, in a famous nineteenth-century maritime cannibalism case, that Dudley and his shipmates should not even consider killing and eating the cabin boy, or that Sophie in *Sophie's Choice* should reject absolutely any option that involves nominating either or both of her children for murder, these truths are, for the morality system, the termini and not the starting points of deliberation. And that is precisely Williams' complaint about them: by the time these dire contingencies have become a matter for deliberation, it is *already too late* for them to have the treatment that virtuous deliberation must give them—which is not to admit them into deliberation in the first place, but to pass over them in deliberative silence.

Alongside the necessity of silence about some options, there is the equal and opposite necessity of seeing some options as salient. What psychological mechanisms bring it about, in people of good character, that the right options are salient to them—and the right other options silenced? To raise this question is to ask for an account of moral perception; and/or to ask for an account of practical wisdom. Such an account will be partly explicit, and partly implicit. I have written plenty elsewhere about the explicit side,[10] but it would take many more pages than I have available here to say much about it. In this context, then, I restrict myself to the implicit side.[11]

Notes

1 *Sic.* Singer presumably means "maximise the satisfaction of the interests" *vel sim.*
2 As I have argued in print before: Chappell 2001.
3 See Foot 1967, Thomson, 1976.
4 The next few paragraphs are unapologetically lifted, with minor revisions, from *Knowing What to Do*, Chapter 2: I include them here as well to display a connection.
5 The fact that the terrorist presumably knows that he is in for it later can hardly be all that important in the case as described. He presumably knows that he's in for it *anyway*.
6 Even more puzzlingly, Levin seems to be contrasting his preferred procedure for the terrorist's *interrogation* with a dispreferred procedure for the terrorist's *prosecution*. I've no idea why.
7 These further reasons are further explored in my longer discussion of them in *Knowing What to Do*, Chapter 2.
8 Retrieved from http://www.imdb.com/title/tt0086831/quotes
9 For a fairly typical, and relatively balanced, presentation of arguments for high-school debates about the alternatives "To torture or not to torture?" see e.g., http://securingliberty.idebate.org/arguments/torture.

10 See in particular *Ethics and Experience* (2009), *Knowing What to Do* (2014), and *Epiphanies* (forthcoming).
11 My thanks to the Leverhulme Trust for the award of a Major Research Fellowship 2017–2020, during the tenure of which this was written.

References

Allhoff, Fritz. 2012. *Terrorism, Ticking Time-Bombs, and Torture*. Chicago University Press, Chicago.
Anscombe, Elizabeth. 1958. Modern Moral Philosophy. *Philosophy* 33: 1–19.
Chappell, Timothy. 2001. Option Ranges. *Journal of Applied Philosophy* 18: 107–118.
Chappell, Timothy. 2009. *Ethics and Experience*. Acumen, London.
Chappell, Sophie Grace. 2014. *Knowing What to Do*. Oxford University Press, Oxford.
Foot, Philippa. 1967. The Problem of Abortion and the Doctrine of Double Effect. In *Virtues and Vices*. Basil Blackwell, Oxford, 1978; originally in the *Oxford Review*, Number 5, 1967.
Levin, Michael. 1982. The Case for Torture. *Newsweek* 99(23): 13.
Pettit, Philip. 1991. Consequentialism. In Peter Singer (Ed.), *Companion to Ethics* (pp. 230–237). Blackwell, Oxford.
Quinton, Anthony. 1971. Views. *The Listener* 2(12): 757.
Singer, Peter. 1993. *Practical Ethics*. Cambridge University Press, Cambridge.
Thomson, Judith Jarvis. 1976. Killing, Letting Die, and the Trolley Problem. *The Monist* 59: 204–217.
Williams, Bernard. 1981. *Moral Luck*. Cambridge University Press, Cambridge.
Williams, Bernard. 1985. *Ethics and the Limits of Philosophy*. Penguin, London.

8 The moral psychology of salience

Christopher Mole

8.1 Attention and salience

Although it is possible to direct attention onto an arbitrary region of peripersonal space – as when you ask how many things currently occupy the six-inch cube that lies two feet below your left hand – we do not usually allocate our attention in this arbitrary way (cp. Evans, 1982, p.172). Our attention more typically attaches to items that make themselves available to it. These items are metaphysically various. They might be objects, shadows, sounds, or tingles. We can attend to a region of space, even in the absence of such an item, but it seems that we do so by imagining there to be something that gives bounds to that region, and then directing our attention onto that imagined thing.

To explain the way in which real and imagined items give structure to our experience, and so make parts of it apt to receive our attention, we need the notion of salience. Attention and salience are distinct: we can pay attention to that which is not salient, and can experience a thing as salient whilst withholding our attention from it, but the connection between these two phenomena is not merely contingent. There cannot be a propensity without there being something to which one is prone, and so – since salience essentially involves a propensity for the receipt of attention – there cannot be salience without there being such a thing as attention.

Although the controversies as to how attention should be explained sometimes extend to debates about whether it really exists (Anderson, 2011; Mole, 2011; Wu, 2014), the attention to which salience is essentially related is a commonplace thing. It has been a topic of much psychological research, and it has sometimes been thought to be morally important. The present essay examines the moral importance, and the contribution of salience to it.

8.2 Attention is morally important

In notebooks that were posthumously edited for publication, Simone Weil writes:

> The authentic and pure values — truth, beauty and goodness — in the activity of a human being are the result of one and the same act, a certain application of the full attention to the object.

DOI: 10.4324/9781351202114-9

> Teaching should have no aim but to prepare, by training the attention, for the possibility of such an act.
>
> All the other advantages of instruction are without interest. (Weil, 1986, p.214)

In these notebooks, Weil attempted to articulate the convictions that motivated her endeavour-filled life. They were not an occasion for rhetoric. Even when she was writing for effect (as when she was writing pseudonymously about the *Iliad*), Weil was unfailingly sincere. We should therefore prefer to understand this assessment of attention's importance as something other than an exaggeration.

Weil was not the only twentieth-century thinker to make the faculty of attention carry so large and so normative a weight. Nor was she the only thinker to emphasise the role of teaching in the cultivation of our capacity for attentiveness. Much the same ideas can be found in some late remarks of W. H. Auden (who, like Weil, had spent a part of his twenties working as a school teacher, prior to the outbreak of war). Writing in *The Episcopalian*, Auden tells us that:

> Choice of attention—to attend to this and ignore that—is to the inner life what choice of action is to the outer. In both cases man is responsible for his choice and must accept the consequences. As Ortega y Gasset said 'Tell me to what you pay attention, and I will tell you who you are'. (Auden, 1974, quoted in Hecht, 2003, p.139)

Although Weil and Auden are both, in their different ways, canonical writers, both stand outside the canon of mainstream Anglophone philosophy. Their claims about the cultivation of attention have seldom been read as philosophical theses. To the extent that our discussions of attention over the last twenty years have had a moral orientation, it has been an orientation towards accounts of attention in the Buddhist tradition (Davis and Thompson, 2015). These discussions have tended to employ the vocabulary of meditation and of mindfulness. Auden was not ignorant of the tradition from which such vocabulary is drawn, but his sympathies on the present point were elsewhere. His temperament here was quite thoroughly Anglican, and when he considered the disciplined exercise of attention he found it natural to employ the vocabulary of prayer. It was a discussion of prayer that gave the context for the remarks that have just been quoted:

> Whenever a man so concentrates his attention—be it on a landscape or a poem or a geometrical problem or an idol or the True God—that he completely forgets his own ego and desires in listening to what the other has to say to him, he is praying.

> Choice of attention—to attend to this and ignore that—is to the inner life what choice of action is to the outer. [...] The primary task of the schoolteacher is to teach children, in a secular context, the technique of prayer. (*op cit*)

Weil's engagement with the Eastern tradition was somewhat more complicated than Auden's, as was her engagement with Christianity (Murdoch, 1956), but again it is in the vocabulary of prayer, rather than in the vocabulary of mindfulness or meditation, that she formulates the present point. She writes that 'Attention, taken to its highest degree, is the same thing as prayer' (p.212). When this equation is combined with the points that were quoted above – about teaching being a preparation for 'a certain act of full attention' – the conclusion that follows is close to Auden's. Weil arrives at that conclusion when she writes:

> Prayer being only attention in its pure form and studies being a form of gymnastics of the attention, each school exercise should be a refraction of spiritual life. There must be method in it. A certain way of doing a Latin prose, a certain way of tackling a problem in geometry (and not just any way) make up a system of gymnastics of the attention calculated to give it a greater aptitude for prayer. (*op cit*, p.214–215)

In these passages, we see Weil and Auden independently identifying an aptitude for prayer with a capacity for attentiveness, and see both of them taking the possession of this capacity to be an achievement that might properly be called 'spiritual', but that is esoteric in only the most minimal sense. This capacity for attentiveness is something that they both take to be cultivated through the everyday discipline of completing a Latin prose, or a problem in geometry. And it is this role in the cultivation of attention, rather than their role in the acquisition of any soon-to-be-forgotten knowledge, that gives these schoolroom disciplines their 'interest' (for Weil), or their 'primary task' (for Auden). To identify this as the source of their interest is to claim that such disciplines are of the very first importance since, for Weil, 'truth, beauty and goodness [...] are the result of [...] a certain application of the full attention to the object', and, for Auden, 'Choice of attention—to attend to this and ignore that—is to the inner life what choice of action is to the outer. In both cases man is responsible for his choice and must accept the consequences'.

8.2.1 Attending without Praying

Several writers have shown themselves to be in sympathy with the position that Weil and Auden were advocating, while also being suspicious of the Christian ideas that informed their advocacy of it. An example can be found in Kathleen Jamie's account of her response to her husband's hospitalisation:

> Could I explain to Phil that – though there was a time, maybe 24 hours, when I genuinely believed his life to be in danger – I had not prayed? But I had noticed, more than noticed, the cobwebs, and the shoaling light, and the way the doctor listened, and the flecked tweed of her skirt, and the speckled bird and the sickle-cell man's feet. Isn't that a kind of prayer? The care and maintenance of the web of our noticing, the paying heed? (Jamie, 2005, p.109)

We shall return to these questions below.

A congenial line of thought can be found in the life-writing of Virginia Woolf. Woolf emphasises the crucial importance, to her character and to her writing, of certain 'shocks', in which her attention had been seized by some particular independent thing – as when, in childhood:

> I was looking at the flower bed by the front door; 'That is the whole', I said; and it seemed suddenly plain that the flower itself was a part of the earth; that a ring enclosed what was the flower and that was the real flower; part earth; part flower. (Woolf, 1985, p.71)

Such 'moments of being' would seem to instantiate the unselfish attention that Auden identified with prayer when he wrote that 'To pray is to pay attention to, or, shall we say, to 'listen' to someone or something other than oneself' (op cit). But the philosophy that Woolf derives from her reflection on these moments– 'what I might call a philosophy; at any rate it is a constant idea of mine' (p.72) – is, nonetheless, one in which 'certainly and emphatically there is no God'. It is based on the realisation:

> that the whole world is a work of art; that we are parts of the work of art. *Hamlet* or a Beethoven quartet is the truth about this vast mass that we call the world. But there is no Shakespeare, there is no Beethoven; certainly and emphatically there is no God; we are the words; we are the music; we are the thing itself. And I see this when I have a shock. (p.72)

Rather than transplanting it from a Judaeo-Christian setting into a quasi-Buddhist one, the present essay asks whether the position advocated by Weil and Auden can be more thoroughly secularised. My sympathies are therefore with Woolf and Jamie, and my project has a great deal in common with that pursued by Iris Murdoch, in her 1964 essay 'On "God" and "Good"'. In that essay, Murdoch's 'central question' was not, in the first place, a question about secularisation. It was a more general question about the techniques that contribute to the crafting of a moral life. Murdoch states her question succinctly, albeit metaphorically:

> [A]re there any techniques for the purification and reorientation of an energy which is naturally selfish, in such a way that when moments of choice arrive we shall be sure of acting rightly? (Murdoch, 1970, p.53)

The 'techniques' that Murdoch considers first (as being, she says, 'much closer and more familiar' than those suggested by Plato) are 'the techniques of religion, of which the most widely practised is prayer'. It is this that leads her to ask 'What becomes of such a technique in a world without God [...]?'(*op cit*). I do not pretend to answer that question here, but – in trying to indicate the moral significance of salience – I do hope to articulate one understanding of the way in which an answer might be approached.

8.2.2 The Need for Moral Psychology

In the formulation of her question, and in approaching it through an enquiry into prayer without God, Murdoch was attempting to find a way of addressing the need that Elizabeth Anscombe had made prominent in her 1958 essay, 'Modern Moral Philosophy'. The need is one that Murdoch herself identifies, in her own essay's first paragraph. Whereas Anscombe began her 1958 essay by telling us that 'moral philosophy [...] should be laid aside at any rate until we have an adequate philosophy of psychology, in which we are conspicuously lacking' (Anscombe, 1958, p.1), Murdoch begins her 1964 piece with the thought that:

> A working philosophical psychology is needed which can at least attempt to connect modern psychology with a terminology concerned with virtue. (p.45)

The 'modern psychology' that Murdoch was attempting to connect with a terminology of virtue was, in large part, the psychology of Freud. She was attempting to bring into view 'a moral philosophy which can speak significantly of Freud and Marx, and out of which aesthetic and political views can be generated' (*op cit*). In the half-century since Murdoch was writing, the psychology that has become established has a very different set of methodological commitments, and a very different set of theoretical aims, but if the integration of Freudian psychology into our moral thinking no longer seems like an urgent need, that is not because the psychology by which Freud's work has been superseded speaks more immediately to the aesthetic and political needs that Murdoch had in mind, or to the casuistical concerns that motivated Anscombe.

I want to suggest that the findings of this recent psychology can nonetheless be 'connected with a terminology concerned with virtue', in much the way that Murdoch hoped. I also want to suggest that it is the concept of salience – with its intimate relationship to the concept of attention – that enables us to make such a connection. To make this last claim plausible, some work needs to be done. The connection between salience and virtue is obscure when we attempt to view it from one secularising perspective. It comes into view only when we see it in the light of some recent results concerning the way in which attention is modulated. In what follows, I first adopt the problematic perspective, since the problems created by it are instructive.

8.3 Do attentive people have different reasons from inattentive ones?

Much recent work in metaethics has been guided by the idea that we *ought* to do whatever we have most *reason* to do, and so has focussed on the attempt to give a naturalistic account of *reasons*, in the hope that we can account for at least some forms of moral importance by explaining the ways in which morally important things contribute to the reasons that we have (Schroeder, 2007). This suggests one way in which we might hope to account for the moral importance of attention and salience, without this account depending on the supernatural considerations that were implicated in Auden and Weil's talk of prayer. It suggests that we might bring the moral importance of attention into view by giving an account of the way in which salience introduces reasons.

Some reasons for action can be studied, both formally and empirically, using the vocabulary of game theory. The theory of two-person coordination games enables us to see that salience does play a role in enabling some of our cooperative achievements, but we shall see that it also reveals an explanatory difficulty: when we adopt the austerely secular stance that game theory affords, any *explanation* of salience's importance disappears from view. Two different lines of enquiry support these points; one empirical and one a priori. I examine both in what follows, before applying the lessons to be extracted from them to the ethical question with which we began.

8.3.1 Actions taken on the basis of their salience

During the first generation of philosophy's encounters with game theory, the role of salience in coordination games was a topic of some debate. The point in dispute was not whether salience contributes to the way in which coordination games are actually played. The experiments of Thomas Schelling provided support for the idea that it does (Schelling, 1960), and a more rigorous investigation by Judith Mehta and her collaborators puts this idea on a strong empirical footing (Mehta et al., 1994). Both lines of work show that, when people need to coordinate their behaviour with one another, they will pursue a course of action that is salient more often than they will when coordination is not required.

To examine this tendency to favour the salient, the participants in Mehta et al.'s experiment were given a questionnaire in which each question allowed for various responses: they were asked, for example, to name any flower, to name any British town or city, and to name any colour. Some participants were told to complete all of the questions so that they would be entered into a lottery. Others were told that they could win money only if their answers matched those that were being given by one of the other participants in the room, with whom they had been anonymously paired. These latter participants were therefore playing a game of non-communicative coordination. Their responses indicate a number of ways in which salience contributes to the coordination of behaviour.

Mehta et al.'s experiment included questions of various sorts, but one especially clear example is seen in the responses that were given to a question asking for the day and month of any day of the year. Of the ninety participants who were attempting to coordinate, forty picked 25th December (the experiment having taken place on the tenth of that month), as compared to five of the eighty-eight participants who were merely trying to answer all of the questions. (The statistically significant difference here is between 44.4% of the coordinating participants and 5.7% of the non-coordinating ones.) On the assumption that, in the UK in the second week of December, Christmas is a salient date, it would seem to be a tactic of favouring the salient that is enabling the participants in this experiment to coordinate. They succeed in doing so far better than they would have done had they been picking a date at random. Mehta *et al*'s experiment therefore illustrates one straightforward way in which salience can make a certain kind of interpersonal achievement possible, albeit in a rather artificial context.

8.3.2 Gilbert's Argument

Although Mehta's experiment shows that salience can facilitate coordination, there is room for disagreement as to how this facilitation should be understood. More specifically, there is room to question whether the role played by salience is one of providing a *reason* for the salient option to be preferred. If salience did indeed provide such a reason then, since reasons have a necessary connection to rationality (and the disregard of reasons to *irrationality*), a normatively laden charge could be brought against those who fail to opt for a salient choice. Their irrational failure to pick the salient option might not be a *moral* failure, but (on the assumption that one ought to do what one has most reason to do) we would at least have taken a step from a merely descriptive 'is' claim, to a normatively loaded 'ought'. Facts about salience would have been shown to have some normative significance, even if the extent of that significance had not yet been established.

But it is not at all clear that the way in which salience facilitates coordination is by providing reasons. The case for thinking that it is not was made in a 1989 article by Margaret Gilbert: Gilbert claims that the influence of salience should not be thought of as a rational influence, since the salience of an option does not suffice to give us any reason for choosing it. She summarises this position (adapting a remark of J. L. Mackie) by saying that 'salience in the sense at issue here is not *intrinsically action-guiding*' (Gilbert, 1989, p.70). Her argument, which I paraphrase below, is a simple and convincing one.

In developing this argument, the scenario that Gilbert considers is one in which two players each have to choose one colour from an array of several, with catastrophic consequences that can be averted only if the colours chosen are the same. If these players are unable to communicate then the best that they can do will be to take a chance that their independent picks coincide. Neither player, in that case, has any reason to prefer any one of the colours. Gilbert asks whether some reason to prefer a colour would be introduced if we added a source of salience to the example, perhaps by having one and only one of these colours be mentioned repeatedly, in a radio announcement that both players hear. Because the game is structured so that there can be no reason to favour a colour unless there are grounds for thinking that the other player will pick it, this salience-introducing announcement can make no rational difference unless it is known by both players that the other player heard it. More precisely: if the announcement is to be capable of making a rational difference then its occurrence must be *common knowledge*, in the sense introduced by David Lewis (Lewis, 1969): Each player must know what the announcement said, know that the other player knows this, know that the other player knows that he knows, and so on. Gilbert's claim is that, even if the salience-introducing announcement is heard by both players, with common knowledge of their both hearing it and of the announcement's effects on salience, this can still introduce no new reason for selecting one colour over the others.

To see Gilbert's argument for this, remember that the game is set up as a game of symmetric coordination, so that the known salience of an option gives each player a reason for choosing that option only if the player takes this salience to increase the other player's chances of choosing it. Any reason to choose the salient option would therefore depend on each player's having grounds for thinking that the other player will also choose it. But this leaves the set of reasons that weigh on each player unchanged. Even in the absence of any salience-introducing announcement, each player would have a reason to choose any option if there were a reason for thinking that this option would be chosen by the other. For each of the options that might be chosen, there was, therefore, a standoff: each would have been a good choice for both players if and only if it were chosen by the other. The salience-introducing announcement has made one of these standoffs conspicuous, but it has not thereby stopped it from being a standoff. The profile of reasons that each player faces remains unchanged, and so, Gilbert concludes, the contribution of salience needs to be understood as something other than a rational contribution:

> It seems that human agents tend to do their parts in a salient combination of action in an otherwise intractable coordination problem [...but...] this tendency cannot be explained as an expression of each agent's knowledge that, if a combination obviously stands out for all, then *ipso facto* each one has reason to do his part in it. (p.73)

Gilbert's point is that this last proposition cannot be known, because it isn't true, and so that knowledge of it cannot explain success.

This argument suggests that the person who finds some things salient has the same reasons as the person who does not, and so that the introduction of salience does not introduce new reasons. If we endorse the metaethicists' plausible assumption that there is always a reason to do what one ought, this suggests that the introduction of salience to our picture of the mind must be something other than a normative matter. Salience can play a helpful role in determining what one is likely to do, but it cannot change one's conception of what one ought to do. No argument of this sort could show that Weil and Auden's ideas must be mistaken. Nor could it show those ideas to be unsecularizable. What Gilbert's argument does show is that a secularised defence of these ideas would need to draw on details that our game-theoretic picture has so far omitted.

8.3.3 Communication and the Problem of Coordinated Attack

One of the things omitted by the game-theoretic picture, as we have so far considered it, is any account of the way in which those who are coordinating their behaviours might communicate. This omission is perfectly sensible, for the purposes of making a game-theoretic point. It is also quite artificial: the possibility of communication is omitted by stipulation from Gilbert's thought experiment, and by design from the real-world experiment of Mehta *et al*. If communication were permitted in an actual experimental setting then the coordination of actions would cease to be problematic (and to that extent the experiment would cease to be interesting). All that would be needed would be for one player to suggest that the date to be named should be Christmas Day, or that the colour to be chosen should be red, and for the other player to agree to this suggestion. A communicated suggestion about any other day, or any other colour, would do just as well, whether or not that option is otherwise salient.

Allowing for communication might therefore seem to have the consequence that salience drops out of our explanation for how coordination is achieved. And this might seem to suggest that salience is much less important than we have been supposing, since salience has a role to play only in the artificial case where communication is suspended. A return to the world of thought-experiment enables us to see why this appearance is misleading, by showing that something similar to the puzzle from Gilbert's case remains, even when communication is possible. Salience does continue to have a role, and the rational basis of that role remains problematic.

To see this, we need to modify Gilbert's thought experiment, so as to create a scenario with the form of a 'coordinated attack problem', of the sort discussed by Joseph Halpern (Halpern, 1986; Halpern and Moses, 1990), and – more recently and more philosophically – by John Campbell (Campbell, 2002). In the scenario that Gilbert originally considered the two players each had to pick an option, something catastrophic would happen unless they picked the same one, and the players were unable to communicate. We can give this scenario the features required for a coordinated attack problem if we introduce the possibility of each player refraining from picking any option, and if we stipulate that the result of both of them refraining is not as bad as the result of their picking different options, and not as good as the result of both players picking the same non-refraining option. We should also introduce the possibility of our players communicating.

Once communication has been introduced it would be quite natural for one player to suggest an option – 'Let's go for the red one!' – and for the other player to agree. It is very likely that coordination would then be achieved, as it very likely would be in Gilbert's original scenario, once an announcement had made one of the options salient. The question, in both cases, is whether the resulting coordination would be a rational achievement, so that a player who failed to play his part in it would be open to the charge of irrationality (and so of not doing what, by his own lights, he *ought*). We have seen Gilbert's argument suggesting that in her scenario the achievement of coordination would not be rational. To see that the achievement of coordination would still fail to be rational in our modified scenario, where communication has been introduced, consider the importance of the first player's suggestion being acknowledged.

It is not yet rational for you to pick an option merely because you have suggested that it be picked. Suggesting an option gives you a reason to then go ahead and pick that option only if your suggestion has been received and agreed to. Equally, for the player who receives a suggestion, agreeing to that suggestion does not yet make it rational to go ahead and pick the suggested option, unless this agreement is itself recognised and understood: if my following through on your suggestion is to be rational, it is not enough for me to privately think that the suggestion is a good one. Suggestions always need to be agreed upon, and agreements always need to be acknowledged. But the problem can then be reiterated, even after these agreements and acknowledgements are in place. The communication of a suggestion and the communication of an agreement to that suggestion are not yet enough to make the selection of the suggested option rational. Nor can any finite number of iterations remove the problem. This is the 'problem of coordinated attack' (Halpern and Moses, 1990).

The problem, in a coordinated attack scenario, is not just that there is some fact of which infinitely iterated common knowledge is required, so that it only becomes rational for me to act on that fact once I know that you know that I know that you know ... the fact in question. Such knowledge *can* be attained, albeit in a tacit form, by a finite route.[1] But the availability of such knowledge does not remove our present problem. Even if all of the facts given in the coordinated-attack scenario are commonly known, we will still need to establish common knowledge of a new fact. The fact needing to be known is not that I have made a suggestion as to which option we might pick, but that this is the option that I *am going to* pick. The difficulty here is not in getting this fact out into the open. The difficulty is that there is no rational basis on which this can become a fact in the first place. It isn't yet true that I am going to pick the suggested option, until I know that the suggestion to pick it has been received and acknowledged, nor until that acknowledgement has been received and acknowledged, nor until that further acknowledgement has been received and acknowledged. And so on. The coordinated attack scenario is one in which communication provides a way of *making* an option salient, but the coordination of behaviour onto that salient option still seems not to be rational. Salience therefore remains at a distance from the normative.

8.3.4 Locating the operations of salience

The conclusion that these game-theoretic considerations force upon us is that, if our secularised picture of the mind is a picture of people acting on the basis of known reasons in order to optimise anticipated outcomes, then it is a picture that struggles to account for the salience-involving way in which we do in fact coordinate our behaviour, both in the absence of communication and in its presence. Since we do in fact coordinate our behaviour successfully and easily, and since many of our actual achievements seem to depend on salience-mediated coordination, this picture of the mind must be one from which something has gone missing. The missing thing is normative, in the sense that it pertains to our reasons for acting, and so pertains to our understanding of what it is that we ought to do.

Taken in combination, the above arguments give us an updated version of the problem that was identified by Murdoch. After having sketched a picture in which 'Our personal being is the movement of our overtly choosing will' (p.7), Murdoch wrote:

> I find the image of man which I have sketched above both alien and implausible. That is, more precisely: I have simple empirical objections (I do not think people are necessarily or essentially 'like that'), I have philosophical objections (I do not find the arguments convincing), and I have moral objections (I do not think people *ought* to picture themselves in this way). [...] it cannot be so, something vital is missing. (p.9)

Our present position, in light of the arguments above, is similar. The picture that game theory sets before us is one in which a range of options is given, each with its expected pay-off attached. The resulting reasons for opting are weighed, more or less intelligently, and some choice is arrived at, which ought or ought not to be made. We have seen that the importance of salience goes missing from this picture. Here too the missing thing appears to be 'something vital', since the empirical studies show (what is already plausible) that salience does play a role.

This should not be taken as a reason to think that our game-theoretic tools have no use here. It is because those tools *do* gauge our reasons for picking amongst given options that their failure to register the importance of salience is revealing. Since game theory gauges our reasons for picking among given options, but does not register the importance of salience, the role of salience cannot be a role that gets played when we are picking amongst the options that have been given. Its role must instead be understood as a role in determining the way in which those options are given. The morally significant phenomenon here is not within the psychology of our choosing, but in the framing of the choices to be made.

This last line of thought corresponds to one of Murdoch's main complaints against the Francophone and Anglophone traditions between which she was working:

> The agent, thin as a needle, appears [in these traditions] in the quick flash of the choosing will. [...] Sartre tells us that when we deliberate the die is already cast, and Oxford philosophy has developed no serious theory of motivation. The agent's freedom, indeed his moral quality, resides in his choices, and yet we are not told what prepares him for the choices. [...]
>
> What we really are seems much more like an obscure system of energy out of which choices and visible acts of will emerge at intervals in ways which are often unclear, and often dependent on the condition of the system in between the moments of choice. (pp.52–53)

The preceding arguments suggest that Murdoch is right about all of this: our attempt to identify the moral quality of salience will not find that quality to reside in an agent's action of choosing. That quality will instead be found in the 'obscure energy' that 'operates in between moments of choice'. The psychological work that has become established since Murdoch was writing casts light on this 'obscure system of energy'. Such work employs methods that are very different from the methods of Freudian psychology, with which Murdoch herself engaged. By enabling us to see what for Murdoch were 'unclear' ways in which our 'visible acts' depend on 'the condition of the system in between the moments of choice', it begins to make clear the connection between salience and virtue.

8.4 Recent Discoveries about the Determinants of Salience

The methods used by cognitive psychologists to study attention typically employ tasks where simple stimuli are presented, and simple responses are made. These tasks do little to engage their participants' sense of the 'authentic and pure values — truth, beauty and goodness', of which Weil wrote. But neither Weil nor Murdoch nor Auden would take this to be evidence that the subject has been changed, so that 'attention' as a term of art in current psychology denotes something other than the morally-significant attention that they were lauding. We have seen that Weil was explicitly concerned with the form of attention that we cultivate when completing a problem in geometry, or when writing a Latin prose. It was central to her position that, despite these being tasks in which nothing morally important would seem to be at stake, the forms of attention that they solicit are morally significant. Auden also mentions attention to geometric proofs (*op cit*). Murdoch inherits this idea from Weil, most immediately, but also, and explicitly, from Plato. It is in connection with the study of mathematics – ('the τέχνη (techne) which Plato thought was most important' (p.87)) – and with the study of language – ('a τέχνη more congenial to myself' (*op cit*)) – that she writes 'studying is normally an exercise of virtue as well as of talent, and shows a fundamental way in which virtue is related to the real world'.

The other authors that we have mentioned are also concerned with the attention that is found in mundane contexts. Jamie's prayer-like attention was directed on the flecked tweed of a skirt; Woolf's 'moment of being' was occasioned by a flowerbed. The things to which attention is paid in our psychological experiments are, in typical cases, morally undistinguished things, but this is no reason to think that those experiments reveal nothing about the form of attention to which moral importance has been attributed, in the tradition of moral thinking that I am here trying to perpetuate. That tradition is one in which the direction of attention onto everyday things *is* taken to be morally significant. It contains no suggestion that attention needs to be paid to morally valuable things, in order to itself be valuable. On the contrary: the paradigms of valuable attention that these writers identify are cases in which attention is paid to things that have little value independently of the attention that they occasion.

Nor is it a disqualification from such moral significance that the attention paid in our psychological experiments is typically a solitary matter, by which no other people are affected for better or for worse. This, again, is a feature that is shared by the paradigm cases that were identified by Woolf, Jamie, and others. It is a feature the significance of which Weil notes, puzzles over, and affirms:

> Solitude. Where does its value lie? For in solitude we are in the presence of mere matter (even the sky, the stars, the moon, trees in blossom), things of less value (perhaps) than a human spirit. Its value lies in the greater possibility of attention. (p.26)

Several decades of psychological experimentation have by now revealed a great deal about the circumstances in which simple sensory attention can be paid. They have revealed a great deal about the effects of its being paid, and about the kinematics of its allocation. Some results of this research pertain to factors contributing to the salience structure that comes to be imposed on the perceived world (where 'salience' is understood, as above, as the propensity for receiving attention). Those results suggest that the form of this salience structure owes something to one's previous perceptual engagements, so that a discipline of geometric proofs or of Latin prose compositions might indeed provide a 'gymnastics of the attention', whereby the mind is prepared for subsequent encounters. This is not simply a matter of things becoming salient because we are in the habit of looking for them: it is, in part, the independent structure of things, and not only our intentions with regard to them, that gives this salience structure its form. Some of the factors contributing to that structure are things of which the attentive person is not aware, even when that person *is* aware of the particular stimuli to which she is attentive. It will be helpful to consider some elementary examples of this. (Further discussion can be found in Mole, 2020 and Kentridge, 2011.)

In a 2007 experiment, Mulckhuyse, Talsma, and Theeuwes examined the way in which the sudden appearance of a thing can call attention to it (Mulckhuyse et al., 2007). The participants in this experiment were asked to respond, as rapidly as possible, to a stimulus that was flashed up on a screen where three grey circles had previously appeared (Mulckhuyse et al., 2007). On some occasions, one or other of these circles appeared 16ms earlier than the others. This difference – (a difference of 1.6% of a second) – is too small to be consciously noticed. It nonetheless seems to influence the speed with which subsequent stimuli get processed: if the stimulus to which participants must respond appears at the location of the circle that had an earlier onset, then the participants' reaction times in response to that stimulus are reduced. Although this fractionally earlier onset time makes no appearance in consciousness, it does seem to make one of the stimuli salient, so that this stimulus is more apt to receive attention than the others.

Such unconsciously registered contributors to salience need not be simple or transient. A recent series of studies by Jiaying Zhao and her collaborators illustrates their potential complexity. In a 2015 experiment, Yu and Zhao sat their participants in front of a computer screen, on which two series of stimuli were presented (Yu and Zhao, 2015). For some participants there was one stream of stimuli at the top and one at the bottom; for others, there was one stream on the left and one on the right. If the participant was being shown stimuli on the left and right then the locations at the top and bottom of the screen contained grey squares (and vice versa, if they were being shown stimuli in the locations at the top and bottom). There were, therefore, four marked locations, and in two of these, a sequence of stimuli was appearing, with the stimuli in these two locations being meaningless symbols of different sorts. Each pair of stimuli appeared for 750ms, followed by a pause of the same duration. These two stimulus streams were intermittently interrupted by three Ls, and one T shape, variously rotated, with one shape in each location. When these interruptions occurred, the participants were to press a button, indicating the direction in which the one T shaped stimulus was pointing. This is illustrated in Figure 8.1.

In each of the two locations where a stimulus stream was being presented, nine different stimuli were used. The ordering of these stimuli was not entirely random. In one location their order was subject only to the constraint that no stimulus was ever followed by itself. In the other location, the nine stimuli were grouped into three triples. The order in which these three triples were presented was random, but the order of stimuli within each triple was never changed: A was always followed by B and then C; D always followed by E and then F.; etc. The participants were not aware of this. By analysing the reaction times to the intermittent, T-orientation task, Yu and Zhao were able to show that the

154 Christopher Mole

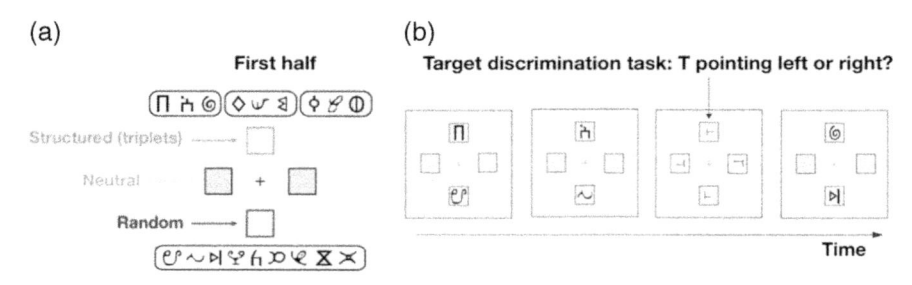

(a)   (b)
         First half   **Target discrimination task: T pointing left or right?**

Figure 8.1 The basic paradigm of Yu and Zhao (2015). Thanks to Jiaying Zhao for providing this figure.

attention of these participants had nonetheless been drawn to the location in which the stimuli were ordered less randomly. The presence of such statistical regularity therefore seems to be a contributor to salience, even when we are not consciously looking for a regularity, are not performing a task in which this regularity is relevant, and have no conscious awareness of any such regularity being present.

Variations on this basic paradigm show that the effect of regularities on salience exhibits a form of inertia. Once the existence of a statistical regularity at one location has made that location salient, it will remain salient, even after the stimuli in that location revert to a random ordering. This regularity-displaying location will also remain salient (although to a lesser degree), even if the other, previously random, stream now starts to display a regularity: new statistical regularities have been observed to pull salience away from previously-regular locations only when these new regularities are displayed by stimuli of previously unseen types.

The factors contributing to the extent and duration of these inertia-like effects are a topic of ongoing research. For our present purposes, the points to notice are just that it is relatively easy to impose a salience structure on the perceived scene; that it is relatively hard to change that structure, once it has been imposed; and that the factors determining such a structure need not figure in conscious awareness, or in the attentive subject's intentions.

The salience structure in Yu and Zhao's experiments prioritises one location over others, where each of these locations corresponds to a perceptibly demarcated region of the screen. In other cases, the salience structure that is determined by an unnoticed regularity does more than this. In a 2017 study, Lau and Zhao presented their participants with stimuli like those that are shown in figure two (Zhao and Yu, 2017). These are stimuli in which a global shape (which might be a square or a diamond) is made up of local shapes, which might or might not match the global shape, but which always match each other. In some conditions the participants were asked to indicate the global shape, in others they were asked to indicate the local shape. Each local square or diamond was given in a different, easily recognisable colour. There were statistical

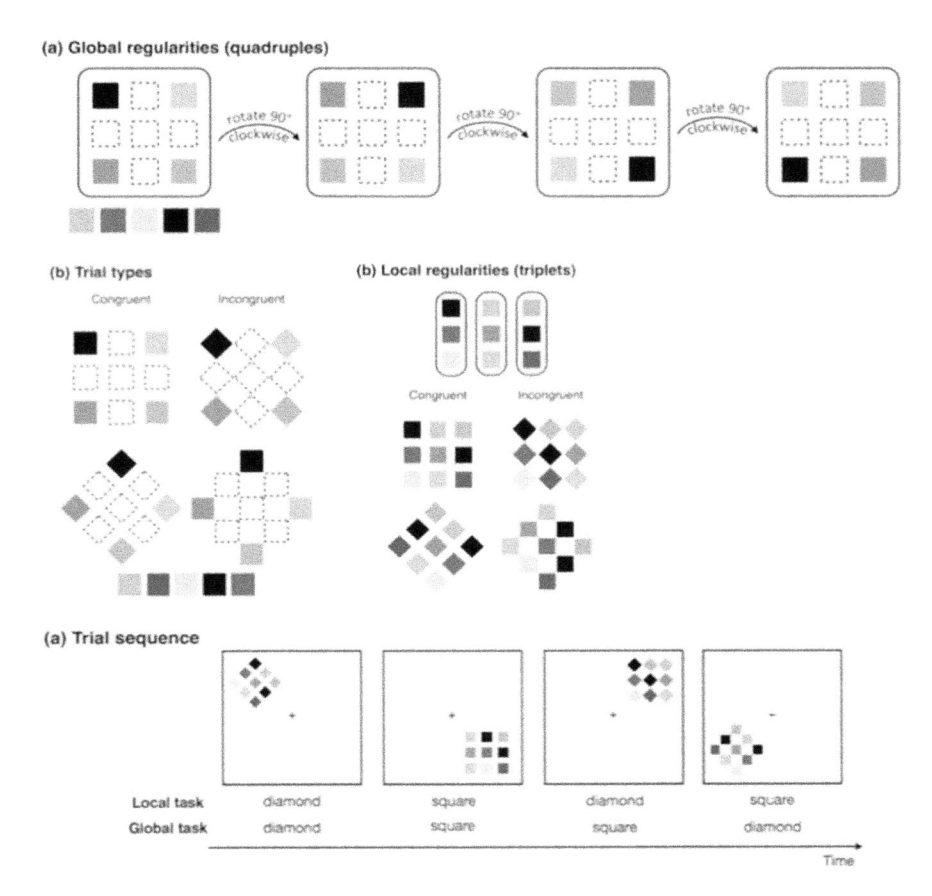

Figure 8.2 Local and global regularities make local or global shapes salient. Reprinted by permission from Springer, Attention, Perception, & Psychophysics "Statistical regularities guide the spatial scale of attention" Jiaying Zhao et al., 2016.

regularities in these colourings, although, as in the previous experiments, the participants were not told about them.

Two different types of regularity were used. For one regularity there were triples of colours that always occurred together in the same sequence, as a row or a column. These triples would appear randomly at the top, middle, or bottom of the global shape. For the other regularity, a quartet of colours always occurred in the four corners of the global shape, with the order of the colours being preserved, although their rotation could vary. (The figure illustrating this can be found here: https://tinyurl.com/v4esp526.) When asked about them at the experiment's end, most of the participants did not claim to have noticed these regularities. Those who did claim to have noticed them were unable to say what the regularities had been (although, in the case of the local regularity, these participants did perform better than chance when asked to distinguish, on the basis of 'familiarity', between those shapes that did and did not display this regularity).

Each of these non-random conditions was compared to a condition in which the colouring was genuinely random. This revealed that the presence of a local regularity increases the speed at which the participants were able to name the local shape, as compared to their speed when there is no regularity, and that the presence of a global regularity increases the speed at which participants were able to name the global shape, as compared to their speed when there is no regularity. Participants are faster to identify the local shape than the global one when there are local regularities. They are faster to identify the global shape than the local one when there are global regularities.

8.5 Salience as a Lab-Model of Moral Attention

The experiments of cognitive psychology are almost always open to different interpretations, depending on whether one takes them to demonstrate some elementary version of a phenomenon that plays a role in life outside of the laboratory, or takes them only as an indication of the way that minds behave when the abnormally sparse conditions of a controlled experiment are imposed upon them. If we do extrapolate from the effects demonstrated by Zhao et al., and take them to be a model of the way in which salience operates in the real world, then this last experiment exhibits two effects that deserve to be regarded as significant, in the context of our earlier discussion. The experiment shows that the question of whether a participant's thinking will prioritise the local or the global features of a situation is determined, in part, by their prior experience of regularities. It thereby confirms that the salience structure of a scene is determined in part by the statistical regularities of that scene, in ways that do not require these regularities to figure in the consciousness of the attentive person. The experiment also shows that this salience structure is not merely a prioritisation of some locations over others.

The salience structure resulting from those regularities imposes constraints on the level of aggregation at which attention's targets will be selected. It therefore operates in the place where our Murdochian considerations suggested valuable attention might be found: It does not give us reasons, but it does modulate the way in which our attention will tend to be directed. This salience structure – this 'web of noticing' in Jamie's phrase – is imposed on the world over the course of our encounter with it, in a way that makes some things more apt to receive our attention than others. The structure displays inertia. Its form is determined in part by the regularities in the things to which we direct our attention, without those regularities needing to figure in our plans or reasoning. Our mere attentive engagement with things can thereby shape the decisions we make about that world, in ways that can be obscure to the person who makes these decisions. To this extent, Zhao's experiments provide a laboratory model for the phenomenon that Murdoch identified when she spoke of the obscure energies that operate between moments of choice. It is, in Murdoch's view, on the operation of these energies that our capacity for moral action depends:

> If we ignore the prior work of attention and notice only the emptiness of the moment of choice we are likely to identify freedom with the outward movement since there is nothing else to identify it with. But if we consider what the work of attention is like, how continuously it goes on, and how imperceptibly it builds up structures of value around us, we shall not be surprised that at crucial moments of choice most of the business of choosing is already over. This does not imply that we are not free, certainly not. But it implies that the exercise of freedom is a small piecemeal business which goes on all the time and not a grandiose leaping about unimpeded at important moments. (Murdoch, 1970, p.36)

I hope it is obvious to the reader that, although I am attempting to vindicate a tradition in which attention is associated with the value of prayer, my intention is not to suggest that participants in a simple laboratory experiment are engaged in a practice that displays the subtleties of any contemplative discipline. The point is only that we should no longer think of the mechanisms by which such disciplines cultivate virtue as if they were 'an obscure system of energies'. 'The work of attention continuously goes on', as Murdoch says, and it 'imperceptibly builds up structures of value around us'. How, then, should we reply, when Jamie asks whether 'the care and maintenance of the web of our noticing, the paying heed' is not a kind of prayer? Considerations of the sort evoked here cannot hope to provide grounds for an unequivocal answer, but they do suggest that the care and maintenance of the web of our noticing is one context in which a value of prayer can be made explicable and apparent.

Note

1 It was David Lewis who first explained this route, in his 1969 book on convention (Lewis, 1969). Lewis notes that one can be credited with knowledge of a fact that one has not explicitly formulated, if one knows facts from which this unformulated fact obviously follows. That principle can be applied recursively, from a basis of commonplace assumptions about other people's cognitive capacities, to secure arbitrarily large iterations of common knowledge.

References

Anderson, B. 2011. There Is No Such Thing as Attention. *Frontiers in Psychology* 2: 246.
Anscombe, G. E. M. 1958. Modern Moral Philosophy. *Philosophy* 33(124): 1–19.
Campbell, J. 2002. *Reference and Consciousness*. Oxford University Press, Oxford.
Davis, J. and Thompson, E. 2015. Developing Attention and Decreasing Affective Bias: Toward a Cross-Cultural Cognitive Science of Mindfulness. In K. W. Brown, J. D.

Creswell and R. M. Ryan (Eds.), *Handbook of Mindfulness* (pp. 42–61). Guilford Press, New York.

Evans, G. 1982. *The Varieties of Reference*. The Clarendon Press, Oxford.

Gilbert, M. 1989. Rationality and Salience. *Philosophical Studies* 57(1): 61–77.

Halpern, J. H. and Moses, Y. 1990. Knowledge and Common Knowledge in a Distributed Environment. *Journal of the ACM* 37(3): 549–587.

Halpern, J. Y. 1986. Reasoning About Knowledge: An Overview. In J. Y. Halpern (Ed.), *TARK '86 Proceedings of the 1986 conference on Theoretical aspects of reasoning about knowledge*. Morgan Kaufmann Publishers Inc, San Francisco.

Hecht, A. 2003. *Melodies Unheard: Essays on the Mystery of Poetry*. The Johns Hopkins University Press, Baltimore.

Jamie, K. 2005. *Findings*. Sort of Books, London.

Kentridge, R. W. 2011. Attention Without Awareness: A Brief Review. In C. Mole, D. Smithies and W. Wu (Eds.), *Attention: Philosophical and Psychological Essays* (pp. 228–246). Oxford University Press, New York.

Lewis, D. 1969. *Convention: A Philosophical Study*. Harvard University Press, Cambridge, MA.

Mehta, J., Starmer, C. and Robert, S. 1994. The Nature of Salience: An Experimental Investigation of Pure Coordination Games. *The American Economic Review* 84(3): 658–673.

Mole, C. 2011. *Attention Is Cognitive Unison: An Essay in Philosophical Psychology*. Oxford University Press, New York.

Mole, C. 2020. Consciousness and Attention. In U. Kriegel (Ed.), *Oxford Handbook of the Philosophy of Consciousness* (pp. 499–519). Oxford University Press, London.

Mulckhuyse, M., Talsma, D. and Theeuwes, J. 2007. Grabbing Attention Without Knowing: Automatic Capture of Attention by Subliminal Spatial Cues. *Visual Cognition* 15(7): 779–788.

Murdoch, I. 1956. Knowing the Void. *The Spectator* (196), 2 November. pp. 613–614. Reprinted in I. Murdoch (Ed. P. Conradi), 1997, Existentialists and Mystics pp. 157–160. Penguin, London.

Murdoch, I. 1970. *The Sovereignty of Good*. Routledge, London.

Schelling, T. 1960. *The Strategy of Conflict*. Harvard University Press, Cambridge, MA.

Schroeder, M. 2007. *Slaves of the Passions*. Oxford University Press, Oxford.

Weil, S. 1986. *Simone Weil: An Anthology*. Grove Press, New York.

Woolf, V. 1985. *Moments of Being: A Collection of Autobiographical Writing*. Harcourt, London.

Wu, W. 2014. *Attention*. Routledge, Oxford.

Yu, R. Q. and Zhao, J. 2015. The Persistence of the Attentional Bias to Regularities in a Changing Environment. *Attention, Perception, and Psychophysics* 77(7): 2217–2228.

Zhao, J. and Yu, L. 2017. Statistical Regularities Guide the Spatial Scale of Attention. *Attention, Perception, and Psychophysics* 79(1): 24–30.

9 The unquiet life: Salience and moral responsibility

Sabina Lovibond

9.1 Too much information

'Human kind cannot bear very much reality', as T. S. Eliot (poetically, but plausibly) observes.[1] This state of affairs, no doubt, can be understood in terms of our psychological as well as our moral limitations. Thus at any given moment, according to Richard Wiseman, we 'only have the processing power to look at a very small part of [our] surroundings'; the brain 'quickly identifies what it considers to be the most significant aspects', and 'focuses almost all of its attention on these elements'.[2] So even at the level of sensory awareness, it would appear that we enjoy some natural defences against the hazard of too much information. In this sense, to say that we automatically restrict or edit our exposure to 'reality' is analogous to commenting on the natural tendency to stabilise our body temperature by seeking warmth when cold, or conversely: to select some of our experiential input, from moment to moment, as 'salient' at the expense of the rest is a functional imperative for the human animal.

But the human animal, being prone to reflection and self-criticism, cannot treat this as the end of the matter. Having noted empirically – and hence raised to consciousness – the selective mechanism just mentioned, one is led to ask: what practical claims, if any, does this consciousness impose? Are there better and worse ways – even, perhaps, right and wrong ways – of regulating the mental powers that determine what is salient for us?

9.2 Salience and practical reason

The potential interest of the idea of salience for moral philosophy – that is, for the normative or idealising (as distinct from the purely descriptive) study of our moral life – has made itself felt most strongly within a neo-Aristotelian frame of reference. Its role here has been to articulate what the 'practically wise' person excels at doing; to specify the skill (which is not of a merely technical kind) possessed by the skilful deliberator. Taking a lead from the Aristotelian tradition, we can think of this person as someone who is good at constructing 'practical syllogisms', or more accurately, good at thinking in the way of which the practical syllogism offers a (however stylised) reconstruction. This means:

DOI: 10.4324/9781351202114-10

drawing upon one's general principles, concerns, or evaluative convictions so as to connect these with the particular, concrete situation at hand. ('One mustn't antagonise people unnecessarily ... it would really annoy her to be reminded about last week ... so I won't mention it.') However, the contrarian feature of this approach (in contrast, for example, to that of consequentialist ethics) is its insistence on the ultimately 'uncodifiable' nature of what is known or understood by someone who can be relied on to get these things right: its acceptance (in effect, from Aristotle) of the thought that you can arrive at practical wisdom only through a process of habituation, which occurs – all being well – in the ordinary course of upbringing; and which prepares you to deal, in the general spirit of that upbringing, with an indefinite variety of real-life practical demands.

Addressing the question of how an uncodified, quasi-Aristotelian practical reason can engage with lived experience, John McDowell has written as follows:

> Acting in the light of a conception of how to live requires selecting and acting on the right concern ... [But] if there is more than one concern that might impinge on [a given] situation, there is more than one fact about the situation that the agent might, say, dwell on, in such a way as to summon an appropriate concern into operation. It is by virtue of seeing this particular fact rather than that one as the salient fact about the situation that he is moved to act by this concern rather than that one ... A conception of how to live shows itself, when more than one concern might issue in action, in one's seeing, or being brought to be able to see, one fact rather than another as salient. And our understanding of such a conception enters into our understanding of actions ... by enabling us to share, or at least comprehend, the agent's perception of saliences.[3]

The 'conception of how to live' that is the main object of interest in this discussion is, of course, the one exemplified by the virtuous or practically wise individual envisaged in Aristotelian ethical theory and its modern analogues – that is, in the kind of approach that understands 'practical reason' as something culturally embedded. It is not that exposure to the inherited values and ideals of our culture is in any way guaranteed, on this view, to equip us with an unerring eye for the morally salient facts of a situation; but to the extent that we make progress in moral understanding, it will become progressively more true to say that what ought to be salient for us in this or that deliberative context actually is salient. This quality of accuracy in the 'perception of saliences' – not just in a spirit of calculation, but by the standard of an *ethically informed* consciousness – is a powerful criterion of good character.

Clearly by invoking the idea of perception in relation to moral phenomena, and thus accepting the implicit suggestion that individuals may vary (among themselves or from one moment to another) in their perceptual capacities, we will be speaking on the basis of some 'moral realist' assumptions: not necessarily on the basis of any controversial metaphysical doctrine, but at any rate on the assumption that one's judgement with regard to the ethically salient can be better or worse, and requires monitoring. Such monitoring may be imagined on paternalist lines: in the original Platonic-Aristotelian picture it is not only children, but a majority of adults too, who need to be steered towards the formation and maintenance of virtuous habits; and these will include the habitual patterns of observation, the intuitive sense of importance, that we bring to bear on our surroundings. But the effort to apply these principles to one's own thinking can also figure in an autonomous 'ethics of vision' (or attention), as developed in recent times by Simone Weil and Iris Murdoch.[4]

9.3 Involuntary wrongs

However, my concern in this paper is not so much with any positive ideal of practical wisdom as with the attempt to avoid wrongdoing – an aspect of the 'good life' that gives rise to some perhaps less familiar issues of salience.

We can begin by considering whether 'wrongdoing' is in fact the most appropriate heading under which to discuss this topic. One might think: if what I want is a clear conscience, surely I can be confident of achieving this by simply not *doing* anything wrong? But that is less of a truism than it may appear. It is not even incontrovertible when modified to take account of the wrongness of (deliberately) 'passing by on the other side'[5] – a modification which yields the seemingly commonsensical view that we are morally responsible only for our voluntary *acts and omissions*: that is, for what we choose (or try, or intend) to do or omit. One philosopher unconvinced by this view is Robert Merrihew Adams, who holds, on the contrary, that there are some states of mind for which we are responsible which are not even within our *indirect* voluntary control – say, by being foreseeable consequences of our acts and omissions in the past. He thus defends the uncomfortable claim that there are 'involuntary sins'.[6]

As befits a philosopher of religion, Adams tells us in a footnote to the relevant paper that he has 'no wish to disavow the theological connotations of the term ["sin"]'. However, he says that he does not mean to base any part of his argument on these, but will use 'sin' simply as a shorthand term for 'any action, omission or state that is inherently blameworthy'.[7] So far as I can judge, he is as good as his word; but since I cannot share his relaxed attitude to the presence of theistic language within general-purpose moral philosophy, I will switch from now on to 'involuntary wrongs' as a label for the item under discussion – acquiescing, though, in the suggestion that 'wrongs' may not be fully accounted for by instances of wrong*doing*.[8]

The claim being put to us, then, has to do with moral responsibility, where an action for which I am 'responsible' means – in respect of bad actions – one for which I am legitimately open to blame; and where 'blame' is co-ordinated with the general idea of moral fault. According to this picture, *reproach* is a form of blame; and we can sometimes be reproached – and hence blamed – for what is involuntary. Thus ingratitude, disrespect and suchlike failings are all liable to incur reproach; and these are not attributes we *choose* to have.

But now of course we need a principle by which the sphere of legitimate reproach can be delimited (since, for example, an accidental injury – though undesirable – will normally fall outside it).[9] In order to motivate drawing the boundary in a way that will warrant the recognition of involuntary wrongs, Adams starts by noting that the candidates for such recognition are all *states of mind*, and moreover, states of mind that have an *intentional object*. He then proceeds to argue that the main idea behind the attempt to tie blame to the voluntary, namely that 'we cannot be responsible for anything unless some of its springs or causes lie within us in an appropriate way', can be retained in a theory of involuntary wrongs by holding that

> among states of mind that have intentional objects, the ones for which we are directly responsible are those in which we are responding, consciously or unconsciously, to data that are rich enough to permit a fairly adequate ethical appreciation of the state's intentional object and of the object's place in the fabric of personal relationships.[10]

So his key move is to '[relate] responsibility to the possibility of ethical appreciation'.[11] And he ends by tentatively envisaging the revival of a doctrine of 'substance causation', according to which 'we as substances, endowed with the power to respond to certain objects with either love or hate, acceptance or rejection, are the causes of the involuntary states for which we are morally responsible' – so that 'the springs or causes of everything for which we are responsible lie within us in an appropriate way'.[12] We should keep faith, therefore, with the intuition that it is wrong to hold a person responsible for what is *not caused by*, and therefore *does not reflect on*, that person–but we should acknowledge that what reflects on us in the relevant way goes beyond the voluntary. In particular, Adams could presumably agree that what reflects on us ethically extends to the quality of our 'perception of saliences'. This appeal to perception would flow from a more general view of ethics as concerned not just with juridical questions of right or wrong action, but with the rectitude of what we are for or against 'in our hearts'.[13]

9.4 Ethical data

Evidently there are some points in the 'involuntary wrongs' model that call for clarification. As Adams acknowledges,[14] the phrase 'data that are rich enough to permit a fairly adequate ethical appreciation' may catch the eye as an obvious trigger for controversy. What sort of ethical appreciation qualifies as 'fairly adequate', and how rich do our data have to be to permit this? But in fact the phrase just quoted raises only the kind of difficulties that occur routinely in the business of conceptual elucidation. Thus (to stay close to the topic in hand) when we try to determine questions of responsibility by asking what a *reasonable person* would have done or believed in some given circumstances, we are not replacing a controversial question with a non-controversial one, but rather with a different – yet putatively equivalent – controversial question on which more progress may be possible. So I shall not baulk at 'rich enough' or 'fairly adequate', which are no more problematic in their bearing on moral epistemology than the idea of (objectively) salient features of a situation. Instead, I want to pause over the notion of states of mind in which we are responding, *consciously or unconsciously*, to ethical 'data' that come up to this (admittedly somewhat indeterminate) standard.

An important question is whether 'responding unconsciously' can include, as a limiting case, failure to respond at all. Some comments by Adams seem to indicate that for him the answer is yes. He says that although his proposal to link responsibility to the possibility of ethical appreciation is to some extent traditional, it parts company with the traditional theories in that 'whereas [these] are concerned with *conscious* recognition of the badness of the act', his own criterion 'demands only that the data to which we are responding be rich enough to *permit* recognition of the relevant values.'[15] This implies, and I think is intended to imply, the following claim: a person is guilty of involuntary wrong whenever they are presented with data rich enough to permit the recognition of certain values, and yet they fail–albeit through inattention, and therefore unconsciously – to register those values, and hence to respond adequately to the data. It now becomes urgent to ask: what constitutes being *presented*, for the purpose of this kind of judgement, with ethical data? Or in the idiom of the present discussion: under what conditions can we say that such data are objectively salient with respect to any given person, so as to exert a moral claim on that person?

The least exacting answer would be that I am 'presented' with an ethical datum *d*, or that I ought to experience it as salient, when–but only when – *d* forces itself upon my awareness. So it would be feasible (on this account) to avoid being 'presented' with *d* by taking evasive action–for example, by crossing the street in order to avoid a beggar, or (better still, as it were, in pharisaical terms) by taking a different route where no beggars are likely to impinge even on one's peripheral vision.[16]

Although Adams touches on this question only glancingly, I think it is clear that his inclination is to deal with it in a more demanding style. He considers, but rejects, the suggestion that someone 'bred up from childhood in the Hitler *Jugend*' might not be culpable for their resulting moral ignorance. So, for instance, we would not accept this from an army officer as an excuse for failing to understand his duties to non-combatants. Adams holds that no matter how such a person came by his evil beliefs, they 'are a part of who he is, morally, and make him a fitting object of reproach'.[17] He explains this view only to the extent of saying that the offender 'has rich enough data in his evidence of the humanity of the non-combatants in question, even if he is never told that they have rights'.[18] In the abstract, this explanation seems rather weak, since it is notoriously possible to condition people for military or colonialist purposes to discount the *prima facie* obvious humanity of the 'enemy' (or of the 'subject race'). But I take it the underlying thought – and this thought is surely not, in itself, a weak one – is that when it comes to attributing moral responsibility, what can be said to be 'presented' to us comprises not only those data with which we are forcibly confronted by personal experience, or spoon-fed by a deliberate process of socialisation, but more ambitiously, *all* the information and *all* the insight that can be assumed to be available at a given time and place to a human being with the normal natural powers of such a being (subject to any necessary adjustments for age, physical or mental *ab*normality, and the like).

In other words: the criterion for our being 'presented' with some ethically significant datum, or for its being objectively salient in our experience, is in the first place an interpersonal or social criterion. What matters is whether it *is known*, for example, that some state of affairs exists which demands remedy – not whether I personally manage to conduct my life so as to minimise the frequency with which I have to confront the unpleasant facts, though I may find it convenient to do that. And in the second place, the relevant conception of the social is not a purely local but, at least in some measure, a cosmopolitan one: it makes each of us responsible for knowing what is there to be known by a member of our own generation equipped with the usual cognitive capacities. Thus the state of mind that consists in *indifference* to morally significant contemporary phenomena such as human rights abuses or environmental degradation would seem to qualify as one in which we are indeed responding – inadequately and badly – to 'data that are rich enough to permit a fairly adequate appreciation of the state's intentional object and of the object's place in the fabric of personal relationships'. No highly specialised enquiry is needed in order to come face to face with data that satisfy this description; on the contrary, as already noted, some evasive action may be necessary if one wants to *avoid* encountering such data. They are salient, for us, whether we like it or not.[19]

9.5 The long reach of blame

The 'involuntary wrongs' position helps to explain how ordinary, reasonably well-meaning people are exposed to blame for their failure (whether individual or collective) to confront various evils to which, most of the time, they are not required to give any thought. It can maintain that that failure, though to a large extent involuntary, nevertheless reflects a culpable lack of appreciation of certain (salient) ethical facts. This looks like a sound basis on which, for example, to denounce the complacency of the rich world towards the sufferings of the poor. At any rate, it implies a certain moral rigour which we may find admirable. Contrast the way this topic has sometimes been treated within consequentialist ethics: step one, assume that good is to be maximised, so that we cannot just shrug off the *prima facie* requirement to commit ourselves to an impartially benevolent worldview and to tireless good works; but then, step two, recognise the psychological impracticality – and hence the excessiveness – of these demands; so that, step three, it turns out after all to be permissible to resort to the use of emotional 'defence mechanisms', which can thus be granted a qualified acceptance on consequentialist grounds.[20]

With regard to current abuses – current states of affairs that are in any way a reproach to us – the view we are developing entails that by failing to pay due attention to these or to be emotionally engaged by them, we are guilty of a wrong, though this wrong will typically be an involuntary one. (That is: it will be involuntary to the extent that it is due to genuine inattentiveness, as distinct from a deliberate decision *not* to pay attention.) So, really, everyone who leads a comfortable life and gets on with that life in forgetfulness – even genuinely involuntary forgetfulness – of wrongs that demand remedy would appear by this standard to be blameworthy, since their behaviour constitutes an ethically inadequate response to 'data that are rich enough to permit' an adequate one. And this claim, one may feel, represents a helpful local contribution to describing the moral shadow that hangs over ordinary (bourgeois) life even when no one seems to be doing anything amiss; I mean the shadow to which Kant, for example, is alluding when he writes in the *Lectures on Ethics*: 'One may take a share in the general injustice, even though one does nobody any wrong by civil laws and practices. So if we now do a kindness to an unfortunate, we have not made a free gift to him, but repaid him what we were helping to take away through a general injustice'.[21]

9.6 An ideal notion of attentiveness

However, the 'involuntary wrongs' view no less than the consequentialist gives rise to a question about the limits of responsibility – in our case, a question about what can and cannot be said to fall within the range of information and insight available, in a given generation, to a human being of normal natural powers. Here one may cast an eye over the long inventory of *past* injustices, and ask: what would count as success in avoiding the wrong (even if it is an involuntary one) of indifference towards matters about which we ought not to be indifferent? There are plenty of historical events about which journalists and scholars can supply us with 'data rich enough to permit a fairly adequate appreciation' of them – of the events themselves and of their 'place in the fabric' of human relationships. Most of the time, needless to say, we fail to seek out any such data, except in so far as we take a general, open-minded interest in the past, the kind of interest that can lead one on from topic to topic in search of a less parochial understanding of the present. But it remains true that the 'data' to which we are responding are 'rich enough to permit recognition' of all sorts of relevant values which, in fact, we obstinately neglect. Does this situation not threaten to bring morality into disrepute, just as consequentialism may be felt to do, by its excessive demandingness: that is, by advancing the intolerable claim that the state of mind (or way of life) of the 'ordinary, well-meaning' person is one of chronic guilt or culpability?

We might think to mitigate the demandingness of the present view by saying that, at any rate, the responsibilities of any given individual are proportional to the extent of his or her knowledge. But note that since education is supposed, eventually, to acquire its own momentum and become spontaneously self-advancing, this would have the seemingly paradoxical consequence that to educate a person is, *pro tanto*, to turn them into someone who is destined by the internal logic of the educational process to feel – and to *be* – responsible for more things than if they had been left to themselves.[22] It may be that, paradox or no, this view is in harmony with some of our intuitions about responsibility, namely those that represent a more modern (though still implicitly patrician or paternalist) take on the aristocratic maxim *noblesse oblige*. Yet, ranged against it, there is also the rival intuition that the availability of ethically significant data to normally competent members of any given human generation is – to repeat – an objective matter. For it seems strange to say that some people can be acquitted, by reason of the poverty of the 'data' to which they are responding, of blameworthy states of mind of which others (possessing richer data) are guilty, when the greater richness of the data available to the latter group may be due in large part to their own superior energy and curiosity. This looks uncomfortably like a policy of conferring penalties rather than rewards on intellectual virtue. And after all, if democratic engagement is a source of duties–including, centrally, the duty to be attentive to the social world in which one's civic rights will be exercised – it does not seem unreasonable to set these duties against the background of the contemporary 'data landscape', and hence to think of them as common property.

In fact, the idea of a *demand of virtue* may well be helpful in explicating the 'involuntary wrongs' view – provided we are careful to remember that according to this view, not all of ethics is practical and that what we can properly be blamed, or reproached, for extends beyond the sphere of actual wrong*doing*. The ethical is just as fundamentally concerned, in Adams's words, with 'what we should be for and against in our hearts, what and how we ought to love and hate'.[23] And to think of such emotional rectitude as issuing in *penalties* might itself be seen as symptomatic of a wrong attitude.

We are contemplating the proposal to relate responsibility to the 'possibility of ethical appreciation'. To take this proposal seriously involves an orientation of the will; it means *wanting* to measure up to the relevant cognitive possibilities, not to evade or repress them. A certain quasi–Kantian idealism seems once again to be in play here: just as we can be required to strive for our own (general) moral perfection, so we can be pointed towards the task of self-perfection with respect to the appreciation of the ethical 'data' available to us at our own historical moment and on the basis of our own natural capacities. And for the purpose of this task, we will need an ideal notion of attentiveness by reference to which our various failures to do justice, 'in our hearts', to the totality of our lived experience can be identified as blameworthy.

It may be that the perfectionist project just mentioned can supply something plausible to say about the limits of responsibility. True, we seem compelled to admit on this basis that since there is no determinate point at which one can be said to have *done enough* in the way of ethical appreciation of the data available to us, there is equally no determinate point at which we can consider ourselves definitively beyond the reach of blame – that is, of reproach – for the kind of *failure* of appreciation that constitutes an involuntary wrong. This admission should not necessarily be regarded as damaging, however, since it is only within a juridical context that one can properly object to the absence of a clear answer to the question: 'What do I have to do to avoid being in the wrong?' By contrast, when it comes to that part of ethics which exceeds the juridical–the part that has to do with how things stand 'in our hearts' – we have no business to press this question, since it would be misguided to imagine that any of us can avoid being 'in the wrong' in the sense of *imperfect* or *open to improvement*. With regard to this latter part of ethics, our objective – 'given finite time', as Kant might put it – has to be, not *maintaining the required standard*, but *progressing in the right direction*.[24] For present purposes, the right direction will be that of a more adequate 'perception of saliences'.

9.7 The surprise attack on conscience

Despite this talk of 'progress', the proposed conception of a responsibility extending beyond the juridical may come across as rather abstract and static – a mere wistful admission of our own shortcomings, supplemented by a pious resolve to do better. The picture changes, though, when we turn to the dynamic aspect of ethical 'salience'.

To allow a foothold for the idea of *progress* in this context at all presumes, as discussed in §9.2, that one can be better or worse at grasping the morally salient facts of a situation: not just at entertaining a lively array of discrete value considerations (though this ability may of course be an asset when engaging, for example, with a work of art or theory), but at recognising, in our capacity as agents, which considerations should be regarded as making the strongest practical claim. What is envisaged is a type of judgement in which our various evaluatively relevant thoughts about the given situation are reviewed and integrated,[25] so as to yield an outcome expressible as: 'The most important thing here is ...; so what I must do is ...' Such judgements may come to us more smoothly with experience; ideally, they are meant to evolve towards some measure of lucidity about the place of obvious (self-interested) 'appearances of the good' in a larger deliberative scheme; or as Iris Murdoch puts it, '[M]oral advance carries with it intuitions of unity which are increasingly less misleading.'[26]

But in agreeing that someone's judgement in these matters can be better or worse – or even in conceding (to a Platonist like Murdoch) that we might find some heuristic value in the idea of a fully determinate lexical ordering of moment-by-moment practical claims – one should not lose sight of the socially contested nature of any such putative ordering. To bring out what I have in mind, it may be helpful to turn to one of the standard moves in moral discussion (in an inclusive or socially diffuse sense of 'discussion'), namely (what I would like to call) the *surprise attack on conscience*.

If there is no determinate inventory of things that one has to pay attention to, in a given socio-historical context, to avoid the reproach of responding inadequately to the available data, or if there is no determinate degree to which we have to keep this or that thing in the forefront of our thoughts in order to qualify as responding adequately, then it will be to some extent a matter for negotiation – that is, for the exchange of opinion and criticism – what we need (in any given context) to pay attention to in order to avoid such reproach: I mean the charge of frivolity in the face of 'data that are rich enough' to tell some important (though possibly neglected) story. This is a form of negotiation which, under conditions of sufficient freedom of expression, we learn to accept as a constant cultural background noise – a background that has presumably existed in some form at least since the invention of the printing press, but that has evolved in the course of modernity with the gradual spread of literacy, and in recent years has mutated dramatically with the advent of the internet. Any means of mass communication, however, can in principle serve as a vehicle of reproach for the moral fault – however involuntary – of indifference to some form of injustice or avoidable suffering. To issue a reproach of this kind, we might say, is to enter the general process of negotiation over the status and ranking of claims to salience: to declare to the relevant public that its current perceptions of salience are, in one way or another, defective.

9.8 The shifting landscape of salience

Two ideas have been invoked in the course of this discussion which may appear to stand quite far apart in the subject-matter of moral philosophy: that of a *deliberative context* or situation, and that of what we are *for or against in our hearts*. I proceed now to consider the argumentative potential of the latter.

Much imaginative literature addresses itself, more or less directly, to our concern to 'see the world aright' – aright as in justly (or less unjustly). This is true in a crude sense of works with propagandist purposes, but also of those that teach us to fine-tune our understanding of the motivation or inner life of the people around us. While it would hardly be convincing to suggest that our incentives to carry out this fine-tuning belong entirely to the domain of ethics (since sheer curiosity, whether psychological, social or sexual, must figure prominently among them), I think we can say – in the spirit of the 'involuntary wrongs' view – that *one* such incentive is the desire (most of the time, no doubt, merely implicit) to avoid wronging others by harbouring unjust thoughts or feelings about them: that is, by responding to our human 'data' in an ethically inadequate way. Admittedly, this picture is complicated by the fact that humorous or satirical writing can often lead us to modify our response to the 'data' in the direction of a less solemn or deferential attitude to certain persons or institutions. But since there is no reason why a change of this kind should not be an improvement, this complication does not constitute a difficulty for the view under consideration. In any case, it seems to be true that our interest in fiction and drama is an ethical one to the extent that it reflects our sense of responsibility for the quality – adequate or otherwise – of our ethical appreciation of the world in which we are placed.[27]

But in the attempt to keep our 'perception of saliences' under critical review, our main concern is likely to be with the impact not of any fictional world but of the real one, as we experience it through various forms of mediation.

Even somewhat remote historical events can be framed as giving rise to issues of conscience, in the sense of demanding fresh effort to rise to an adequate ethical appreciation – one that will lead us to 'love and hate as we ought'. To take an example that is unlikely to ruffle many feathers today: Macaulay, writing his *History of England* in the middle of the nineteenth century, has the very clear objective of making his readers appreciate the blessing constituted by the 'Glorious Revolution' of 1688-9 which brought William and Mary to the throne after the abdication of James II. The 1689 Declaration of Right, he says, 'though it made nothing law which had not been law before, contained the germ [of all subsequent progressive legislation up to Macaulay's own day, and] of every good law which may hereafter, in the course of ages, be found necessary to promote the public weal, and to satisfy the demands of public opinion'.[28] In using this sort of language – hyperbolical as we may find it – the historian is making an ethical intervention, which we can characterise as being designed to save us from the involuntary wrong (for that is what it would be in Macaulay's eyes) of ingratitude for the sanity and good faith of those who helped to secure the 1689 settlement, and so to save England from a subsequent, more violent revolution on the pattern of 1789 or 1848.

However, more contemporary – and contentious – material is not far to seek. Thus it would be hard to deny that with regard to the colonial and imperial phase of European history, we have 'data that are rich enough to permit a fairly adequate appreciation' of the relevant events – and hence to demand that we take ownership, morally speaking, of our *actual* reception of those data. And indeed it may be that no one is denying this, in the sense of maintaining that we just don't know enough to venture an opinion. But this leaves the field open for conflicting accounts of what it might mean, from the standpoint of later generations, to attach one's love and hatred to the right objects. Was the legacy of the British empire to the Indian subcontinent essentially one of progress and enlightenment, or rather of 'economic exploitation and ruin for millions'?[29] Should 'Australia Day' (26th January) be understood as a signifier of national unity or of racist violence?[30] Is it true that, as the UK Treasury has apparently claimed, 'Millions of [us] helped end the slave trade through [our] taxes', or would this merely be a feelgood gloss on the fact that Britain spent an enormous amount of public money on compensating slave-owners for the loss of their property?[31]

9.9 Democratic dialogue

I want to return now to the question of how these challenges to the postcolonial conscience might relate to our 'deliberative situation', this latter being the point where the idea of salience – and of a more or less sharp perception of saliences – gains entry to our reflection on practical reasoning. Here it may be pointed out that efforts to make us search our 'hearts' for involuntary wrong, in the guise of an inadequate response to the available ethical data, confront the obstacle of a certain natural inertia. For example, as the matters to which the data refer become more remote from us in time, it seems to become easier to

170 Sabina Lovibond

disclaim responsibility for having the right attitude. Our attitude, we may feel, can make no difference, so how can it be blameworthy to be indifferent? ('What's Hecuba to him, or he to Hecuba ...?'[32])

True, the range of issues on which it is my business to strive towards a correct attitude must depend – at least at the periphery – on the general intellectual responsibilities I have taken upon myself through my prior decisions to direct my attention in certain ways. In academic life, this might take the form of a decision to study one subject rather than another. But if there is a periphery in this respect – that is, if there are matters in regard to which my responsibilities to the ethical data are contingent on my own prior choice of orientation – then perhaps there is also a core: a body of knowledge and experience such that it can be said of each one of us, 'If you are not interested in arriving at an (ethically) adequate appreciation of this or that episode, then you ought to be; it is not a specialist matter but part of (what we ought to regard as) our ordinary common culture.' As to the substantive question of what belongs to the 'core' for this purpose, so that we cannot neglect it except at the cost of committing an involuntary wrong – this (I have suggested) is a zone of contention, and of gestures calculated to *make* people question their conscience about things which, for them, do not normally appear on the radar; considerations which may not (or not *yet*) be among those generally registered as salient, but which are being promoted as (objectively, or *de iure*) salient by certain parties to the general democratic dialogue.

At this point, someone might protest that the very idea of a *deliberative situation* is at risk of disappearing from view. Shouldn't this term be reserved for more recognisable successors to the Aristotelian paradigm in which I try to connect a desired end with *something I can do here and now*? What bearing can it be expected to have on a 'situation' as abstract as our total historical predicament – the predicament (no longer of a specific individual or local deliberator, but) of some correspondingly abstract subject of reflection?

The protest is understandable, but it has to be faced down. That is: a line of communication has to be maintained between what I have called the 'general democratic dialogue' – the testing ground, as it were, for claims of ethical salience – and the deliberative situation of individual agents in their capacity as citizens, piecing together whatever scraps of actual democratic participation may be available to them. We have accepted that ethics is concerned not only with action but with what we are for or against 'in our hearts'; still, the condition of our 'hearts' is not entirely *disconnected* from action but will periodically find expression in it. This applies, or could in principle apply, even to the historic injustices mentioned in §9.8 above.[33]

9.10 The big picture

But how is that connection to be made? Doesn't the enlarged (civic) view of our deliberative situation introduce new difficulties? Most obviously, perhaps, it means we can no longer think in terms of the more or less surveyable array of value-claims confronting the Aristotelian practical reasoner. Instead, we have to adjust ourselves to an ethical 'data landscape' of which the adequate appreciation, captured in some eventual 'intuition of unity', looks permanently out of reach. The big picture defeats our powers of integration; any number of moral demands can impress one, individually, as salient in some given deliberative context, yet the attribution of salience may be scarcely more than momentary; closure is achieved through acquiescence in some version of the idea of 'my station and its duties', where those duties may flow from nothing more complicated than the demands of local crisis-management. And yet the non-surveyability of the big picture is not clearly sufficient to acquit us of 'involuntary wrong' in relation to various more specific (and relatively surveyable) abuses; these latter parts of the picture, at least, constitute 'data that are rich enough' in themselves to permit adequate appreciation, even if we are at a loss to draw them into a gathered field.

But if it isn't enough to acquit us – won't that amount to a *reductio ad absurdum* of the 'involuntary wrongs' view? How can we acquiesce in a position that convicts us all indiscriminately, if not of chronic wrong*doing*, yet still of chronic moral *fault*?

Our attitude to this objection will depend on how far we are prepared to enter into the idea of a 'general injustice' or 'moral shadow' overhanging what we experience as social normality (§9.5 above). As mentioned earlier (§9.3), there is undoubtedly some inclination to seek a place of moral safety by ensuring that what one *does* (or tries, or intends to do – or to avoid doing) is above reproach. But there is also an incentive to leave that place, in that outside it – if we can develop a certain toleration of the thought that our normal, continuing condition (or 'place') is *in the wrong* (compare §9.6) – new possibilities of moral discovery and progress may be found. By 'toleration' of this thought I mean an ability to entertain it somewhat coolly, without being paralysed by neurotic guilt over the inadequacy of one's response to the available ethical data. Of course, for obvious reasons, one had better not get too comfortable with the consciousness of occupying a chronically false moral position. But between this (cynical) outcome and, on the other hand, the (hyper-cautious) refusal to raise our 'general injustice' to consciousness at all – here, we might think, lies the creative potential of a state of alertness to the hazard of involuntary wrong; or more modestly, a state of *willingness* to be alerted to it by others.

A public–spirited or indeed cosmopolitan conception of responsibility holds out the promise of improvement, but also the threat of an ever-present sense of failure. However, this sense of failure can be tempered by a certain acceptance of finitude and of the 'situated' character of all particular claims on our moral attention. It is not the case that if we are suitably attentive to the various voices raised, as it were, in warning against the involuntary wrongs of ingratitude, complacency and the like we will eventually win through to a condition of total rectitude in which the whole of moral reality, so far as we have cognitive access to it, is correctly appreciated. This ideal, as specified, is probably about as empty as that of, say, 'a complete description of physical reality at a given moment in time'. Our responsibilities to the data set before us for ethical appreciation are, surely, endless.[34] All the same, the idea of involuntary wrongs – and of the fallibility of our perceptions of salience – does seem to succeed in capturing something of that mixture of optimism and existential anxiety with which we lay ourselves open to whatever history, and literature, have to teach us. Anxiety, because there is a standing expectation of being confronted by new evidence of our own stupidity–that is, of the inadequacy of our ethical appreciation of what is already (actually or virtually) before our eyes. But also optimism of a kind, in that to be shown such evidence is to be offered the means of correcting this or that specific fault, and so of becoming less morally stupid, even if only in a piecemeal way.[35]

Finally, though, it is worth remembering that our relation to the 'surprise attack on conscience' is not a purely passive one, but can also offer interesting possibilities of discursive agency. The attack does not issue from nowhere, but is mounted by specific commentators on an existing moral outlook or consensus. Sometimes, in fact, the idea of salience seems strikingly conducive to the description of this process. An example might be the current resurgence of indignation over sexual harassment (and related, more extreme forms of abuse). It is not that we have only just become aware of this pattern of behaviour: even the term 'sexual harassment', brilliant linguistic innovation though it was, goes back half a century.[36] Rather, what seems to have varied over time is the place of that awareness in our overall 'perception of saliences'. Is it a matter for surprise, denunciation and urgent action that there are so many (more or less powerful) men around us who apparently feel entitled to practise sexual coercion on vulnerable young people, typically women and girls? Or is that just the way of the world, which only a naïve or hypersensitive person would bother to challenge? To seek to tilt the balance towards the first of these alternatives can be understood as a political intervention with respect to what we perceive as morally salient. And in the same moral-realist spirit that prompted the use of this terminology in the first place, one can add with a final touch of bravado: it is an attempt to bring home to people, to make people *acknowledge* as salient, what has been (objectively) salient – perhaps not literally 'always', but for far too long. If we have failed to give due weight in our thinking to the abuses in question, whether against ourselves or others, that represents a shortfall in 'practical wisdom'. The term 'wisdom' reflects a conviction that there is something here for us to *get right*. 'Practical' – in contrast to (merely) 'theoretical'– should speak for itself.[37]

Notes

1 'Burnt Norton' (1935), in T. S. Eliot, *The Complete Poems and Plays* (London: Faber and Faber, 1969), p.172.
2 *Paranormality: The Science of the Supernatural* (Basingstoke and Oxford: Pan Macmillan, 2015; first published 2011), pp.124–125. Despite its unnerving title, this popular-science text aims to debunk rather than promote the supposedly 'paranormal'.

3 John McDowell, 'Virtue and Reason', in his *Mind, Value, and Reality* (Cambridge, MA: Harvard University Press, 1998), pp.68–69. McDowell mentions in a footnote that his use of the word 'salient' here is indebted to David Wiggins: an obvious source for the idea would be 'Deliberation and Practical Reason', in Wiggins, *Needs, Values, Truth* (3rd edn: Oxford, Clarendon Press, 1998), p.233. Another representative of this approach would be Martha C. Nussbaum, who cites the relevant paper by Wiggins and comments on 'the way in which the "matter of the practical" appears before the agent in all of its bewildering complexity, without its morally salient features stamped on its face' (*Love's Knowledge: Essays on Philosophy and Literature*, New York and Oxford: Oxford University Press, 1990, pp.141–142, with note 18). However, a distinct reference point for Nussbaum is Henry James, who in one of his prefaces describes the novelist – qua 'intelligent painter of life' – as one for whom 'the flat grows salient and the tangled clear' (quoted, *Love's Knowledge*, p.165).
4 Thus Murdoch, *The Sovereignty of Good* (London: Routledge and Kegan Paul, 1970), p.37: 'I can only *choose* within the world I can see, in the moral sense of "see" which implies that clear vision is a result of moral imagination and moral effort.'
5 Luke 10:25–37 (the parable of the 'good Samaritan').
6 Robert Merrihew Adams, 'Involuntary Sins', *Philosophical Review* 94 (1985), pp.3–31.
7 Ibid., note 2 (pp.3–4).
8 I also acquiesce in Adams's apparent indifference to the Aristotelian distinction between 'involuntary' and 'non-voluntary' action (see *Nicomachean Ethics* 1110b18–24). Although he follows Aristotle in holding that 'we voluntarily do only what we know we are doing' ('Involuntary Sins', p.5), Adams has no special reason to dwell on the contrast between caring and not caring about, say, the news that one has inadvertently brought about some bad *result* (which for Aristotle would determine whether one did so *akôn*, 'involuntarily', or alternatively *oukh hekôn*, 'non-voluntarily'). His main concern is with certain *states of mind* which it is morally bad to be in, whether or not we are aware of the fact – and moreover, whether or not we care when someone ventures to tell us.
9 'Normally', because some injuries – in common with some forms of illness – are due at least in part to behaviour for which a person can be called to account, such as excessive drinking: cf. Aristotle, *Nicomachean Ethics* 1114a 12–19.
10 Adams, 'Involuntary Sins', pp.25–26.
11 Ibid., p.26.
12 Ibid., pp.30–31.
13 Ibid., p.12.
14 Ibid., p.27.
15 Ibid., pp.26–27.
16 Strictly speaking, of course, I must already have noticed the beggar some way off or I would not have that particular motive for crossing the street. Still, it makes a difference (to the state of one's moral consciousness) how much of an effort is needed in order to walk past the person in question *without looking him or her in the face*. See Emmanuel Levinas, 'Ethics as First Philosophy', in Seán Hand, ed., *The Levinas Reader* (Oxford: Blackwell, 1989), pp.75–87, especially at pp.82–84.
17 Ibid., 19.
18 Ibid., p.27.
19 The conception of objective ethical salience developed in this section probably requires some tweaking to accommodate the experience of a digitally connected world, in which (i) the enhancement of our natural (cognitive) powers by vast resources of online information is as 'normal' as the enhancement of our eyesight by glasses, while at the same time (ii) genuine and spurious information are sometimes worryingly hard to distinguish. But these points must wait for another occasion.
20 Thus Jonathan Glover, *Causing Death and Saving Lives* (Harmondsworth: Penguin, 1977), ch. 20. More topically, these remarks may also be applicable to the literature

of 'effective altruism', where again the objective proposed to us as conscientious individuals is to work out a personal regime or course of action that will be defensible in consequentialist terms, relative to our own socio-economic situation: see William MacAskill, *Doing Good Better: Effective Altruism and a Radical New Way to Make a Difference* (London: Guardian Books, 2015). What seems to go missing here is the idea of the *structural* wrongness of a way of life, where this wrongness is something in which one can be implicated through an acquiescence that never crosses the threshold of the voluntary. (Though having said this, it is only fair to pause for a moment over MacAskill's principle of 'neglectedness'. In deciding what good cause or causes to support, he somewhat explosively suggests on his final page, we do well to ask: 'Is there reason to expect that markets or governments won't solve this problem unaided?' (p.252). That criterion, if taken seriously, seems to have the – possibly unintended – effect of promoting structural injustices straight to the top of our moral agenda.)

21 Immanuel Kant, *Lectures on Ethics*, eds. Peter Heath and J. B. Schneewind, trans. Peter Heath (Cambridge University Press, 1997), p.179.
22 Compare the situation of the conscientious enquirer who, through unwearying sceptical scrutiny of what he or she would initially have put forward as claims to knowledge, appears to end up knowing less than they did at the outset. For a striking exploration of this difficulty, see David Lewis, 'Elusive Knowledge', *Australasian Journal of Philosophy* 74 (1996), pp.549–567.
23 'Involuntary Sins', p.12.
24 Kant actually says: 'Here [that is, as regards one's own moral disposition] the command is "Be perfect" [Matthew 5:48].' He continues, however: 'It is a human being's duty to *strive* for this perfection, but not to reach it (in this life), and his compliance with this duty can, accordingly, consist only in continual progress' (*The Metaphysics of Morals*, trans. and ed. Mary Gregor (Cambridge University Press, 1996), p.196; 6:446). Or as Christine Korsgaard observes, explaining Kant's idea of the duty to adopt morally good ends: 'Adopting an end is a definite, though internal, action. But ... making that end the motive of your conduct is not something a human being can *decide* all at once to do' (*Creating the Kingdom of Ends*, Cambridge University Press, 1996, p.21).
25 Wiggins writes in his explanatory paraphrase of Aristotle, *de Anima* (*On the Soul*) 434a5–10: '[A] rational animal is one with the power to arbitrate between diverse appearances of what is good and integrate the findings into a unitary practical conception' (*Needs, Values, Truth*, p.258).
26 *The Sovereignty of Good*, p.93.
27 This sense of responsibility is what Nussbaum undertakes to foster in *Love's Knowledge*, where she argues that moral philosophy requires for its own completion 'the experience of loving and attentive novel-reading' (p.27).
28 Thomas Babington Macaulay, *The History of England* (Harmondsworth: Penguin, abridged text, ed. Hugh Trevor-Roper (1979)), pp.293–4. The wrong of ingratitude in relation to the past can also figure as a theme for the historical novelist: thus Helen Dunmore's *The Siege* (London: Viking, 2001), which is a fictionalised account of events in the city of Leningrad after the breach of the Hitler-Stalin pact in 1941, seems calculated in a quiet way (though the author is evidently no Stalinist) to remind British readers of an often understated factor in the Allied victory, namely that Hitler inflicted great damage on his own forces by attacking the Soviet Union.
29 Shashi Tharoor, 'The Myth of Britain's Gifts to India: A Legacy of Exploitation and Ruin', *The Guardian*, 9th March 2017.
30 Calla Wahlquist, 'Massacres and Protest: Australia Day's Undeniable History', *The Guardian* (online), 23rd January 2018. The date is the anniversary both of the planting of the Union Jack in Sydney Cove (1788) and of a massacre in which at least 40 native people were killed (1838).

31 David Olusoga, 'The Treasury's Tweet Shows Slavery is Still Misunderstood', *The Guardian*, 13th February 2018. Olusoga reports that the payment concerned - £20 million, or 40% of the national budget at the time – was made in 1833 and involved a debt that was not discharged until 2015.
32 Shakespeare, *Hamlet*, Act II, scene 2.
33 The application is of more than academic interest. Thus J. Angelo Corbett, 'Reparations', in Jay L. Garfield and William Edelglass (eds.), *The Oxford Handbook of World Philosophy* (2011), pp.596–609, at p.608: '[W]ithout rectification [of past wrongs] there can be no apology, no forgiveness, and no reconciliation' – though it is a 'presumptuous mistake' to think that 'reparations are sufficient for reconciliation or forgiveness, or … that [they] are contingent on either for their moral justification.'
34 Apart from anything else, one has to deal with the intimate juxtaposition of good and bad in so many of the persons, states of affairs and other objects that constitute our ethical data. But that problem is tangential to the present discussion.
35 As Adams says, 'The appropriate purpose of reproach, and of judgements of blame, directed at others or at oneself, is not to crush us but to lead us to repentance, and to acknowledge moral realities' ('Involuntary Sins', p.24). 'Repentance' – in secular terms–must mean something like the acknowledgement that our scheme of values is at fault, and the will to correct it. Recall however (§9.3 above) that the existence of this forward-facing power of self-correction does not, in Adams's view, imply that the faults which have been present in us up to now are blameworthy only in so far as they are attributable to our *voluntary* actions and omissions in the past.
36 See Miranda Fricker, *Epistemic Injustice: Power and the Ethics of Knowing* (Oxford University Press, 2007), pp.149–152.
37 Thanks to Sophie Archer as editor of the present collection, and to S. G. Williams, for helpful comments on an earlier draft; and to all who took part in the discussion of this paper at the Graduate Symposium on Imagination, Society, and Culture at the University of Bergen, Norway in January 2019.

References

Adams, Robert Merrihew. 1985. Involuntary Sins. *Philosophical Review* 94(1): 3–31.
Aristotle. 2009. *Nicomachean Ethics*. Translated by David Ross, revised by Lesley Brown. Oxford University Press, Oxford.
Corbett, J. Angelo. 2011. Reparations. In Jay L. Garfield and William Edelglass (eds.), *The Oxford Handbook of World Philosophy* (pp. 596–609). Oxford University Press, Oxford.
Dunmore, Helen. 2001. *The Siege*. Viking, London.
Eliot, T. S. 1969. *The Complete Poems and Plays*. Faber and Faber, London.
Fricker, Miranda. 2007. *Epistemic Injustice: Power and the Ethics of Knowing*. Oxford University Press, Oxford.
Glover, Jonathan. 1977. *Causing Death and Saving Lives*. Penguin, Harmondsworth.
Kant, Immanuel. 1997. *Lectures on Ethics*. Edited by Peter Heath and J. B. Schneewind. Translated by Peter Heath. Cambridge University Press, Cambridge.
Korsgaard, Christine. 1996. *Creating the Kingdom of Ends*. Cambridge University Press, Cambridge.
Levinas, Emmanuel. 1989. Ethics as First Philosophy. In Seán Hand (ed.), *The Levinas Reader* (pp. 75–87). Blackwell, Oxford.
Lewis, David. 1996. Elusive Knowledge. *Australasian Journal of Philosophy* 74(4): 549–567.
MacAskill, William. 2015. *Doing Good Better: Effective Altruism and a Radical New Way to Make a Difference*. Guardian Books, London.

Macaulay, Thomas Babington. 1979. *The History of England*. Abridged text, edited by Hugh Trevor-Roper. Penguin, Harmondsworth.

McDowell, John. 1998. Virtue and Reason. In Mind, Value, and Reality. Harvard University Press, Cambridge, MA.

Murdoch, Iris. 1970. *The Sovereignty of Good*. Routledge and Kegan Paul, London.

Nussbaum, Martha C. 1990. *Love's Knowledge: Essays on Philosophy and Literature*. Oxford University Press, New York and Oxford.

Olusoga, David. 2018. The Treasury's Tweet Shows Slavery Is Still Misunderstood. *The Guardian*, 13th February.

Shakespeare, William. 1977. *The Complete Works of William Shakespeare*. Abbey Library, London.

Tharoor, Shashi. 2017. The Myth of Britain's Gifts to India: A Legacy of Exploitation and Ruin. *The Guardian*, 9th March.

Wahlquist, Calla. 2018. Massacres and Protest: Australia Day's Undeniable History. *The Guardian*, 23rd January (online).

Wiggins, David. 1998. Deliberation and Practical Reason. In Needs, Values, Truth. Third edition. Clarendon Press, Oxford.

Wiseman, Richard. 2015. *Paranormality: The Science of the Supernatural*. Pan Macmillan, Basingstoke and Oxford.

10 On salience and sneakiness

Mary Kate McGowan

10.1 Introduction

Salience does a lot of philosophical work.[1] For this reason, it ought to be the focus of more explicit philosophical attention than it currently receives. Although philosophers acknowledge their reliance on the related notion of relevance and although relevance has been the focus of considerable direct philosophical attention[2], the same cannot be said for salience. It, by contrast, is comparatively under-discussed and under-recognized.

That salience plays an essential role in so many areas of philosophy should not be that surprising. After all, we are in the business of explaining how we understand the world around us and it stands to reason that that which is salient to us will play a key role in those explanations. Moreover, this is true across explanandum. As a result, the essential role of salience will be ubiquitous.

That said, salience also has unexpected and (ironically) quite hidden consequences. Although salient things are, of course, salient, there often are covert consequences of that salience. Drawing attention to this phenomenon and spelling out some of its philosophical, normative, and social consequences is the main aim of this paper.

The paper proceeds as follows. In the next section, sneaky results of salience altering actions are explored and a variety of preliminaries are presented. One of those preliminaries concerns the distinction between constituting harm and merely causing it. Then, in §3, a specific instance of speech that alters salience facts is presented. In §4, we explore how that utterance might constitute harm in a sneaky and surreptitious manner and, in §5, we explore how it might merely cause harm in a potent and yet hidden way.

10.2 Sneaky consequences

Although salient things are salient, some of the work done by salience is significantly less apparent. In particular, when actions alter salience facts and those actions are contributions to a broader (norm-governed) practice, then those actions actually enact fresh norms and this has important consequences for what counts as appropriate in that particular practice going forward. Such moves can

DOI: 10.4324/9781351202114-11

be harmful, neutral, or good. In what follows, I will explore the possibility that norm-altering actions are harmful and that they are harmful in an especially sneaky and hidden way.

10.2.1 Preliminaries

Before presenting the argument for the (hidden) consequences of salience altering actions, some preliminaries are warranted.

10.2.1.1 Speech and action

In what follows, I shall be focused on speech actions that alter salience facts. When I bring up my favorite restaurant, I thereby make that restaurant the most salient restaurant in the context of that conversation. Non-speech actions can also change what is salient in a conversation. Were we to walk past a restaurant while it is on fire, that restaurant would be conversationally salient. In the remainder of this chapter, though, I shall nevertheless focus on speech actions that alter salience facts.

The term 'speech' is used in different ways. In the context of free speech, the term is used in a special technical sense that cuts across the ordinary sense.[3] Some speech in the ordinary sense is not speech in the technical free speech sense. 'I'll pay you ten thousand to kill him and bury the body', uttered sincerely and seriously to a known assassin is speech in the ordinary sense but it is not given any free speech protections. It thus does not appear to be speech in the technical sense of a free speech principle. Moreover, some actions that are not speech in the ordinary sense are speech in this technical free speech sense. Burning a draft card, for example, is not a use of language and thus it is not speech in the ordinary sense but it is nevertheless within the scope of a free speech principle. I am not here concerned with 'speech' in this technical free speech sense.

As I am using the term, 'speech' is a communicative act that also involves the use of a conventional language. Speech can certainly be understood in a broader way (such that the use of a conventional language is not required). Suppose, for example, that I lick my lips and hum while I look intently at my friend's box of Belgian chocolates. Doing so clearly communicates my desire that she share them with me but it is not speech in this narrow sense. Although much of what I say in what follows applies also to speech in the broader sense, I nevertheless use 'speech' in the narrow sense. I do this both in order to simplify discussion and to stick closer to ordinary usage.

It is also worth stressing at the outset that speech is itself an action. In addition to whatever physical action is involved in the use of language (e.g., pressing pen to paper, pronouncing words), using words to express content also performs distinctly linguistic acts. When I say that the clarinet is in the guest room, I am making sounds and vibrating air but I am also describing a state of affairs and committing myself to the truth of the claim that the clarinet is in the guestroom. Since speech is action, I will sometimes refer to an utterance as a speech action or a speech act.

10.2.1.2 Cause vs constitute

There is an important distinction between speech actions that (merely) cause harm and those that constitute it. Before attempting to define the difference, an example might help.

Suppose that I convince my friends that redheaded people are genetically inferior, disposed to evil, and a threat to all things decent and good and, as a result of coming to believe these things, my friends discriminate against redheaded persons.[4] In this case, my utterance causes discrimination against those redheaded persons. My words cause my friends' beliefs (attitudes, and dispositions) to change and these changes in turn cause my friends' harmful discriminatory conduct. The connection between the speech and the harm, in this case, is (by hypothesis merely) causal.

Contrast that with a different case. Suppose instead that I am an employer and I implement a company hiring policy when I say, 'From now on, we no longer hire anyone with red hair'. This utterance will no doubt cause discriminatory conduct on the part of my employees. Despite this, since that discriminatory conduct is brought about by my employees' adherence to a policy that I put into place with my utterance, my utterance enacts the policy that prescribes the harmful discriminatory practice in question. As a result, we shall say that my utterance constitutes (and does not merely cause) the harm of discrimination.

Thus, to say that the speech action causes harm is to say that it causes harm but it does not also constitute it; the speech action in question merely causes harm. By contrast, to say that a speech action constitutes harm is to say that it brings the harm in question via the enacting of a permissibility fact (or norm) that prescribes the harm in question.

Clearly 'constitution' is here being used in a special technical sense. It does not mean what it means in other philosophical contexts. To say that the employer's (hiring-policy-enacting) utterance constitutes the harm of discrimination is not to say that the employer's utterance happens at the exact same time as the discriminatory harms. The harm of discrimination is causally downstream from the utterance that enacts the discriminatory policy. It is also not to say that the employer's utterance is sufficient for that harm either. Others need to follow the policy for the discriminatory harms to obtain.[5] Constitution talk here, unlike elsewhere in philosophy, is not akin to an equals sign; it is instead a distinct norm-driven way of causing.

In sum then, in order for an utterance to constitute harm, three conditions are required. The utterance enacts a norm; that norm is followed, and harm results from following that norm.

One way (but not the only way) for a speech action to enact a norm is through an exercise of speaker authority. In the above case, for example, the employer (and only the employer) is able to verbally enact a new policy for her employees because she has and is exercising her authority to do just that. (She also intends to be doing so and she is recognized as intending to do so and so forth.) Such sorts of cases are fairly familiar, but this is not the only way for a speech action to enact a norm. As we shall see, speech actions that contribute to norm-governed practices enact norms for those practices and they do so via a very different norm-enactment mechanism.

One might wonder what motivates this distinction between causing and constituting harm. There are several reasons but here are two. This difference between causing and constituting harm matters to the law. In the United States, for example, speech that (merely) causes discrimination is protected by a free speech principle but speech that constitutes discrimination is not. Furthermore, being as clear as possible about the relationship between speech and its associated harms will aid attempts to remedy those harms. Thus, if a speech action brings about harm via adherence to a norm enacted by that utterance, then effective remedies ought to attend to the crucial role of the norms enacted.

Since harm constitution depends on the enacting of norms, a bit more information is required both about norms and about enactment.

10.2.1.3 On enactment

Some forms of enacting are really easy to do. In fact, we enact facts all the time. Simply by being and doing things, we thereby routinely affect what's true of the world and thereby enact these truths about it. Very roughly, enacting is a fairly direct way to make something true. When I skip to work, for example, I change what is true about the world; I make it the case that I skipped to work. That I skipped to work is directly enacted by my skipping. Although enacting involves an immediate way of making truths true and it is thus 'truth-making' in this minimal sense, I am here entirely agnostic about the underlying metaphysics.[6]

Some forms of enacting depend on institutional structures. When Leo dies, for example, his death enacts the fact that his wife Sue is a widow. That this widowhood fact is enacted by this death event depends, among other things, on the institution of marriage. Consequently, it is dependently enacted by it.[7]

Finally, a single speech action can enact several different facts and it can do so via quite different mechanisms of enactment. Suppose, for example, that I verbally set a new bedtime for my children. When I do so, I thereby enact various facts. I directly enact the fact that I spoke; I also dependently enact a new bedtime. Moreover, these different facts are enacted in different ways.

10.2.1.4 Permissibility facts/norms

Permissibility facts are facts about what is permissible or appropriate in some realm. The rules of baseball are permissibility facts in that game and norms about how much physical space to give a conversational partner are culturally specific permissibility facts. This notion of permission does not require that some agent(s) grant the permission. What is permissible is just what is appropriate in the practice. Permissibility facts also include prohibitions (and thus what is impermissible) as well as what is required (that is, what it is impermissible to refrain from doing). Permissibility is also a matter of degree and may function along more than one axis.

In much of what follows, we shall be primarily interested in the enacting of social norms; these are the norms that guide our social practices. Although social norms guide our actions, we are typically barely conscious of them. An American may remain blissfully ignorant of the personal space norms that have been guiding her life in the U.S. until, that is, those norms are violated by a European friend when she is an adult. Social norms are not mere regularities. Being right-handed is the norm (in a purely descriptive sense) in my current logic class but this does not mean that the left-handed students really ought to be right-handed. Social norms, by contrast, are prescriptive: they give rise to talk about what a person ought to do; they afford incentives and reasons for action; they are used to explain behavior, and they ground criticism of those who do not comply.

Whether or not certain social norms apply to someone is typically a function of that person's social role and position; the application of a norm to a person does not require that that person be consciously awareness of that norm and it does not require that that person endorse that norm.[8] A woman who emphatically rejects the (patriarchal) norms of femininity, for example, will nevertheless be evaluated in terms of her response to those norms. Because she socially counts as a woman, the norms are relevant to her and this is so whether she agrees with those norms or not.

Bicchieri argues that social norms are "behavioral rules that are supported by a combination of empirical and normative expectations".[9] They are behaviors we expect others to follow (empirical expectation) and we believe that others believe that we ought to follow them too (normative expectations).[10] This means that we expect plenty of compliance and we expect negative social consequences for failures to comply. The prescriptive force of these social norms is considerable. Individuals routinely go against self-interest in order to avoid the social censure of non-compliance and even practices that seem collectively irrational (or at least suboptimal) nevertheless persist because of the self-propelling nature of these norms.[11] Clearly, social norms are action-guiding.

Thus far, we have one example of speech constituting harm. When I enacted a discriminatory hiring policy and a discriminatory hiring practice ensues, my utterance constitutes the harm of discrimination. In this case, the enacted harmful norm is my company's hiring policy. This norm is both official and explicit. The focus in the remainder of this chapter, by contrast, is on the enacting of harmful social norms that are neither. When I enacted that policy, I also did so via an exercise of my authority over my company. My policy-enacting utterance was an authoritative speech action. The focus in what follows, by contrast, is with a different much sneakier mechanism of norm-enactment.

In the remainder of this paper, I explore how speech actions that alter salience facts can be harmful and how they can be harmful in an especially covert and sneaky manner. We shall consider both how speech actions that alter salience facts can constitute harm and how they can merely cause harm. The exploration begins in conversational kinematics. In later sections, I argue that the phenomenon generalizes to other broader (that is, extra-conversational) social practices.

10.2.2 Conversations

In recent work, I have argued that speech enacts norms in a ubiquitous but highly hidden manner. Here, I will highlight the role that salience sometimes plays in this sneaky way that speech routinely enacts norms. One way to see this phenomenon of sneaky norm enactment concerns the salience component of the conversational score.

10.2.2.1 On salience component of conversational score

Conversational score is a specification of a conversational context.[12] It tracks that which is relevant for the proper development and assessment of that conversation. This includes, among other things, the presuppositions, the appropriate standards of accuracy, and the relevant topics. Since the various components of conversational score affect such a wide variety of linguistic phenomena (which may not be familiar to some readers), it is worthwhile to consider some examples.

Definite descriptions are one such linguistic phenomenon; they are descriptions that purport to uniquely refer.[13] In other words, definite descriptions seem to refer to exactly one thing. Examples include 'the tallest student in my 207 class', 'Helen McGowan Gardner's oldest son' and 'my favorite color'. Each of these descriptive expressions is routinely used on particular occasions to uniquely refer; on each occasion, it seems that these expressions refer to one and only one thing.

As is well known, many definite descriptions appear to succeed in uniquely referring even though these descriptions fail to uniquely describe their referent. The expression 'the desk', for example, may pick out a particular desk even though there are many desks in the universe and there may even be several desks in the room in question. Salience appears to account for this.[14] On this account, a definite description refers to the most salient satisfier of the description.[15] Suppose, for example, that Bobby mentions that his dog has just been to the vet and I ask if the dog is healthy. Bobby's dog is certainly not the only dog in the universe and his dog may not even be the only dog present, but I have nevertheless managed to refer to his dog with this use of the expression 'the dog'. This is because Bobby's dog is the most salient dog in the context of this particular conversation. Salience is a component of the conversational score and this salience component of the conversational score helps to settle the appropriate use of definite descriptions in the conversation at hand by fixing the unique referent of such descriptions. Salience is doing work by both fixing the referent of the definite description and by guiding our proper use of such expressions.

10.2.2.2 Conversational exercitives

This all seems fairly straightforward but there are hidden mechanisms at play: whenever one adds to a conversation in a way that alters facts about what is most salient, one thereby directly enacts changes to the salience components of the conversational score and this, in turn, enacts facts about what is conversationally permissible. Let's see how this works.

Suppose that, in response to Bobby's claims about his dog, I mention my own dog by saying, 'Our dog Braun has the cutest markings above his eyes; it is just impossible NOT to love him!'. By bringing up my dog, I make Braun the most salient dog in the context of this particular conversation; my act of saying what I said (in the conversational context in which I said it) enacts a change to the salient-dog component of the conversational score.[16] Just as any action enacts the fact that that action took place, bringing up my dog enacts the fact that my dog is thereby the most conversationally salient dog. Whenever we speak, we enact a variety of facts: the fact that we spoke, the fact that we uttered the words we did, the fact that air vibrated in a certain (audible) manner, the fact that the speaker expressed a particular content and so forth. Some of these enacted facts are intended by the speaker and some are not. Some of these enacted facts are such that we are fully aware of them and some we are not.

Whether we consciously intend to do so or not and whether we are consciously aware of doing so or not, enacting score-altering facts has permissibility consequences. When one enacts new salience facts for the conversation, one thereby changes what is subsequently permissible or appropriate in that conversation. By making my dog the most salient dog, I thereby changed the proper way to use the expression 'the dog' in this particular conversational context. Once Braun is the most salient dog in the context of this conversation, it is conversationally inappropriate to try to refer to any other dog using that expression. Although enacting this particular conversational permissibility fact was far from my primary intent in saying what I said, my utterance nevertheless enacts this particular conversational permissibility fact.

When conversational contributions enact conversational permissibility facts in this way, they are, what I call conversational exercitives.[17] Exercitives enact permissibility facts (or norms) in some arena. I have argued elsewhere that most conversational contributions are conversational exercitives in virtue of enacting conversational permissibility facts (via enacting changes to the conversational score).

10.2.2.3 Harmful conversational exercitives

That salience altering conversational contributions enact permissibility facts about the appropriate use of some definite descriptions in a particular conversation seems rather unlikely to harm anyone. Although conversational harms are not the focus here, it is nevertheless possible for conversational permissibility facts to harm. If, for instance, the conversational permissibility facts prevent a certain speaker from successfully communicating, then those permissibility facts might silence that speaker. Since there are many ways for one's communicative capacities to be systematically impeded, there are many different types of silencing.[18]

10.2.2.4 How it generalizes: Covert exercitives

This phenomenon (of sneaky norm-enactment) generalizes. Conversational exercitives are a special case of a more general phenomenon and the real reason I first focus on conversational permissibility facts is that doing so highlights this more general phenomenon of norm enactment. Conversational contributions to a particular conversation enact permissibility facts in that conversation simply because conversations are norm governed activities. Since adding to the conversation directly enacts a change to the score, and since the score affects what is subsequently permissible (because conversations are norm governed), changing the conversational score thereby changes what is conversationally permissible. It is the norm-governed nature of conversation making it the case that conversational contributions are sneakily norm-enacting in this way.

This norm-enactment phenomenon generalizes exactly because other social practices are also norm-governed. How we interact with one another in social spaces, for example, is governed by a variety of social norms. Thus, whenever we make contributions to such activities, we sneakily enact mini token-activity specific permissibility facts for that particular instantiation of that type of activity.

There are different sorts of norms at play and they ought to be distinguished. There is an important difference between norms that govern all instances of the (sort of) activity in question and those norms that govern only a particular instance of that (sort of) activity. Consider first the general or global norms. I call them 'g-norms'.[19] G-norms govern all instances of the norm-governed activity in question and the performing of any particular such activity does not enact them. Consider, for example, conversations. The g-norms governing conversations include the (relatively rigid) rules of grammar and (the accommodating norm of) Grice's cooperative principle.[20] Note that these conversational g-norms apply to all conversations and they are not enacted by any particular conversation.[21] These are the norms that make norm-governed activities norm-governed.

Some of these g-norms are very general and others are more localized. The norms of cooperation that Grice stresses, for example, are very general norms of conversation. One ought to speak in a manner that enables one's interlocutor to understand what one means by what one says. This is a very general norm of conversation. Of course, the appropriate way to do this can vary from one context to another. In other words, there are more localized g-norms of manner that are operative in different contexts. Using technical philosophical language while conversing with a supermarket teller is likely to violate local g-norms of the manner of expression while failing to use that technical language would likely violate those local g-norms at an APA session on indexicals. G-norms can be more or less localized.

Other norms, by contrast, are quite specific and they are enacted by the performing of the very token-instance of the norm-governed activity over which they preside. I call such (token-activity-specific) norms 's-norms'.[22] When I made my dog the most salient dog in the context of the conversation, for example, I thereby enacted an s-norm for that conversation; I enacted a conversation-specific permissibility fact regarding the appropriate use of the expression 'the dog': the appropriate way to use the expression 'the dog' is to refer to Braun. When I said this, I changed the salience facts for the conversation (making Braun the most salient dog) and this, in turn, changes what is subsequently permissible in that conversation. My utterance constitutes a move in the conversation that makes it conversationally impermissible (for the time being anyway) to try to refer to any other dog with the expression 'the dog'. My utterance enacts a new s-norm for the conversation.

Notice that when our actions enact these permissibility facts (or s-norms), we are barely aware of doing so; we typically do not have a conscious and explicit intention to do so; our fellow participants barely realize that we are doing so, and we are not exercising authority in doing so.[23] Clearly, this mechanism of norm enactment works very differently from the authoritative cases discussed earlier.

How might this mechanism shed light on the possibility of salience-altering speech actions either constituting or merely causing harm? To focus on ideas, we shall consider an example.

10.3 The case: Medical group meeting

Imagine that Hawthorne and Associates is a medical practice in southeastern Massachusetts and that they have just hired Dr. Pamela Tilson, a new pediatric oncologist trained at Boston Children's Hospital. Dr. Green is head of staff at Hawthorne and Associates and he was the chair of the hiring committee that hired Dr. Tilson. At the reception welcoming Dr. Tilson to the practice, the following exchange takes place:

Dr. Green: Welcome, Dr. Tilson. We are delighted that you have decided to join our practice here on the south coast.
Dr. Tilson: Thank you but the pleasure is all mine. This area is just gorgeous and my family loves to sail so it was a very easy decision for us.
Dr. Green: For us too. We wanted to diversify our staff and many of our patients are also Black. They'll relate to you.

Although it might have been well-intentioned, Dr. Green's second utterance is problematic in lots of ways. In particular, he seems to assume that all (or most) Black people are alike. I tend to doubt that he also believes that all (or most) white people would relate to him! Dr. Green could also be taken to be insinuating that Dr. Tilson was hired simply because she is Black and that the standards were lowered in order to hire her. To keep our discussion focused, however, we shall attend only to the salience-altering aspects of his speech action. By saying what he said, Dr. Green made Dr. Tilson's race salient (or more salient) in this particular social context. And the questions before us are: How might doing so constitute harm? How might doing so merely cause harm? I turn now to these questions.

10.3.1 On the possibility of harm constitution

In this section, we shall consider the possibility that by altering the salience facts in this way, Dr. Green's utterance constitutes harm. Recall that the harm constitution requires enacting a norm that prescribes a resulting harm. Since Dr. Green's utterance is a contribution to a conversation, it is a conversational exercitive and it thus enacts norms for the conversation. By bringing up the patients of the practice, Dr. Green's utterance affects the proper way to use the pronoun 'they' in this particular conversation. Such subtle conversational permissibility facts are constantly altered during the course of a conversation. Again, I am not here concerned with the possibility of harmful conversational s-norms. Rather, I am concerned with the s-norms enacted in broader (extra-linguistic) norm governed practices.

Note that, in addition to contributing to a conversation, Dr. Green's utterance is also a contribution to the norm-governed activity of social interaction. As such, whether it directly enacts a score change in that activity and thus it dependently enacts permissibility facts or s-norms in it. What remains to be shown is that the enacting of those s-norms constitutes harm.

Whether a speech action that makes someone's race salient is harmful or not will, of course, depend on the context. In some situations, doing so could facilitate inclusion in a way that harms no one. In other situations, however, making a person's race salient can be harmful.

Proving that this is the case and proving it completely would require identifying the precise social norms (g-norms) governing the social space in question as well as a complete and accurate specification of the score at the time of the contribution. These are each empirical matters and they are not settled here. Moreover, the medical meeting case is underspecified. There are (and there always will be) further contextual details that could change the effects of particular moves. That said, we can, and we can with some degree of confidence, make plausible judgments about various possibilities.

Suppose, for example, that there are g-norms operative in our society that interfere with the recognition of the medical expertise of Black women doctors. There is certainly evidence of this and (appalling) behavior on airplanes draws our collective attention to the existence of such norms.[24] Thus, if such g-norms are operative, then actions that make a Black woman doctor's race salient (or more salient)[25] will enact s-norms (relevantly similar to the g-norms activating them), and, so long as the s-norms are followed, harm will ensue. If this happens, then Dr. Tilson might suffer from credibility deficits; her expertise might be undermined; she could be subject to increased demands to justify her judgments, and her professional standing might be perpetually insulted. Since Dr. Green's remark enacts the s-norms prescribing these harms, his utterance constitutes (rather than merely causes) the harms in question. This is just one way that actions altering salience facts can constitute harm.

Now, notice how sneaky and hidden this phenomenon can be. Suppose, for instance, that Dr. Green did not intend to bring about any of these results. Furthermore, there is a good chance that he also remains blissfully (even if culpably) unaware of them. We are constantly doing things with our speech actions that far outstrip either our conscious intentions or our conscious awareness. Since our actions are always socially situated, they are routinely moves in norm-governed practices. By enacting score changes in those activities, we are also thereby enacting s-norms in them. Therefore, what we do routinely have permissibility consequences for ourselves and for those around us. In sum, Dr. Green's remark makes Dr. Tilson's race salient but the fact that doing so has such impactful consequences is far from salient (even if the consequences themselves are salient to some).

10.3.2 On the possibility of merely causing harm

As we have just seen, actions that directly enact changes to salience facts thereby dependently enact s-norms and when those s-norms prescribe harmful actions, the salience altering action constitutes the harm in question. Now, we will focus on the possibility of salience-altering actions having (merely) causal consequences. What follows highlights just some of the possibilities.

10.3.2.1 Stereotype threat

Altering salience facts can trigger stereotype threat. Stereotype threat, the "real-time threat of being judged and treated poorly in settings where a negative stereotype about one's group applies",[26] is a well-documented psychological phenomenon. Persons made aware of their membership in negatively stereotyped social groups underperform on some cognitive tasks. The data suggests that one's awareness of the relevance of one's social group membership both taxes working memory and triggers psychological defense strategies, each of which undermines performance. By drawing attention to Dr. Tilson's race then, Dr. Green's remark could well have the causal effect of undermining Dr. Tilson's performance by triggering stereotype threat. This is one way that Dr. Green's remark could have not so salient causal effects.

Furthermore, in addition to making Dr. Tilson's race (more) salient to her, Dr. Green's remark also makes the salience of Dr. Tilson's race salient. In other words, everyone is aware of everyone else's awareness of the salience of Dr. Tilson's race. That the salience of her race is made mutually manifest in this way is likely to enhance the negative effects of stereotype threat.

10.3.2.2 Implicit associations

Actions that change salience facts can also activate implicit associations. In some contexts, it seems to take precious little to activate implicit associations.[27] Consequently, there is good reason to believe that making race salient will sometimes bring to mind and thus make salient a broad set of racist associations.[28] The sorts of racist associations I have in mind here connect Black women with negative characteristics like servitude (domestic or sexual), low intelligence, immorality, laziness, and incompetence.[29] Moreover, the evidence demonstrates that these associations affect our ability to reason well and fairly; they do so unconsciously, and they are perniciously difficult to shield oneself from.[30] If even any of these associations are activated by Dr. Green's remark, then it stands to reason that Dr. Tilson will be negatively affected by the activation of such associations. Clearly, the activation of these sorts of implicit associations is another sneaky and hidden consequence of salience-altering actions. Although the salience change itself might be apparent, the consequences of so doing are certainly not.

10.4 Conclusion

Salience is a ubiquitous but under-theorized philosophical concept. As we have seen, although salient things are salient, the fact that altering salience facts has such potent consequences is not salient; the mechanisms involved can be quite veiled. Moreover, these consequences can be harmful and they can be harmful in ways that perpetuate and even exacerbate antecedent patterns of group-based injustice. Consequently, shedding light on the subtle mechanisms involved is all to the good. Bringing those harms and their covert causes to the surface can open up new possibilities for positive social change.

Notes

1 Salience plays a central role (via exemplification) in Elgin's reconceptualized epistemology. See her *True Enough* (Cambridge, MA: MIT Press, 2017). It is front and center in Lewis's classic work on convention. Davis Lewis, *Convention* (Cambridge, MA: Harvard University Press, 1969). Salience plays an essential role in coordinating behavior. Richard Brooks has recently argued that how we address one another highlights (i.e. makes salient) certain social roles in context thus helping to avoid conflict by guiding or coordinating behavior. See Richard Brooks, *The Law of Address*, unpublished manuscript. Contextualism in epistemology relies crucially on salience. See especially David Lewis, "Elusive Knowledge," *Australasian Journal of Philosophy*,

74: 549–567, 1996 and Keith DeRose, "Solving the Skeptical Problem." *The Philosophical Review*, 104: 1–52, 1995. Salience also plays a critical role on the phenomenology of religious experience. Peter Goldie, *The Emotions: A Philosophical Exploration* (Oxford: Oxford University Press, 2000).
2 See, for example, the classic H.P. Grice, "Logic and Conversation," in *Studies in the Way of Words* (Cambridge, MA: Harvard University Press, 1989): 22–40; Dan Sperber and Deirdre Wilson, *Relevance: Communication and Cognition* (Oxford: Blackwell, 1986).
3 For a discussion of this scope issue in criminal law, see Kent Greenawalt, *Speech, Crime, and the Uses of Language* (Oxford: Oxford University Press, 1989). For a more general discussion of the First Amendment, see Frederick Schauer, "The Boundaries of the First Amendment: A Preliminary Exploration of Constitutional Salience," *Harvard Law Review* 117 (6): 1765–1809, 1972; Frederick Schauer, *Free Speech: A Philosophical Enquiry* (Cambridge: Cambridge University Press, 1982). For a sufficient disqualifying condition, see Ishani Maitra and Mary Kate McGowan, "The Limits of Free Speech: Pornography and the Question of Coverage," *Legal Theory* 13 (1): 41–68, 2007; and Ishani Maitra and Mary Kate McGowan, "On Racist Hate Speech and the Scope of a Free Speech Principle," *Canadian Journal of Law and Jurisprudence* 23 (2): 343–372, 2009. Finally, for an exploration of the possibility of several different free speech principles, see Robert Simpson, "Defining 'speech': Subtraction, Addition, and Division," *Journal of Law and Jurisprudence* 29 (2): 457–494, 2016.
4 This would not be an instance of discrimination in the legal sense (because redheaded persons are not a protected group) but it is an instance of discrimination in the moral sense (since it disadvantages persons in virtue of morally irrelevant characteristics of those persons). For a discussion of various types of discrimination (or senses of 'discrimination'), see Ch. 7 of Mary Kate McGowan, *Just Words: On Speech and Hidden Harm* (Oxford: Oxford University Press, 2019) and Andrew Altman. "Discrimination," in Edward N. Zalta (ed.), *The Stanford Encyclopedia of Philosophy* (Spring 2011 Edition) http://plato.stanford.edu/archives/spr2011/entries/discrimination/.
5 One might be tempted to say that certain norms are such that the mere enacting of them is harmful (and thus constitutes harm). Consider, for example, the employer's verbal enacting of this discriminatory hiring policy. Even if a discriminatory hiring practice does not result from the enacting of this policy (because, say, the business is shut down shortly thereafter), that policy in place might be harmful in a counterfactual way. Options are unjustly limited and this is so even if no particular redheaded person is denied employment. I have sympathy with this line of thinking, but build resulting harms into the conditions of the constitution in order to simplify the discussion. Langton, by contrast, defines harm constitution in terms of enacting harmful norms. See her *Sexual Solipsism: Philosophical Essays on Pornography and Objectification* (Oxford: Oxford University Press, 2009).
6 What truth-makers are ontologically (states of affairs, tropes, …), which sorts of things bear truth-value (sentences, propositions, …), which relation obtains between truth-makers and truth-bearers (necessitation, entailment, grounding….) and even which truths, if any, require their own truth-maker are here left entirely open.
7 For further discussion of the distinction between direct and dependent enacting, see my *Just Words: On Speech and Hidden Harm* (Oxford: Oxford University Press, 2019).
8 See Charlotte Witt, *The Metaphysics of Gender* (Oxford: Oxford University Press, 2011); Sally Haslanger, "Race and Gender: (What) Are They? (What) Do We Want Them to Be?" *Nous* 34 (1): 31–55, 2000; Sally Haslanger, *Resisting Reality: Social Construction and Social Critique* (Oxford: Oxford University Press, 2012); Asta Sveinsdottir, *Categories We Live By: The Construction of Sex, Gender, Race, and Other Social Categories* (Oxford: Oxford University Press, 2017).

9 See Christine Bicchieri and Hugo Mercier, "Norms and Beliefs: How Change Occurs," in Maria Xenitidou and Bruce Edmonds (eds.), *The Complexity of Social Norms* (Heidelberg: Springer, 2014): 37–54. This is a gloss on Christine Bicchieri, *The Grammar of Society: The Nature and Dynamics of Social Norms* (Cambridge: Cambridge University Press, 2006).

10 According to Bicchieri, social norms are constituted by the (empirical and normative) expectations of individual people and this opens up the possibility of changing them. Altering our expectations in the right way will transform social norms. For a discussion about altering social norms, see Christine Bicchieri and Hugo Mercier, "Norms and Beliefs: How Change Occurs," in Maria Xenitidou and Bruce Edmonds (eds.), *The Complexity of Social Norms* (Heidelberg: Springer, 2014): 37–54.

11 Lessig discusses dueling in the American South. See his "The Regulation of Social Meaning," *The University of Chicago Law Review* 62 (3): 943–1045 at 1001, 1995. Bicchieri and Mercier discuss female genital cutting. See Christine Bicchieri and Hugo Mercier, "Norms and Beliefs: How Change Occurs," in Maria Xenitidou and Bruce Edmonds (eds.), *The Complexity of Social Norms* (Heidelberg: Springer, 2014): 37–54.

12 I am working with a Lewisian conception of conversational score. It tracks everything relevant. See his "Scorekeeping in a Language Game," *Philosophical Papers Volume I* (Oxford: Oxford University Press, 1983): 240–243. Common ground is a different way to specify conversational context. It tracks only what is accepted (for the purposes of the conversation) by all participants. See Robert Stalnaker, 1998. "On the Representation of Context," *Journal of Logic, Language, and Information* 7: 3–19 and his "Common Ground," *Linguistics and Philosophy* 25: 701–721, 2002. For a discussion of the difference (and why I prefer score), see ch 2 §§ 4–5 of my *Just Words: On Speech and Hidden Harm* (Oxford: Oxford Unievrsity Press, 2019).

13 I leave it open whether this uniqueness condition is required for reference and I also leave it open whether this uniqueness condition is a semantic or pragmatic one. See Bertrand Russell, "On Denoting," *Mind* 14 (56) (Oct. 1905): 479–493; Szabo, Zoltan Gendler, "Descriptions and Uniqueness," *Philosophical Studies* 101: 29–57, 2000; and Craige Roberts, "Information Structure: Towards and Integrated Formal Theory of Pragmatics, in Yoon, Jae-Hak and Andreas Kathol (eds.), *Ohio State University Working Papers in Linguistics No. 49*, Papers in Pragmatics, 2012. Available at https://linguistics.osu.edu/sites/linguistics.osu.edu/files/workingpapers/osu_wpl_49.pdf

14 There are other ways to try to account for this. Perhaps 'the desk' is shorthand for a longer description that satisfies the uniqueness condition. Russell himself used this ellipsis strategy by taking proper names to be shorthand for definite descriptions. See Bertrand Russell (1918/1956), "The Philosophy of Logical Atomism," in R. Marsh (ed.) *Logic and Knowledge* (London: Allen and Unwin, 1956): 29. Alternatively, one might argue that the objects under consideration are restricted in such a way that this uniqueness condition is met. For an especially accessible discussion of this uniqueness problem, see William Lycan, *Philosophy of Language: A Contemporary Introduction* (London and New York: Routledge, 2000): 24–25. For further details see, for example, Stephen Neale, *Descriptions* (Cambridge, MA: MIT Press, 1990) and Stanley and Szabo (2000), "On Quantifier Domain Restriction," *Mind and Language* 15 (2 and 3): 219–261. For criticisms of salience-based accounts of reference fixing for demonstratives, see Nowak and Michaelson (this volume).

15 Many theorists appeal to salience. Lewis does. See his "Scorekeeping in a Language Game," *Philosophical Papers Volume I* (Oxford: Oxford University Press, 1983): 240–243. So does Herbert Clark although his account is a bit more detailed. See Herbert Clark, *Using Language* (Cambridge: Cambridge University Press, 1996): 62–70.

16 The salience component of the score will itself have many components; one for each type of thing under consideration.

17 The term 'exercitive' comes from Austin. J. L. Austin, *How to Do Things with Words* (Cambridge, MA: Harvard University Press, 1975): 155–157. Although Austin's terminology is not widespread in the mainstream philosophy of language, linguistics, or pragmatics literatures, my work has arisen out of a separate literature that does use the term. Moreover, the category of exercitive is both helpful and illuminating. The speech act approach to free speech literature (mainly arising from Langton's work) uses the category of exercitive. See Rae Langton, 1993. "Speech Acts and Unspeakable Acts," *Philosophy and Public Affairs* 22 (4): 293–330.
18 Silencing can occur before communication is even attempted when, for example, a speaker decides against speaking (and certain further conditions are met). Doston calls this testimonial smothering. Kristie Dotson, 2011. "Tracking Epistemic Violence, Tracking Practices of Silencing," *Hypatia* 26 (2): 236–257.

Silencing can occur when there is a recognition failure during an attempted communication (and that recognition failure is brought about in a systematic way). Rae Langton. 1993. "Speech Acts and Unspeakable Acts," *Philosophy and Public Affairs* 22 (4): 293–330; Jennifer Hornsby, 1993. "Speech Acts and Pornography," *Women's Philosophy Review* 10: 38–45; Ishani Maitra, 2009. "Silencing Speech," *Canadian Journal of Philosophy* 39 (2): 309–338; Mary Kate McGowan, 2014. "Sincerity Silencing," *Hypatia* 29 (2): 458–473. Finally, silencing can occur after communication has succeeded, when, for example, a speaker's speech act is (systematically) prevented from having its intended effect. Group-based credibility deficits are an example of this. Women might be silenced if, for example, they are systematically discredited when speaking about their experiences with sexual violence. Dotson calls this testimonial quieting; Fricker calls it testimonial injustice. Kristie Dotson, 2011. "Tracking Epistemic Violence, Tracking Practices of Silencing," *Hypatia* 26 (2): 236–257; Patricia Hill Collins, *Black Feminist Thought: Knowledge, Consciousness, and the Politics of Empowerment*, second edition (New York. Routledge, 2000); Miranda Fricker, *Epistemic Injustice: Power and the Ethics of Knowing* (Oxford: Oxford University Press, 2007).
19 See my "Oppressive Speech," *Australasian Journal of Philosophy* 87 (3): 389–407.
20 H.P. Grice, "Logic and Conversation," in *Studies in the Way of Words* (Cambridge, MA: Harvard University Press, 1989): 26–31.
21 To say that these norms are conversational does not require that they be peculiar to conversation. These "conversational" norms may just be more general norms of cooperation.
22 See my "Oppressive Speech," *Australasian Journal of Philosophy* 87 (3): 389–407. The distinction between g-norms and s-norms may not be a sharp one and there is likely to be a complex feedback system between the two sorts of norms. (G-norms clearly affect which s-norms are enacted by any particular move. Moreover, s-norms may (collectively) affect the g-norms.) Although interesting, such details are not pursued here.
23 For a discussion of authority versus standing, see *Just Words: On Speech and Hidden Harm* (Oxford: Oxford University Press, 2019): 64–66.
24 Richard Brooks, *The Law of Address*, unpublished manuscript. Pamela Wible, "Her Story Went Viral. But She is Not the Only Black Doctor Ignored in an Airplane Emergency," *Washington Post*, October 20, 2016. Available at https://www.washingtonpost.com/national/health-science/tamika-cross-is-not-the-only-black-doctor-ignored-in-an-airplane-emergency/2016/10/20/3f59ac08-9544-11e6-bc79-af1cd3d2984b_story.html?utm_term=.534ef6c58314
25 It could be that race is salient by default (especially in contemporary U.S. culture). There is reason to think, for example, that this is true for non-whites especially in social contexts traditionally reserved for whites. If that is the case, then Dr. Green's utterance renders Dr. Tilson's race more salient (than it already was) and this has consequences for which g-norms are activated. For a discussion of this, see my *Just Words: On Speech and Hidden Harm* (Oxford: Oxford University Press, 2019).

26 C.M. Steele, S.J. Spencer, and J. Aronson, "Contending with a Group Image: The Psychology of Stereotype and Social identity Threat," in M.P. Zanna (ed.), *Advances in Social Experimental Psychology*, Vol. 34 (San Diego, CA: Elsevier, 2002): 385. Quoted in Cordelia Fine, *Delusions of Gender* (New York: Norton, 2010): 30.
27 For a discussion of this, see Robert Mark Simpson, 2013. "Un-ringing the Bell: McGowan on Oppressive Speech and the Asymmetric Pliability of Conversation," *Australasian Journal of Philosophy* 91 (3): 555–575. For empirical work on this, see Jeff Greenberg and Tom Pyszczynski, 1985. "The Effect of an Overheard Slur on Evaluations of the Target: How to Spread a Social Disease," *Journal of Experimental Social Psychology* 21 (1): 61–71; Jeffery A. Goodman, Jonathan Schell, Michelle G. Alexander, and Scott Eidelman, 2008. "The Impact of a Derogatory Remark on Prejudice Toward a Gay Male," *Journal of Applied Social Psychology* 38 (2): 542–555; Claude M. Steele and Joshua Aronson, 1995. "Stereotype Threat and the Intellectual Test Performance of African Americans," *Journal of Personality and Social Psychology* 69 (5): 797–811. It is important to note that associations are context-sensitive and malleable.
28 If these harms are brought about by adherence to norms enacted, then the harms are constituted rather than merely caused. Whether the causal process is norm-guided in this way is an empirical matter left open here.
29 Collins identifies "controlling images" of Black women (such as the mammy, Jezebel, and welfare mothers) each of which, according to Collins, serves to make the oppression of Black women seem justified and natural. See Collins, Patricia Hill, and *Black, Feminist Thought: Knowledge, Consciousness, and the Politics of Empowerment* (New York: Routledge, 2000). By focusing on Black women, we are at the intersection of race and gender. For work on intersectionality, see especially Kimberlé Crenshaw, 1989. "Demarginalizing the Intersection of Race and Sex: A Black Feminist Critique of Antidiscrimination Doctrine, Feminist Theory and Antiracist Politics," *University of Chicago Legal Forum* 1 (8). Available at: https://chicagounbound.uchicago.edu/uclf/vol1989/iss1/8 and Kimberlé Crenshaw, 1991. "Mapping the Margins: Intersectionality, Identity Politics, and Violence Against Women of Color," *Stanford Law Review* 43 (6): 1241–1299.
30 See, for example, Robert Mark Simpson, 2013, "Un-ringing the Bell: McGowan on Oppressive Speech and the Asymmetric Pliability of Conversation," *Australasian Journal of Philosophy* 91 (3): 555–575; Lawrence Blum, 2004, "Stereotypes and Stereotyping: A Moral Analysis," *Philosophical Papers* 33 (3): 251–289; Daniel Kelly and Erica Roeder, 2008. "Racial Cognition and the Ethics of Implicit Bias," *Philosophy Compass* 3(3): 522–540.

11 Harmful salience perspectives*

Ella Whiteley

11.1 Introduction

Can certain patterns of salience be harmful? I want to consider a normative side to salience. I will argue that we can harm someone simply in virtue of making certain things salient about them. This may be surprising. Whilst a great many factors, from physical and psychological violence, to false beliefs and credibility deficits, have already been identified as potentially harming an individual or group, facts about *salience* have not seemed particularly relevant to harm. I shall argue, however, that certain salience patterns can indeed be harmful.[1]

A woman can be harmed, for example, when what she is wearing is more salient in her interlocutor's mind than her conversational abilities. A philosopher can be harmed when what others find most salient about her is her identity as an ethnic minority, as opposed to her philosophical expertise. For an athlete who has been raped, it can be in her best interests for her athletic achievement to be her most salient feature, and not the fact that she was raped.

In what follows, I will begin, in §11.2, by distinguishing linguistic and cognitive salience perspectives. Certain uses of language make some properties more linguistically salient than others. This tends to make those properties more salient in the minds of its audience, producing a counterpart *cognitive* salience perspective. Linguistic and cognitive salience perspectives can be harmful. They can be instrumentally harmful, as I show in §11.3, when they produce certain beliefs, ideologies and actions. They can be harmful in a constitutive way, as I show in §11.4, for example, when they are in themselves objectifying, or disrespectful of personhood. I conclude that certain salience perspectives can both cause and constitute particular kinds of harm. This has wider ramifications for existing debates in ethics, such as for hate speech, as I show in §11.5.

11.2 Salience perspectives

When we communicate, we try to get our audience to adjust their attitudes in various ways. If I say 'Jane is excellent at philosophy', I may be trying to produce a certain belief.[2] If I say 'Jane's book will open up your mind; you won't regret buying it!', I may be aiming to produce a certain desire. Sometimes, we simply

DOI: 10.4324/9781351202114-12

encourage our audience to make something more *salient*. If I say 'yes Jane is a little socially awkward, but we shouldn't forget that she gives an awful lot to charity', I encourage my audience to make Jane's charitable side more prominent in their minds.

11.2.1 Cognitive salience perspectives

When something is salient in our minds, we notice it, remember it, and find it cognitively accessible. Think about listening to a band. You might find yourself focussing on one instrument over the others. That synth is really grabbing your attention! You hear the drums, but they've melted into the background of your experience.[3] Because you've noticed the synth, it also sticks in your memory—a week later, it's the synth that you've remembered the sound of better than the other instruments. When you think about the band, then, you find the synth particularly cognitively accessible, in the sense that it takes little cognitive labour to think of it—it easily pops into your mind.[4] The drums, on the other hand, require a lot more processing power to think of—they're not 'at the top of your mind', so to speak: instead you really have to imagine yourself back in the room, and so on.

When we are disposed to find a property particularly noticeable, memorable, and cognitively accessible, we can be said to have a particular 'cognitive salience perspective'. (The terminology of 'perspective' is borrowed from Elisabeth Camp.)[5] A cognitive salience perspective is constituted by dispositions that structure our *attention*. It structures how properties are foregrounded and backgrounded in our attention by giving some *relative* salience over others.[6] So, whilst the synth *and* drums in the band enter into your attention, it's the synth that is given *relative* salience over the drums.

We can also talk about how cognitive salience perspectives determine how *mental states* such as beliefs are structured in our attention. Whilst I hold various beliefs about a subject, it is a further question whether one of those beliefs has relatively more salience in my mind than another. I might believe that Jane is both socially awkward and charitable, but we can still ask which of these beliefs better captures my attention. Cognitive salience perspectives are individuated by how they *structure* mental content: they are not about *what* is represented in our cognition, but rather *how* that content is organised.[7]

It is this structural nature of attention that makes it a good candidate for an account of salience in the mind. Definitions of salience often hinge on the idea of structure; something is salient when it *stands out relative to the background*.[8] Salience, according to this definition, is about the structural relations between various contents so that certain of those contents stand out as more prominent than others. Attention has also been explicated in similar ways; indeed, Sebastian Watzl's 2017 book on attention is titled *Structuring Mind*. In it, he offers what he calls the 'priority structure view of attention', which refers to how our mind orders the parts of one's mental life so that certain parts are prioritised over others.[9]

The cases that I will be focussing on in the following sections concern someone recognising all relevant properties of, or having all relevant beliefs about, a subject, but nevertheless having one of those properties or beliefs more salient in their mind—namely, of that person giving *relative salience* to one of those properties or beliefs over another. Let's say, then, that Arif recognises Jane's social awkwardness and her charity. When I implore Arif to attend more to Jane's charity work, I am not claiming that he is *unaware* of this trait of hers, or that he is *ignoring* it. I am instead imploring Arif to give it *relative* salience over her awkwardness—to attend to it *more* than he currently is.

Whilst attention can take many forms, cognitive salience perspectives are characterised by what one might call *habitual* attention. In particular, they are constituted by dispositions to find, *intuitively* and *automatically*, certain properties more salient than others.[10] In and of the moment, Arif is not following a rationalised decision to focus on Jane's social awkwardness. He has developed a habit over time so that his attention simply gravitates towards this trait of hers. Attentional dispositions, then, often bypass our conscious deliberation. As with most habits, we are limited in our voluntary control over our cognitive salience perspectives. Arif, in and of the moment, might be unable to prevent himself from attending primarily to Jane's awkwardness. Despite this, he still possesses what Jules Holroyd would call 'long-range' control over which attentional dispositions he cultivates over time.[11] If he is so motivated, Arif might look to various habit-breaking techniques in order to stop himself intuitively and automatically attending more to Jane's awkwardness. For instance, he might look to the implicit bias literature's suggestions regarding how to change one's automatic, unconscious cognitive patterns. To borrow one technique from this literature, shown to be effective in reducing one's implicit biases, he might repeat certain intentions to himself such as 'when I see Jane, I will think 'charitable''.[12]

Finally, attention is distinct from belief. I might *believe* that the achievements and successes in my life should be salient in my attention—that I should find them noticeable and memorable—but I might nevertheless *attend* more to my worries and flaws.[13] My achievements simply don't intuitively leap out as salient in my own mind. Attention, then, is non-doxastic, and therefore lacks truth conditions.

11.2.2 Linguistic salience perspectives

There are lots of ways that we might explicitly use language to encourage our audience to adopt a certain cognitive salience perspective, as when we say 'well, yes Jane is a little socially awkward, but let's not forget how much she gives to charity'. Here, by explicitly using phrases such as 'but let's not forget *x*', we imply that our audience should make *x* (i.e., Jane's charitable side) more salient in their minds. Alternatively, we might explicitly say 'Jane is very charitable!' If our audience already believes this proposition, this utterance might be an explicit effort to get them to *attend* more to Jane's charitable side.

There are more subtle ways of encouraging our audience to adopt a particular cognitive salience perspective. One is by using what we can call a *linguistic salience perspective*. Linguistic salience perspectives too are individuated by how they *structure* content, in this case, linguistic content.

Consider a journalist making decisions about how to present the costs and benefits of Brexit in a newspaper article. They are obliged, let's say, to include both a cost and a benefit of Brexit—for instance, the increased hate crime since the vote, and the benefits associated with no longer having to pay the EU membership fee. They are obliged, then, to include a particular set of linguistic contents. Even with this constraint on what content they can communicate, the journalist can decide which of these facts to *head-line*—namely, which of these facts they make most salient.[14] They mock up two articles, the only difference between them being which implication of Brexit is at the top of the page. We can say, in this case, that the two articles invoke different linguistic salience perspectives. A linguistic salience perspective refers to the *structuring* of linguistic contents so that certain contents stand out more than others.

The aim of this sort of linguistic salience perspective is to inculcate its cognitive counterpart in its audience. So, the newspaper that makes hate crime headline is encouraging its audience to attend primarily to the socio-political costs of Brexit. It is encouraging its audience to make these properties of Brexit more salient in their minds, so that they better notice, remember, and find cognitively accessible, such costs.

Even in an article that discusses the benefits of Brexit in just as much detail as the costs, invoking a linguistic salience perspective that involves simply head-lining the costs can successfully encourage its audience to pay more attention to those costs. While the article explicitly recognises both the costs and benefits of Brexit, it nevertheless encourages its audience to come away with the costs looming larger in their minds.

One important thing to flag about linguistic salience perspectives is that they have an *under the radar* quality. They do not make their requests explicit, such as through the phrase 'pay attention to the costs of Brexit'. Instead, they subtly play with the presentation of information. This gives them a manipulative quality, insofar as they do not, in Cass Sunstein's words, '*sufficiently engage or appeal to [people's] capacity for reflection and deliberation*' (emphasis in original).[15] Instead, they attempt to *bypass* a person's conscious awareness. Language like this can have a special power in shaping a person's cognitive and behaviour state. In particular, because we are not *aware* of what this language is getting us to do (in this case, shift our attentional patterns such that we make a certain content particularly salient in our minds), we do not consciously monitor our attentional patterns. As such, we do not attempt to suppress any attentional patterns that we might reject, if given the opportunity to reflect. This can make linguistic salience perspectives especially *effective* in shaping people's attentional dispositions, something I will discuss further below.

In what follows, I will argue that mere salience perspectives, both cognitive and linguistic, can have significant moral implications.

11.3 Salience perspectives and instrumental harms

Imagine a man, let's call him Terry, who, when interacting with men, tends to notice their voice and face more than their body. He easily remembers what they say, as well as their facial expressions. When he considers an individual man that he has met, he tends to find these aspects of them more cognitively accessible than memories of their biceps or chest size. By contrast, when Terry interacts with women, he often notices and remembers a woman's figure or chest more than their face and voice, finding these attributes most accessible in his mind when he later reflects on what they were like. Terry still notices and remembers other aspects of the women he meets; he does notice and remember their conversational contributions and personality quirks. They are simply less prominent in his mind than these other features.

Terry is systematically attending to women differently from men. Is this a problem? Well, you might think that this could be a problem if Terry's cognitive salience perspective on women is helping him to objectify women in what he believes, and in how he acts. Sexual objectification involves treating a person as a thing in some way. Perhaps Terry's cognitive salience perspective is helping him to think things like 'women are reducible to their bodies'. Perhaps it is helping him to act in objectifying ways, for example by touching women inappropriately, as though women are physical objects to be enjoyed, instead of agents with personal space to be respected.[16]

Can these patterns of attention really be enough to activate such substantive beliefs and actions, though? Evidence from cognitive psychology suggests that they could. Let's consider some of this evidence.

11.3.1 Framing effects

Framing effects occur when people respond differently to informationally equivalent contents when those contents are presented in subtly different ways.[17] Consider the question: 'How do women lead differently to men in boardrooms?' Now consider the same question, phrased slightly differently: 'How do men lead differently to women in boardrooms?' Surely, this change in word order is too trivial to evoke different responses from us?

Not so, say Susanne Bruckmüller and colleagues.[18] They found that study participants answering the former question were, amongst other things, more likely to endorse gender stereotypes, attributing a greater number of stereotypical traits to men (such as self-confidence, independence, and decisiveness), and a greater number of feminine stereotypic traits to women (such as being emotional, compassionate, and warm). Why?

Although a full answer to this question is relatively complex, we can give a brief analysis.[19] The two questions differ not in content, but in the *structuring* of that content. More specifically, the only difference between the phrases is the order in which 'men' and 'women' occur in the sentence. These questions differ in virtue of linguistic salience perspective only. By talking about women *first* in the question 'how do *women* differ from *men* in the boardroom', this question makes women more salient than men. This triggers a linguistic norm, that treats women as more salient in the *explanation*. They are the *effect-to-be-explained*, whilst men are positioned as the implicit norm for comparison.[20] As discussed, a salience perspective in language tends to cultivate its counterpart salience perspective in our cognition. This salience perspective suggests that we, as the audience, position women as the group that we *attend* to when giving our explanation as to how men and women differ in the domain of leadership.

By drawing the audience's attention to women in this way, various cognitively accessible, pragmatic associations and beliefs concerning women in leadership are activated that *also* treat women as salient in this domain—namely, that treat women as *striking* and *unusual* in the domain of leadership. In particular, they are striking insofar as they *do not fit the stereotype of a leader*. In our culture, the stereotype of a leader is a man. Leadership qualities are masculine qualities—rationality, assertiveness, lack of emotion, and so on.[21] These clash with stereotypes associated with women; women are stereotyped to be illogical, compassionate, emotional, nurturing, and so on. Indeed, in Bruckmüller and colleagues' pre-test, they found that men were called to mind much more easily when participants were asked to imagine a leader.[22]

By making women salient in our minds when comparing the genders in the domain of leadership, then, we activate the cognitively accessible gender stereotypes that make them salient in that domain.[23]

Whilst this can have various epistemic consequences, what is relevant to my purposes is the *harm* that stereotypes can engender.[24] Although Bruckmüller et al. do not discuss this issue, activating inferences to stereotypes can mean also activating various forms of *behaviour* that are consistent with these stereotypes.[25] For instance, research suggests that, thanks to the stereotype that leaders are men, employers are more likely to hire a man as a manager.[26] Research has also shown that men are also more likely to get promoted over women, and receive larger bonuses and variable pay, even when these men's and women's performance evaluations are identical.[27]

Further, it has been shown that where women display assertiveness, a trait stereotypically associated with leadership, and a trait that Laurie Rudman and Julie Phelan describe as 'necessary for success in the business world', they tend to get viewed and evaluated more negatively, and this comes with significant financial setbacks for women leaders.[28] It has been suggested that these factors combine to explain why fewer women put in for leadership roles.[29] Not only do stereotypes tell women that they do not fit the bill of a leader, but the prescriptive side of these stereotypes means that they will likely be penalised if they *do* try to lead, which dissuades them from pursuing leadership roles.[30] Where women *do* pursue leadership roles, research suggests that negative stereotypes associated with women leaders can engender stereotype threat effects, affecting how well women leaders perform. For instance, research conducted on

American adults found that when these negative stereotypes are implicitly activated (e.g., where feminine-coded traits, such as empathy, are linked to poor negotiation outcomes), women tend to underperform men in leadership tasks.[31]

It might be helpful, then, to see this stereotype of men leaders as part of a wider *ideology* about leaders. Ideologies, according to Eric Swanson, encompass a great range of mutually supporting components.[32] Some are doxastic, but many are non-doxastic. These non-doxastic components might involve associations, affective dispositions, codes of interaction, values, practices, and so on. An ideology about leaders might involve associations between men and presidents. It might involve feelings of unease at leaders who are women, and codes of interaction that encourage one to behave in distrustful, patronising ways towards women leaders. It might involve valuing cold, unemotional behaviour.

Simply making women salient in the context of a gender comparison of leadership styles, then, can activate problematic stereotypes (and, arguably, ideologies) associated with women leaders being salient (read: striking) in our culture. In other words, a mere salience perspective can activate stereotypes. The action-engendering consequences of these stereotypes make vivid the far-reaching, material consequences that can come with salience perspectives.

11.3.2 Terry and his salience perspective on women

In the example above, no cultural beliefs, associations and ideologies are explicitly discussed, and yet the audience ends up endorsing them. How does this happen? When certain beliefs, associations and ideologies are cognitively accessible, we risk activating them simply by making salient content that is central to those beliefs, associations and ideologies. In the example above, there is a cognitively accessible stereotype that women are unusual because women are too emotional and illogical to lead. Simply making *salient* content that is central to this stereotype (namely, women), in the context of a comparison of gendered leadership styles, is sufficient to activate this stereotype.

Further, it is precisely the fact that the beliefs and ideologies are not explicitly asserted that can explain why framing effects are so successful at altering our responses. Framing effects work in an *under the radar* way, which, as discussed earlier, can make them especially effective in manipulating our thought and behavioural patterns. Research shows that where the sort of implicit stereotype activation above occurs, more people respond in stereotype-congruent ways, in the sense that their responses are consistent with them *endorsing* stereotypes. For instance, I would be responding in stereotype-congruent ways if, when shown a video of a black man behaving in an ambiguous way (e.g., bumping into someone), I am likely to evaluate that man's behaviour as aggressive (i.e., as fitting with harmful stereotypes that black men are threatening).[33] In particular, it is not just high-prejudiced individuals (i.e., those who, according to psychological tests, indicate that they accept and endorse stereotypes)[34] who respond in these ways. Implicit stereotype activation also succeeds in getting *low*-prejudiced individuals (i.e., those who, whilst they have knowledge of stereotypes, indicate that they reject them) to respond in stereotype-congruent ways. When stereotypes are activated explicitly, such as where a stereotype is *asserted*, fewer people have these stereotype-congruent responses. Again, because our ability consciously to monitor our thought patterns is precluded in cases of implicit stereotype activation, we do not attempt to suppress the activation of the stereotype, or the behavioural codes associated with it.[35]

What can this tell us about Terry and his cognitive salience perspective on women? Well, given that our culture is saturated in objectifying images and narratives that encourage us to think of women in terms of their bodies, objectifying beliefs and ideologies about women are plausibly cognitively accessible.[36] Terry, in virtue of having a cognitive salience perspective on women that makes salient content central to these beliefs and ideologies—i.e., by making women's bodies salient—risks activating those beliefs and ideologies. The behavioural dimension of ideologies is important to emphasise here; Terry's cognitive salience perspective might activate behavioural codes that encourage him to *act* in objectifying ways, such as by touching women inappropriately.

Further, Terry's cognitive salience perspective on women need not be one that he is conscious of having. Where Terry is not conscious of his salience perspective, its activation of any objectifying beliefs and ideologies (and their component behavioural codes) would occur in an under-the-radar way. As such, his cognitive salience perspective would be likely to be *especially successful* in activating these beliefs and ideologies.

What is the problem here? Leaving aside their epistemic issues, objectifying beliefs and ideologies can themselves be harmful; they are ways of treating a person as an object, and of disrespecting their personhood, as we shall see in §11.4. Objectifying beliefs and ideologies have a range of harmful consequences, from decreased self-esteem of those who are objectified, to behaviour that includes sexual harassment and rape.[37] So, Terry's mere salience perspective on women could harm women in just these ways. (One might also consider how his salience perspective on women harms Terry himself. For instance, finding women's bodies more salient than their personalities might limit the meaningful relationships he is able to cultivate in his life.)

In this section, I have argued that certain salience perspectives can be *instrumentally* harmful.[38] They can be damaging because of their *effects*, including the beliefs, ideologies and actions that they are liable to activate.

11.4 Salience perspectives and constitutive harms

Is there a more direct way in which salience perspectives can be harmful? Can a certain salience perspective be harmful *independently of its effects*? I think that it can.

11.4.1 People who have experienced rape[39]

Many women have experienced sexual violence. 85,000 women are raped in England and Wales alone every year.[40] Many cases are not brought to trial.[41]

There are multiple reasons that these women might want to avoid testifying in the courts. The exceedingly low conviction rate is one. The emotional distress of having to recount a horrific attack to a room full of people is another.[42] A different reason, however, might be that these women do not want the fact that they were raped to become the most salient thing about them. They do not want it to be what others find most noticeable, memorable, and cognitively accessible.

A common concern raised by those who have been raped is that this experience ends up masking other aspects of one's identity. Monika Korra, who was kidnapped and raped when she was out on a run, has said that she wants to be known as a runner, not a rape victim. Calling running her passion, Korra describes it as 'the thing that gave me identity in life', and that her rape threatened the primacy of that identity.[43] Similarly, Simone Biles, seven-time Olympic gymnastics medalist cited similar concerns when she announced that she had been sexually abused by her USA Olympic national team doctor. In a statement published on social media, Biles stressed that 'this horrific experience does not define me. I am much more than this. I am unique, smart, talented, motivated, and passionate. I have promised myself that my story will be much greater than this...[emphasis in original]'.[44]

Many complex issues around identity, and the 'victim' status in particular,[45] no doubt play a role in Korra and Biles' thoughts here. One way of thinking about their statements, though, is by invoking cognitive salience perspectives. Let's think back to what cognitive salience perspectives involve. What would having Korra's experience of rape, for example, be most prominent amongst her various characteristics mean? Amongst other things, this would involve people *noticing* properties connected to the fact that she was raped more than others; for instance, they might notice others discussing her experience of rape more than they would notice others discussing her skills, her interests, and so on. Further, the fact that Korra was raped would be the most remembered feature of her life by others. It would involve the fact that she was raped being at the top of people's minds when considering Korra's other traits.

This is a problem when it is in one's interests to have *different* features of one's person most salient in the minds of others (and one's own mind).[46] Korra and Biles would do better having 'runner' and 'Olympic gymnast' respectively more salient than 'person who has experienced rape' in people's minds. They would do better having their athletic successes noticed and remembered more easily than reports of their rape, and for their determination and commitment to their sport to be at the top of people's minds when they come to think about them, contemplate their behaviour, and act towards them.

Why? Consider sexual objectification again. A common feminist explanation as to why phenomena like objectification harm women, have referenced the idea that we deserve to be recognised as agents with personhood—with, amongst other things, rationality, a capacity to set and pursue our own ends, integrity and personality.[47] Objectification is harmful because it involves *disrespecting* an individual's personhood. Rachel Fraser has noted the importance of this idea in feminist writing about rape: 'feminists have long argued for the importance of recognising the complex personhood and agency of those who have experienced rape'.[48] This is especially important when people who experience rape are understood and portrayed as passive and lifeless. In Susan Brison's powerful philosophical paper detailing her experience of rape, she talks about how crime novels and detective films portray the rapist as agential, whilst the victim is treated as 'a merely passive pretext for our entertainment'.[49] Fraser herself cites rape metaphors as evidence for this way of seeing those who experience rape. Metaphors such as 'Germany is raping Brazil in the football right now' are prevalent and successful in part *because* of the ease of seeing those who experience rape as powerless and passive—as *lacking* personhood.[50]

We can harm a person by disrespecting their personhood. How does this apply to salience perspectives? Attending to a person so that their personhood-related traits are their most salient attributes looks to be one way of *respecting* their personhood. Having 'athlete' at the top of our minds when considering Korra and Biles helps us to notice and remember an identity that they have autonomously chosen, displays their individuality, reflects their ability to set their own goals, reflecting their rationality and agency. Conversely, attending to a person so that their *non* personhood-related traits are their most salient features is a way of disrespecting their personhood, and of *harming* them. Having 'person who has experienced rape' most prominent in our minds directs our attention to their passive status as someone who has been attacked: a status they did not choose, and so does not reflect their individuality, their agency, and so on.[51]

Disrespecting an individual's personhood is harmful not just instrumentally, but in itself, independently of its further effects. If a certain cognitive salience perspective is a way of disrespecting someone's personhood, it *constitutes* a harm.

11.4.2 Women and their bodies

The example of Terry illustrates this constitutive harm, as well as the instrumental harms discussed earlier. Attending to men so that their conversational contributions are their most salient feature is a way of *respecting* their personhood. Attending to women so that their body parts are their most salient feature is a way of *disrespecting* their personhood.[52]

The particular type of harm seems connected to *objectification*, treating a person as a thing. There are many ways of 'treating' a person as a thing, in actions, or in attitudes. I suggest that objectifying treatment includes mere attention. Making an individual's *thing*-like properties more salient than their personhood-related properties is a form of objectification. Attending to a person in this way might count as a way of treating a person as a thing. Martha Nussbaum's influential account of objectification details seven ways of treating a person as a thing, including, for instance, denying a person's autonomy, and treating them as fungible.[53] Other ways have been added since.[54] The speculative suggestion being made here is that *attending* to a person so that their thing-like properties are their most salient feature is another way of treating them as a thing.

This proposal resonates with existing ideas in the literature on objectification.

Bartky, for instance, claims that women are 'too closely identified with [their body]'.[55] Paraphrasing her words, Evangelina Papadaki phrases Bartky's view in a way quite consonant with the idea that attentional patterns can objectify: '[a]ll the focus is placed on a woman's body, in a way that her mind or personality are not adequately acknowledged'.[56] The particularly *minimalist* dimension of mere *salience* perspectives is never made entirely explicit, however. Further, Bartky goes on to expand on her view in ways that indicate that something beyond mere salience is at issue. For instance, she uses words like 'infatuation' synonymously with her idea of a 'focus' on the body, as well as using phrases such as '[being objectified] is to have one's entire being identified with the body'.[57] The sort of objectification being discussed here—let's call it *attentional* objectification—is not as strong as this. Aspects of one's person beyond one's body (such as personality and autonomy) are recognised by the objectifier; it is simply that the objectifier *better* attends to one's body. They give it *relative salience* over one's personality.

Leaving aside this question—namely, whether one can specifically *objectify* a person in virtue of making salient their thing-like properties—we can borrow an important qualification commonly made by those discussing objectification. Diagnosing whether harm results from the various ways in which one can treat a person as a thing often requires examining the particular case and context.[58] A doctor arguably reduces her patient to his body, but various considerations concerning the patient's goal of health, and the role of a doctor, mean that harm does not occur.[59] The same goes for cognitive salience perspectives. We need knowledge of the particular case and context to decide whether *attending* to a person so that their non-personhood-related traits are their most salient feature does in fact harm them.

Do the agent's desires count as one of these contextual variables? What if a woman, let's call her Chun, desires for her appearance to be her most salient feature? She might find others attending primarily to her figure to be empowering, and desires for her body to be given relative salience over her personality.[60] In other words, Chun wishes for (what I am calling) a non-personhood-related trait of hers to be most salient in the minds of others. Although we are attending primarily to a non-personhood-related trait of Chun's, does the fact that we are respecting her wishes mean that we avoid harming her?

How one adjudicates these sorts of cases depends on to what extent one thinks that agents can be *wrong* about what contributes to their well-being.[61] Can we say that Chun is *wrong* to say that having others attend to her body is empowering? An important point to note in this context is that a great many feminists have argued that our choices, preferences and desires are socially constructed, in the sense that society shapes them.[62] Where society is sexist, women can internalise sexist ideologies and end up choosing and desiring things that are congruent with sexism. For instance, due to internalising sexist body ideals for women, many women desire to be so thin that a medical professional would consider them seriously underweight.[63] Although these women's weight is often a result of their choices and desires, we can see in this instance how society has perniciously influenced these women, such that they end up choosing and desiring something unhealthy and harmful.

We must be alive to the fact, then, that the woman who desires for her appearance to be her most salient attribute may not be aware of how society has perniciously shaped her desires in a way that harms her. Whilst an individual can arguably be harmed when she is not attended to in the way in which she wishes,[64] we may well do that individual *greater* harm by heeding her wish, if that wish is for us to attend to her in a way that disrespects her personhood. This sort of conclusion is not an uncommon one. Many feminists recognise that a balancing act is necessary regarding respecting agent's desires, choices, and preferences on the one hand, whilst, on the other hand, being critical of what has *caused* those desires, choices, and preferences.[65] We might conclude, then, that we should indeed respect individuals' desires regarding how they are to be attended to, *but only to a certain extent*.[66] We also want to be able to point out where those individuals have internalised oppressive ideologies.

To summarise, simply attending to a person so that their non-personhood-related traits are their most salient feature can *constitute* (as opposed to cause) harm. Merely making a trait of an individual's *salient* in one's attention can by itself harm that individual, by disrespecting their personhood.

11.5 Salience perspectives and hate speech

What is the significance of this suggestion? Well, we do not usually think of salience or attention being relevant to harm. Acknowledging that it is would have implications for existing debates in ethics. Consider the topic of hate speech, for instance. This sort of speech tends to receive criticism on two grounds. Firstly, it is criticised for its liability to inculcate false and harmful beliefs in its audience. Jeremy Waldron, for instance, suggests understanding hate speech as group libel. As such, its harm consists in defaming members of a group through making *false* statements about them. Waldron considers a leaflet published in 1950s Chicago which urges people to protect the white race from being 'mongrelised' and terrorised by the 'rapes, robberies, guns, knives, and marijuana of the negro'.[67] The harm of this hate speech, he suggests, is primarily in its *falsity*, and the damage that false assertion does to the reputation of black people.

Alternatively, hate speech is often criticised on the basis of the violence that it causes and licences (i.e., legitimises). Lynne Tirrell, for instance, focuses on how hate speech can '[open] the door to previously prohibited [and violent] actions'.[68] Looking at the Rwandan genocide of 1994, Tirrell considers hate speech targeted at the Tutsi people. She notes that Tutsi people are regularly called '*inyenzi*' (Kinyarwanda for 'cockroach'). Tirrell suggests that partly because of the social meanings associated with the word 'cockroach' (e.g., that they are dirty and disgusting), uses of this word ended up licensing actions consistent with the Tutsi people *actually being* cockroaches, such as the mutilation of their bodies. Tirrell locates one harm of hate speech, then, in its ability to license violent, even genocidal, actions. Hate speech, can, in an important sense, *kill*.[69]

These are both important ways in which hate speech can be harmful. The suggestion in this paper, however, is that we should consider the possibility of another harm. We should consider whether hate speech might be harmful simply by inculcating a wrongful pattern of attention in its audience. The Chicago leaflet, for instance, arguably helps its audience to find any instances of crimes committed by black people particularly cognitively accessible—more so than, say, any good deeds they might do. The Rwandan hate speech arguably helps its audience better to notice and remember traits associated with cockroaches in Tutsi people—more so than traits associated with their personhood. For instance, cockroaches are taken to be ubiquitous, dirty and disease-ridden. Calling Tutsi people 'cockroaches' can serve simply to help one to notice crowds of Tutsi people, and to help one remember instances of unclean or unwell Tutsi people. In other words, hate speech might succeed simply in making certain traits of an individual, qua their group membership, particularly *salient*. This, as we have suggested, can *constitute* a way of harming them.

11.6 Conclusion

Salience perspectives can be harmful instrumentally, and harmful in themselves. They can produce harmful beliefs or ideologies. But in themselves, they can *constitute* a harm when they disrespect someone's personhood. Harm can extend beyond the material, behavioural, or doxastic level, then, to include mere salience patterns in our attention.

There is a great deal more to find out about salience perspectives. One question that this chapter has not addressed is whether harming someone in the manner discussed is a way of *wronging* them. Can making the wrong thing salient about a person involve a violation of their rights?[70] We might also ask if, and how, we can successfully change our cognitive salience perspectives. Perhaps the fact that our culture regularly depicts women as sex objects means that Terry, for instance, will struggle to adopt new attentional dispositions on women. Material changes in society may be necessary, therefore, for individuals successfully to cultivate new attentional dispositions.[71] I hope that these issues can be addressed in future discussions.

Notes

* This chapter was submitted in 2019. Since then, others have written on the ethical dimensions of salience. Jessie Munton's account of salience in connection to prejudice has some particularly interesting parallels with the ideas discussed in this chapter, which would be fruitful to investigate (Munton, 2021).
1 The type of harm being considered in this chapter is what Feinberg (1987, Ch. 1) calls 'setbacks to interests'. I am asking, therefore, if patterns of salience can hinder our interests. Our interests, Feinberg suggests, are those things in which we have a stake. They are components of our well-being, insofar as one 'flourishes or languishes

as [one's interests] flourish or languish' (ibid. 34). The sorts of interests that Feinberg judges to be morally relevant are those with some stability, and those that reflect a deep-rooted concern. A person can set back my interest, and thus harm me, by making it difficult for me to achieve my interest.

2 Langton (2012) identifies additional functions of speech beyond merely attempting to get the audience to *know* something they didn't before. She suggests that this occurs through a process of psychological accommodation.

3 This example is a version of one discussed by Sebastian Watzl (2017, p.74), whose work to has influenced of the ideas in this chapter.

4 This definition is inspired by Rachel Fraser's (2018) phraseology.

5 Camp (2017). A Campian perspective is partly constituted by mental dispositions that make certain properties stand out more than others. Campian perspectives also include other dimensions that go beyond salience, including dispositions to find certain properties more *causal and explanatory* than others (ibid. 80). I use the phrase 'cognitive salience perspective' to highlight how my account of perspectives is narrower than Camp's.

6 This view is inspired by Watzl's (2017, Ch. 4) 'priority structure view of attention'.

7 Camp (2017, p.77) is also largely concerned not with *what* content is represented in our thought, but rather *how* that content is represented.

8 Inspired by Amos Tversky's analysis of salience, Camp (2017, p.80) defines salience as in part being about how much a feature 'sticks out relative to the background'.

9 Watzl (2017, Ch. 4). This focus on the *structural* side of attention can be contrasted with what Watzl refers to as inquiries into the *manner* in which one attends (Watzl, 2022: §5.6). For instance, whilst I am interested in how the synth is *foregrounded* in my attention over the guitar (i.e., I am interested in attentional *structure*), those interested in my attentional *manner* might question the *way* in which I attend to the guitar; is my attention sensitive and insightful, appreciative of the nuances of the sound of the instrument, or am I blankly and uncritically attending to it? As Watzl suggests, the reader can look to Murdoch (1970) for discussions of this manner-based dimension of attention, including suggestions as to how ethically to evaluate the manner in which one attends. For ethical discussions of salience that are closer to the type of *structural* salience that interests me, see Chappell and Yetter-Chappell (2016) and Watzl (2022).

10 This type of intuitive, sub-conscious attention is discussed by Camp (2017, pp.80–83). See Watzl (2017) for a discussion of various other forms of attention, including attention that is under conscious control.

11 Holroyd (2012, p.284) uses this term to describe the type of control that we have over the skills, habits, and biases that we cultivate over time.

12 According to research by Stewart and Payne (2008), one effective way of reducing an implicit bias that involves associating black people with danger is to repeat the intention 'when I see a black face I will think 'safe''. See Saul (2012) for other techniques.

13 One might wonder if attention is instead captured by something like Gendler's (2008) notion of *alief*, which is also distinguished from belief. Crucially, aliefs encompass affective and behavioural dimensions; for instance, one might *alieve* that the characters in a film are real insofar as one feels emotions about them, and one is disposed to cry about the bad things that happen to them. It is precisely these dimensions that distinguish aliefs from cognitive salience perspectives. The latter are more minimal, simply involving the structuring of our attention so that we find certain properties more noticeable and memorable than others.

14 Watzl (2017, p.70) also compares our mind to a newspaper when explicating his account of attention.

15 Sunstein (2016, p.82) is talking about modes of manipulation more generally here, as opposed to linguistic salience perspectives in particular.

16 There are many different forms of objectification, as I touch upon later in §11.4.2. The form in question here relates best to treating women as though they do not have boundary integrity (Nussbaum, 1995, p.257).
17 Kahneman and Tversky (1979).
18 Bruckmüller et al. (2012).
19 See Bruckmüller et al. (2012) for a fuller analysis, which includes a discussion of the linguistic norms that tend to govern such comparative questions.
20 Ibid. (210).
21 See Bruckmüller et al. (2012, p.212) and the references therein. Also see Hegarty & Bruckmüller (2013, p.457).
22 Bruckmüller et al. (2012, p.2013).
23 These stereotypes are cognitively accessible in part because they are repeated so often in our culture. We hear them in the media, in everyday conversations and so on, so that they are increasingly familiar to us (Rudman & Glick, 2008, p.81).
24 For instance, a stereotype might be false, misleading, unwarranted, and so on. See, for example, Blum (2004), Langton (1993, 2004), Elgin (1996), and Puddifoot (2017) for these sorts of ideas.
25 Tirrell (2013, p.165), Wheeler & Petty (2001, p.820).
26 Heilman (2012).
27 Castilla (2008).
28 See Rudman and Phelan (2008, pp.65–66) and the references therein.
29 Hoyt and Murphy (2016).
30 Ibid. (388).
31 Kray et al. (2001). This also makes vivid one of the epistemic costs of this particular gender stereotype; it can have the wrong direction of fit with its subject matter (see Langton, 1993).
32 Swanson (forthcoming).
33 Devine (1989, p.7).
34 Psychological studies often use what is called the *Modern Racism Scale* to assess whether an individual counts as high- or low-prejudiced (Devine, 1989, p.7).
35 See Bornstein (1990) and Wheeler & Petty (2001, p.820).
36 Goh-Mah (2013).
37 See Choma et al. (2010) for connections between objectification and low self-esteem, and Vasquez et al. (2017) for connections between objectification and sexual violence.
38 This echoes one of the ways in which Watzl 2022: §5.7 suggests judging our attentional patterns—attentional patterns that I am calling *cognitive salience perspectives*.
39 I use the term 'person who has experienced rape' as a form of 'person-first language', which aims to emphasise the personhood of these individuals, by emphasising that they are first and foremost *people* (as opposed to victims/survivors of rape). The importance of emphasising the personhood of those who have experienced rape is discussed in §11.4.1.
40 Office for National Statistics (2013, p.6).
41 For instance, the crime survey for England and Wales found that around 5 in every 6 individuals who experienced rape did not report their experiences to the police (Office for National Statistics, 2018). Only 5.7% of reported rape cases result in a conviction for the perpetrator (Kelly et al., 2005).
42 See these and other issues eloquently discussed in an open letter by the person who was raped in the Stanford University rape case (Anonymous, reprinted in Osborne, 2016).
43 Korra, in Lopez (2016).
44 Biles, S., Twitter statement, reprinted in Lutz (2018).

45 See Jean-Charles (2014) and Kelly, Burton and Regan (1996) for discussions of the issues surrounding both words, 'victim' and 'survivor', in the context of rape.
46 As with stereotype threat, damage can be done through internalising salience perspectives. A person who has experienced rape can harm herself through making her experience of rape her most salient feature in her own mind.
47 The first two features of this list are borrowed from Kant (*Lectures on Ethics*), who many theorists writing about objectification cite (see Papadaki, 2018, §1). The latter features come from Dworkin (2000, pp.30–31) and Bartky (1990, p.130), who expand upon Kant.
48 Fraser (2018).
49 Brison (1993: 11).
50 Fraser (2018).
51 Some individuals who have experienced rape may find their status *as* a person who has experienced rape to be powerfully connected to their personhood. Instead of being something that is passive, it might have allowed them to, for instance, create support networks for others in similar positions, and to spread awareness of their experience. There are at least two ways of explaining this scenario. One is to suggest that these individuals are benefitting from others attending primarily to their status as an *informed political activist*, as opposed to *person who has experienced rape*. They look to be drawing attention to their experience of rape only in order to highlight the political and/or social goals that they wish to achieve, such as to improve the welfare of those who experience rape. It is their informed activism oriented towards these goals that demonstrate their agency, rationality, and so on. Considered by itself, the identity *person who has experienced rape* does not demonstrate these personhood-related traits. In fact, it is an identity that these activists are working hard to erase from the world, precisely *because* of the harm it does to those to whom it has been bestowed. An alternative explanation of this scenario suggests that whether a given trait is a '(non) personhood-related trait' depends on how it is functioning in a given case/context. In the case at hand, *person who has experienced rape* might be functioning as a personhood-related trait.
52 This idea might helpfully be applied to other examples, too. For instance, a common complaint from artists from minority backgrounds is that they are seen primarily in terms of their ethnicity, race, or nationality, instead of primarily as an artist. The fact that these artists are regularly referred to as e.g., 'Indian artists', while white artists are typically referred to simply as 'artists', gives credence to this complaint (Pollock & Parker, 1981: xix). Using the prefix 'Indian' serves to make these artists' nationality their most salient feature. Understanding that we can be harmed when a non personhood-related feature of ours is made our most salient attribute can help to identify the harm occurring in these cases. Indeed, the professional identity of these individuals (i.e., artist) seems a better candidate for a personhood-related trait than the nationalities, ethnicities or genders of these individuals. (For those who wish to argue that our nationalities, ethnicities and genders can count as personhood-related traits, we may be able to give a response that parallels that in fn. 51.)
53 Nussbaum (1995, p.257).
54 See Langton (2009, pp.228–229).
55 Bartky (1990, p.130).
56 Papadaki (2018, §3).
57 Bartky (1990, 35).
58 Langton (2005) and Nussbaum (1995) advocate this view. For a contrasting view, see MacKinnon (1987).
59 There are exceptions. Patients can be harmfully objectified by their doctors where their emotions, and personal perspectives on their health, are ignored, for instance (see Berglund et al., 2012).
60 This is indeed the message that many 'women's magazines', for instance, push.

One example of this is *Glamour* magazine's article on beauty products that empower women (Kay, 2018).
61 Perhaps, following prevalent positions in contemporary ethics (see Crisp, 2017, §4), one decides to be an objectivist about what counts as a personhood-related trait. Alternatively, one might opt for a softer 'informed desire' account, which takes personhood-related traits to be those that an individual would desire to be made most salient about them if they were fully informed. Or, one might opt for a middle ground, a version of which is indicated on p.204.
62 See, for example, Hirschmann (1996) and Hirshman (2006).
63 McCarthy (1990).
64 See, for instance, Korsgaard (1996) for the general argument that we can be harmed when others do not see us in the way in which we wish.
65 See, for instance, Hirschmann (1996) and Snyder-Hall (2010).
66 Defending precisely to *which* extent we should respect individuals' desires regarding how they are attended would take me beyond the scope of this chapter.
67 Waldron (2012, p.48).
68 Tirrell (2012, p.175).
69 For this phraseology, see Tirrell's participation in the podcast *Can Speech Kill?* (Philosophy Talk, 2017).
70 In fn. 1, I mentioned a notion of harm introduced by Feinberg—that of a *setback of interests*. This can be contrasted with another version of harm that Feinberg identifies, namely, harm in the sense of *wronging* someone (Feinberg, 1987, pp.34–35). This sort of harm consists of the violation of rights.
71 See similar advice from Sally Haslanger (2015) on how to change our implicit biases.

References

Bartky, S. 1990. *Femininity and Dominaion: Studies in the Phenomenology of Oppression.* Routledge, New York.
Berglund, M., Westin, L., Svanström, R. and Sundler, A. 2012. Suffering Caused by Care—Patients' Experiences From Hospital Settings. *International Journal of Qualitative Studies on Health and Well-Being* 7: 1–9.
Blum, L. 2004. Stereotypes and Stereotyping: A Moral Analysis. *Philosophical Papers* 33(3): 251–289.
Bornstein, R. F. 1990. Critical Importance of Stimulus Unawareness for the Production of Subliminal Psychodynamic Activation Effects: A Meta-Analytic Review. *Journal of Clinical Psychology* 46(2): 201–210.
Brison, S. 1993. Surviving Sexual Violence: A Philosophical Perspective. *Journal of Social Philosophy* 24(1): 5–22.
Bruckmüller, S., Hegarty, P. and Abele, A. 2012. Framing Gender Differences: Linguistic Normativity Affects Perceptions of Power and Gender Stereotypes. *European Journal of Social Psychology* 42: 210–218.
Camp, E. 2017. Perspectives in Imaginative Engagement with Fiction. *Philosophical Perspectives* 31: 73–102.
Castilla, E. 2008. Gender, Race, and Meritocracy in Organisational Careers. *American Journal of Sociology* 113(6): 1479–1526.
Chappell, R. Y. and Yetter-Chappell, H. 2016. Virtue and Salience. *Australasian Journal of Philosophy* 94(3): 449–463.
Choma, B., Visser, B., Pozzebon, J., Bogeart, A., Busseri, M. and Sadava, S. 2010. Self-

Objectification, Self-Esteem, and Gender: Testing a Moderated Mediation Model. *Sex Roles* 63: 645–656.

Crisp, R. 2017. Well-Being. *The Stanford Encylopedia of Philosophy* (Fall 2017 Edition). https://plato.stanford.edu/entries/well-being/ (Accessed 5 September).

Devine, P. 1989. Stereotypes and Prejudice: Their Automatic and Controlled Components. *Attitudes and Social Cognition* 56(1): 5–18.

Dworkin, A. 2000. Against the Male Flood: Censorship, Pornography, and Equality. In D. Cornell (Ed.), *Feminism: Feminism and Pornography* (pp. 19–44). Oxford University Press, Oxford.

Elgin, C. 1996. *Considered Judgement*. Princeton University Press, Princeton.

Feinberg, J. 1987. *The Moral Limits of the Criminal Law Volume 1: Harm to Others*. Oxford University Press, Oxford.

Fraser, R. 2018. The Ethics of Metaphor. *Ethics* 128(4): 728–755.

Gendler, T. 2008. Alief and Belief. *Journal of Philosophy* 105(10): 634–663.

Goh-Mah, J. 2013. The Objectification of Women Goes Further Than Sexy Pictures. *HuffPost*, 09 June. https://www.huffingtonpost.co.uk/joy-goh-mah/objectification-women-sexy-pictures_b_3403251.html (Accessed 28 August 2018).

Haslanger, S. 2015. Distinguished Lecture: Social Structure, Narrative and Explanation. *Canadian Journal of Philosophy* 45(1): 1–15.

Hegarty, P. and Bruckmüller, S. 2013. Asymmetric Explanations of Group Differences: Experimental Evidence of Foucault's Disciplinary Power. *Social and Personality Psychology Compass* 7(3): 176–186.

Heilman, M. 2012. Gender Stereotypes and Workplace Bias. *Research in Organizational Behaviour* 32: 113–135.

Hirshman, L. 2006. *Get To Work: A Manifesto for Women of the World*. Viking, New York.

Hirschmann, N. 1996. Toward a Feminist Theory of Freedom. *Political Theory* 24(1): 46–67.

Holroyd, J. 2012. Responsibility for Implicit Bias. *Journal of Social Philosophy* 43(3): 247–306.

Hoyt, C. L. and Murphy, S. E. 2016. Managing to Clear the Air: Stereotype Threat, Women, and Leadership. *The Leadership Quarterly* 27: 387–399.

Jean-Charles, R. M. 2014. Toward a Victim-Survivor Narrative: Rape and Form in Yvonne Vera's *Under the Tongue* and Calixthe Bayala's *Tu t'appelleras Tanga*. *Research in African Literatures* 45(1): 39–62.

Kahneman, D. and Tversky, A. 1979. Prospect Theory: An Analysis of Decision Under Risk. *Econometrica* 47: 263–291.

Kant, I. 1963. *Lectures on Ethics*. Translated by Louis Infield. Harper and Row, New York.

Kay, C. 2018. Our Favourite Beauty Product Heroes That Give Back to Empower Women. *Glamour Magazine*, 8 March, [online]. Available at: https://www.glamourmagazine.co.uk/article/empowering-beauty-products (Accessed 10 September 2018).

Kelly, L., Burton, S. and Regan, L. 1996. Beyond Victim or Survivor: Sexual Violence, Identity and Feminist Theory and Practice. In L. Adkins and V. Merchant (Eds.), *Sexualising the Social: Power and the Organisation of Sexuality*. Palgrave Macmillan, London, Ch. 4.

Kelly, L., Lovett, J. and Regan, L. 2005. Gap or Chasm?: Attrition in Reported Rape Cases. *Home Office Research Study No. 293*. Home Office, London. http://webarchive.

nationalarchives.gov.uk/20110218141141/http://rds.homeoffice.gov.uk/rds/pdfs05/hors293.pdf (Accessed 20 August 2018).
Korsgaard, C. 1996. *The Sources of Normativity*. Cambridge University Press, Cambridge.
Kray, L. J., Thompson, L. and Galinsky, A. 2001. Battle of the Sexes: Gender Stereotype Confirmation and Reactance in Negotiations. *Journal of Personality and Social Psychology* 80: 942–958.
Langton, R. 1993. Beyond a Pragmatic Critique of Reason. *Australasian Journal of Philosophy* 71: 364–384.
Langton, R. 2004. Projection and Objectification. In B. Leiter (Ed.), *The Future for Philosophy* (pp. 285–303). Oxford University Press, Oxford.
Langton, R. 2005. Feminism in Philosophy. In F. Jackson and M. Smith (Eds.), *The Oxford Handbook of Contemporary Philosophy*. Oxford University Press, Oxford, Ch. 9.
Langton, R. 2009. *Sexual Solipsism: Philosophical Essays on Pornography and Objectification*. Oxford University Press, Oxford.
Langton, R. 2012. Beyond Belief: Pragmatics in Hate Speech and Pornography. In: I. Maitra and M.K. McGowan (Eds.), *Speech and Harm: Controversies Over Free Speech* (pp. 72–93): Oxford University Press, Oxford.
Lopez, T. 2016. Following Rape, 'Runner' Rather Than 'Victim' Defines Survivor's Identity. *U.S. Army*, 21 April. https://www.army.mil/article/166506/following_rape_runner_rather_than_victim_defines_survivors_identity (Accessed 2 August 2018).
Lutz, T. 2018. Simone Biles: I Was Sexually Abused by USA Gymnastics Doctor Larry Nassar. *The Guardian*, 15 January. https://www.theguardian.com/sport/2018/jan/15/simone-biles-larry-nassar-sexual-abuse-allegations-usa-gymnastics (Accessed 3 August 2018).
MacKinnon, K. 1987. *Feminism Unmodified: Discourses on Life and Law*. Harvard University Press, Cambridge, MA.
McCarthy, M. 1990. The Thin Ideal, Depression, and Eating Disorders in Women. *Behavioural Research and Therapy* 28(3): 205–215.
Munton, J. 2021. Prejudice as the Misattribution of Salience. *Analytic Philosophy* 00: 1–19.
Murdoch, I. 1970 [2013]. *The Sovereignty of the Good*. Routledge, London.
Nussbaum, M. 1995. Objectification. *Philosophy and Public Affairs* 24(4): 249–291.
Office for National Statistics. 2013. *An Overview of Sexual Offending in England and Wales*. UK. http://webarchive.nationalarchives.gov.uk/20140711232238/https://www.gov.uk/government/publications/an-overview-of-sexual-offending-in-england-and-wales (Accessed 1 September 2018).
Office for National Statistics. 2018. *Sexual Offences in England and Wales: Year Ending March 2017*. UK. https://www.ons.gov.uk/peoplepopulationandcommunity/crimeandjustice/articles/sexualoffencesinenglandandwales/yearendingmarch2017 (Accessed 1 September 2018).
Osborne, S. 2016. Stanford University Rape Case: Victim's Letter in Full. *The Independent*, 06 June. https://www.independent.co.uk/news/world/americas/stanford-university-rape-case-the-victims-letter-in-full-a7067146.html (Accessed 2 August 2018).
Papadaki, E. 2018. Feminist Perspectives on Objectification. *The Stanford Encylopedia of Philosophy* (Summer 2018 Edition). https://plato.stanford.edu/cgi-bin/encyclopedia/archinfo.cgi?entry=feminism-objectification (Accessed 15 July 2018).
Philosophy Talk. 2017. Can Speech Kill? 10 December. [podcast]. https://www.philosophytalk.org/shows/can-speech-kill (Accessed 15 August 2018).
Pollock, P. and Parker, R. 1981. *Old Mistresses: Women, Art, and Ideology*. Routledge & Kegan, London.

Puddifoot, K. 2017. Dissolving the Epistemic/Ethical Dilemma over Implicit Bias. *Philosophical Explorations* 20 (Sup. Vol. 1): 73–93.

Rudman, L. and Glick., P. 2008. *The Social Psychology of Gender: How Power and Intimacy Shape Gender Relations*. The Guilford Press, New York.

Rudman, L. and Phelan, J. E. 2008. Backlash Effects for Disconfirming Gender Stereotypes in Organizations. *Research in Organizational Behaviour* 28: 61–79.

Saul, J. 2012. Scepticism and Implicit Bias. *Disputatio* 5(37): 243–263.

Snyder-Hall, C. 2010. Third-Wave Feminism and the Defence of 'Choice'. *Perspectives on Politics* 8(1): 255–261.

Stewart, B. D. and Payne, B. K. 2008. Bringing Automatic Stereotyping Under Control: Implementation Intentions as Efficient Means of Thought Control. *Personality and Social Psychology Bulletin* 34: 1332–1345.

Sunstein, C. 2016. *The Ethics of Influence*. Cambridge University Press, New York.

Swanson, E. Forthcoming. Slurs and Ideologies. In R. Celikates, S. Haslanger and J. Stanley (Eds.), *Ideology: New Essays*. Oxford University Press, Oxford.

Tirrell, L. 2012. Genocidal Language Games. In I. Maitra and M. K. McGowan (Eds.), *Speech and Harm: Controversies Over Free Speech* (pp. 174–221). Oxford University Press, Oxford.

Tirrell, L. 2013. Studying Genocide: A Pragmatist Approach to Action-Engendering Discourse. In G. Hubbs and D. Lind (Eds.), *Pragmatism, Law, and Language*. Routledge, London.

Vasquez, E., Osinnowo, K., Pina, A., Ball, L. and Bell, C. 2017. The Sexual Objectification of Girls and Aggression Towards Them in Gang and Non-Gang Affiliated Youth. *Psychology Crime and Law* 23(5): 459–471.

Waldron, J. 2012. *The Harm in Hate Speech*. Harvard University Press, Cambridge, MA.

Watzl, S. 2017. *Structuring Mind: The Nature of Attention and How It Shapes Consciousness*. Oxford University Press, Oxford.

Watzl, S. 2022. The Ethics of Attention: An Argument and a Framework. In S. Archer (Ed.), *Salience: A Philosophical Inquiry*. Routledge, Abingdon. Ch 5.

Wheeler, S. C. and Petty, R. E. 2001. The Effects of Stereotype Activation on Behaviour: A Review of Possible Mechanisms. *Psychological Bulletin* 127(6): 797–826.

12 Salient alternatives and epistemic injustice in folk epistemology

Mikkel Gerken

12.1 Introduction

The notion of salience figures prominently in contemporary epistemology and some empirical evidence suggests a *salient alternatives effect* on folk epistemological ascriptions of knowledge: People are less inclined to ascribe knowledge that p to a subject when a possibility, q, that is incompatible with p is salient.

Sometimes epistemologists use the term 'salience' as synonymous with 'salient alternatives.' This is a mistake since salience is a *property of* alternatives and of other epistemically relevant phenomena. For example, practical factors such as stakes or urgency may be salient or non-salient in a given context. Likewise, it may be salient or non-salient that a subject has strong evidence, is in an inhospitable environment, has formed her belief on a lucky basis etc. The salience or lack thereof of such factors should be expected to affect folk judgments about knowledge, evidence, rationality etc. Thus, salience does not solely concern alternatives to someone's knowledge. However, in the present paper, I restrict the discussion to the salient alternative effect on knowledge ascriptions with the aim of highlighting how it may lead to epistemic injustice (Fricker, 2007, 2017).

The paper builds on previous work in which I argue that the salient alternative effect on knowledge ascriptions is best understood as a cognitive bias (Gerken, 2012, 2013, 2015, 2017a; Gerken and Beebe, 2016; Gerken et al. 2020). I continue this approach by considering a number of questions for foundational epistemology that arise from further reflection on the salience of alternatives and epistemic position. On this basis, I turn to more applied issues. First, I will consider work in social psychology to motivate the working-hypothesis that social stereotypes will make some alternatives more, and some less, salient. A related working-hypothesis is that social stereotypes may lead to both overestimation and underestimation of a subject's epistemic position. If these working-hypotheses are true, the outcome may be a distinctive route to epistemic injustice.

12.2 Salient alternatives in epistemology and folk epistemology

Epistemologists conceive of various error-possibilities as alternatives to possession of knowledge. In this section, I briskly present this idea via *relevant alternative* epistemology and the distinction between salient alternatives and epistemically relevant ones. I then turn to folk epistemology and consider some puzzling patterns of ascriptions of knowledge and sketch an epistemic focal bias account of them.

12.2.1 Salient alternatives vs relevant alternatives

The idea of a salient alternative may be approached by way of relevant alternative theories of knowledge (Dretske, 1970, 1971). An epistemically relevant alternative is a proposition, q, that is incompatible with S's knowing that p unless S has ruled out that q is true. The simplest example is one in which q (the tree is a beech) is incompatible with p (the tree is an elm). Since knowledge is factive, a knowledge ascription is falsified by every true proposition that is incompatible with its complement clause. For example, it is false that S knows the tree is an elm if it is true that the tree is a beech. However, an *epistemically relevant* alternative, q, is such that in order to know that p, S must rule out that q is true.[1]

A crucial aspect of relevant alternatives theory is that not every alternative is epistemically relevant. Consider, for example, the alternative that the elm has been uprooted overnight and replaced with an indistinguishable but different tree-type, a schmelm, invented in a lab. Such an unlikely alternative is an epistemically *irrelevant* one which S does not need to rule out in order to know that the tree is an elm.

However, epistemically relevant alternatives may be salient. For example, they may be part of the description of the case to be evaluated, part of the conversational context or otherwise highlighted to someone evaluating whether S knows. The relationship between salient and epistemically relevant alternatives is debated among epistemologists. Some theorists think that the salience of an alternative renders it an epistemically relevant one. For example, Lewis sets forth the following *Rule of Attention*: 'No matter how far-fetched a certain possibility may be, no matter how properly we might have ignored it in some other context, if in *this* context we are not in fact ignoring it but attending to it, then for us now it is a relevant alternative.' (Lewis, 1996: 559).

If we take attending to q as equivalent to or entailing q being salient, salience will entail epistemic relevance. If we merely take it that salience will mostly make the speaker attend to q, salience will only mostly yield epistemic relevance. In either case, Lewis uses the *Rule of Attention* to motivate contextualism about 'knows' – the view that the content expressed by 'knows' varies with conversational context (see Blome-Tillmann, 2014 for a critical discussion). So, the salience of an alternative in the conversational context can – via attention – result in a change in what is expressed by 'S knows that p.' For example, the fantastic alternative that the elm has been uprooted and replaced with a schmelm may, once it is salient in the conversational context, result in a change in the content of the utterance of 'S knows that the tree is an elm.' Specifically, it may result in a change in content such that the sentence is false.

In contrast, strict invariantists argue that 'knows' does not vary its truth-conditional content with conversational context.[2] In consequence, many strict invariantists argue that salient alternatives and epistemically relevant alternatives may come apart. Here is how I put it (Gerken, 2017a, p.70):

Salience-Relevance Distinction
Not all salient alternatives are epistemically relevant ones.

Thus, even if the schmelm alternative is salient in the relevant conversational context, it is not thereby epistemically relevant. So, 'S knows that the tree is an elm' may remain true even if S can't rule out the schmelm alternative that is salient to the evaluator (Dretske, 1970; Gerken 2017a).

Thus, the epistemological debate between contextualist and strict invariantists is partly a debate concerning the relationship between salience and epistemic relevance. Contextualists take their view to be supported by patterns of intuitive judgments about knowledge that appear to be sensitive to the salience of alternatives. Such a pattern is called a *salient alternative effect*. There is now a good deal of empirical work supporting the existence of salient alternative effects in lay ascriptions of knowledge (Schaffer and Knobe, 2012; Nagel et al., 2013; Alexander et al., 2014; Buckwalter, 2014; Buckwalter and Schaffer, 2015; Turri, 2015; Waterman et al., 2018; Gerken et al., 2020)

According to strict invariantists the salient alternative patterns of knowledge ascriptions are misleading because they only reflect something pragmatic or because they reflect a psychological bias. This view will be *assumed* in the present paper. More specifically, I assume, for the purpose of the present investigation, a psychological account of salient alternative effects – the epistemic focal bias account. I have argued for this account elsewhere and now I want to explore its ramifications for epistemic injustice (Gerken, 2012, 2013, 2015, 2017a; Gerken and Beebe, 2016; Gerken et al. 2020). For criticism, see Stoutenburg, 2017; Langford, 2020).

12.2.2 Epistemic focal bias and the Principle of Contextual Salience

According to the epistemic focal bias account of salient alternative effects, it is a mistake to move uncritically from salience to epistemic relevance. While doing so may be a reasonable cognitive heuristic insofar as salient alternatives are typically epistemically irrelevant, it leads to systematically misleading – that is, biased – judgments (Gerken, 2017a). When an epistemically irrelevant alternative is salient, we tend to mistakenly process it as an epistemically relevant one.

The epistemic focal bias account explains this via two principles that are descriptive of our folk epistemological processes:

Principle of Contextual Salience
Normally, for an agent, A, q is a contextually salient alternative to S's knowledge that p iff A processes q as an epistemically relevant alternative to S's knowledge that p.

Principle of Epistemic Satisficing
Normally, an agent, A, forms epistemic judgments on the basis of a prima facie reason that is arrived at by processing only a limited part of the evidence that is available to A.

In conjunction, the two principles predict biased judgments in cases that feature a mismatch between psychologically salient and epistemically relevant alternatives. For example, if a salient alternative is *not* epistemically relevant, *Principle of Contextual Salience* has it that it will be mistakenly processed as an epistemically relevant alternative. According to *Principle of Epistemic Satisficing* the verdict will normally be made on this basis without reflecting on whether the alternative is really epistemically relevant. So, the account in *On Folk Epistemology* highlights how some of the judgments that constitute the salient alternative effect amount to *false negative* judgments due to their being governed by the two principles (Gerken 2017, Ch. 10). That is, someone who *does* know may mistakenly be judged to *not* know when an epistemically irrelevant alternative is salient.

I will not repeat the details here although it will be important to note that according to the focal bias account of salient alternative effects, we may misjudge in different ways. In *Relevance Cases*, such as the one sketched above, the mistake consists in misjudging that a salient alternative (e.g., the schmelm one) is epistemically relevant and consequently we mistakenly regard S as not knowing that the tree is an elm. In *Rebuttal Cases*, the mistake consists in failing to recognize that S has in fact ruled out the alternative and, again, the consequence is that we mistakenly regard S as a non-knower. (For more on the distinction between *Relevance* and *Rebuttal* cases, see Gerken, 2017a, pp.70–74 and Ch. 10.2).

The *Principle of Contextual Salience* can be developed by specifying the factors that determine whether a proposition is salient to the relevant agent. Indeed, it will increase the principle's predictive power to add specific claims about when an alternative is salient. For example, if a factor, X, is argued to be a determiner of salience, it will *ceteris paribus* be the case that when X obtains in the context of a knowledge judgment, the *Principle of Contextual Salience* will be operative and affect the judgment. Yet more specifically, if X is argued to be unrelated to the *epistemic* relevance of the alternative, we have a more concrete and, hence, more testable prediction about when a type of biased folk epistemological judgment obtains. As I will argue, this is important for diagnosing cases of epistemic injustice. So, I will conclude the section with a brief reflection on the determiners of whether an alternative is salient.

12.2.3 The determiners of salience

What are the features that determine whether an alternative is salient in a context of epistemic assessment? This is a complicated question but an important one to understand the relationship between salient alternative effects, folk epistemology and epistemic injustice. On this occasion, I focus on one kind of determiners – namely, social ones. But this focus should be initiated with recognition of more commonly discussed determiners of salient alternatives – namely, conversational and psychological ones.

Conversational determiners of salience may include simply what is explicitly mentioned as a defeater of knowledge in a conversational context as well as subtler linguistic features of conversational context. For example, evidence suggests that semantic, syntactic and further contextual features may bear on sentence processing by rendering various aspects of a given sentence more or less salient (Sanford and Sturt, 2002; Sturt et al., 2004; I discuss in Gerken, 2017a, Ch. 8).

I conjecture that psychological determiners of whether an alternative is salient include factors such as familiarity and surprise. Likewise, research on priming and framing effects would suggest that these are important psychological determiners of salience. Often it makes more sense to classify a determiner of salience as psycho-linguistic than to try to keep linguistic and psychological determiners apart. For example, priming may be semantic, and framing may be syntactic.

Psycholinguistic determiners of what makes an alternative salient should be explored further. But here I will consider the idea that social factors and social cognition may determine the salience of alternatives in judgments about knowledge. Such determiners of salience are highly relevant to understanding the interplay between folk epistemology and epistemic injustice. For example, I will argue that judgments about knowledge may be influenced by social stereotypes' effect on the salience of alternatives. Likewise, whether someone is regarded as having ruled out a salient alternative may be affected by social stereotypes, social scripts and heuristics (for more on these notions, see Section 3).

If these factors bear on epistemic assessment, the assessed subjects may suffer epistemic injustices. Or so I will argue. My argument comes in two moves. In the next section, I consider some of the relevant social stereotypes and categories in relation to our general ability to *mindread* – i.e., to make judgments about other peoples' mental and epistemic states. In the section thereafter, I consider epistemic injustice and how it may arise from misjudgments arising from social stereotypes.

12.3 Salience and social stereotypes

In order to navigate the social world that we inhabit, we need to categorize it. However, we are cognitively capacity-limited and must make judgments about social groups and types on the fly. Since we cannot consider all the available information when we need to make a judgment, we rely on modes of social categorization that are cognitively cost-effective. Consequently, we rely on cost-effective but systematically fallible heuristics and imperfect social stereotypes in making judgments about our social reality (Hassin et al., 2005; Bargh, 2007; Uleman et al., 2008, Ames et al., 2012; Spaulding, 2018). Ascriptions of knowledge play an important role in our navigation of social life (Gerken, 2017a). So, it is natural to suppose that they are interwoven with social stereotypes.

12.3.1 Social stereotypes, heuristics, scripts and categories

Social properties such as gender, race and age are among the most salient ones in our social cognition. For example, we are extraordinarily fast in categorizing individuals according to such properties (Ito et al., 2004; Kubota and Ito, 2007). However, evidence suggests that social categorization in terms of gender, race and age is interwoven with our ascription of personality traits. Importantly, for the present purpose, these traits include cognitive ones such as competence or trustworthiness (Porter et al., 2008; Rule et al., 2013; Todorov et al., 2015). It is debated whether such social attributions from faces is generally reliable. Some studies indicate accurate attribution of social categories such as sexual orientation from face perception (Rule et al., 2009). However, a recent literature review suggests that the accuracy has been overstated and that attribution of social categories is highly inaccurate and determined by a host of contextual factors (Todorov et al., 2015). So, even if some of the social judgments we form on the fly have some degree of reliability, it must be highlighted that they are highly and systematically fallible.

Examples of such fallibility include cases in which the individual is judged to be in the evaluator's *in-group* or *out-group*. We are generally more inclined to trust and cooperate with in-group than out-group members (see Balliet et al., 2014 for a meta-analysis). We are particularly prone to rely on crude stereotypes in our assessment of out-group individuals whereas we are more inclined to extrapolate our own perspective to members of in-groups (Ames, 2004; Robbins and Krueger, 2005; Ames et al., 2012). Neuroimaging studies have indicated that neural responses associated with empathy for pain are significantly stronger when the observed pain is in racial in-group members than in racial out-group members (Xu et al., 2009). Furthermore, some evidence suggests that we tend to attribute achievements (including cognitive ones) of out-group individuals to circumstantial and environmental facts beyond the individual's control whereas we tend to attribute (cognitive) achievements of in-group members to personality traits (Brewer, 2001). All of these cognitive strategies serve important social functions. For example, they may help to ensure that one remains included in one's in-group. Moreover, these cognitive strategies may be effective heuristics that allow us to make rapid social judgments and decisions. However, from the standpoint of accuracy, they are biased in various ways. In particular, the in-group/out-group dynamics may lead to the overestimation of members of one's in-group and the underestimation of members of one's out-group (Brewer, 2001; Spaulding, 2018).

Evidence for social stereotypes comes from a large body of work. For example, gender stereotypes are indicated by the effect of gender in participants' judgments about negotiators in strategic interactions (for a survey, see Kray and Thompson, 2004). Similarly, studies on an ambiguity task provide evidence that racial stereotypes impact interpretations of whether an item is a weapon or a tool (Payne, 2001). Evidence also suggests that more general social properties such as power affect social cognition. For example, power (as measured by asymmetric dependence) has been found to have an effect on the social distance which affects the cognitive mode of mental state inference – roughly by reducing projection of one's own mental states to high-power individuals (Magee and Smith, 2013). Power may also affect overtly cognitive categories insofar as evidence suggests that power holders were found to have increased subjective certainty in their judgments (See et al., 2011; Magee and Smith, 2013). Moreover, high power individuals appear to rely on stereotypes on the condition that they are *available* (Chen et al., 2004). This is interesting for the present purpose given that availability is likely determined by contextual salience of the stereotype (see Taylor and Fiske, 1978 and ensuing work).

The mentioned effects of social stereotypes and categories on social cognition are mere examples in the vast and complex area of social cognition research. Specific sources of evidence, such as the Implicit Association Test, have been challenged (Brownstein et al., 2017; Lai et al., 2014). Moreover, general methodological worries, such as replication failures, have been raised. These concerns are legitimate and call for caution. Nevertheless, converging evidence provides reason to assume that social stereotypes may bear on epistemic assessment. On the basis of this broad assumption, rather than specific instances of it, I will set forth some fairly generic descriptive principles of folk socio-epistemological judgments.

12.3.2 Some principles of folk socio-epistemology

I have only scratched the surface of the empirical work on stereotypes in social cognition and folk epistemology. However, even the selective survey provides reason to think that many folk epistemological assessments are impacted by social stereotypes and heuristics we use in navigating social life. This broad idea is widely recognized. For example, Spaulding concludes that 'Simply in virtue of being part of a particular social category we may upgrade or downgrade a person's knowledge or competence' (Spaulding, 2016, p.436). In *On Folk*

Epistemology, I articulated a similar idea in terms of the following principle (Gerken, 2017a, p.104):

Principle of Epistemic Stereotyping
Normally, A judges that S knows that p (and otherwise that S does not know that p) iff A represents S as possessing a p-relevant knowledge-stereotypical property and no stereotypically knowledge-defeating circumstances are salient to A.

As in the case of the previous folk epistemological principles, epistemic judgments governed by the *Principle of Epistemic Stereotyping* leads to systematically fallible judgments since the stereotypes may be inaccurate. Two corollary *non-entailment* principles explicate this assumption (Gerken, 2017a, pp.104–105):

Stereotype Non-entailment I
S is a stereotypical knower that $p \not\to$ S knows that p.

Stereotype Non-entailment II
S knows that $p \not\to$ S is a stereotypical knower that p.

The *Principle of Epistemic Stereotyping* and its two corollaries predict mistaken knowledge ascriptions. However, the more specific mechanisms by which someone is downgraded or upgraded as an epistemic agent remain to be explored. To begin such an exploration, I will set forth two pairs of more specific hypotheses concerning how social stereotypes may explain biases in knowledge ascriptions. These more specific hypotheses will help to integrate epistemological work on salience with empirical work on social stereotypes, categories, scripts and heuristics.

A broad lesson from the literature on social cognition is that important psychological mechanisms for epistemic assessment of others include scripts and heuristics that are integrated into mindreading and other forms of social cognition. For example, we may overestimate someone's epistemic position if she is categorized as a member of our in-group or as belonging to a social category associated with epistemic competence. Conversely, we may underestimate someone's epistemic position if she is categorized as a member of an out-group or as a member of a social group associated with epistemic incompetence.

Given the variation in underpinnings of such socio-epistemic cognition, it will be instrumental to the following discussion to articulate these assumptions as a pair of principles. Here they are:

Epistemic Overestimation
Both *accurate and inaccurate* social stereotypes may lead evaluators to overestimate a subject's epistemic position.

Epistemic Underestimation
Both accurate and inaccurate social stereotypes may lead evaluators to underestimate a subject's epistemic position.

Epistemic Overestimation and *Epistemic Underestimation* concern the assessment of agents' epistemic position based on the salience of social properties such as race, gender and age. However, it is plausible that social stereotypes may also bear on the salience of alternatives in the sense operative in relevant alternative epistemology. The surveyed empirical work on social cognition suggests that some alternatives will be more closely associated with some social groups than with others. Likewise, some social scripts that are only activated in some social contexts may involve alternatives that would otherwise be non-salient. I will, once again, articulate this hypothesis as a pair of general principles.

Amplification of Salience
Both accurate and inaccurate social stereotypes may amplify, or even generate, the salience of some alternatives.

Diminishment of Salience
Both accurate and inaccurate social stereotypes may diminish, or even eliminate, the salience of some alternatives.

The quartet of principles is *not* normative but rather empirically informed descriptive hypotheses about our folk epistemological judgments and presuppositions. While the principles are fairly generic, they are more specific than the overarching *Principle of Epistemic Stereotyping*. Hence, they have a good deal of predictive power. First, they predict that intuitive judgments about individuals' epistemic position will align with how the individual is socially categorized. Second, the principles predict that our intuitive and quasi-intuitive judgments about epistemic position may come apart from our more reflective judgments. Finally, given that the principles have it that also *inaccurate* social stereotypes may affect epistemic assessments, they predict systematically inaccurate – that is *biased* – judgments about individuals' epistemic position. Of course, even more, specific predictions will require even more specific assumptions about the relevant stereotypes and cognitive mechanisms. But the present quartet of principles may be put to use in a more general explanation of why socio-epistemic cognition may lead to epistemic injustice.

However, before we are in a position to examine the relation between these folk epistemological considerations and epistemic injustice, a brief characterization of the latter is in order

12.4 Salience and epistemic injustice

I begin my discussion of how epistemic injustice may be generated by the combination of the salient alternative effects on knowledge ascriptions and our reliance on social stereotypes with a brief discussion of epistemic injustice.

12.4.1 Epistemic injustice

In her 2007 book on epistemic injustice, Fricker characterizes the phenomenon as 'a wrong done to someone specifically in their capacity as a knower' (Fricker, 2007, p.1). One species of it – *distributive* epistemic injustice – is a consequence of 'the unfair distribution of epistemic goods such as education or information' (Fricker, 2013, p.1318). However, the species of epistemic injustice that I will consider here is *discriminatory* epistemic injustice which is paradigmatically explained by *identity prejudices* that pertain to gender, class, race or social power.

Since Fricker's initial work, the characterization of epistemic injustice has been broadened to consider epistemic agency generally. Indeed, Fricker herself has now substituted the knowledge-centric formulation to a broader one (Fricker, 2013, p.1320, 2017).[3] While knowledge is central to epistemology and folk epistemology, it is not the only epistemic phenomenon that one may be wronged with regard to.[4] Discriminative epistemic injustice sometimes concerns the comparison between degrees of epistemic competence, trustworthiness or reliability and it is implausible that all of these phenomena can be reductively analyzed in terms of knowledge (Gerken, 2017b). So, here is my favorite generic characterization of discriminatory epistemic injustice ('DEI' for short (via Gerken, 2019)):

> **Generic DEI**
> S suffers a discriminatory epistemic injustice if (and only if) S is wronged specifically in her capacity as an epistemic subject.

This is not the place to pursue a taxonomy of the kinds of 'epistemic wronging' that may constitute discriminatory epistemic injustice. The main assumption that I will rely on is that social stereotypes, scripts, categories and heuristics may constitute epistemic wronging and, thereby, discriminatory epistemic injustice. Varieties may be more or less direct. I will assume that the wronging is *direct* if it pertains to the epistemic evaluation or treatment of S herself or himself. Hence, I will work with the following sufficient condition for direct discriminatory epistemic injustice (following Gerken, 2019).

> **Direct DEI**
> If S is systematically and distinctively judged or treated as being in a weaker epistemic position than S is in fact in and paradigmatic unjust features explain this, then S is wronged specifically in her capacity as an epistemic subject.

The second conjunct of the antecedent of *Direct DEI* ensures that it is paradigmatic unjust features such as prejudice, bias and stereotyping that explain the epistemic misjudgment or mistreatment of S. The directness of this type of wronging lies in the fact that it is the *subject* that is misjudged or mistreated. Note, however, that *Direct DEI* is only a sufficient condition for epistemic injustice. So, although it captures a central case of direct discriminatory epistemic injustice, there are arguably several other varieties of it. Moreover, discriminatory epistemic injustice may also occur indirectly. For example, someone else, S*, may be systematically and distinctively judged or treated as being in a *stronger* epistemic position than S* is in fact in. (Cf. the discussion of credibility excess in Fricker, 2007, p.17ff). However, it may be paradigmatic unjust features that explain this as phenomena such as white male privilege exemplify (McIntosh, 2007). S* and an accurately assessed epistemic subject, S, may be competitors in what Fricker calls 'the credibility economy' (Fricker, 2007, Ch. 2).

So, in some cases, I think it is reasonable to say that S suffers an indirect epistemic injustice in virtue of the fact that S* is epistemically favored due to paradigmatically unjust factors such as white male privilege.[5] This idea of indirect discriminatory epistemic injustice calls for further discussion than space permits. For example, it is unclear what to say about cases where S* is unaware of the epistemic advantage he enjoys. My initial sense is that it does not matter much. S can still suffer a discriminatory epistemic injustice even though S* is not culpable for it. However, such cases merit discussion. Likewise, the notion that S* and S are competitors in the knowledge economy calls for further specification. Despite such complications, I hope that the basic provisional idea of indirect epistemic injustice is sufficiently clear to relate to the cases I will discuss.

A fuller account of the varieties of epistemic injustice requires an account of the harm it involves. Since providing such an account is an immense task, I will only make some modest assumptions. In the examples of epistemic injustice that I will focus on, the epistemic injustice has negative consequences for the wronged individual. For example, there are often tangible negative consequences of not being taken seriously as a testifier, and these are part of the harm of testimonial injustice. However, I do not think that such consequences exhaust the distinctive harm of epistemic injustice. Humans are social creatures and an important part of our social life is epistemic. It is valuable to tell and be told. It is valuable to trust and be trusted. It is valuable to question, inquire and justify. This is not merely because of what we can achieve by these acts. Rather, the epistemic agency is a valuable part of human nature in its own right. So, constraining or devaluing someone's epistemic agency is distinctive harm associated with epistemic injustice. It is well beyond this essay to defend this assumption or to provide a deeper explanation for it (but see Fricker, 2007; Maitra, 2010). But I note this dimension of epistemic injustice to indicate that practical consequences are only one dimension of the overall harm in wronging someone in their capacity as an epistemic subject.

Let's sum up: I will mainly be concerned with *discriminative* epistemic injustice and, like Fricker herself, I reject the knowledge-centric conception of epistemic injustice in favor of the more inclusive formulation, *Generic DEI*. However, to avoid begging any questions against reductive knowledge-first theorists, I will focus the discussion on cases in which someone is unjustly treated as a non-knower although she or he is in fact a knower. Finally, I will consider both cases of direct and indirect epistemic injustice. Given these remarks about epistemic injustice, I will turn to how each member of the new quartet of principles may lead to discriminatory epistemic injustice.

12.4.2 How Amplification of Salience may lead to epistemic injustice

Assume that Tyra has calculated that she and her partner can afford to rent an apartment on just one of their salaries and concluded that they can afford to rent an apartment. However, Tyra and her partner belong to a particular social group, X, which is stereotyped as unreliable. This stereotype may render the remote possibility that they simultaneously lose their jobs a salient alternative. Assume that this alternative is epistemically irrelevant since both S and her partner are reliable employees in fields where there is strong evidence of job security in the foreseeable future. So, we have a *Relevance Case* on our hands: Tyra knows that p even though she properly ignored an epistemically irrelevant alternative, q.

However, due to a social stereotype, the epistemically irrelevant alternative (simultaneous job loss) is rendered contextually salient to someone evaluating whether Tyra really knows that they will have the means to pay rent. So, according to the *Principle of Contextual Salience*, it is processed as epistemically relevant. By the *Principle of Satisficing*, a knowledge-judgment is then made on the basis of the presumption that Tyra has not ruled out an epistemically relevant alternative. So, Tyra is mistakenly judged as not knowing that they can afford to rent the apartment.

Such a situation often exemplifies discriminatory epistemic injustice although it does not invariably do so. Perhaps it would be an alleviating circumstance if the social stereotype were accurate of members of Tyra's group and Tyra and her partner were exceptions to it (Gendler, 2011). But it is highly controversial that this would alleviate the epistemic injustice. For example, Puddifoot has argued on empirical grounds that the epistemically best judgment does not come apart from the ethically best one (Puddifoot, 2017). Moreover, it may be argued that even if the members of the group that Tyra belongs to were in general unreliable, Tyra still deserves to be judged on her own merits. So, I am inclined to think that even if it is an accurate social stereotype that renders the epistemically irrelevant alternative salient, discriminatory epistemic injustice may still occur.

However, a more clear-cut case of a *Relevance Case* that generates discriminatory epistemic injustice is one in which an inaccurate social stereotype renders an epistemically irrelevant alternative salient. In such cases, someone belonging to the social group in question is mistakenly regarded as a non-knower and this may be epistemically unjust. After all, unjust social prejudices encoded in social stereotypes and social scripts explain why Tyra is mistakenly deemed a non-knower. Thus, Tyra is mistakenly deemed a non-knower in a systematically and distinct manner that is due to paradigmatically unjust features. So, by *Direct DEI*, Tyra suffers a discriminatory epistemic injustice. An important aspect of her agency – namely, her epistemic agency – is violated. Moreover, being regarded as not knowing that one can afford to rent the apartment may have severe consequences – for example if the landlord concludes that Tyra might have the cash now but not later.[6]

Perhaps, inaccurate social stereotypes may amplify the salience of an epistemically irrelevant alternative without leading to discriminatory epistemic injustice. For example, the evaluator may have strong misleading evidence that the stereotype is accurate, or the evaluator may be excused from relying on the inaccurate social stereotype. However, S may still suffer a discriminatory epistemic injustice even if the evaluator should not be blamed for making it. Moreover, it is important to be cautious in exculpating the evaluator. He might be *culpably ignorant* of the inaccuracy of the social stereotype that he relies on. Moreover, the very reliance on stereotypes in assessing individuals may be problematic.

12.4.3 *How Diminishment of Salience may lead to epistemic injustice*

When social stereotypes lead to diminishing or eliminating the salience of epistemically relevant alternatives, the consequence may be that someone who does not in fact know may be regarded as a knower. Assume for example, that a white male, Christian, is interviewing with a landlord in order to rent an apartment. Our protagonist confidently asserts: 'I'll get my Ph.D. in philosophy this spring. So, I know that I will be able to pay the rent for years to come.' In fact, it is a highly relevant epistemic alternative that Christian will not get a job and, hence, be unable to pay rent in the years to come. It may be far more likely that Christian will have to move home to his parents awaiting referee number two's rejection of his journal submission. Nevertheless, the landlord may be so impressed by the combination of male, white confidence and the pedigree of a PhD that the epistemically relevant alternative does not occur to her. Thus, social stereotypes may render an epistemically relevant alternative non-salient. So, by *The Principle of Contextual Salience*, the epistemically relevant alternative is not processed as such and Christian may be deemed a knower of something that he does not in fact know. Note that this case exemplifies how *Principle of Epistemic Stereotyping* (and its corollary *Stereotype Non-entailment I*) is integrated with epistemic focal bias: The social stereotypes explain the lack of salience of a relevant alternative whereas the focal bias account explains why the consequence is a mistaken judgment about knowledge.

In some cases, Christian's competitors may suffer an *indirect* discriminative epistemic injustice, if Christian enjoys a competitive advantage due to a judgment explained by paradigmatic unjust features. Christian who is mistakenly regarded as a knower may have an unfair advantage in the competition for fairly abstract goods such as trust and attention as well as fairly concrete ones such as jobs and apartments. More concretely, another wanna-be tenant who does in fact know that she can pay the rent might not get the apartment.

12.4.4 How Epistemic Underestimation may lead to epistemic injustice

Underestimation of an individual's epistemic position may occur when he is represented as belonging to a social stereotype that is associated with ineptness at some cognitive task. Assume that Hilary is represented as belonging to stereotype X and that members of X are presupposed to be inept in matters botanical.[7] When the fact that Hilary belongs to X and Xers' botanical ineptness is salient, the result may well be that he is represented as botanically inept simply due to the fact that he is represented as belonging to X.

Assume that Hilary sees a beech and the alternative that the tree might be an elm is rendered salient. Assume moreover that this is a *Rebuttal Case* – i.e., one in which Hilary has successfully ruled out that the tree is an elm. However, due to the stereotyping, Hilary is mistakenly judged to be unable to rule out that the tree is an elm. So, by *The Principle of Contextual Salience* and *The Principle of Satisficing*, Hilary is mistakenly deemed a non-knower.

According to *Direct DEI*, this situation will be epistemically unjust insofar as Hilary's systematically and distinctively judged as being in a weaker epistemic position than she is in fact in and paradigmatic unjust features explain this. This will be so in some but not all cases in which her epistemic position is underestimated. For example, one brand of *Rebuttal Case* is one in which the subject's evidence is not salient to the evaluator because it is not even available. So, the resulting misrepresentations of the subject's epistemic position may be unfortunate without being epistemically unjust. Cases in which the subject is regarded as in a poor epistemic position due to belonging to an accurate stereotype are more debatable (Gendler, 2011; Puddifoot, 2017). But I have sympathy for the view that at least some such cases represent discriminatory epistemic injustice. For example, it strikes me as unjust to treat an individual as sharing negative traits of a group that she belongs to solely on the basis of belonging to the group.

However, for the present purpose, I will highlight more clear-cut cases of epistemic injustice. Those are cases in which Hilary's epistemic position is underestimated due to her being represented as belonging to a social group which is inaccurately stereotyped as epistemically deficient. Such cases typically exemplify discriminatory epistemic injustice. This is most clear when the evaluator actively disregards, or is culpably ignorant of, evidence that the stereotype is inaccurate. However, even if the evaluator is excused from or even reasonable in relying on the inaccurate stereotype, *the subject* might still suffer a discriminatory epistemic injustice. Generally, epistemic injustice may not be explained by specific individuals as much as by unjust social structures.

12.4.5 How Epistemic Overestimation may lead to epistemic injustice

As in the case of *Diminishment of Salience*, the principle *Epistemic Overestimation* may lead to occasions of discriminatory epistemic injustice when the consequence is that a subject, Matthew, who does not in fact know something may be mistakenly regarded as a knower. Hence, Matthew will have an unfair competitive advantage in the credibility economy (Fricker, 2007). Matthew's competitors may suffer an indirect discriminatory epistemic injustice even if they themselves are epistemically assessed in an accurate manner.

More specifically, *Epistemic Overestimation* leads to discriminatory epistemic injustice in cases where Matthew's epistemic position is overestimated because he belongs to a certain social category that is associated with epistemic competence or to the evaluator's in-group. The upshot of such overestimation may be that Matthew is mistakenly regarded as having ruled out an epistemically relevant alternative that he has, in fact, not ruled out. So, even if this epistemically relevant alternative is salient, the evaluator will have a reason to regard Matthew as knowing that *p*. According to *The Principle of Satisficing* a judgment that Matthew knows that *p* will be made on this basis. Typically, an evaluator will rely on the relevant stereotype in a non-reflective and, hence, uncritical manner. However, being inaccurately represented as a knower gives Matthew a significant competitive advantage over his competitors. Insofar as this advantage is explained by systematical and distinctive due to paradigmatic unjust features, Matthew's competitors may suffer an *indirect* discriminative epistemic injustice. This is so even if Matthew is faultless with regard to the competitive advantage he enjoys. Central instances of this phenomenon involve phenomena such as male privilege and white privilege.

12.4.6 *In-group and out-group scripts and epistemic injustice*

In the previous four sections, I have focused on social stereotypes. In this section, I will briefly consider how in-group/out-group psychology may interact with folk epistemology in a manner that results in discriminatory epistemic injustice. There may be important interaction of in-group/out-group cognition and diminishment and amplification of salient alternatives. But here I will focus on how these aspects of social psychology interact with *Epistemic Underestimation* and *Epistemic Overestimation* and epistemic focal bias to produce discriminatory epistemic injustice.

Compared to in-group members, we are more inclined to regard the cognitive success (true belief) of an out-group member as explained by circumstantial factors. So, alternatives that are salient in the description of an out-group member who holds a true belief may be more likely to negatively impact our epistemic assessment of her than when an alternative is salient in the description of an in-group member holding a true belief. In particular, it may be more likely that the out-group member's true belief is explained in terms of epistemic luck. Similarly, a salient alternative may be more likely to be regarded as epistemically relevant when environmental factors are judged to be more important than individual competencies. So, according to the epistemic focal bias account of relevant alternative effects, out-group members may be deemed non-knowers in cases where in-group members are judged to know. Many such cases will, in accordance with *Direct DEI*, amount to discriminatory epistemic injustice since the relevant judgments often manifest a systematically and distinct pattern that is explained by paradigmatically unjust features of our social cognition. As above, there are complex questions about whether blame should be ascribed to the misjudging evaluator of out-group members. But even in cases where no blame is ascribable to the specific evaluator, the subject may suffer a discriminatory epistemic injustice.

The flipside of the in-group/out-group social cognition is that we are inclined to attribute the cognitive achievements of in-group members to their cognitive traits. Therefore, we may be inclined to overestimate their epistemic position whenever they have formed a true belief. Likewise, we are more inclined to extrapolate our own awareness that the salient alternative is a non-obtaining possibility to in-group than to out-group members. Hence, we may be likely to mistakenly regard an in-group member as having ruled out salient alternatives. Such a judgment would be an instance of *Epistemic Overestimation* arising from in-group/out-group social cognition. Consequently, we may be more inclined to mistakenly take a *Rebuttal Response* to be applicable to an in-group member than to an out-group member. That is, we may be more likely to regard in-group than out-group members to have ruled out salient alternatives that they have not in fact ruled out. According to the epistemic focal bias account, we are in such cases more likely to regard in-group individuals as knowers than out-group individuals in the same epistemic position. Many such cases exemplify discriminatory epistemic injustice of the indirect kind in which the out-group individuals are unjustly suffering a comparatively unfavorable epistemic assessment. So, instances of *Epistemic Overestimation* that are caused by the in-group/out-group dynamic may, according to the epistemic focal bias account, lead to discriminatory epistemic injustice.

12.4.7 An epistemological corollary

The present accounts exemplify how the epistemic focal bias accounts may be interrelated with social cognition. In particular, I have exemplified the impact of specific instances of the general *Principle of Epistemic Stereotyping* according to which ordinary judgments of whether S is a knower tend to depend on whether S has salient knowledge-stereotypical properties. In fact, the present accounts make for specific examples of both *Stereotype Non-entailment I*, according to which the stereotypical knower does not always know, and *Stereotype Non-entailment II*, according to which not all knowers exhibit knowledge-stereotypical features. Thus, the present development integrates various independently motivated principles of folk epistemology. This is valuable, in part, because the accounts sketched above are far more specific than the general *Principle of Epistemic Stereotyping*.

A further epistemological corollary of the discussion is worth highlighting. According to the present analysis, both *Diminishment of Salience* and *Overestimation of Epistemic Position* may cause *false positives* – that is, knowledge ascriptions to someone who does not know. This marks an important development of the discussion in *On Folk Epistemology* (Gerken, 2017a). Here salient alternative effects were argued to be false negatives (Chapter 10). However, the present discussion indicates a novel type of salient alternative cases while generating false positives.[8] These include cases where the subject of evaluation, S, belongs to a certain social category that is associated with positive epistemic stereotypes or in which S belongs to the evaluator's in-group, S may mistakenly be deemed a knower. So, salient alternative cases may, in conjunction with heuristics operative in social cognition, lead to both instances of false negative and false positive knowledge ascriptions. It turns out, then, that applying the epistemic focal bias to the phenomenon of epistemic injustice yields a novel insight concerning the epistemic focal bias account itself. How nice![9]

12.4.8 Further interrelations between folk epistemology and epistemic injustice

I have sought to distinguish between importantly different ways in which judgments affected by the salience of alternatives and epistemic competence may lead to epistemic injustice. If the proposals are on the right track, they explain some of the mechanisms underlying familiar examples of discriminatory epistemic injustice that arise from epistemic underestimation and overestimation. This deepens our understanding of the sources of epistemic injustice. Moreover, the present investigation also reveals some less recognized routes to discriminatory epistemic injustice that arise when social stereotypes amplify or diminish the salience of alternatives. This widens our understanding of the sources of epistemic injustice.

That said, I have not provided a full map of this complex territory. As mentioned initially, salience is not merely a property of alternatives to someone's knowledge. Salience may also be a property of competence, stakes and environmental factors etc. Thus, there is reason to suspect that folk epistemological judgments mediated by salience of these things may also bias judgments about knowledge and that the consequence may, in some cases, be epistemic injustice of various kinds.

Moreover, the interaction between social cognition and folk epistemology does not stop with ascriptions of knowledge. Judgments of reliability, trustworthiness, epistemic competence, sincerity and so on may also be biased in very similar manners. Neither epistemology nor folk epistemology begins or ends with knowledge. However, I have focused on intuitive knowledge ascriptions because they are central to folk epistemology (Gerken, 2017a). However, other cases are very important. For example, Spaulding has argued that social cognition may bias assessments of epistemic peerhood in a manner that is highly relevant to the epistemology of disagreement (Spaulding, 2016, 2018). Another extremely important case is laypersons' selective uptake of scientific experts' testimony (Gerken, 2020a, 2020b; Kovaka, 2021). In general, the intersection between social cognition and folk epistemology is an extremely rich and complex area.

12.5 Conclusion

I have explored some aspects of the complex interface between folk epistemology and social cognition. However, I have not approximated anything like a survey of such intersections. Rather, I have selectively considered the role of salience in ordinary judgments about knowledge and how such judgments may be affected by social stereotypes, scripts and categories. In doing so, I have argued that the heuristics that we rely on in navigating the social world we inhabit may cause biased judgments about who knows and who does not. However, since the concept of knowledge plays a central role in our social life, such judgments have very significant consequences. Indeed, I have argued that they may lead to severe and tenacious types of epistemic injustice. In consequence, the present considerations should encourage attempts to consider debiasing measures (Devine et al., 2012; Lai et al., 2014).

Thus, I hope that the present paper exemplifies how foundational work on something as abstract as salient alternatives in foundational epistemology may contribute to more concrete empirical and philosophical work on issues of considerable societal consequence.[10]

Notes

1 The precise meaning of 'ruling out' is debated. The idea may be taken to concern S's ability to discriminate between beeches and elms but – you guessed it – the precise meaning of 'discriminate' is also debated. Here I'll steer clear of these epistemological debates (but see Gerken, 2017a, p.13ff).
2 In Kaplanese, contextualists claim that 'knows' has an unstable character whereas strict invariantists argue that it has a stable character (Kaplan, 1989).
3 Thanks to Fricker for helpful correspondence on this point.
4 I argue for this specific point in Gerken, 2019. I argue against knowledge-first epistemology in Gerken, 2011, 2012, 2014, 2017a, 2017b, 2018, 2020c.
5 Fricker discusses whether credibility excess may generate (discriminatory) epistemic injustice but she mainly considers whether it may incur to the subject who is epistemically overestimated – for example, because that subject has to carry unreasonable cognitive or emotional burdens (Fricker, 2007, pp.18–21).
6 This would be an instance of implicit discrimination that would add to the explicit racism involved in apartment rental funkily described in (Wonder, 1980).
7 X might be philosophers who are, sadly, in unfair disrepute as tree categorizers due to (Putnam 1974). Thanks Putnam…
8 In previous work I argued that another type of case involving non-salient alternatives – so-called *contrast cases* – yield false positives (Gerken, 2013, 2017 Ch. 11). But this case type differs from the ones discussed here.
9 There is a methodologically interesting aspect to this. At least it is striking that reflecting on more empirically inspired cases than the thought-experiments that are usually the input to reflection about salient alternatives has led to the novel insight. Just as meta-ethics and normative ethics have benefitted from the rise of applied ethics, I believe that foundational epistemology may benefit from the development of applied epistemology.
10 The paper was presented at the International Network for Danish Philosophers, University of Copenhagen (Sep. 2018), University of Uppsala (Nov. 2018)

University of Stanford's Variety of Agency workshop (Jan. 2020) where Jared Parmer provided helpful comments. I am grateful to the audiences on these occasions for very helpful feedback. Sophie Archer provided very helpful substantive and editorial comments.

References

Alexander, J., Gonnerman, C. and Waterman, J. 2014. Salience and Epistemic Egocentrism: An Empirical Study. In J. Beebe (Ed.), *Advances in Experimental Epistemology* (pp. 97–118). Bloomsbury, London.

Ames, D. R. 2004. Inside the Mind-Reader's Tool Kit: Projection and Stereotyping in Mental State Inference. *Journal of Personality and Social Psychology* 87: 340–353.

Ames, D. R., Weber, E. U. and Zou, X. 2012. Mind-Reading in Strategic Interaction: The Impact of Perceived Similarity on Projection and Stereotyping. *Organizational Behavior and Human Decision Processes* 117(1): 96–110.

Balliet, D., Wu, J. and De Dreu, C. K. 2014. Ingroup Favoritism in Cooperation: A Meta-analysis. *Psychological Bulletin* 140(6): 1556.

Bargh, J. A. 2007. *Social Psychology and the Unconscious: The Automaticity of Higher Mental Processes*. Psychological Press, New York.

Blome-Tillmann, M. 2014. *Knowledge and Presuppositions*. Oxford University Press, Oxford.

Brewer, M. B. 2001. Ingroup Identification and Intergroup Conflict. *Social Identity, Intergroup Conflict, and Conflict Reduction* 3: 17–41.

Brownstein, M. et al. 2017. What Can We Learn from the Implicit Association Test? A *Brains Blog Roundtable*. http://philosophyofbrains.com/2017/01/17/how-can-we-measure-implicit-bias-a-brains-blog-roundtable.aspx.

Buckwalter, W. 2014. The Mystery of Stakes and Error in Ascriber Intuitions. In J. Beebe (Ed.), *Advances in Experimental Epistemology*. Bloomsbury Academic, London.

Buckwalter, W. and Schaffer, J. 2015. Knowledge, Stakes, and Mistakes. *Noûs* 49(2): 201–234.

Chen, S., Ybarra, O. and Kiefer, A. K. 2004. Power and Impression Formation: The Effects of Power on the Desire for Morality and Competence Information. *Social Cognition* 22: 391–421.

Devine, P. G., Forscher, P. S., Austin, A. J. and Cox, W. T. 2012. Long-Term Reduction in Implicit Race Bias: A Prejudice Habit-Breaking Intervention. *Journal of Experimental Social Psychology* 48(6): 1267–1278.

Dretske, Fred I. 1970. Epistemic Operators. *Journal of Philosophy* 67(24): 1007–1023.

Dretske, Fred I. 1971. Conclusive reasons. *Australasian Journal of Philosophy* 49(1): 1–22.

Fiske, S. T. and Taylor, S. E. 2013. *Social Cognition: From Brains to Culture*. Sage, Thousand Oaks, CA.

Fricker, M. 2007. *Epistemic Injustice: Power and the Ethics of Knowing*. Oxford University Press, Oxford.

Fricker, M. 2013. Epistemic Justice as a Condition of Political Freedom? *Synthese* 190(7): 1317–1332.

Fricker, M. 2017. Evolving Concepts of Epistemic Injustice. In *The Routledge Handbook of Epistemic Injustice* (pp. 53–60). Routledge, London.

Gendler, T. S. 2011. On the Epistemic Costs of Implicit Bias. *Philosophical Studies* 156(1): 33.
Gerken, M. 2011. Warrant and Action. *Synthese* 178(3): 529–547.
Gerken, M. 2012. On the Cognitive Bases of Knowledge Ascriptions. In B. Jessica and G. Mikkel (Eds.), *Knowledge Ascriptions*. Oxford University Press, Oxford. DOI: 10.1093/acprof:oso/9780199693702.003.0007
Gerken, M. 2013. Epistemic Focal Bias. *Australasian Journal of Philosophy* 91(1): 41–61.
Gerken, M. 2014. Same, Same but Different: The Epistemic Norms of Assertion, Action and Practical Reasoning. *Philosophical Studies* 168(3): 725–744.
Gerken, M. 2015. The Roles of Knowledge Ascriptions in Epistemic Assessment. *European Journal of Philosophy* 23(1): 141–161.
Gerken, M. 2017a. *On Folk Epistemology. How We Think and Talk About Knowledge*. Oxford University Press, Oxford.
Gerken, M. 2017b. Against Knowledge-First Epistemology. In Benjamin Jarvis, Emma C. Gordon, and J. Adam Carter (Eds.), *Knowledge-First Approaches in Epistemology and Mind* (pp. 46–71). Oxford University Press, Oxford.
Gerken, M. 2018. The New Evil Demon and the Devil in the Details. In Veli Mitova (Ed.), *The Factive Turn in Epistemology* (pp. 102–122). Cambridge University Press, Cambridge, MA.
Gerken, M. 2019. Pragmatic Encroachment and the Challenge from Epistemic Injustice. *Philosophers' Imprint* 19(15): 1–19.
Gerken, M. 2020a. How to Balance *Balanced Reporting* and *Reliable Reporting*. *Philosophical Studies* 177: 3117–3142.
Gerken, M. 2020b. Public Scientific Testimony in the Scientific Image. *Studies in History and Philosophy of Science A* 80: 90–101.
Gerken, M. 2020c. Truth-Sensitivity and Folk Epistemology. *Philosophy and Phenomenological Research* 100(1): 3–25.
Gerken, M. and Beebe, J. R. 2016. Knowledge in and out of Contrast. *Noûs* 50(1): 133–164.
Gerken, M., Alexander, J., Gonnerman, C. and Waterman, J. 2020. Salient Alternatives in Perspective. *Australasian Journal of Philosophy* 98: 792–810.
Hassin R. R., Uleman, J. S. and Bargh, J. A.(Eds.). 2005. *The New Unconscious*. Oxford University Press, New York.
Ito, T. A., Thompson, E. and Cacioppo, J. T. 2004. Tracking the Timecourse of Social Perception: The Effects of Racial Cues on Event-Related Brain Potentials. *Personality and Social Psychology Bulletin* 30(10): 1267–1280.
Kaplan, D. 1989. Demonstratives. J. Almog, J. Perry and H. Wettstein (Eds.), *Themes from Kaplan* (pp. 481–563). Oxford University Press, Oxford.
Kovaka, K. 2021. Climate Change Denial and Beliefs About Science. *Synthese* 198: 2355–2374.
Kray, L. J. and Thompson, L. 2004. Gender Stereotypes and Negotiation Performance: An Examination of Theory and Research. *Research in Organizational Behavior* 26: 103–182.
Kubota, J. T. and Ito, T. A. 2007. Multiple Cues in Social Perception: The Time Course of Processing Race and Facial Expression. *Journal of Experimental Social Psychology* 43(5): 738–752.
Lai, C. et al. 2014. Reducing Implicit Racial Preferences: I. A Comparative Investigation of 17 Interventions. *Journal of Experimental Psychology General* 143(4): 1765–1785.

Langford, S. 2020. Knowledge Judgements and Cognitive Psychology. *Synthese* 197: 3245–3259.
Lewis, D. 1996. Elusive Knowledge. *Australasian Journal of Philosophy* 74(4): 549–567.
Liberman, Z., Woodward, A. L. and Kinzler, K. D. 2017. The Origins of Social Categorization. *Trends in Cognitive Sciences* 21(7): 556–568.
Magee, J. C. and Smith, P. K. 2013. The Social Distance Theory of Power. *Personality and Social Psychology Review* 17(2): 158–186.
Maitra, I. 2010. The Nature of Epistemic Injustice. *Philosophical Books* 51(4): 195–211.
McIntosh, P. 2007. White Privilege and Male Privilege. *Race, Ethnicity and Gender: Selected Readings*: 377–385.
Nagel, J., San Juan, V. and Mar, R. A. 2013. Lay Denial of Knowledge for Justified True Beliefs. *Cognition* 129(3): 652–661.
Payne, B. K. 2001. Prejudice and Perception: The Role of Automatic and Controlled Processes in Misperceiving a Weapon. *Journal of Personality and Social Psychology* 81(2): 181.
Porter S., England, L., Juodis, M., ten Brinke, L. and Wilson, K. 2008. Is the Face a Window to the Soul? Investigation of the Accuracy of Intuitive Judgments of the Trustworthiness of Human Faces. *Canadian Journal of Behavioral Science* 40: 171–177.
Puddifoot, K. 2017. Dissolving the Epistemic/Ethical Dilemma over Implicit Bias. *Philosophical Explorations* 20: 73–93.
Robbins J. M. and Krueger, J. I. 2005. Social Projection to Ingroups and Outgroups: A Review and Meta-analysis. *Personality and Social Psychology Review* 9(3): 2–47.
Rule, N. O., Ambady, N. and Hallett, K. C. 2009. Female Sexual Orientation is Perceived Accurately, Rapidly, and Automatically from the Face and Its Features. *Journal of Experimental Social Psychology* 45: 1245–1251.
Rule, N. O., Krendl, A. C., Ivcevic, Z. and Ambady, N. 2013. Accuracy and Consensus in Judgments of Trustworthiness from Faces: Behavioral and Neural Correlates. *Jersonality and Social Psychology Review* 104: 409–426.
Sanford, A. J. and Sturt, P. 2002. Depth of Processing in Language Comprehension: Not Noticing the Evidence. *Trends in Cognitive Sciences* 6(9): 382–386.
Schaffer, J. and Knobe, J. 2012. Contrastive Knowledge Surveyed. *Noûs* 46(4): 675–708.
See, K. E., Morrison, E. W., Rothman, N. B. and Soll, J. B. 2011. The Detrimental Effects of Power on Confidence, Advice Taking, and Accuracy. *Organizational Behavior and Human Decision Processes* 116(2): 272–285.
Spaulding, S. 2016. Mind Misreading. *Philosophical Issues* 26(1): 422–440.
Spaulding, S. 2018. *How We Understand Others: Philosophy and Social Cognition*. Routledge, London.
Stoutenburg, G. 2017. Strict Moderate Invariantism and Knowledge-Denials. *Philosophical Studies* 174(8): 2029–2044.
Sturt, P., Sanford, A. J., Stewart, A. and Dawydiak, E. 2004. Linguistic Focus and Good-Enough Representations: An Application of the Change-Detection Paradigm. *Psychonomic Bulletin & Review* 11(5): 882–888.
Taylor, S. E. and Fiske, S. T. 1978. Salience, Attention, and Attribution: Top of the Head Phenomena. *Advances in Experimental Social Psychology* 11: 249–288.
Todorov, A., Dotsch, R. and Mende-Siedlecki, P. 2015. Social Attributions from Faces: Determinants, Consequences, Accuracy, and Functional Significance. *Annual Review of Psychology* 66.

Turri, J. 2015. Skeptical Appeal: The Source-Content Bias. *Cognitive Science* 38(5): 307–324.

Uleman, J. S., Adil Saribay, S. and Gonzalez, C. M. 2008. Spontaneous Inferences, Implicit Impressions, and Implicit Theories. *Annual Review of Psychology* 59: 329–360.

Waterman, J., Gonnerman, C., Yan, K. and Alexander, J. (2018). Knowledge, Subjective Certainty, and Philosophical Skepticism: A Cross-Cultural Study. In S. Stich, M. Mizumoto and E. McCready (Eds.), *Epistemology for the Rest of the World: Linguistic and Cultural Diversity and Epistemology* (pp. 187–214). Oxford University Press, Oxford.

Wonder, S. 1980. Cash in Your Face. *Hotter Than July*. Motown Tamla, Los Angeles.

Xu, X., Zuo, X., Wang, X. and Han, S. 2009. Do You Feel My Pain? Racial Group Membership Modulates Empathic Neural Responses. *Journal of Neuroscience* 29(26): 8525–8529.

13 Salience principles for democracy*

Susanna Siegel

> A cynical, mercenary, demagogic press will produce in time a people as base as itself.
> — Joseph Pulitzer, 1904

For a significant segment of people, to focus mainly on their own interests, interactions, and social pressures means living within horizons that leave politics and state institutions in the background. Political life may become salient through elections, contact with the government on a special occasion such as jury duty, or by the need for a license to drive, build, hunt, buy or sell things, or a with the law. But in this mode of life, absent any large-scale political crisis, political consciousness largely stays in the background of consciousness.

John Rawls seems to endorse such a stark division of attention between the private and the political. 'In a well-governed state', he wrote, 'only a small fraction of persons may devote much of their time to politics. There are many other forms of human good'.[1]

By contrast, Walter Lippmann saw the diversion of attention from politics as an unavoidable yet seriously problematic consequence of attempts to govern democratically on a large scale. For Lippmann, exactly the kind of epistemic situation Rawls points to would make a mockery of democratic governance. 'In the cold light of experience', he wrote in his 1927 book *The Phantom Public*, 'the private citizen knows that his sovereignty is a fiction':

> The private citizen today has come to feel rather like a deaf spectator in the back row, who ought to keep his mind on the mystery... but who cannot manage to keep awake. He knows he is somehow affected by what's going on. Rules and regulations continually, taxes annually, and wars occasionally remind him that he is being swept along by great drifts of circumstance.
>
> Yet these public affairs are in no convincing way his affairs. They are for the most part invisible. They are managed, if they are managed at all, at distant

DOI: 10.4324/9781351202114-14

centers, from behind the scenes, by unnamed powers. As a private person he does not know what is going on, or who is doing it, or where he is being carried.... He lives in a world which he cannot see, does not understand, and is unable to direct...

Contemplating...his actual accomplishments in public affairs, [he can] contrast...the influence he exerts, with the influence he is supposed according to democratic theory to exert. (p.3)

Where Rawls seems to suggest that directing attention to public affairs is optional in a nearly-just democracy, Lippmann suggests that everyone's doing so is all but impossible - to the detriment of democratic aspirations.

The informational disconnect that Lippmann highlights can be bridged only by means of mass communication. Modern democracy, on this view, needs mass communication.[2] But what kind does it need?

Lippmann thought it needed newspapers overseen by an editor who would select and oversee news stories shaped by the goal of finding out hidden truths about complex things that matter to the public. Journalists would need to draw on another institution at the interface between journalism and government: 'political observatories', designed to pre-digest the technical expertise that the politicians draw on, and to make the complexities of governing legible to nonexperts. Political observatories would enable journalists to convey complex issues of everyday governance to the public, and would give them the information they'd need to hold both governmental officers and corporations accountable to the public.

The deaf spectator is politically bewildered, Lippmann thought, because 'no newspaper reports his environment so that he can grasp it' (p.4). By publicly presenting simplified technical information, journalists could begin to rectify this situation. And by using information about the processes of governance to hold officials accountable to the people, journalists could bridge the epistemic gap between government and the public. In this picture, professional journalists become second-hand experts whose role is to un-bewilder an otherwise clueless population. They address the public from the distance of an informed commentator – as Lippmann was himself.

Though Lippmann's paradigm of a 'deaf spectator' is someone who is only 'occasionally reminded' by war or taxes that the political order impacts everyday life, the need for journalism he identified applies equally to people with an ongoing awareness of this basic fact. In a crisis, such as a ground war, a hurricane, or a pandemic, the fact that everyday life can be made steady or unsteady by political order or disorder is glaringly plain. And absent crises like these, there are at least two sets of people for whom the impact of political institutions regularly occupies the foreground of consciousness: political elites, whose job relates them directly to the government, and incarcerated persons or others living under frequent or even constant surveillance by the state. Whether the precarities involved in large-scale social coordination are hidden or evident, the need for journalism remains.

Professional print journalism as it emerged in the 1920s in the US was shaped by Lippmann's vision of mass communication.[3] It institutionalized a *salience principle of importance*: make salient information that is important for the public to know about. In this principle, which I'll call the importance principle for short, 'newsworthiness' is a normative notion, tied to whatever is actually important for the public to know about. I'll use 'newsworthiness' in this normative sense. A different notion (more common among journalists) would define newsworthy content as whatever content will in fact attract attention if reported in a news outlet, whether it is *important* to know about or not. In a digital context, the newsworthy in this other sense would align with being likely to be 'shared'. But this use is not the one at work here.

What would the news be like, if it lived up to the importance principle? In the ideal defined by the principle, the news would be full of things worth paying attention to, and it wouldn't be the case that most newsworthy things are left out of the news.

This paper is about a problem that arises from this ideal. I call it the problem of democratic attention. The problem is that some roles for journalism in democracy depend on readers actually taking in the information that would be made salient by journalism, when journalism fulfills the importance principle. But for much important information, many readers have no antecedent interest in it, feel no prior motivation to learn it, and face substantial obstacles to paying attention to information even when it is widely available, and even when it would yield knowledge that would be useful to have. The problematic upshot is that democracy imposes an attentional demand that can't easily be met.

Democracy in many of its guises has frequently been held to be too demanding. Does representative democracy rely on a population with stable, well-formed opinions about public policy, who are disposed to select representatives ready to respect their preferences? Achen and Bartels (2016) argue that people simply don't have such stable preferences, so any democratic scheme on which they guide voters in selecting representatives demands more of voters than they can give. Does democracy's ideal of political equality rely on sidelining powerful group affinities, even when doing so would yield political losses? Delany (1852) had his doubts that white supremacy in America would ever allow democracy there to flourish - doubts felt forcefully by some theorists today.[4] Would true self-governance require citizens to deliberate and discuss political matters with one another? Mansbridge (1980) argues that in practice, deliberation historically ended up distinctly *un*democratic, leading to domination by better-educated citizens - a generalization echoed by Mutz (2006).

These criticisms point to ways in which representative, deliberative, and liberal democracy seem to ask a lot of our abilities to detach from group allegiance, or deliberate, or form policy preferences. By contrast, the problem of democratic attention concerns our capacity to take in the information on the basis of which we would do any of those things. The challenge finds obstacles to forming even our most basic understandings of public political life - a precondition for our forming opinions, preferences, or allegiances regarding our political arrangements.

The problem of democratic attention arises in part from the importance principle. I'll argue that a different, more specific salience principle can help address it: the public-as-protagonist principle.

In Part I of this paper I develop the challenge of democratic attention. Since there is little point in addressing a merely apparent problem, it is worth considering the point of view from which the purported problem isn't really a problem, either because the roles for journalism in democracy do not, after all, exert normative pressure on attention, or because respecting the importance principle is enough to ensure that the public pays attention to the degree it has to. Against these perspectives, I argue that the problem is indeed a challenge for journalism in aspirational democracies.[5]

In Part II I develop the public-as-protagonist principle. I'm presuming without argument that it would be a good thing for democracy - and a good thing, period - if news was selected and framed by this principle, and if readers saw themselves and all their fellow denizens of the polity in the ways the principle invites them to: as political protagonists with a stake and a say in the political future. On this assumption, the principle is worth developing, regardless of whether it helps solve the problem of democratic attention. But I'll argue that there are reasons to think it would help.

13.1 Part 1: The problem of democratic attention

I'll explicate the problem of democratic attention for the specific case of the United States, where most of my examples will be drawn from. But the problem is general. It could face any aspirational democracy that contains journalism in the professionalized form born in the early twentieth century United States. It arises from the combination of three points:

1. Professional journalism is governed by an importance principle of salience.
2. Some roles for journalism in democracy depend on readers actually taking in information that would be made salient by journalism, if journalism fulfilled the importance principle.
3. For much important information, many readers have no antecedent interest in it, and feel no prior motivation for taking it in.

I'll argue that taken together, these points create a problem: large swaths of any public are liable to lack the disposition to pay attention to important information made salient by journalism, even though they face pressure to do just that by virtue of living in an aspirational democracy.

To feel the force of the problem, and to recognize potential solutions to it, its central notions need to be unpacked. Regarding point (1): what exactly is the importance principle and how does it regulate the news? Regarding point (2):

what are journalism's roles in a democracy, and what kinds of demands do they place on the public's attention? Regarding point (3): what principles of salience in news journalism facilitate or anti-facilitate democratic forms of political engagement?

13.1.1 Journalism and the importance principle

Salience and attention are closely related. To make something salient is to put it forward as both demanding attention and deserving it. On the receiving end, when something becomes salient to us we experience it as demanding our attention. Whether we experience it as also deserving attention is a further question.[6] The more salient something is to someone, the more easily available to them it is, so that they can react to it.

When a newspaper publishes a story or an image, it presents that content as something that calls for attention, and makes it available to be noticed. A news story is more easily available, and therefore more salient, if it is on the front page of a print or digital newspaper than if it is several clicks or pages away. In a digital context, a story is more salient, the more places a link to the story appears.

Salience is distinct from actual uptake. In principle, a news story can be salient without anyone actually noticing it, let alone reading it, understanding it, remembering it, reacting to it, drawing any conclusions from it, or otherwise integrating it with anything else they know, suspect, want, feel, or believe.

Some stimuli capture attention as soon as they become salient. Think of bright flashes or honking horns. News stories are not quite in this category. No matter how salient they are, their salience is not a guarantee of their uptake.

A principle of salience for a type of communication system is a guide to what should be made salient and what should not be. In the context of professional news journalism, the principle of salience is the importance principle. The importance principle says to make salient the things that are important for the public to know about.

The formal aspect of this principle applies to journalism in any type of regime, whether it is democratic or not. As I'll now clarify, the formal aspect is distinct from procedural and substantive aspects, which can reflect political values.

The formal aspect of the importance principle is that merely by including a story, image, or information under the guise of 'news' in a newspaper, its content is presented as important for readers to pay attention to. The formal aspect is evident in a structure of presenting information that makes it more prominent than others. Print media reserves a 'front page' for the stories presented as most important. Digital media preserves a structure that uses degrees of prominence to mark degrees of importance. A digital version of a newspaper treats the first things you see as more important than stories found several clicks away within the newspaper's interface.[7]

In its formal aspect, the importance principle applies to journalism in any type of regime. Consider the role of mass communication in the type of autocracy led by a strongman, as described by Ruth Ben-Ghiat:

The strongman has turned politics into an aesthetic experience, with him as the star. The communication codes and celebrity cultures of film, television, and now digital storytelling shape the leader's self-presentation and the images he releases of both followers and enemies.[8]

Such leaders aim to develop a cult of personality in which they remain the central spectacular protagonist. Often they are demagogues who purport to have a special direct relationship to 'the people' in the polity that they aim to govern. A newspaper, newsreel, radio or television program that facilitates these narratives fulfill the formal aspects of the importance principle, by circulating stories that satisfy the leader's modes of self-presentation, while presenting them under the guise of information that is important for the public to understand.

In its formal aspect, the importance principle is compatible with the types of mass communication made for pointedly *anti*-democratic politics. A demagogic strongman refuses to treat 'the people' as an abstraction that can only be evoked indirectly by the principles of government that should unite it, and instead tries to present the public as a palpable crowd that he addresses directly in rallies, where he brings the narratives conveyed by newsreels, radio addresses, or Twitter feeds to life. Mass rallies build a direct emotional connection between the strongman and follower, giving the impression that the public can be seen and felt. In the live crowd bewitched and unified by the strongman's speeches, the public becomes whole. This kind of public is not *represented* by the leader, but partly constituted by him.[9]

These observations bring out an unstated assumption in Lippmann's construal of the need for journalism, an assumption that Dewey made explicit: the public is nebulous and cannot be perceived or grasped directly.[10] It takes an act of imagination for the public to figure in its members' minds. As Danielle Allen puts it:

> Democracy's basic term is neither 'liberty' nor 'equality', but 'the people'. But where and what is this thing, the people?...How can one even hold an idea of this strange body in one's head? Only with figures, metaphors, and other imaginative forms.[11]

The elusiveness of the public presents a challenge: what features of society will enable people to grasp the polity to which they belong?

In the character of mass communication, we find completely opposite answers to this question. The mass rallies essential to fascist demagoguery purport to make the public concrete, by generating enormous crowds that give the impression of being so massive as to include nearly everyone who matters in the region. The leader tries to stoke their feelings of righteousness, using chants and jeers against political enemies construed as illegitimate and deserving of violence. As the epigraph from Pulitzer suggests, professionalized journalism can echo this way of imagining the public. But when it does, it plays second fiddle to the direct channels of communication that strongman leaders depend upon to cultivate their idea of a public made whole by the leader.

The democratic potential of professionalized journalism derives from its capacity to portray a pluralistic public, and for its reports to involve protagonists other than and even opposed to a strongman. That is why fascist politics is hostile to journalism. Its democratic potential comes from further constraints on the importance principle, which can be found in the structures and genres of professional journalism. In 'Liberty and the News', Walter Lippmann writes:

> The newspaper is in all literalness the bible of democracy, the book out of which a people determines its conduct...Now the power to determine each day what shall seem important and what shall be neglected is a power unlike any that has been exercised since the Pope lost hold on the secular mind.

Here, Lippmann makes explicit that newspapers select things that should be treated as important *for democracy*. His guiding idea of democracy is that 'a people determines its conduct'. What kinds of things are important, given this construal of democracy?

As Lippmann recognized, in the American context, the guiding democratic idea that 'a people determines its conduct' involves a delicate balance between popular preference, constitutional constraints, and expertise . People who lack expertise of various kinds would have little idea which cooperative schemes would be best; but leaving all terms of coordination up to experts would remove any pretense to political equality or accountability. In Lippmann's vision, journalism can help to strike this balance, by building channels of communication between experts and everyone else, and by making public the stakes and challenges of social coordination. That makes journalists a locus of mediation between overlapping publics, figures of political establishments, and experts - the very forces whose balance determines the extent of liberal democracy.

Lippmann took for granted a political structure in which leaders were representatives of the people, and therefore accountable to them. The roles for journalism he outlined stem from this assumption.

How is journalism supposed to contribute to the correct balance? For a start, the organizational structure of newspapers traditionally divided the "news side" from the 'business side' (sometimes denoted using exalted terminology of 'Church and State', where the business side is the Church, a force whose influence has to be contained). Institutionally, the news and business sides traditionally had separate modes of management, different offices, and different staff.[12] For the many decades in which print newspapers were lucrative, newspapers would not typically be financially threatened by running stories critical of their advertisers, and they did. A famous case from 1950 illustrates this: the Wall Street Journal published an article that offended General Motors, who then pulled their ads from the paper. The paper was unapologetic, and said ultimately no one would read the newspaper if they thought its content was controlled by their advertisers.[13]

This institutional division is a procedural aspect of the importance principle. It is a negative constraint: don't let the news be unduly influenced by advertisers. But beyond the negative constraint, what substantive constraints are there on the importance principle?

The major substantive constraint is in professional journalism's brief to 'follow the story', and the skills needed to carry it out. A 'story' is something that has to be followed - not invented by a strongman or demagogue. A story is built of facts - not of lies that suit the teller or promote a campaign of persuasion. Given this conception of a story woven from facts, it follows that the skills journalists need are both literary and epistemic. The literary skill is knowing how to tell a story that unfolds from questions, and the epistemic skill is knowing how to verify reliable sources, how to establish which things are true. Taken together, these skills amount to an ability to inquire. To follow a story, one needs to know which questions to ask, and how to determine which answers to them are correct. Once again, we can see why journalism construed in this way falls out of favor with modes of government that shun transparency and have no structure of accountability, and why conversely it is essential for democratic modes of governmentoriented around accountability.

Other substantive constraints are evident in the main genres of news journalism. There is accountability or watchdog journalism, and reporting on the workings of government or political campaigns. There are portraits of a neighborhood or a subpopulation; reporting focused on problems that arise from sharing public space, or disputes about which things are public goods, or public health concerns; and investigations of possible crimes,[14] especially 'white-collar' ones occurring within powerful institutions.[15] The prevalence of these genres of reporting in American journalism shows that the substantive constraints in the importance principle have been clearly operative, and that they are designed for a multitude of publics and plurality of points of view.

Substantive constraints on the importance principle are also evident in public criticisms of journalism charged with failing to make salient important events, facts, or inquiries. Consider the six-part retrospective series by the Kansas City Star re-examining how the newspaper has covered issues affecting Black Kansas Citians for the past 140 years.[16] One of its starkest self-criticisms concerns reports about the newspaper's neglect to investigate the underlying reason that a local school district made dozens of boundary changes during a two-year period, some of which were only a single block. These reports could not be faulted for inaccuracy or lack of verification, but are now criticized for what they failed to make salient: that it was an attempt to bypass desegregation laws. Mará Rose Williams, the reporter who instigated the retrospective review, voices the criticism like this:

> We may have written about a boundary change as it occurred at a school board meeting. But what we didn't do was make the connection as to why they were making these boundary changes. We didn't dig in deep enough to make the connection that it was to keep the schools segregated, to keep

white children in one part of town and Black children in another part of town, which was also a violation of federal law at the time.[17]

This example illustrates that sometimes for journalists to make important information salient to the public, questions that open important lines of inquiry must first be salient to the journalists.

The same retrospective review notes other examples of omissions that failed to report on things that were important for the public to know about. In his introduction to its six-art series, editor Mark Fannin describes how the newspaper covered the devastating 1977 flood by reporting on property damage of J.C. Nichols, a wealthy white developer. Fannin writes:

> The Star [and its then-sister paper, the Times] quickly dubbed it 'The Plaza Flood'. That set the stage for the papers...to focus mainly on property damage at the Country Club Plaza, not so much the 25 people who died, including eight Black residents.[18]

He adds: 'White businessman J.C. Nichols got plenty of ink. His advertisements promoting segregated communities ran prominently in The Star and Times. Nichols, who developed the Country Club Plaza, was a protege of The Star's founder, William Rockhill Nelson, who enthusiastically supported his effort'. Fannin is suggesting here that the newspaper failed to respect the importance principle twice over. Procedurally, it failed to insulate judgments of newsworthiness from business interests; and substantively, it neglected to include stories it should have reported.

Another type of criticism based on the importance principle focuses on the inclusion of facts and pursuit of inquiries that should not have been made salient, but were.

For example, during the U.S. Presidential campaign in 1992, the talk show host Phil Donahue focused his interview with Bill Clinton on his marijuana use, and the recent revelations by Gennifer Flowers to a tabloid of an extra-marital affair lasting many years. The focus on those 'personal' things was roundly criticized, even by some of Clinton's opponents, for being the wrong kind of thing for the press to focus on during a presidential campaign.[19] Where was the discussion of his platform and principles and policies? How would the focus on 'character' help people understand how this candidate would connect politics to government, if he were elected? The Phil Donahue type of questioning added to US political journalism's poor reputation at that time. People thought news coverage wasn't focused on the right things.

For the importance principle to operate in a culture of journalism, there need not be consensus on what is important to include or exclude, even in retrospect. Consider the e-mails hacked by Russian intelligence operatives in the summer of 2016.[20] Once the emails were released, much of the press coverage focused intensely on the content of the emails – not on the fact that Russia, a rival power, had infiltrated one of the two main political parties of the US. By focusing on the contents of the emails treated those contents as information that was important for the public to know, instead of focusing the story on the electoral interference itself.

When media commentators debated whether the contents of the emails should have been revealed, the debate illustrated that the importance principle operates in the culture of news production. Both sides assumed the importance principle. They disagreed about which information was important to reveal.[21]

13.1.2 Journalism's roles in democracy and their demands on public attention

The importance principle is the first ingredient in the puzzle of democratic attention. The second ingredient is a set of demands on public attention.

News stories are addressed to any readers of the newspaper. We could say that they address the superset of politizens: denizens of a polity, of any size ('politizens' – a contraction of 'denizens of a polity').[22] Some news stories will be important for all politizens, other stories will be most important to some and less important to others. But for any story, there is a public it most closely concerns.

Phenomenologically, like anything salient, a story, image, or headline in a newspaper is presented as something that deserves attention of readers – whether it really does deserve such attention, or not. When contents that do not deserve attention are presented as if they do, we could say its demand is a sham. It exerts no genuine normative pressure on readers to pay them any attention.

When news stories fulfill the importance principle, by contrast, we can ask: what kind of attention do they demand, and of whom?

One extreme response rejects the presumption that news stories demand anything at all of the readers. It is enough simply for news to be salient, and that happens as soon as it is published. Availability is enough. On this view, the role of a newspaper in a democracy is analogous to a public records office, and that role is complete once information is available, regardless of whether anyone actually reads it.

This extreme response is at odds with the central roles for journalism in democracy envisaged by Lippmann. If one of journalism's roles is to provide simplified technical information such as explaining the basic points of a health care or police reform bill, or the reasons for a new traffic safety measure, or how to prevent or stem the tide of a pandemic, this role will be incomplete if hardly anyone actually learns about these things. If such information was presented in the news but got no uptake from the public, the public could easily remain just as bewildered as they would be without the information.

A different role, associated more with John Dewey than with Lippmann, is to make a public aware of problems that affect a range of different stakeholders, and in doing so, make visible which people are stakeholders and how they are connected to one another by those problems.[23] For journalism to help politizens become aware of the different stakeholders who are connected by a problem, there is no way for it to play this epistemic role without actual uptake. This point holds at large scales and small: in a company, a school community, a group of people who want or need to use the same space in multiple and potentially conflicting ways, a city, a country, and so on.

What about accountability or watchdog journalism? Does it demand any actual uptake? And if it does, from whom?

In discussing journalism's watchdog role, Michael Schudson suggests that only an 'inner circle' of citizens have to pay attention to accountability reporting:

> Journalism performs its institutional role as a watchdog even if nobody in the provinces is following the news. All that matters is that people in government believe that some people somewhere are following the news. All that is necessary to inspire this belief is that an inner circle of attentive citizens is watchful. This is sufficient to produce in the leaders a fear of public embarrassment or public discrediting, public controversy, legal prosecution, or fear of losing an election.[24]

If Schudson is correct, the problem of democratic attention might seem to dissolve for the crucial case of accountability journalism. In this picture, watchdog journalism's demands on attention are both mild and easy to meet, because the demand on attention affects only those people who are disposed to pay attention anyway. For journalism to play a watchdog role, it is enough for the news in this category to be known by the 'inner circle' that matters for politics. Their attention is enough to effectively monitor the workings of powerful leaders.

Is this picture correct?

Let's distinguish reports on actual cases of grift and corruption from the regular presence of journalists at meetings of school boards or city councils. The mere presence of journalists at government meetings lowers the cost of local governance, and helps prevent corruption.[25] It plays its preventive role in part by affording the possibility of publicizing corruption, were it to occur. This role is also played by reporting on ho-hum proceedings. Public records of such meeting proceedings are important for record-keeping, but few people read them, and arguably the reports don't even exert pressure on anyone to read them. Does this kind of reporting then undermine the idea that fulfilling the importance principle generates demands on the reading public's attention?

No, because reports of uneventful meetings, or reports made for record-keeping, often do not fulfill the importance principle. It is not important for the public to know that nothing untoward happened in the day to day business of governing. If this reassuring fact is proven by publishing a story that notes the ho-hum proceedings, and such a story counts as part of watchdog journalism, then we should conclude that the importance principle is not the only principle of salience. This fact does not undermine the problem of democratic attention, because the problem arises only if much of the public is *not* disposed to pay attention to news that *does* fulfill the importance principle.

Is Schudson's picture correct for reporting on actual corruption? Schudson mentions people 'in the provinces' Let's assume they are voters to whom the leaders are officially accountable. If the leaders could be confident that these voters would not learn about their grift or other forms of corruption, why should they fear public embarrassment? Schudson's picture assumes if the voters outside the inner circle have any political role at all, their role is fully determined by the power of the inner circle to discredit a corrupt leader in the eyes of those voters, without the voters ever hearing about the corruption. And this pushes the question back one step: if voters 'in the provinces' are not paying attention to the leader, they are presumably also not paying attention to the watchful inner circle, which makes it hard to see how the inner circle could influence them.

The watchdog role in making offenses costly to powerful leaders requires that the leaders' fear of public embarrassment is reasonable. They lose any reason to fear embarrassment, if they can be confident that the population at large won't care about the offense, either because they don't know about it, or because they but don't know its significance.[26] So the watchdog role seems to require actual uptake. When Mark Meadows was Trump's chief of staff, he defended the repeated violations of the Hatch Act by high-ranking members of the Trump administration by asserting 'No one outside the Beltway cares' about such offenses.[27] As Meadows and the administration he worked for knew, convincing the public not to believe, listen to, or care about reported violations of the Hatch Act is a good way to make such violations seem like no big deal.

13.1.3 Can the public meet journalism's demands?

So far, I've highlighted several roles for journalism in democracy: monitoring powerful leaders, closing informational gaps, and making different segments of overlapping publics visible to one another. For news stories to play these roles, I've argued, they require actual uptake on a wide scale.

If some of the things that are important to know about lie entirely outside our concerns, then it's an open question what, if anything, might motivate us to actually pay attention to them. And here there are at least two major obstacles to mobilizing attention.

The first obstacle is the mere cognitive load that meeting every demand on attention that important news would impose. Here, important news is on par with much else that's worthwhile to know about. It would be worthwhile for me to know more about the many amazing regularities captured by the periodic table of elements. The same is true for countless histories, problems, stories, poems, and facts that live between the covers of the books, journals, and archives in libraries all over the world. I am unlikely to pay any attention to most of it, given how much of it there is. The library is full of good books, and the sad fact is that none of us will ever read them all.

The cognitive load would be far less significant an obstacle to taking in important news if we found the news to be readily engaging. This observation brings us to the second and perhaps even bigger obstacle to journalism's demands on attention. Stories about things that are important to know about may lack the features that tend to engage attention readily. Important news is often not sensational. It only sometimes provokes fear, indignation, offense, humor or joy – all things that prompt 'viral' circulation in modes of mass communication that are governed by different salience principles from the one governing professional journalism. Social media platforms highlight content that tracks the time spent with a browser occupied by a website. There is no editor deciding what is important *for the public* to make salient, no entrenched culture of an institution meant to serve an essential role in democracy, and no libel laws criminalizing the publication of harmfully false information.[28]

Few people have to be urged to check their social media accounts. Instead, we are sometimes admonished (and sometimes admonish ourselves) not to spend so much time on those platforms.[29] Virality is a measure of one kind of engagement, but the markers of virality are not co-extensive with information that is important for the public to know about.[30] Journalism's importance principle and social media platforms' engagement principle each select different content to bring to salience.

So there appears to be a mismatch. Professional journalism purports to generate importance norms of attention, while social media does not; but attention gravitates much more readily to social media platforms governed by principles of engagement than it does to news outlets governed by the importance principle – even when conformity with the importance principle is far from perfect. The mismatch suggests an uphill battle when it comes to drawing wide attention to things that are important for the public to understand.

13.2 Is the problem merely apparent?

A skeptic might propose that the problem is merely apparent, because it is actually an artifact of the failure of news media to live up to its own importance principle. On this view, the only problem in the vicinity is that too often, the importance principle *isn't* actually fulfilled. Even though news outlets present their content under that mode of presentation of importance, the things they deem newsworthy are frequently not actually important for the public to understand, and that is why people devote less attention to them. Truly important information is also always engaging, on this view, and that is why there is no real problem of democratic attention. The appearance of such a problem is merely an artifact of news media's failure to live up to its own importance principle.

This approach to the problem of democratic attention evokes Aristotle's idea that we are essentially political animals.[31] All you have to do is show us the information that matters to our political life, and we will be interested in it, because it is in our political nature to be so interested.

Whatever elements of truth this oversimplified, vaguely Aristotelian picture may contain, there are strong reasons to think that the problem of democratic attention would not automatically dissolve if the importance principle were consistently fulfilled.

The first reason is that as any student of style knows, there are many ways to convey the same basic information. Compare the style of the report by special counsel Robert Mueller on then-president Trump's dealings with Russian operatives, with the concise, straightforward op-ed written by Anonymous in the early days of the Trump administration written as a warning to the public.[32] Both pieces of writing aimed to convey serious crimes committed by Trump and other central figures in the administration. But the op-ed was easy to understand, whereas the report was full of indirection and legalese. The difference was not only in content and length, but in style.

The second reason to think the puzzle of democratic attention could challenge even a news media that fulfilled the importance principle was acknowledged by both Lippmann and Dewey in their discussions of the complexity of democratic society. In *The Public and Its Problems*, Dewey emphasizes the indirect consequence of interactions in society that affect people who cannot trace those consequences back to their source. For instance, before the 1970s, it was not known that the acidic rain and snow falling in the northeastern U.S. was caused by industrial sites in the Ohio Valley. This discovery helped identify the health impact of people living in Sweden and Norway from factories in Germany and England.[33]

Dewey observed that we remain unaware of many of the laws, practices, and interactions that shape our lives. Given these epistemic limitations, we are often unaware of the set of people whose lives are all affected by the same factors. We don't know with whom we share a stake in a problem, or who has different or opposing stakes in the same problem. When decisions taken in one place by one set of actors affect the health of people in a different place, these people form a 'public' in Dewey's sense. In this sense, modern publics are often invisible, and it takes journalism, among other types of institutions and practices, to make them visible.[34] As we saw from the Kansas City *Star*'s retrospective overview, journalists can distort their portrait of the public through their choices about which inquiries to pursue and which stories to make salient.

Taken together, these observations show that the category 'information that is important for the public to know about' leaves open how that information is presented, how it is framed, which parts are emphasized, and whether or not its importance is made manifest. The puzzle of democratic attention is not therefore merely an artifact of the failure of news outlets to fulfill the importance principle. The importance principle can be fulfilled in ways that make the importance of the content relatively more manifest or relatively less so.

An informal observation may help illustrate this point for readers familiar with a mainstay of television news in the mid-1970s and 1980s: the MacNeil-Lehrer News Hour. Many momentous things occurred during these years, and on the show they were discussed at length. But the discussions always sounded the same, regardless of the topic. The two unflappable anchors with the same demeanor never reacted much differently from one occasion to the next, regardless of what anyone else said. If you weren't already interested in the topics under discussion, you would probably not become interested in them from listening.

But boring news shows are not the root of the problem of democratic attention. If they were, the problem would be analogous to the one faced by some parents: their young children should eat vegetables but they much prefer to eat cupcakes. This type of problem concerns only what to ingest: vegetables or cupcakes. The nutritive results of ingestion take care of themselves.

If the problem of democratic attention concerned merely what information to ingest, the solution would be infotainment: the genre that packages information in short spurts without extensive narratives, but still aims to convey supposedly important facts. As the parent of a picky toddler might coat brussels sprouts in maple syrup but avoid broccoli which can't plausibly be sweetened, infotainment partly compromises importance, selecting only the important content that can be fit into an entertaining frame.

Ingestion is a poor model for the underlying problem, because the problem concerns a type of uptake that involves more than merely consuming information. As the case of the Hatch Act suggests, for the mechanisms of accountability to work fully, the publics to whom a leader is accountable have to feel invested in the outcomes. They have to feel that they have a stake in whether the leader governs properly or not. In the case of how public money is used, these stakes are straightforward: instead of using it to maximize public goods, a leader may use it extremely inefficiently, or use it to further his political career, or at an extreme, simply put it in his pocket. Merely staring at the television or website while it broadcasts reports that speak to whether this is happening or not may be a good start, but if the information had no further interactions with anyone's attitudes toward politics, the broadcasting would have no more effect than a sit-com or a movie.[35] Entertainment is the wrong model of accountability journalism.

When looked at this way, the problem of democratic attention looks more specifically like a problem of standing attitudes that facilitate democracy, not occurrent intake with no further impact on a listener's mind. To solve it, what's needed is a way to orient the reader. The crucial questions then become: which attitudes are democracy-facilitating attitudes? And which principles of selection and framing of news stories can cultivate them?

Viewing the problem in this way has implications for how to measure the kind of uptake that would constitute democratic attention. Occurrent engagement can be measured by how much time one spends taking it in, because by definition it lasts only as long as it occupies attention. When digital sites estimate occurrent engagement with content by measuring how much time one spends on a website displaying it, they don't measure directly whether people actually take in the information, let alone whether they remember it or whether it affects how they feel or think about their political communities.

By contrast, *attitudinal* engagement makes a more lasting impact by surviving in memory, where it remains available for further inferences and action. Attitudes are lasting mental states. They contribute to the standing dispositions a person has. To measure attitudinal engagement, instead of asking how much time people spend taking content in, we would ask how the person's attitudes were affected by it. If one never spends any time with the content at all (zero occurrent engagement), it will not engage one's attitudes, either. But there may be no further correlation between time spent and attitudes affected.

I'll argue that the core democratic attitude is seeing oneself and one's fellow politizens as potential political protagonists - a role excluded, I'll argue, by the strongman principle of salience, which tailors messages to construe listeners as loyalists to the strongman who remains the seat of political agency. The principle is to frame and select stories in a way that invites readers to see themselves as on a par with other politizens as potential political protagonists in public affairs. I'll call this principle of salience the public-as-protagonist principle.[36]

This reorientation of the problem does not sidestep the pitfalls of boredom and the challenge of how to capture attention in the first place. Practically anything can be made boring or uninviting, including news articles that address readers as potential political protagonists. But if the problem of democratic attention is ultimately a problem of democratic attitude, then merely capturing attention is not sufficient to address it.

To make the case that the public-as-protagonist principle helps solve the problem of democratic attention, in the rest of this paper I explain what the principle says and illustrate it with three kinds of examples. Since the principle itself is independent of the dialectical role in the problem that I'm claiming for it, even readers who think there is no problem of democratic attention, or who come to doubt that the public-as-protagonist principle helps address it, may nonetheless be interested in exploring and evaluating the principle as a potential guide for selecting and framing of news stories.

13.3 Part 2: The public-as-protagonist principle

The public-as-protagonist principle recommends framing and selecting information to invite readers to view themselves and one another as potential political participants. Whatever else a news story reports, it should make explicit, when it can, the ways in which the reading public has a stake in how the situation reported unfolds; and it should make explicit the ways in which they could affect its outcome. The stakes can be economic, political, or affective.

In this general form, the principle may sound simple. But many complexities arise, including well-known imprecisions of the very idea of a public. Is there just one public or are there many? If two people belong to the same public, will they necessarily be aware of this fact? Will they necessarily share the same 'public interests' in the important situation being reported? If there are multiple publics, or publics with different interests, what do the principle's recommendations amount to?

The rest of this paper works with the following general answers. There are many publics. Two people (call them A and B) belong to the same public only if the outcome of a situation matters to them (not necessarily in the same way). A and B need not know each other. They need not know what stakes they hold in a problem, and need not know that an outcome matters to them, or how. In general, A and B can belong to the same public, while being quite epistemically impoverished about the situation that affects them.

Removing epistemic limitations like these results in a type of political consciousness. Lifting such limitations leaves one aware of one's interests, or one's potential interests in an outcome. It also brings to light relationships with other people in the polity. As often happens in inquiry, removing one layer of ignorance may introduce another. For instance, learning that one is susceptible to the effects of acid rain may leave one with a rash of questions, including which industries are responsible, whether any measures can be taken to guard against its ill effects, what the prospects are for future prevention, and so on.

Not every reader will be a potential protagonist in every story. But if the importance principle is fulfilled and the public-as-protagonist is applied consistently, then every regular reader is likely to encounter a story in which they feel addressed as a potential protagonist eventually.

13.3.1 *Examples*

I'll draw on three types of examples to illustrate the public-as-protagonist principle at work, representing three major types of stories that connect news journalism directly to democracy: elections, accountability, and loss of life. These examples are meant to illustrate the principle at work. The reasons to think that applications of the principle can meet the challenge of democratic attention will come in section 4.

13.3.1.1 *Elections*

A common approach to election coverage regards the campaigns as determined primarily by the candidates and their interactions. The role of journalists is to decipher the criticisms the candidates launch at one another, and convey the state of play to the public. Like reporting on a horse race that provides a continuous stream of information about which horse has forged ahead and which has fallen behind, this approach highlights who is ahead in the polls.

The 'horse race' approach treats the voting public as an audience who is interested in the micro-dynamics of the campaign. By contrast, according to the public-as-protagonist principle, the purpose of election coverage is to help voters set the agenda for the campaign by communicating which issues they think the candidates should address. This approach treats the voting public as stakeholders who need to make a decision and may have questions about how policy will connect with government. It does not matter whether journalists undertake this kind of opinion polling or rely on other outlets, so long as the opinions about which issues candidates should address are made salient.[37]

Another way to portray voters as inquirers as opposed to people who simply react is to make explicit how candidates' positions unfold over the course of a campaign. Rosen (1999) gives an example of election coverage by the *Wichita Eagle* that elegantly created a way to display these responses by displaying campaign statements chronologically. Each week, the newspaper added updates to a list of commitments of each candidate, including whether the candidate restated a position as an issue, or adjusted it. Using this format, the newspaper could highlight questions from the public and answers by the candidates.

By having an entry for each week and displaying the whole timeline, the newspaper made it possible to report if nothing had changed that week, if anything was clarified, or if any new positions had been taken. By creating a space in which a candidate's responsiveness or failures to respond to voters' reactions could be made salient, it implicitly treated candidates' positions as changeable in response to voters' reactions.

13.3.1.2 Accountability

A second illustration of the principle concerns reporting on grift or other forms of corruption, such as using public resources to fund a political campaign. In reporting on misuses of taxpayer money, the taxpaying public figures as a protagonist just by virtue of the focus of the story. But there are further choices that can either foreground the specific communities who may be harmed by the misuse of funds, as the public-as-protagonist principle recommends, or leave them out of the picture altogether.

Consider the multiple charges of corruption made against the Republican politician Josh Hawley during his term as Attorney General of Missouri. All of the charges were based on information uncovered and reported by the Kansas City *Star*. This reporting gives us several examples of the public-as-protagonist principle at work, as well as examples where it could have been applied more extensively.

Hawley was investigated by Missouri Secretary of State for using taxpayer money to hire political consultants from Massachusetts and Louisiana during 2017 and 2018 to set the agenda for the Attorney General office.[38] The agenda they set seemed to be geared toward raising Hawley's national profile in preparation for his run for senate against Democrat Claire McCaskill, whom he eventually defeated in the 2018 election. His office was also charged with violating Missouri open-records laws after he both declined to use government email and declined to turn over records of communications between the Attorney General's office and political consultants, which would help determine the extent and nature of the role of political consultants.[39]

Because it played a major role in instigating the investigations and in publicizing the results, the Kansas City *Star*'s reporting was successful accountability journalism, by the standard set by the importance principle. It could have played this role without doing much to successfully engage readers' attention. But the reports took a step toward highlighting the potential political roles of readers by including the email address and telephone number of the whistleblower hotline at the state auditor's office, in case any readers had further information, and noting that under state law whistleblowers can remain anonymous.[40]

Most members of the public are not in a position to blow any whistles. But by including this information in the article, the journalists are highlighting that any such whistleblowers are regular members of the public, rather than political insiders to whom journalists have special access. In these ways, the coverage was treating the public as potential contributors in an inquiry that matters to everyone, and as people with a stake in how the inquiry turns out.

In other ways, the Kansas City *Star*'s accountability reporting on Hawley kept the reading public at a distance from the situation it reported. It focused repeatedly on the disconnect between Hawley's statement that he was 'not the type of ladder-climbing politician who would continually seek higher office', and his behavior as an official who allegedly devoted public resources to his own political campaign.[41] In the same vein of identifying instances of hypocrisy, the *Star* reminded readers that Hawley 'had criticized Hillary Clinton's use of a private server for sending and receiving emails while she was U.S. secretary of state' while campaigning for election to Attorney General, even though he appears to have done the same thing himself. 'Sec. Clinton's outrageous conduct & lack of prosecution shows we need an AG who knows how to win for the rule of law', they reported him as having tweeted during his campaign.[42]

Pointing out this kind of hypocrisy is a way of discrediting the politician, and inviting the public to do the same.[43] In a story that highlights politicians' hypocrisy, the reading public is implicitly framed as a spectator of disappointing politics.[44] The disappointment may be warranted, and it may justifiably make readers angry. But leaving things there relegates the reading public to the background. If the Attorney General has served his own political career at taxpayer's expense, and that's the end of the story, then the story treats it as an open possibility that there is no other way things could be.

A more extensive application of the public-as-protagonist principle could list pending allegations, or past known infringements that were never litigated, or controversies over potential corporate, governmental or environmental infringements that affect the readers. This point of focus would make the monitoring function itself salient, instead of highlighting a politician's failure to perform it. The monitoring function turns the focus onto what the office is supposed to do for the public.

13.3.1.3 Life and death

Election coverage and watchdog reporting focus on relationships between politicians and the people they aim to govern. Because elections and accountability in government are two defining features of a democracy, journalism plays an important role in facilitating democratic politics when it is designed to bolster accountability and participation in elections.

The third defining feature of democracy is political equality among the governed. Political equality is a relationship between members of the public, rather than the relationship between the government and the governed.

The decisions made by journalists about how to narrate losses of life and property can facilitate or anti-facilitate a sense of political equality. How?

When a newspaper publicizes deaths from traffic fatalities, an epidemic, natural disaster, or homicide, it can depict those deaths as losses by making salient *what* was lost when the people died: the people, places, and activities they cared about; the reactions of the people who cared about them; the roles they played in their community, and so on.

If the people lost happened to occupy a position of public service, such as being a janitor in a public school, the loss would be a loss of a public servant, and to that extent a loss to the public. But what if the people weren't officially public servants? Is publicizing what is lost simply satisfying to the people who knew the deceased? It is likely to affect them most strongly. It may also affect people who didn't know them, if they identify in some way with their situation. But there will often be scores of people who remain relatively indifferent to losses distant from their concerns. So what role could depicting such losses play in a democracy?

If the depiction of lives lost aim to evoke a feeling of loss, no matter who the deceased people are, then those depictions reflect an assumption of equal value of life. Consider reporting on the 1977 flood by the Kansas City *Call*. Unlike the *Star*, the *Call* featured stories and photos about the eight Black flood victims, interviews with residents who survived the flood, and stories about damage to the Bo Dollar riding club, where twenty-five horses drowned. The *Call* estimated that in losing the horses and the club, 250 young people from the east side of Kansas City lost the place where they learned to ride and care for horses. This story makes salient what the property damage means to the people most directly affected by it.[45]

This example illustrates a type of loss and a depiction of it that makes the losses legible as losses, even to readers who had never even heard of the riding club and had no interest in horses.

Why does it matter for everyone, even those who are socially distant from a loss like this, how the loss is depicted, and whether it is depicted at all?

First, the various political roles of journalism that we've considered here are interdependent. The premise of a newspaper is that there is a constant stream of events passing by a large population of readers who need to be kept up to date. From one issue of a newspaper to the next, some things are held constant while other things vary. The stories reported vary. The format of the newspaper stays constant, with its structure that gathers stories into one digital or printed location, making some stories in the unity more salient than the others.

The unity is most palpable in a print version, when a reader has to interact with the entire newspaper in order to read any part of it. But whether a newspaper is in print or digitized, the same reading public is addressed by all the stories in it. When the Kansas City *Star* photographs a white fellow who managed to rescue his cat from the flood, they aim to elicit sympathy from anyone who can understand what it's like to care about saving their cat.[46] They are implicitly including this fellow and anyone who identifies with him as members of polity. When the same newspaper sidelines or omits losses of Black Kansas Citians, or presents them as undeserving of sympathy, the newspaper is excluding them from the reading public.[47] But the reading public is presumed to be the same as the political public addressed by watchdog reporting and election coverage. So in excluding Black Kansas Citians from narratives of losses, the type of asymmetry criticized in the *Star's* retrospective overview manifests an attitude of political inequality.[48]

The second reason that public depictions of loss matter for democracy concerns the epistemic situation of people belonging to the same polity. In a democratic polity, each politizen is supposed to have a say in decisions that affect fellow politizens. But if the losses of people on your side of town are not legible as losses to the people on the other side of town, why should you trust them to make decisions that will affect you? By making losses and their meaning publicly legible, a newspaper helps to foster trust among citizens in a political process.

Here it may be useful to contrast the public-as-protagonist principle with the strongman principles of salience. As a guide to what to make salient and what to background, the strongman principle does not focus on losses to a pluralistic public. The public is addressed and presented as reactive loyalists. If it is a protagonist at all, it gets that status from being imaginatively merged with the leader. In proto-fascist political culture, communications are meant to cultivate a range of hostile negative reactions to those politizens who according to the ideology do not belong in the polity at all.

The communications guided by the strongman principle of salience do not foreground any other differentiation within the public, besides the division between the people in the base and the others who supposedly do not belong in the polity. Here, an authoritarian style of governing that is served by the strongman principle has no need to highlight the varied contours of a pluralistic public, with a range of hopes and fears, losses and setbacks, aspirations and milestones. Whatever differences they have are eclipsed by their emotionally charged relationship to the leader, who claims to come from them, be part of them, and therefore especially well-placed to lead them.[49]

When it is applied to narrating losses, the public-as-protagonist aims to make the varieties of loss legible to the entire public, both for the readers for whom the losses are most proximate, and the readers to whom they are most distant, because deaths are an occasion to depict what was lost in losing the life.

13.4 How does the public-as-protagonist principle meet the challenge?

I've attempted to illuminate the public as protagonist principle both by characterizing its values and the attitudes it attempts to cultivate, and by illustrating how it would orient three types of reporting. We're now in a position to consider whether it helps address the problem of democratic attention. We can break down the probe into two questions. One question concerns how journalism cultivates readers' attitudes, and another whether it contributes to capturing attention at all:

Q1 Does journalism conforming to the public-as-protagonist principle cultivate attitudes that facilitate democracy?

Q2 Is journalism conforming to the public-as-protagonist principle more likely to attract attention in the first place, compared to journalism that respects the importance principle but does not highlight the roles for members of the public as potential political protagonists?

Regarding Q1, the democracy-facilitating attitudes in question are: an awareness of the different public stakes in a problem; the presumption that one is a potential protagonist; and a disposition, or at least a psychological possibility, of inquiring further into at least some of the problems highlighted in the news that respects the importance principle. The public-as-protagonist principle is designed to cultivate those attitudes. Are there reasons to think it actually will cultivate them?

An experimental approach to testing whether it works would have to operationalize both salience principles - the importance principle and public-as-protagonist principle – and then find a way to measure the self-conception of readers of the two experimentally relevant categories of important news stories: those that conform to the public-as-protagonist principle and those that do not. This type of experiment would have to be conducted over an extended period, in which participants were shielded from one type of journalism while being exposed to another. It would also need to control for other factors that could influence that self-conception. For instance, it could turn out that to have any effect, such journalism needs reinforcement from other modes of encouraging civic engagement through education or other organizations. If it turned out that the journalism guided by the public-as-protagonist principle contributed nothing to democratic attitudes, then that would be a reason to think it doesn't fully address the challenge posed by the problem of democratic attention.

Independent of any such experiment's results, plausibility considerations make it reasonable to hypothesize that applying the principle could have some effect on attitudes. Treating audiences as consumers seeking entertainment made infotainment seem like a normal guise for the news, so that in seeking news one could also be seeking entertainment. By analogy, treating audiences as if it were culturally normal for them to consider themselves and one another as political protagonists might make it seem more culturally normal to consider oneself in this way. Lasch (1990) claims that people in the US were never more politically engaged than they were during the era of 'partisan' journalism, which addressed people as if they were politically opinionated. If he is right, that conclusion may favor the idea that journalism conforming to the public-as-protagonist principle would cultivate democratic attitudes.

More specifically, it seems reasonable to expect different effects on attitudes depending on the starting state of the audience. Consider three categories: (a) people tuned out of politics entirely, who tend not to take in much news media; (b) people involved in local organizing in which they respond to threats they feel to their own security or well-being, or that of their communities, but tuned out of most national and international politics; (c) political hobbyists who follow all sorts of news closely, because for them it is entertaining or otherwise emotionally engaging, or intellectually satisfying, or both.[50]

These categories are obviously not exhaustive. A community organizer could also be well-informed about issues beyond the ones they are focused on, and nothing stops a news junkie from joining political organizations. But at least one political scientist, Hersh (2020), claims that groups (b) and (c) are cultural archetypes: people from group (c) primarily seek power to influence how the government operates; people from group (b) primarily track how power is distributed. People from group (a) do neither.

When journalism respects both the importance principle and the public-as-protagonist principle, it is reasonable to expect differential effects on each of these groups. On the people tuned out of politics entirely, it would seem to have a better chance at cultivating the attitudes it aims to cultivate, compared with journalism that doesn't try to show readers why they should care about the stories if they don't already. By contrast, for people who already see themselves as political protagonists, it might simply reinforce this presumption. It may have less effect on hobbyists, if they are determined to maintain the stance of an ironist, observing the political scene from a distance. I put these ideas forward as plausibility considerations, subject to adjustment from experimental or other considerations.

Regarding Q2, there is indirect evidence that systematically failing to treat the public as protagonists will drive readers away. Consider the Kansas City *Star-Times*' retrospective verdict that for over a century, their coverage systematically excluded Black Kansas Citians as political protagonists, both in the ways that losses were narrated (as the flood example shows) and in the omission of reporting 'the achievements, aspirations and milestones of an entire population'. The Kansas City *Call* did not have this problem, and it had greater credibility with Black readers - presumably a precondition for more occurrent engagement.[51] Between 1915 and 1925, the Chicago *Defender*, the Black newspaper with the largest circulation in the US during the twentieth century, played a major role in the Great Migration through its coverage of violence in the south and job and housing opportunities in northern cities. Here, they were urging Black Americans to leave one polity and join another. Their readers were addressed as political protagonists. The fact that *Defender*'s circulation rose steadily during these years and after reinforces the natural suggestion that readers are indeed attracted in part by being treated as members of a polity whose lives, decisions, and options matter.

For the case of watchdog journalism, a similar argument may apply. Suppose the only people with a major role in holding powerful leaders accountable were journalists who ask 'tough questions' at hearings. If the effects on the public of accountability or unaccountability are left out of the news story, then the links to the stakes for various publics have to be drawn by readers who may be unable to draw them, putting them into a position analogous to Lippmann's deaf

258 Susanna Siegel

spectator. Journalists who frame their stories in a way that comports with this picture do not offer readers any way to locate themselves in relation to the event reported as people affected adversely or positively, as people who can have any effect on the political future. By contrast, if journalism makes clearer along the way why it matters to the public, there is at least something explicit in the story that a reader could identify as a reason for her to be taking it in.

I conclude with a leftover question.

I've focused on a specific kind of journalism: the kind produced by the professionalized apparatus developed in the early twentieth century in the US. Its professional structure includes newspapers that gather different kinds of stories in one print or digital place; editors who by their own lights are supposed to publish news that is important for the public to know about; a profession that trains writers in methods and inculcates them into a code of ethics; and institutions that grant press passes.

Both the problem of democratic attention and the public-as-protagonist principle are separable from this specific kind of journalism. As the example of the Chicago *Defender* shows, journalists before professionalization produced stories that fulfilled both principles, and in recent times, citizen journalism has played similar roles. The professional structure of newspapers made familiar in the last century is clearly not the only way to fulfill these principles. A residual question raised by this discussion is what the relative advantages and drawbacks are, compared with other forms that journalism could take.[52]

Zooming out even further, journalism's roles in a democracy are unified by the ways their contribution to building a set of overlapping publics through what it chooses to make salient and how it selects and frames its stories. Professionalized journalism can do this, and so can its adjacent forms. Seen in this light, journalism is but one means among others of shaping the contours of civic engagement and education and defining the publics that operate in aspirationally democratic polities. But a society without an entrenched culture of following a story where it leads, whether that culture is found in professionalized journalism or not, would be vulnerable to profoundly anti-democratic principles of salience.

Notes

[*] I first began thinking about the types of norms that might govern salience and attention in 2015 through many extensive and illuminating discussions with Sebastian Watzl. My initial writings about this topic in (2017) ' focused on norms of rationality that apply to individual minds. Sebastian Watzl and I discussed for years whether there might be some sort of rational pressure on individuals to pay more attention to what's more important, but we struggled to pinpoint the kind of importance at issue. The microstructure of the world is important, and so are fire departments; but there seem to be no general rational pressures to pay attention to fire departments, and the sense in which everyone faces a rational pressure to study the periodic table and other wonders of the world remained elusive to me. Since the examples that struck me as illustrating the general idea that what's important should be attended had always involved journalism, I came to suspect that journalism itself might best illuminate importance norms of salience. At that point, the target of my thinking shifted from

norms of rationality to norms that constrain us by virtue of the type of political community some of us live in, which I call an aspirational democracy. For help in thinking through this idea, I'm indebted to Justin Pottle, Emma Ebowe, Denish Jaswahl, Kevin Troy and Danielle Allen.
1 Rawls, *Political Liberalism*, section 36.
2 By 'modern democracy' I mean representative democracies at a large enough scale that each member of the polity is personally acquainted with only a small fraction of everyone else in it.
3 On the emergence of professional journalism and its contrast with the 'partisan' press that preceded it in the nineteenth century US, see Schudson (1978) and (2020).
4 Hooker (2017). And in considering 'the security [white Americans'] identity provide [s]', Rogers (2018) asks pointedly: 'who among us would readily give up such security, even for the noble values of equality, freedom, and justice?...[W]e must grapple with...the possibility that white supremacy generates far too many psychological, libidinal, cultural, political and economic goods to be sufficiently destabilized or decentered' (p.181).
5 What is an aspirational democracy? I mean a society with democratic political institutions, such as regularly holding free and fair elections to determine political succession, with a history full of actors claiming to aspire to democratic political culture that will fulfill the promise of those institutions. Long-standing debates in US history concern which political actors, among those who expressed such aspirations, were genuinely committed to them, and which have used aspirational language as a guise. A parallel question arises about the functions of purportedly democratic institutions. As many writers have shown, aspirational democracies in this sense are compatible with political cultures that are deeply anti-democratic in many respects (a point developed recently using examples from many parts of the world by Keane 2020, Ben-Ghiat 2020). For the democratic roles of journalism to get their purchase, however, the cultural entrenchment of claims to democratic aspiration is enough.
6 In Siegel (2014) I discuss nuances surrounding the phenomenology of salience, including the possibility of experiencing something as *demanding* attention without experiencing it as *deserving* attention. For more on the phenomenology of salience see Munton (2021), Watzl (2019) and Watzl (this volume), and for comprehensive discussion of the differences between salience in linguistic contexts (where salience of linguistic content can explain framing effects) and contexts of cognition, see Whiteley (2019).
7 Using spatial structure to mark importance was an innovation of professionalizing journalism. During the nineteenth century, in newspapers in the US and Europe, the contents of newspapers were a miscellany of poems, fiction, verbatim reports, and often the order in which things appeared reflected the order in which these items arrived at the news office. Schudson (1978) and (2020).
8 Ben-Ghiat 2020, p.93.
9 'We won the election', said Trump after he lost the election. 'It was stolen from us' (Egan, 2021). Winners and losers of elections are candidates. But in narratives shaped by this grammar, there is no public protagonist distinct from the leader.
10 Dewey (1927) characterized the nebulous nature of the public when he wrote 'If a public exists, it is surely as uncertain about its own whereabouts as philosophers since Hume have been about the residence and make-up of the self' (p.150).
11 Allen (2004), p.69.
12 A separate topic, sidelined here, is the ways the economics of news helps construct a public (see Strömberg (2002)). Ads that reach more people are more effective and therefore more lucrative for newspapers, a fact that may pressure the news to become 'bland' and avoid 'extremes'. An older example: National Organization for Women began with a protest against the New York Times' sex-segregated ads, in which the

same job was advertised for men and women in different places so that different wages could be listed - also lucrative for the newspapers (Rosen, 2000).
13 Abramson (2019) paints a vivid picture of the pressures on this traditional division in the digital age, making evident the weight of the tradition. The GM example is on p.70.
14 In a paper keyed to American democracy and aptly titled 'Six or seven things news does for democracy', Schudson (2008) gives a related list: (i) inform about doings of powerful leaders; (ii) investigate doings of elected officials; (iii) simplify complex information about government; (iv) portray the many modes life in a polity in a way that casts them with a pall of acceptability; (v) provide a public forum, e.g. via letters to the editor and op-eds; (vi) mobilize and advocate; (vii) report on the workings and findings of accountability mechanisms internal to the executive branch, or their dissolution, including (in the U.S.) the offices overseeing Freedom of Information Act requests, the General Accounting office, Federal Election Commission, and the Department of Justice.
15 This last example includes government accountability but is not limited to it. A contemporary example is Miami Herald reporter Julie K. Brown's reporting on the Jeffrey Epstein's large-scale sex trafficking operation, which was used by the prosecution (a point made by Sullivan in her (2020)).
16 Fannin (2020).
17 NPR interview with Mará Rose Williams and Mark Fannin about Kansas City Star, December 20, 2020. See also Williams (2020b).
18 Fannin (2020).
19 Reprinted in Kurz 1992, cited by Rosen and Taylor, 1992, who discusses these criticisms. At the time, Clinton's liaison with Flowers was viewed simply as part of his personal life, and not as potential locus of sexual domination. A quarter-century later, in 2018, Gennifer Flowers told Fox News host Laura Ingraham that although she didn't see it that way at the time, the liaison began as what she would now consider sexual harassment (Mikelionis, 2018). Had the issue been framed that way in 1992, it might not any longer have seemed merely to be sensational facts about Bill Clinton's personal life. It might have been considered a political matter: does this person understand sexual forms of domination and will he oppose them?
20 Shortly after the release of the Access Hollywood tape in which the Republican presidential candidate boasted of sexual assault, and just before the Democratic National Convention in July which would kick off Hilary Clinton's presidential campaign, Russian intelligence operatives released to Wikipedia a trove of emails that had been sent to Democratic Party Chair John Podesta. The emails had been hacked by Russia's Internet Research Agency, one branch of the successor to the Soviet-era KGB. They detailed the inner workings of the Clinton campaign.
21 In the specific case, some people took the contents of the emails to be important to publish because they provide a window in the workings of a party that had long seemed impenetrable and insidery, while others argued that a political party has a right to decide how to present itself at its convention (Shimer, 2020; Snyder, 2018, p.234). The latter position sees the invasion of the DNC emails as comparable to an invasion of personal privacy by a voyeur who invades a family's privacy, planting a camera in their bathroom and bedroom, spying on people in their private moments. It would be grotesque if the press reported on what the camera saw, as part of the report of the crime. If anything is a matter of public concern it is the fact that privacy was invaded.

On the ethics of reporting on information obtained unethically, see Shafer 2017; Sullivan 2019.
22 This handy term avoids the overly specific implications of 'citizens', and allows us to

describe polities at any scale - school, company, neighborhood, city, country, international organization, etc.
23 Dewey (1927). An example of reporting that does this is Nanos and Leung (2020).
24 Schudson (2008), p.14.
25 On lowering costs, see Gao and Murphy, 2018. For evidence of links between local accountability journalism, civic engagement, and corruption, see Sullivan 2020 and (for a discussion focused on Missouri) Kendzior, 2020.
26 A related problem is that powerful leaders are not embarrassed at all by corruption, even if people all over do know about it because they are confident that they will not face consequences for illegal actions (see Burgis (2020), Keane (2020)). On the role of journalism in monitoring such anti-democratic divisions, Schudson's seventh role for news in his (2008) is relevant: reporting on the internal systems of accountability in government, or on the need for such systems if they have been dismantled. When framed by the public-as-protagonist principle, such reporting would highlight the consequences for the public of losing such institutions and making vivid for readers what it could be like if such institutions were in place.
27 Choi (2020).
28 On this last issue, see D. Citron and M. Franks (2020) 'The internet as a speech machine and other myths confounding section 230 speech reform'. Boston University Law School, Public Law and Legal Theory paper 20–28.
29 J. Lanier (2018); Center for Humane Technology (https://www.humanetech.com/).
30 That virality will not track importance is evident from the factors that prompt virality. These factors include formats of lists ('10 tactics to help you find a husband', '29 things I learned from spending two days with Rick Santorum') and quizzes ('which Muppet/Billionaire Tycoon/etc are you?'), and short-lasting, low-impact modes of affect: images or stories that 'restore faith in humanity', nostalgia, the short arousals expressed by LOL, cute, Fail, WTF. Content markers of virality include celebrities, animals, and food. These examples come from the excellent historical analysis of BuzzFeed in Abramson (2019). As Snyder (2018) points out, when combined with political content, some of these types of arousal produce an illusion of becoming informed.
31 Aristotle, *Politics* (1958).
32 Anonymous (2018). On the style of the Mueller report, see Toobin (2020).
33 Likens, 1999, Oreskes and Conway, 2010.
34 There are two ways to describe the removal of these epistemic limitations, and Dewey uses them both. If you describe it by saying that the public exists all along but is invisible until the epistemic limitations are removed, then you're talking about the public as a sets of people whose lives are affected by the same things (laws, interactions, practices) - whether or not they care about those things, and whether or not they know which things affect what they care about. When a sign is posted at a construction site that says 'Notice of public hearing', the operative meaning of 'public' is roughly 'anyone who may be affected'. When Dewey talks about the public's 'eclipse' and 'submergence' (chapter 4, 1927), he is talking this way.

At other times in (1927), he talks about the public coming into being only when the indirect consequences of interactions are made visible (chapter 2). Here, 'the public' includes a type of political consciousness: one's awareness of a whole defined by the interlocking consequences. Becoming aware of the factors that affect you indirectly makes you aware of belonging to a whole. It's that awareness that constitutes a public, which is, therefore, more than just the set of people who are affected by a set of laws, practices, and interactions.
35 A different point against infotainment is implicit in Snyder's (2018) observation that in the US, presenting news as national entertainment made news vulnerable to

political opportunists who exploit the tools of entertainment to create harmful political fictions (p.247).
36 The movement known as 'public journalism' has a similar label, but the major difference is that the public-as-protagonist principle concerns the way that news stories are framed and selected, whereas public journalism is a larger class of efforts, on the page and off, to mobilize readers in civic participation. On the varieties of approaches to public journalism and criticisms of it see the papers in Glasser (1999), especially Schudson (1999).
37 As an example of public journalism, Rosen (1999) describes an effort in Charlotte, North Carolina, undertaken jointly by the *Charlotte Observer*, a local television station and the Poynter institute for Media Studies, that undertook telephone polling of readers to find out which issues they wanted candidates to discuss in an upcoming election, and then directed campaign coverage to those issues.
38 Wise et al., 2018.
39 Government email unlike private email becomes part of the public record. Ultimately Hawley was found not to have violated election law. See Hancock 2019, Hancock et al 2019a.
40 Wise and Hancock, 2019.
41 Hancock et al., 2019b.
42 Wise and Hancock, 2018; Hawley, 2016.
43 This position was reflected in the *Star*'s editorials that were highly critical of Hawley. It is an example of a newspaper's editorial outlook shaping the selection and framing of stories it reports. I discuss the relationships between outlook and selection including its epistemic dimensions in Siegel, (2017).
44 As theorists over the years have noted, hypocrisy in politics is hardly ever the main problem (Shklar, 1984; Dover, 2019; Siegel, 2020).
45 The contrast between reporting by the *Star* and the *Call* noted in the Star's retrospective mirrors a contrast found in *The East St Louis Massacre*, a pamphlet submitted by Ida B. Wells in 1919 to then-Governor L of Illinois which included both her own reporting during the aftermath of the mob attacks on Black people and their property, and eyewitness reporting from the Chicago *Tribune* during the attack. In Wells-Barnett's reporting, the reader meets the people whose houses were ransacked and stolen from: we learn their names, how long they lived in East St Louis, their families and jobs, and sometimes what their house looked like and some of the things that were in it. From the *Tribune*'s reporting, one learns only about the death of nameless persons, that they were Black, the location of crimes committed against them, and finally (and this was the reason for including it in the pamphlet) the indifference and inefficacy of the National Guard.
46 Williams (2020a).
47 According to the Kansas City *Star*'s former architecture critic Donald Hoffman, who worked for the paper when it was paired with the *Times*, 'When I first came to the papers, I worked at police headquarters, and we were instructed not even to pay attention to Black murders or Black traffic fatalities. They just weren't reported'. Cited in Adler (2020).
48 It is well-documented how cultivating attitudes of political inequality degrade, erode, undo or preclude democracy. For examples outside the American context, see P. Pomerantzev (2019), chapter 1 on Rodrigo Duterte in the Philippines; and A. Applebaum (2020) chapter 4 on the rise of Spain's Vox Party.
49 Ben-Ghiat, 2020; Posner, 2020.
50 Hersh (2020) draws a useful distinction between two kinds of political engagement, by focusing on the distinction between people in groups (b) and (c). One of his examples of type (b) is a bus monitor from Haverhill, MA who leads the Latino

Coalition, a community organization that monitors its local government (police, school superintendent, mayor) on issues related to its residents who have immigrated from the Spanish-speaking parts of Latin America, such as how the city will interact with ICE under the Trump administration and whether there will be Spanish-speaking staff at schools. He contrasts this type of organizing with the mode of political engagement done by college-educated people, which consists primarily in informing themselves about a large range of political issues by reading about them online where they interact with others by sharing reactions, and argues that while type (c) may feel like political engagement and may even superficially appear that way, it has little effect on actual political change.
51 Eligon and Gross, 2020.
52 Abramson (2019) can be read as an historically rich exploration of this question.

References

Abramson, J. 2019. *Merchants of Truth: The Business of News and the Fight for Facts*. Simon and Schuster, New York.

Achen, C. and Bartels, L. 2016. *Democracy for Realists*. Princeton University Press, New Jersey.

Adler, E. 2020. 'Brutes' and Murderers: Black People Overlooked in KC Coverage—Except in Crime. *Kansas City Star*, December 20. https://www.kansascity.com/news/local/article247235584.html

Allen, D. 2004. *Talking to Strangers: Anxieties of Citizenship since Brown v. Board of Education*. University of Chicago Press, Chicago.

Anonymous. 2018. I Am Part of the Resistance Inside the Trump Administration. *New York Times*, September 5.

Applebaum, A. 2020. *Twilight of Democracy*. Doubleday, New York.

Aristotle. 1958. *The Politics of Aristotle*. Edited and translated by Ernest Barker. Oxford University Press, New York.

Ben-Ghiat, R. 2020. *Strongmen: Mussolini to the Present*. W.W. Norton, New York.

Burgis, T. 2020. *Kleptopia*. HarperCollins, New York.

Choi, M. 2020. Meadows Dismisses Hatch Act Concerns at RNC: 'Nobody Outside the Beltway Really Cares'. *Politico*, August 26. http://www.politico.com/news/2020/08/26/mark-meadows-hatch-act-rnc-402194

Citron, D. and Franks, M. 2020. The Internet as a Speech Machine and Other Myths Confounding Section 230 Speech Reform. Boston University Law School, Public Law and Legal Theory paper 20-8.

Delany, M. R. 1852. *The Condition, Elevation, Emigration and Destiny of Colored People in the United States*. Public domain book.

Dewey, J. 1927/1954. *The Public and Its Problems: An Essay in Political Inquiry*. Ohio University Press, Athens, Ohio.

Dover, D. 2019. The Walk and The Talk. *Philosophical Review* 128(4): 387–422.

Egan, L. 2021. 'We Won': Trump Spreads Misinformation About 2020 Election During Final Georgia Rally. NBC News, Jan 5. https://www/nbcnews.com/politics/2020-election/we-won-trump-spreads-misinformation-about-2020-election-during-final-n1252802

Eligon, J. and Gross, J. 2020. Kansas City Star Apologizes for Racism in Decades of Reporting. *New York Times*, December 21. https://www.nytimes.com/2020/12/21/us/kansas-city-star-apology.html

Fannin, M. 2020. The Truth in Black and White. *Kansas City Star*, December 20. https://www.kansascity.com/news/local/article247928045.html

Gao, C., Lee, J. and Murphy, D. 2018. Financing Dies in Darkness? The Impact of Newspaper Closures on Public Finance. Brookings, September 24.

Glasser, T. (Ed.). 1999. *The Idea of Public Journalism*. Guilford Press, New York.

Hancock, J. 2019. Ashcroft Ends Investigation of Josh Hawley, Says He Didn't Violate Election Law. *Kansas City Star*, February 28. https://www.kansascity.com/news/politics-government/article226917029.html,

Hancock, J., Vockrodt, S. and Wise, L. 2019a. Hawley Insider Had Seat at Table in Secretary of State Inquiry That Cleared Senator. *Kansas City Star*, March 06. https://www.kansascity.com/news/politics-government/article227121274.html

Hancock, J., Wise, L. and S. Vockrodt. 2019b. 'Astonishing Development': Hawley AG Office May Have Violated Mo. Open Records Laws. *Kansas City Star*, February 01, 2019. https://www.kansascity.com/news/politics-government/article225334655.html

Hawley, J. 2016. twitter.com/HawleyMO/status/750467243763466240

Hersh, E. 2020. *Politics Is For Power*. Simon and Schuster, New York.

Hooker, J. 2017. Black Protest, White Grievance: On the Problem of White Political Imaginations Not Shaped by Loss. *South Atlantic Quarterly* 116(July): 3.

Keane, J. 2020. *The New Despotism*. Harvard University Press, Cambridge.

Kendzior, S. 2020. *Hiding in Plain Sight*. Flatiron Books, New York.

Kurz, H. 1992. Reports on Clinton Post Quandary for Journalists. *Washington Post*, January 30, p. A14.

Lanier, J. 2018. *Ten Arguments for Deleting Your Social Media Accounts Right Now*. Picador, New York.

Lasch, C. 1990. *The Lost Art of Political Argument*. Harper's Magazine.

Lerman, A. and Weaver, V. 2014. *Arresting Citizenship: The Democratic Consequences of American Crime Control*. University of Chicago Press, Chicago.

Likens, G. E. 1999. The Science of Nature, the Nature of Science: Long-Term Ecological Studies at Hubbard brook. *Proceedings of the American Philosophical Society* 143(4): 558–572.

Lippmann, W. 2010/1920. *Liberty and the News*. Harcourt Brace and Howe, New York. Republished by Dover Publications, Mineola, New York.

Lippmann, W. 1927. *The Phantom Public*. Transaction Publishers, New Brunswick.

Mansbridge, J. 1980. *Beyond Adversary Democracy*. University of Chicago Press, Chicago.

Mikelionis, L. 2018. Gennifer Flowers Accuses Bill Clinton of Sexual Harrassment Before Their Consensual Relationship. *Fox News*, June 6. http://www.foxnews.com/politics/gennifer-flowers-accuses-bill-clinton-of-sexual-harrassment-before-their-consensual-relationship

Munton, J. 2021. Prejudice as the Misattribution of Salience. *Analytic Philosophy*.

Mutz, D. 2006. *Hearing the Other Side: Deliberative Versus Participatory Democracy*. Cambridge University Press, New York.

National Public Radio Interview on All Things Considered with Mike Fannin and Mará Rose Williams, December 22, 2020. npr.org/2020/12/22/949309308/kansas-city-star-publishes-apology-for-its-coverage-of-black-community

Nanos, J. and Leung, S. 2020. One Block, One World. *Boston Globe*, December 19. https://apps.bostonglobe.com/business/2020/12/water-street/

Oreskes, N. and Conway, E. 2010. *Merchants of Doubt: How a Handful of Scientists Obscured the Truth on Issues from Tobacco Smoke to Global Warming*. Bloomsbury, New York.

Pomerantzev, P. 2019. *This Is Not Propaganda*. Hachette Book Group, New York.
Posner, E. 2020. *The Demagogue's Playbook: The Battle for American Democracy from the Founders to Trump*. St. Martin's Press, New York.
Rawls, J. 1993. *Political Liberalism*. Columbia University Press, Cambridge, MA.
Rice, M. S. 2012. *Images of America: Chicago Defender*. Arcadia Publishing, Charleston, SC.
Rogers, M. 2019. White Supremacy, Fear, and the Crises of Legitimation. In C. Howard-Woods, C. Laidley and M. Omidi (Eds.), *#Charlottesville: White Supremacy, Populism, and Resistance* (pp. 176–181). Public Seminar Books, New York.
Rosen, J. 1999. *What Are Journalists For?* Yale University Press, New Haven.
Rosen, J. and Taylor, P. 1992. *The New News v. the Old News: The Press and Politics in the 1990s*. The Twentieth Century Fund Press, New York.
Rosen, R. 2000. *The World Split Open: How the Modern Women's Movement Changed America*. Penguin, New York.
Schudson, M. 1978. *Discovering the News: A Social History of America's Newspapers*. Basic Books, New York.
Schudson, M. 2008. Six or Seven Things News Does for Democracy. In M. Schudson (Ed.), *Why Democracy Needs an Unlovable Press* (pp. 11–26). Polity Press, Malden.
Schudson, M. 2020. *Journalism: Why It matters*. Polity Press, Malden.
Shafer, J. 2017. Oui, Journalists Should Report on Hacked Emails. *Politico.com*, May 08. https://www.politico.com/magazine/story/2017/05/08/journalists-report-hacked-emails-macron-clinton-wikileaks-215112
Shimer, D. 2020. *Rigged: America, Russia, and One Hundred Years of Electoral Interference*. Alfred Knopf, New York.
Shklar, J. 1984. *Ordinary Vices*. Harvard University Press, Cambridge, MA.
Siegel, S. 2014. Affordances and the Content of Perception. In B. Brogaard (Ed.), *The Contents of Perception*. (pp. 39–76). Oxford University Press, Oxford.
Siegel, S. 2017. *The Rationality of Perception*. Oxford University Press, Oxford.
Siegel, S. October 30, 2020. Here's How to Hack Hypocrisy, *Tampa Bay Times*.
Snyder, T. 2018. *The Road to Unfreedom: Russia, Europe, and America*. Penguin Random House, New York.
Strömberg, D. 2002. Mass Media Competition, Political Competition, and Public Policy. *Review of Economic Studies*. Oxford University Press, vol. 71(1): 265–284.
Sullivan, M. 2019. Journalists Can't Ignore Hacked Data Meant to Disrupt Election. But Here's What They Can Do. *Washington Post*, April 28. https://www.washingtonpost.com/lifestyle/style/journalists-cant-ignore-hacked-data-meant-to-disrupt-elections-but-heres-what-they-can-do/2019/04/26/4ff6a0fa-6785-11e9-a1b6-b29b90efa879_story.html
Sullivan, M. 2020. *Ghosting the News: Local Journalism and the Crisis of American Democracy*. Columbia Global Reports, New York.
Toobin, J. 2020. Why the Mueller Investigation Failed. *The New Yorker*, July 6 & 13.
Watzl, S. 2019. *Structuring Mind*. Oxford University Press, Oxford.
Watzl, S. 2022. The Ethics of Attention: An Argument and a Framework. In S. Archer (Ed.), *Salience: A Philosophical Inquiry* (pp. 89–112). Routledge, Abingdon.
Whiteley, E. 2019. Salience Perspectives. PhD dissertation, Cambridge University.
Williams, M. R. 2020a. As Floodwater Upended Black lives, Kansas City Newspapers Fixated on Plaza, suburbs. *Kansas City Star*, December 20. https://www.kansascity.com/news/local/article247164484.html

Williams, M. R. 2020b. Kansas City Schools Broke Federal Desegregation Law for Decades. *The Star Stayed Quiet. Kansas City Star*, December 20. https://www.kansascity.com/news/local/article247821130.html

Wise, L. and Hancock, J. 2018. Hawley Champions Open Government. *So why doesn't he use email the public can see? Mccaltchydc.com.* October 22. https://www.mcclatchydc.com/news/politics-government/election/midterms/article220225615.html

Wise, L. and Hancock, J. 2019. Missouri Auditor Galloway Beings Review of Josh Hawley's Attorney General Office. *mcclatchydc.com*, January 10. https://www.mcclatchydc.com/article 224159555

Wise, L., Hancock, J. and Vockrodt, S. 2018. Out-of-State Political Consultants Helped Direct Josh Hawley's Missouri AG office. *Kansas City Star*, October 31. https://www.kansascity.com/news/politics-government/election/article220870465.html

Index

Page numbers followed by "n" indicate a note

aberrant salience 2, 53
Abramson, J. 263n52
accountability 5
Achen, C. 237
Adams, Robert 6
adaptability 15
aesthetics: attention 10, 11; attitude 12; demands 21; formalism 10; judgements 10, 12, 20, 21; trait virtues 16, 18
affordance 2, 3, 60; anticipated actualization 63; intelligibility of 63; landscape of 67n12; patterns of 64
affordance-concept lack 64
agent's psychology 13
alief, notion of 206n13
Allen, Danielle 240
Anscombe, Elizabeth 136
Antico, Concetta 77
Archer, Sophie 48n52, 87n16
Aristotle 107, 173n8, 247
aspirational democracy 259n5
attention: in age of distraction 93; attentional repulsion/capture 14; choice of 141, 142; cognitive science of 95; consciousness 94; content-based attention 100–2; decision making 94; descriptive centrality of 89, 92, 94; descriptive significance 94; emotions 95; instrumental attention norms 103–6; intentional agency and agentive control 94; introspection 95; involuntary shifts of 13; manner-based attention 102–3; memory 95; mental activity 96; mind and agency 89; neuronal/psychological mechanisms 98; non-instrumental attention norms 103–6; non-perceptual forms 95; normative pressures on 90; normative significance 94, 97; normative source of 106–9; object objection 99; perception 94; primitive and constitutive norms 109; problem of democratic attention 238–44; psychological research on 6; psychological theory 89; and salience 140; self 94; self-control 94; social bonding and human development 102; unselfish attention 143
attention-grabbing 1, 2, 13, 19, 22
attentiveness 165–7
attitudes 249
attitudinal engagement 249
Auden, W. H. 141, 142, 145, 148
Aurelius, Marcus 107
autonomous rational awareness 136

Bartels, L. 237
Beck, J. 45n26
belief: ethics of 90; and ideologies 199, 200; and transitions 98
Bell, Clive 10
Ben-Ghiat, Ruth 239
Berridge, K.C. 51, 67n3
Bicchieri, Christine 190n10
Block, N. 45n25
Blum, Lawrence 107
blurry vision 46n27
Boyle, M. 128n7
Broome, Matthew 2, 3, 68n15
Bullough, Edward 10

Campbell, John 26, 148
Camp, E. 206n7

carefulness 15
Carel, H. 68n15
Carrasco, Marissa 30, 43n9, 47n45
Cartier-Bresson, Henri 13, 17, 18, 19, 22
Cavedon-Taylor, Dan 1, 2
Chappell, Sophie-Grace 5, 14, 103
Chemero, A. 60
Christianity 142
Clark, Andy 66n2
Clifford, William 4, 90
Clinton, Bill 243
Clinton, Hillary 253
Close, Chuck 16
cognitive attention 26, 75
cognitive bias 8, 213
cognitive psychology 156
cognitive salience perspectives 207n38
coherence-attention theory 86n1, 86n4
Colombetti, G. 67n11
conceptual connection 12
conceptual ethics 91
conscious recognition 163
conscious visual experience 44n20
consequentialism 165
contemporary ethics 209n61
content-based attention 100–2
contextualism 188n1
contextual variables 203
conversational norms 191n21
Crowther, Thomas 48n52
cultural authority 108

decision theory 5
De Haan, S.E. 61, 67n12, 67n13
Delany, M. R. 237
deliberative situation 170
delusions 50, 51
democracy: journalism in 237–8; modern democracy 236; political elites 236; political equality 237; political institutions 236
democratic dialogue 169–70
demonstratives: competent, attentive, reasonable hearer 72; de facto mutual salience 76–80; further thoughts 73; guarantee reference 78; Kaplan's formal model 71; occurrence of 73; reference failure 79; referential success 80; speaker-intention theory of 73; speaker's reference 71, 86n8
descriptive centrality 97

descriptive psychology 92
Dewey, John 244, 248, 259n10
Dietz, Richard 48n52
Dings, Roy 61
discrimination 189n4
distinctiveness: attended and unattended properties 35; attentional modulations 34; right-hand patch 35; subject-level 34; subject-level focused visual attention 39; test cases 37, 38; types of changes, in appearance 38, 39
distribute attention 46n37
Donahue, Phil 243
dopamine dysregulation 52
Dutton, Denis 16

Eilan, Naomi 48n52
Eliot, T. S. 159
emotional distress 201
epistemic injustice: diminishment of 225; discriminative epistemic injustice 222–4; distributive epistemic injustice 222; in-group and out-group scripts 227–8; overestimation 226–7; social group 226; social stereotype 224–5
ethical data 162–4, 175n34
ethical thinking 138
evaluative control 4, 117–18
existential feeling, concept of 68n16
experienced affordances 63

fairness 15
Fannin, Mark 243
feelings of righteousness 240
Feinberg, J. 205n1
Fletcher, P.C. 67n6
folk epistemology 229
formal linguistic theories 85
fovea 28
framing and nudging techniques 134
framing effects 197–9
Fraser, Rachel 201
Freud, S. 144
Fricker, Miranda 230n5
Frith, C.D. 67n6
functional salience 45n26

Gallagher, S. 65, 67n11
game-theoretic tools 150
game theory 150
Ganeri, Jonardon 95

Gauker, Christopher 72, 73
Gaut, Berys 12
genuine inattentiveness 165
Gerken, Mikkel 8
Gibson, J. J. 53, 60, 65
Gilbert, Margaret 146–8
g-norms 191n25
grab attention 51
group-based injustice 6

hallucinations 50, 52
Halpern, Joseph 148
harmful salience: cognitive salience 194–5; linguistic salience 195–7
Haslanger, Sally 209n71
Hatch Act 249
hate speech 205
Hersh, E. 257
Hieronymi, P. 128n7
Hirschmann, N. 209n65
Hoffman, Donald 262n47
Hooker, J. 2594
Howes, O.D. 67n5
human agents 147
human beauty 21
human rights abuses 164
humility 15

imagination 47n39
incentive salience 51, 53, 60, 62, 67n3
indirect voluntary control 4
informed political activist 208n51
in-group/out-group psychology 8
integration 171
intellectual virtue 15
intentionality: modalities of 64
intention-based theory 72
interpersonal regulatory processes 68n15
interpersonal/social criterion 164
intrinsic formal qualities 16
introspection 2; dependence of 28; identical Gabor patches 28f; left-hand patch 28; overlapping figures 26f; reliability of 28; right-hand patch 28; unattended object 27
intuitions 78, 162
Iris, Murdoch 107

James, William 90
Jaspers, K. 67n4
journalism: accountability journalism 245; anti-democratic politics 240; culture of 243; demands on public attention 244–6; digital media 239; government/political campaigns 242; print media 239; professional journalism 247; public journalism 262n36; public meet 246–7; self-presentation 240; substantive constraints 242

Kant, Immanuel 103, 104
Kant's concept of aesthetic disinterest 11
Kaphar, Titus 93
Kaplan, David 71, 82
Kapur, Shitij 50, 51
Kiverstein, J. 60, 61
Korsgaard, C. 209n64
Krueger, J. 67n11

Lasch, C. 256
legal sense 189n4
Lerman, Hemdat 2
Levin, Michael 138n6
Levinson, Jerrold 10
Lewis, David 147, 157
Lippmann, Walter 235, 236, 237, 241, 248
Longworth, Guy 48n52
Lovibond, Sabina 6

Macaulay, Thomas Babington 174n29
Mack, A. 43n7
manner-based attention 102–3
Mansbridge, J. 237
Marx 144
McDowell, John 107, 160, 173n3
McGowan, Mary Kate 6
meditation practices 93
Mehta, Judith 145, 146
memory 18
mental dispositions 206n5
mesolimbic dopamine 51
meta-ethics 230n9
Michaelson, Eliot 3, 4, 43n6, 77
mind 162; and agency 89; blameworthy 166; normative evaluation of 91; targeted normative analysis 96
mindfulness: meditation and 104, 141; training 93
mind-independent qualities 45n23
mind-wandering 106
modern democracy 259n2
Mole, Christopher 5
moral epistemology 163
morality system 138

moral orientation 141
moral phenomena 160
moral philosophy 168
moral psychology 144–5
moral responsibility 161
moral sense 189n4
moral significance 107
moral theory 94
moral thinking 152
Moran, R. 128n7
motivational elements 15
motivational value 16, 18
Mount, Allyson 3, 75, 76, 87n16
Mueller, Robert 248
Mulckhuyse, M., D. 153
Munton, J. 258n6
Murdoch, Iris 5, 102, 150, 151, 156, 157, 161
Mutz, D. 237
myth of option ranges: ideological function of 135; at random 136–7

Nanay, Bence 10
negotiation 168
Nelson, William Rockhill 243
neuroscience 52
Nichols, J.C. 243
Nickel, B. 46n28
non-aesthetic attention 11
non personhood-related traits 202, 203, 204
non-visual phenomenology 41
non-voluntary attention-grabbingness 14
normative assessment 98
normative constraint 21
normative ethics 230n9
normative innovation 93
normative inquiry 92
normative pressures 90, 91
norm-governed practices 187
Nour, M.N. 67n5
Nowak, Ethan 3, 4, 43n6, 77
Nussbaum, Martha C. 7, 173n3

objectification 202, 206n16
object objection 99
Olusoga, David 175n31

Parmer, Jared 231n10
perception 91
perceptual attention 13, 96
personal decision-making 93

personal interests/desires 10
personhood-related trait 7, 208n52, 209n61
perspectival objectification 203
phenomenological distinctions 53
phenomenology, of visual attention: attended and unattended objects 31; behavioral and neurobiological findings 29; distinctiveness 33–41; distinctive saliency effect 25; effect of attention 33; experimental research 29–33; introspection 26–9; masking 31; neural activity 30; priming 31; timescale phenomena 31
photographer's aesthetic appraisal 20
photography 17
physical/mental abnormality 6
Plato 152
political engagement 262n50
political intervention 6
political protagonists 257
predictive coding 66n2
psychological experimentation 152
public-as-protagonist principle 250, 262n36; accountability 252–3; elections 251–2; life and death 253–5

Quesada, Daniel 48n52

randomness 136–7
Ratcliffe, Matthew 2, 3, 68n16
Rawls, John 235
regularities 155f
Reimer, M. 86n1
reliabilism 15
responsibilism 15
Rietveld, E. 60, 61
Robinson, T.E. 51, 67n3
Rock, I. 43n7
Rosen, R. 262n37
Russell, Bertrand 80, 190n14

salience: and attention 1, 140; cause vs constitute 179–80; contextual salience 215–17; conversational exercitives 183–4; conversational score 182–3; covert exercitives 184–5; de facto mutual salience 76–80; de facto speaker/hearer salience 80–4; for democracy (see democracy); determiners of 217; dysregulation 2, 50, 52, 60, 67n6; on enactment 180; and epistemic injustice

(see epistemic injustice); evaluative control model 117–18; experiences of 51; harmful salience (see harmful salience); human life 22; implicit associations 188; indirect voluntary control 114, 115–17; lab-model of moral attention 156–7; moral concerns 107; moral quality of 151; moral significance of 144; Naïve Constitutive View 118–19; norms of fittingness 99; notions of perceptual attention 11; objective ethical salience 173n8; passive force 115; passive salience 51; perception of 162, 168; permissibility facts/norms 180–2; physical attractiveness 114; salience-relevance distinction 215; salient alternatives vs relevant alternatives 214–15; Separate States View 119–23; and silence 137–8; and social stereotypes 218–21; Sophisticated Constitutive View 123–5, 127; speech and action 178–9; stereotype threat 187–8; strongly salient 1; subtleties of 53–60; weakly salient 1
Schelling, Thomas 145
schizophrenia 66n1
Schneider, K.A. 45n26
Schudson, Michael 245, 246
self-conception 256
self-conscious 136
self-help 93
self-perfection 166
semantic reference 86n8
sensory attention 152
sensory perception 79
sex and sexual orientation 14
sexual desires 11
sexual harassment 172
sexual objectification 197, 201
sexual violence 200
Shiffrin, Seanna 107, 108
Siegel, Susanna 1, 8, 14, 19, 20, 21, 109n1, 259n6
silencing 191n18
Smith, A. 128n7
s-norms 187
Snyder-Hall 209n65
social cognition 229
social coordination 241
social interaction 186
social media 93, 247
social norms 190n10

social stereotypes 8, 213, 224–5, 230
Soteriou, Matthew 48n52
speaker-intention theory 73
speaker's reference 86n8
Spinoza 130
spiritual 142
Sripada, Chandra 104
Stalnaker, Robert 70
statistical regularity 154
Stazicker, J. 42n1
stereotype threat 208n46
Stolnitz, Jerome 10
strongly salient 14
sub-conscious attention 206n10
subject-level focused visual attention 48n51

Talsma, J. 153
technological affordances 63
Theeuwes 153
Tirrell, Lynne 204
trait aesthetic virtues 16
traits of open-mindedness 15
trolleyology 131–4
truth-bearers 189n6
truth-makers 189n6
Turatto, M. 44n16
Tversky, Amos 206n8

unattended objects 27, 44n11, 44n20

violation: of Hatch Act 246; of rights 205, 209n70
violence 8; physical and psychological violence 193; sexual 200
virtue aesthetics: aesthetic trait virtues 16; concept of authenticity 16; hyperrealistic portraits 16; motivational facts 17; reliabilism 15; trait aesthetic virtues 16
visual attention 2; effects of 42n1; empirical data 43n6; phenomenology (see phenomenology, of visual attention); simple vision-based demonstrative thoughts 43n6
visual constancy 38
visual system 2

Waldron, Jeremy 204
Watzl, Sebastian 2, 4, 34, 35, 36, 39, 42, 42n1, 45n23, 46n34, 47n40, 115, 127n4, 206n3, 258n1

weakly salient 14
Weil, Simone 140, 141, 142, 145, 148, 151, 161
well-being 106
Werner, P. 102
Wettstein, H.K. 76
Wettstein, Howard 74, 75
Whiteley, Ella 7
Wiggins, David 174n8

Williams, Bernard 137
Woolley, Bernard 134
Wu, W. 41, 42n1, 46n34, 48n51

Yetter-Chappell, H. 103
Yi Jiang 14
Yu, L. 154f

Zhao, J. 153, 154f

For Product Safety Concerns and Information please contact our EU representative GPSR@taylorandfrancis.com
Taylor & Francis Verlag GmbH, Kaufingerstraße 24, 80331 München, Germany